PE

BRYCE COURTENAY
Storyteller

Christine Courtenay (nee Gee) was born in north-eastern Victoria in 1954 and grew up on a cattle property before graduating with a Bachelor of Arts from the Australian National University.

In 1975 she co-founded Australian Himalayan Expeditions, which offered trekking trips to the Himalayas, and became a world leader in adventure travel. In 1989 she created her own marketing company and was engaged by several pioneering tourism projects. She also worked alongside acclaimed authors, world-renowned mountaineers and polar explorers.

Christine served as the Nepalese honorary consul-general in NSW from 1987, and as Nepal attaché during the Sydney 2000 Olympic Games, and was a founding director of the Australian Himalayan Foundation. She was awarded an Order of Australia Medal in 2013.

Christine was Bryce Courtenay's partner from 2005, and they married in 2011. She has a son called Nima, and continues to enjoy travelling, writing, and walking in wild and beautiful places.

She lives in Sydney.

BRYCE COURTENAY

Storyteller

*A memoir of Australia's
most beloved writer*

CHRISTINE COURTENAY

PENGUIN BOOKS

UK | USA | Canada | Ireland | Australia
India | New Zealand | South Africa | China

Penguin Books is part of the Penguin Random House group of companies
whose addresses can be found at global.penguinrandomhouse.com.

Penguin
Random House
Australia

First published by Viking, 2022
This edition published by Penguin Books, 2023

Cover photography by Tim Bauer: timbauerphoto.myportfolio.com
Cover design by Adam Laszczuk © Penguin Random House Australia Pty Ltd
Text design by Tony Palmer © Penguin Random House Australia Pty Ltd
Typeset in 12pt Goudy Oldstyle by Post Pre-press Group, Brisbane
Colour separation by Splitting Image Colour Studio, Clayton, Victoria
Printed and bound in Australia by Griffin Press, an accredited
ISO AS/NZS 14001 Environmental Management Systems printer

A catalogue record for this
book is available from the
NATIONAL LIBRARY OF AUSTRALIA National Library of Australia

ISBN 978 1 76134 353 7

penguin.com.au

MIX
Paper | Supporting
responsible forestry
FSC® C018684

'In the end, if someone says,
"Here lies Bryce Courtenay, a storyteller",
my life will have been worthwhile.'

Bryce Courtenay
The Age, 1997

CONTENTS

PREFACE

'We have been storytellers since the dawn of time. I simply see myself as sitting under the Banyan tree, and saying, "This is what happened" and starting to tell a story.'

Bryce Courtenay, May 2012

BRYCE COURTENAY'S ICONIC DEBUT novel, *The Power of One*, opens with the simple but unforgettable line, 'This is what happened.' A born storyteller, Bryce claimed that these words formed the beginning of the eternal story we have wanted to hear since the dawn of time. Yet he never chose to write his autobiography. He would say, 'What would be interesting about it?' and he would then quote his friend and fellow Australian writer Morris West, who said, 'There's just one problem about writing an autobiography: I don't much care for the central character.' Perhaps Bryce also agreed with the sentiments of his great literary hero, Charles Dickens, who wrote, 'I rest my claims to the remembrance of my country upon my published works . . .'

In April 2020 I sat down at my desk in Sydney and began to write a memoir of sorts of my own – the story of having co-founded in 1975 a pioneering adventure travel company called Australian Himalayan Expeditions. I eventually came to write a chapter that told the story of how Bryce and I first met in 1993. I wrote a second chapter, and then a third and a fourth! It was clear that I had unexpectedly veered away from writing my own story to writing a memoir about my late husband.

It was a nerve-racking revelation at the time, but I felt encouraged when recalling Bryce's words from *The Power of One*: 'First with the head and then with the heart, you'll be ahead from the start.' I had in fact considered writing about Bryce's life while he was still alive, but he had retorted to this idea, with a loving grin, 'Darling, don't you think one writer in the family is quite enough?' But ultimately the timing felt right, and the urge to continue writing about Bryce's life grew stronger. Slowly, chapter after chapter, the book began to take shape. I hoped that somehow, I might even end up securing a tick of approval from the spirit of the master storyteller himself.

To be Bryce's wife was both a joy and a privilege, and I remain proud of the contribution I made to our years together. Not long after we became a couple, he said, 'I love you very deeply, and we make a fantastic team, but you do realise you have taken on a full-time job looking after me? Plus, for seven months a year you're a writer's widow while you wait for me to finish each book.'

In writing Bryce's memoir I wanted to reveal the story of his life as I came to know it, as well as reflect on his astonishing literary legacy. Bryce's generous support of countless charities, his passion for wildlife and the environment, and his efforts in championing the next generation of writers were also important for me to acknowledge. I was mindful of his advice to others who were planning to write a memoir: 'Whitewashing a family when writing a story is not a story at all!' While this is fair comment, I quickly realised that writing a memoir is a big responsibility and not for the fainthearted. I also came to appreciate why Bryce preferred to write fiction, which allowed his imagination to roam free.

From his humble beginnings in Africa to his dazzling success in advertising and as a bestselling author, Bryce's rags-to-riches life story resembles one of the epic tales of his books. And perhaps it took a life like his to conjure the stories he wrote. Material was no problem – there were so many stories to incorporate from how he survived his tough childhood to the international acclaim that followed the publication of his debut novel, *The Power of One*, in 1989.

Since Bryce passed away in 2012 a few people have approached me seeking to write his biography, but I never felt comfortable with any of their proposals. It began to make sense for me to undertake the task myself. I recognised I was in a unique position, having for many years been his closest confidante.

But the task did not come without its challenges. Whilst I had known Bryce since 1993, we didn't come together as a couple until the middle of 2005. There were sections of his life I had not been a part of, and this meant I had to spend months researching archives and putting together the pieces of the jigsaw. I drafted copious notes about our years together, read and listened to hundreds of media interviews, and organised our extensive archive of photographs. I re-read Bryce's books, and in doing so appreciated even more how he had woven aspects of his own life into them. I also spoke with some family members and people who had known Bryce for decades, and I am indebted to them for sharing their time and candid insights. There were inevitable gaps, but I felt I had enough material to write an authentic story told with integrity, humour and love.

In the middle of 2020, I found a battered, unmarked cardboard box in my garage containing over 120 letters written by Bryce to his mother. At first I didn't realise what they were and came close to throwing them out, but I quickly came to see the discovery provided a cache of pure gold for my manuscript. I only wish I had found them while Bryce was alive: I would have loved to have asked him countless questions about their contents. These precious letters also made me appreciate even more what he had gone through in his life. I have included excerpts from these letters in this book, and have retained Bryce's misspellings for authenticity.

Bryce was an amazing but complex person, and uncovering the events that defined his true self has been challenging and, at times, even heartbreaking. He endured a chaotic childhood with tenuous relationships with both of his parents, which he sometimes described as being 'short on love, lonely, and brutal'. Nonetheless he never failed to acknowledge that his parents had done their best, living through difficult times and circumstances themselves. Bryce was blessed with a positivity and a great sense of humour from an early age, which enabled him to keep hope in his heart. Even still, emotional deprivation endured in his childhood left deep scars that never fully healed. While he was consistently Australia's number-one bestselling author, in his own eyes it was perhaps never enough. At times his psychological scars led him down pathways that caused him to be a bit reckless – and, later, regretful. Admittedly, we have all done or said things that on reflection we wish we hadn't.

Bryce's life wasn't defined by fame or money. He did, however, struggle to feel a sense of self-worth, and perhaps no one person could give him the amount of love he craved. But he was an extraordinary, generous and loving husband and I cherish the precious years we shared. I miss him dreadfully, and always shall, while remembering what he said to me in the last few days of his life: 'Darling, I want you to embrace the gift of life as I have.'

Bryce was devoted to his family and his three children, Brett, Adam, and Damon, and frequently said, 'The most important and meaningful aspect of my life is being a father.' It was a sentiment that carried greater poignancy given he did not find out who his own father was until he was fifteen years old. Bryce also took care of his mother, Maud Jessamine Greer, and provided her with financial assistance from an early age.

His passion for life, humour and positive attitude provides an enduring tale of someone who never lost hope, and who held fast to his dream of becoming a writer. The events of his own life inspired many of the themes of his books: triumph against adversity, and holding tight to a dream.

At times Bryce had to pay a price for the unrivalled success he achieved both in the advertising industry and as a bestselling author. His personal courage, resilience and humour were a constant source of inspiration to me, to his family and to almost everyone he met. He was always able to summon the courage to carry on, even through difficult times or when tragedy struck. The most devastating example of this was on 1 April 1991, when his youngest son, Damon, passed away aged just twenty-four.

Bryce was a gifted storyteller. With the application of truckloads of 'bum glue' he managed to write twenty-one books in twenty-three years. Most of them became number-one bestsellers, and some went on to sell millions of copies worldwide. It has been estimated that something like one in three Australian households owns a Bryce Courtenay novel. He used to say with pride, 'My books belong with the socks and the chocolates under the Christmas tree.' Bryce's books sometimes received unflattering reviews from literary critics, but he was far more interested in the opinion of his readers, and would say, 'The reader is always right', even referring to the reader as 'the fourth protagonist' in his books.

Bryce was diagnosed with gastric cancer in late 2010. In the last months of his life he kept writing even though his illness was extracting a terrible toll. He rarely complained, and at the end of July 2012 the final chapter of his novel Jack of Diamonds was completed, a year later than he had intended. At that point he then pretty much turned off his computer. He wanted to spend the time he had left with me, and with Brett and Ann, Adam and Gina, and his beloved grandchildren. It was an intense experience, but I know how much it meant to him to share this time with those he cared about most. Bryce passed away on 22 November 2012 at the age of seventy-nine, just ten days after the publication of Jack of Diamonds.

I hope he would approve of my decision to write the story of his extraordinary life. He always knew that one day a biography would be written, of that I am sure. I have often felt his guiding hand on my shoulder from the portrait of him by Paul Newton, which hangs on the wall behind my desk. I can't tell you how many times I have gazed at this artwork and said, 'I wish I had asked you more questions about your life!' Throughout, I have tried to keep uppermost in my mind the words he cherished from his grandfather, that 'Good storytelling must include a bucketful of tears and a bellyful of laughs.'

This book was written to present to Bryce's three grandchildren, Ben, Jake and Marcus, and to my son, Nima. It was also written for the millions of readers around the world who continue to inspire me to champion Bryce's legacy. Their outpouring of love and kindness has been remarkable, and many have begged me to write Bryce's life story. There is no question that in every respect Arthur Bryce Courtenay AM was a force of nature. My hope is that this book will be received as a fair testament to his life, and an inspiring celebration of all that he achieved.

In advance, I extend my apologies for any errors in my book. I have truly given it my best. I have poured my heart into writing it over an eighteen-month period, and am both grateful and honoured that Penguin Random House Australia decided it was worthy of publication. I especially wish to thank their CEO, Julie Burland, and my publisher and editor, Rachel Scully, who believed in me and whose contribution as my editor has been extraordinary. It is my hope that people reading it will be pleased with this tribute, the first biographical work of Bryce's life. It is especially poignant that it is being released on the tenth anniversary of his passing. I invite you to turn the page and commence reading *Bryce Courtenay: Storyteller*.

My warmest wishes,

Christine Courtenay

Christine Courtenay AM
1 August 2022

1

A TOUGH START

Can you remember when you were a kid
and you'd lie in the grass on your back and
watch the clouds scud above you and dream of what
you were going to be when you grew up?
Well, what happened?
– *A Recipe for Dreaming*

ARTHUR BRYCE COURTENAY was born at the Queen Victoria Hospital in Johannesburg on 14 August 1933 and was not expected to live. He weighed 3.5 pounds (1.6 kilograms), having been born several weeks premature, and was said to be 'bluish in colour'.

His mother, Maud Jessamine Greer, known affectionately as Paddy, may have felt mixed emotions as she was almost penniless and, in those days, would have been labelled 'a fallen woman' for having a child out of wedlock. The tiny boy was her second child born in these circumstances – a daughter named Rosemary Ann had been born sixteen months earlier in the same hospital, on 5 April 1932.

Separation from his mother came early for Bryce. Soon after his birth, Paddy needed to have an emergency appendicitis operation and Bryce was taken back to the hospital while I gather Rosemary was sent to stay with some relatives.

Before Bryce had turned one year old, Paddy moved to Durban, a coastal town located in Natal (now KwaZulu-Natal), six hours' drive from Johannesburg – most likely to be closer to Arthur James Ryder, the father of both of her children, who had secured a job with the Colonial Mutual insurance company. However, soon after her arrival in Durban Paddy suffered a stroke. Bryce was later told by both his mother and Rosemary that it took her months to recuperate as she had to relearn how to walk and speak.

During Paddy's recovery, Bryce was placed in a boarding house while Rosemary was apparently sent to stay with one of Paddy's friends. He was taken care of by an African Zulu nanny called Violet, who reappears as Mary Mandoma in *The Power of One*. Mary is the only maternal figure in the character Peekay's childhood:

> Before my life started properly, I was doing the usual mewling and suckling, which in my case occurred on a pair of huge, soft black breasts. In the African tradition I continued to suckle for my first two and a half years after which my Zulu wet nurse became my nanny. She was a person made for laughter, warmth and softness and she would clasp me to her breasts and stroke my golden curls with a hand so large it seemed to contain my whole head.

Violet's affection was a source of great comfort for baby Bryce, just as it was for Peekay, and for both it was a love soon to be extinguished from their lives. Indeed, many aspects of Bryce's chaotic early life were described in *The Power of One*. He said of his debut on many occasions, 'It was a novel, but it was also in part autobiographical.'

Paddy was born on 8 June 1905 in Springs, a famous goldmining city in the former Transvaal, some 50 kilometres east of Johannesburg. Her mother, Edith Ida Greer (nee West and known as Edie), was pregnant with her sixth child when she tragically died from a burst appendix in 1914 – an unimaginable loss for her surviving children. Paddy was then only nine years old. Edie loved to paint, and I still have a pretty flower study in oils by her hanging on the wall in my bedroom. Bryce confirmed that Edie's tragic death meant that Paddy's father, Robert Bryce Greer, was left with five children to care for: Paddy and her four brothers, James Courtenay, Charles Arthur, Robert Bryce and Archibald Campbell.

In a letter written to Paddy on 2 July 1939, Robert discussed the loss of his wife: 'I dearly loved her and it left me with no desire ever to marry again. Her long illness, three operations – and the final – left me with accounts to meet, of three hundred pounds.' He was advised to send all of his children to a Presbyterian orphanage but couldn't bear to do this: 'I did not think that this course would mean a happy childhood for you all, and I wanted to keep you with me, so I shouldered the burden and engaged Mum as housekeeper.' 'Mum' turned out to be a hardworking but rather stern housekeeper called Mrs Jackson whom Robert later married. He wrote to Paddy of his choice:

I found her everything I could wish in that position, but you children would not recognize her authority over you – and trouble eventuated. I could see a constant succession of housekeepers, my children growing up wild, and so I gave her the powers in the only possible way. It took a brave woman Paddy, to take on the upbringing of you five: Archie just a toddling baby and Bryce little more – and debt in the offing. Thanks to her careful management and hard work, in which I think she wore herself out for us, I got clear of debt . . .

Desperate to secure income, Robert established a grain mill, but this too ended in failure with an outbreak of foot-and-mouth disease and farmers fearing his grain may be contaminated. He had to then search for a variety of jobs including at the Consort Mine near Barberton (Mpumalanga Province) while leaving his children at home with Mrs Jackson.

This entire situation can't have been easy for Bryce's mother, left in the care of her stepmother, and she left school and home as soon as she could. Her hopes and dreams of gaining a qualification were also left behind. Being a talented dressmaker at least meant she could earn a living from her prized Singer sewing machine – but she had aspired to more. More often than not, Paddy ended up taking jobs as a sales assistant in a series of clothing stores being paid wages that weren't exactly generous. Bryce always remarked on her 'good head for business', and it's likely she would have been an asset for her employers.

Upon reaching adulthood, she experienced a broken engagement before falling madly in love with Arthur James Ryder, seventeen years her senior. Arthur was born in Newcastle in Natal on 1 April 1888 to Frank Morel Ryder and Frances Henrietta Ryder (nee Cunningham). He was the eldest son of their eight children and due to his father's poor heath acquired adult responsibilities from an early age. His forebears had been Cunningham-Ryders, but Bryce told me that for some reason Arthur had chosen to be known simply as 'Ryder'. He and Paddy met at a clothing store in Barberton in the Eastern Transvaal where she was working and where he was employed as a commercial traveller. Arthur was married and – Paddy soon discovered – already a father of six.

'Pat', as Arthur called her, may have believed his assurances that he would divorce his wife, Ivy, and in 1931 she and Arthur ran away to live together in Johannesburg. This would have been considered outrageous in those days and Paddy probably knew it was going to be a tenuous arrangement. A short time later Paddy fell pregnant with Rosemary, and when Rosemary was born she was given the surname of Courtenay after Paddy's great-grandmother Agnes Courtenay (1810–1877), who was the daughter of John Courtenay (1782–1815). Agnes's grandfather was called Sampson Courtenay and she went on to marry Thomas Arthur Greer (1808–1890). Arthur Greer their son was the father of Robert Bryce Greer, who was Bryce and Rosemary's grandfather. Paddy must have decided to call her only son Arthur Bryce, after his father Arthur, and in deference to her own father, Robert Bryce.

Arthur Ryder, known as AJ, was known for being a handsome and charming man with impeccable manners and who was always immaculately dressed. At first, he did well in the world of business and public life and was seen as one of Newcastle's most eligible bachelors. At some point he was even appointed deputy mayor, and he co-founded a department store with his brother-in-law John 'Jack' Walsh called Walsh & Ryder that was said to be ahead of its time. Captain Jack was killed in action in Halazin, Egypt on 23 January 1916 while serving with the British forces, and Arthur's youngest brother, Robert, was killed in action on 15 July that year during the Battle of Delville Wood in France. Arthur always felt guilty for having stayed home to mind the business while the boys went off to fight. Sadly, the once-thriving Walsh & Ryder fell victim to the economic firestorm of the Great Depression. Times were hard, and Arthur's fortunes continued to decline until eventually he lost everything.

Arthur's wife, Ivy (nee Ivy Hilda Merrick), had come from a wealthy family in Pietermaritzburg in Natal; she enjoyed a charmed life while growing up and was known for being 'A tiny, dainty and sweet-natured young woman, who was loved by everyone who knew her throughout her life.' Arthur was never really accepted by the Merricks, and his youngest daughter Eirene confirms further details in a letter written to Bryce in 1994: 'They had married in 1913 . . . (but) from the outset she and Dad were not suited.' Ivy was said to have hated having to play hostess at the elaborate social occasions Arthur insisted upon.

Arthur's worsening drinking habit proved to be his undoing. It became too much for Paddy to cope with, and not long after Bryce's birth she reluctantly dispatched Arthur back to his wife and children. Consequently, she was all alone with two young children and barely a penny to her name. Bryce told me that when his mother was in her senior years, she shared a dark secret with him that made him feel desperately sad: Paddy had been so consumed with anxiety while pregnant with him that she had contemplated taking her own life. He understood she didn't take this drastic step because she would lose everything in the world precious to her.

To provide for herself and her children Paddy took on several jobs, including being a boarding-house matron, a shop assistant and a housekeeper. With no one to mind her children while she worked, she had little choice but to place Bryce and Rosemary in a series of hostels, boarding houses and orphanages. For the children these institutions became harbingers of emotional deprivation, loneliness and punishment. As Bryce wrote in *The Power of One*:

> Deep inside me the loneliness bird sat on its crude stone nest and laid a large and very heavy stone egg.

In an interview with Jane Cadzow in the *Good Weekend* published on 17 March 2012, Bryce shared that 'People who worked in orphanages were pretty rough. We got beaten so often on our bums that we got these permanent marks. We used to call it Chinese writing.' The food was also less than inviting as it was for Peekay in *The Power of One*:

> Then began a time of yellow wedges of pumpkin, burnt black and bitter at the edges; mashed potato with glassy lumps; meat aproned with gristle in grey gravy; diced carrots; warm, wet, flatulent cabbage; beds that wet themselves in the morning; and an entirely new sensation called loneliness.

In all it was a harsh, frightening and bewildering experience for a child so young. I suspect it was also why Bryce never grew cabbages in our vegie garden!

There was no social welfare available to Paddy. She told Bryce that when she was growing up she had dreamt of becoming a teacher, but in addition to her difficult home life she suffered from the gender privations of her era. Like many young women back then, she was forced to leave school early as families primarily focused on finding their daughters a husband of means and social standing.

Being a hardworking and well-spoken woman offered Paddy no protection from the perceived shame of being an unmarried mother. During both her pregnancies she fled to stay with friends, well away from prying eyes. Once her babies were born, and to fend off the town gossips, Bryce said she would tell strangers she was a widow. He told me that for a long time, he believed that his father had in fact died in a car crash.

Rosemary and Bryce endured the verbal blows of their peers, who used to call them 'little bastards' – a wound that scarred deeply. Bryce reflected, 'I started life by being born illegitimately and that meant the curse was put on you.' Not having a father around meant he and Rosemary grew up feeling different to other children, whom they viewed as living in 'normal' families. Bryce said he always remembered how people would avert their gaze or shoot disapproving looks in their direction. Being a young child, he never understood why.

For years after her stroke Paddy continued to suffer from ill health, including bouts of malaria and increasingly frayed nerves, all of which made holding down a job more difficult. She would take in sewing to do in the evenings to supplement her meagre wages. She made her children's clothes from cloth remnants, second-hand curtains and even from flour sacks. Bryce recalled in an interview with Diana Ritch recorded by the National Library of Australia in 1991, 'I was actually barefoot, but again this wasn't a big deal because so was everybody else, and my total wardrobe consisted of two pairs of khaki pants and two shirts and, if I remember correctly, one was less patched than the other so it was my best shirt, the one I wore to Sunday school.' It is little wonder, therefore, that Bryce had a lifelong passion for beautifully crafted shoes, which he looked after meticulously.

Even haircuts were something of a luxury. Bryce told me that Paddy would take him to a local barber to get his head shaved so that the haircut would last longer.

As the years went by Paddy and her children continued to drift between Johannesburg and several small towns in Natal that were close to where she could find work and to where Arthur and Ivy were residing with their children. Bryce and Rosemary continued to be placed in a series of spartan institutions where they were at the mercy of carers who were occasionally kind but far too often cold and cruel. It was often the Africans working in these institutions who became their only friends. Many of these experiences were included in the harrowing stories Bryce included in *The Power of One*. In Chapter 9 he describes how Peekay dealt with his mother's anger: 'Of course, she did not know she was dealing with a veteran of interrogation and punishment and since I had suddenly grown up on the hill, I was uncrackable. A real hard case.' When she tries to make him apologise to her before breaking down in tears of self-pity, he responds by saying, 'I'll get you a nice cup of tea and an Aspro and then you must have a good lie-down.'

Now and then, people Paddy had met would take pity on the children. Occasionally both Bryce and Rosemary would be taken out for a meal at a local tearoom – a welcome reprieve from the rigours of institutional life, and a glimpse into a more comfortable world they had never known.

Bryce told me they would quite often be split up and Rosemary would be sent to stay for long periods of time with friends of her mother, or with one of Paddy's four brothers. At other times Rosemary would return to live with her mother but Bryce would be left behind at a boarding house or an orphanage. This meant that he languished all alone, without even Rosemary to turn to for comfort. It is hard to imagine the sheer terror and confusion Bryce must have gone through, especially as he was still such a young child. He confirmed his memories of these times to me on several occasions and said, 'I never quite understood why Rosemary was able to go home more often than me.' Inevitably he came to believe that his mother felt closer to Rosemary than she ever did to him. 'I would sometimes feel that my mother never really liked me.' Rosemary saw his relationship with his mother somewhat differently. This often happens with siblings who grow up to hold contrasting perceptions of their childhoods.

The letters written by Bryce to his mother and the few I have from her back to him do not entirely confirm this situation, as they are invariably imbued with loving refrains. Bryce remained unfailingly loyal and dutiful towards his mother but there is no doubt that he believed there was an emotional chasm between them. The long periods he spent living apart from her would have understandably contributed to him feeling a sense of rejection. Regardless of this ambivalence, Bryce's love and generous financial support of his mother never wavered. He wrote a little about this in a letter to Rosemary on 29 October 2008: 'While we have led very different lives and, in fact, spent only a short period of childhood together, this period we shared under the same single parent differs entirely in the impact it has had on our subsequent personalities.'

Bryce kept many of these experiences buried in his memory, and rarely spoke about them. Soon after he passed away in 2012, I was told that he was once locked in a small dark cupboard by a school or boarding-house matron. Perhaps unravelling the details in his novels provided a more bearable way for him to deal with them. This process was likely to have been cathartic for him, and I am sure he felt it allowed him to set the record straight. In May 2006 he was a guest on *Talking Heads*, an ABC TV program hosted by Peter Thompson. He said, 'I never wanted anybody to know that I had no background, that there was just this darkness, a vacuum in the back of me, and that I came from nothing and no one.'

Paddy didn't often seek help from her brothers, although they did stay in touch and Bryce confirmed that now and then they did provide her with some financial assistance. What a difference it would have made for her and her children if she had reached out to them more. Her two small children were carted from pillar to post, never knowing where their next meal was coming from or where they were going to rest their heads. It is possible her siblings also carried some residual misgivings towards her for having had her two children out of wedlock.

*

In the middle of 1937, when Bryce had turned four, they moved to Krugersdorp, a goldmining city of the West Rand in the former Southern Transvaal (now Gauteng Province) an hour's drive north-west of Johannesburg. Paddy had secured a job there in a store called Foschini's, and she placed the children in an orphanage.

During this time a man called Frederick Roberts began to court her and it wasn't long before she agreed to become his wife, presumably desperate for some security and the respectability afforded to a married woman. It can't have been an easy decision as she was still deeply in love with Arthur. Unfortunately, Fred turned out to be an absolute scoundrel and a drunk – a violent one, at that. She was trapped, her only respite being reunited with her children on the weekends when they were allowed to leave the orphanage. Eventually, after an allegedly violent incident, Paddy fetched the children and fled to live in the relative anonymity of the big city of Johannesburg.

Rosemary remembered these events and has described how they spent their first night after they fled huddled together on a bench in Joubert Park, in the heart of the city. At least they were free from Roberts, who would have undoubtedly wreaked further havoc on their lives. Sadly, this scenario continues to be played out in communities around the world. Bryce regularly donated to women's shelters, having never forgotten the harrowing experiences his mother went through.

The only benefit of this dreadful marriage was that their mother was now able to call herself Mrs Maud Roberts, and claiming to be a widow offered her some protection. It was a surname she continued to use for the rest of her life. She enrolled the children in a local primary school as Rosemary and Bryce Roberts. Some of Bryce's early school reports show that he was registered in the name of 'Arthur Bryce Roberts'.

It was to be another twenty-three years before Paddy was finally freed from the fear of Fred Roberts finding her: she discovered he died on 14 June 1960 at the age of sixty-five. Bryce told me he had almost no recollection of this man, being such a small child at the time, and because Paddy only stayed with him for a short period. What isn't clear is whether she ever managed to formally secure a divorce.

Before long Paddy moved again, this time to the mining city of Tzaneen, about four hours north of Krugersdorp. Tzaneen lies at a height of 719 metres in the Mopani district of Limpopo Province and is known as 'Land of the Silver Mist' because of the mists that descend from the mountains above it. Even though they were now living in an especially beautiful part of South Africa, it's unlikely the landscape gave Bryce and his sister much joy. For a time they all lived together in one room, and the children were left on their own for long periods while their mother went out to work

One of Bryce's most touching stories was about their first Christmas in Tzaneen. Six-year-old Rosemary, knowing there would be no money for presents from their mother, wrapped a brick in crumpled yellow paper so that on Christmas morning Bryce would have a gift to open. Even though, like many siblings, they apparently squabbled a great deal, she was devoted to Bryce and immensely proud of all of his later achievements.

As an adult Bryce adored Christmas and always made it extra special, with roast lamb cooked in yoghurt with rosemary, piles of roast potatoes, and a festive salad made with strawberries and greens from the garden. He indulged everyone with thoughtful and beautifully wrapped gifts, no doubt determined that his childhood memories of spartan Christmas Days were well and truly behind him. I am sure that Paddy did her best; it must have been painful for her to see her children going through many of the privations she had endured as a child. I am also mindful that she had lived through the era of the First World War and the Great Depression, and her expectations would have been commensurate with a life of unrelenting frugality.

In 1938 they moved again, this time to the town of Duiwelskloof (now Modjadjiskloof), 18 kilometres north of Tzaneen at the foot of the escarpment in Limpopo Province. In Afrikaans the town's name means 'Devil's Gorge'. Rosemary and Bryce were placed in yet another orphanage, undoubtedly the worst of the institutions Bryce lived in as a young child. I am certain it was the place he referred to as 'the Boys Farm' in his novels and subsequent media interviews. He soon raised the ire of the staff there, whom he told me were particularly sadistic:

> I couldn't do a single thing right. The heavy-handed punishments regularly meted out to me were invariably explained as being "for my own good", or "in the name of our Lord".

In his interview with oral historian Diana Ritch he confirmed:

> So the germ, the germ of fear – *are you good enough?* – was sown. I think you have to remember that here I was, the five-year-old who'd had a quite awful time in this boarding school and who really knew what it was like to be scared and afraid and feel inadequate and know that you were, to put it crudely, a piece of shit.

Eventually Paddy moved them to another boarding house in the same town, which Bryce faintly recalled was slightly better but still far from being an ideal place for a small child. In his final years, it was hard for him to precisely recall the dizzying number of institutions he had been placed in for varying amounts of time, or the countless times his mother moved. The only breaks from these places he referred to as 'children's prisons' was when he was sent to stay for short periods with his mother, his uncles and their families, or his mother's friends. Years later Bryce could easily be moved to tears if he watched a program on television about abuse meted out to innocent children placed in institutions, in the care of people unfit to look after them.

It has been a heartbreaking process for me to read the childhood letters written by Bryce to his mother while he was incarcerated in these boarding houses. You can feel his sense of longing to be back with her and his loneliness accompanied by the faint hope that somehow, he might make it home for Christmas: 'I have ben working really hard at school but mommy nothing seems to go right. Everything seems to go wrong. I am so worried I dont know what to do.' And, 'Dearest Mummy, We both terribly sorry it won't be a Christmas with our Mommy.' 'I hope you have a happy birthday on Sunday. We did not have any present to send you.' Bryce would sign these letters with, 'Tons of love mommy, your Sunny Bun Bun.'

Learning to read and discovering books became Bryce's saviour during these years of misery, giving him the chance to lose himself in a world of adventure and fantasy. He later drew from this experience in *Whitethorn:* 'Soon the books became longer and more exciting, and reading became a life for me where there was no sjambok, no Mevrou, no Boys Farm.' In *Jack of Diamonds*, Bryce wrote, 'Reading had been the mainstay of my life. It had more or less conquered my loneliness after my mother had landed her job as a night cleaner.' He revealed in an interview with Writers Write, Johannesburg, in 2006, that his favourite book character was Oliver Twist, 'because Dickens made me realise that I was not alone at the age of seven'.

In interviews and public lectures Bryce often related the story of being incarcerated in the 'Boys Farm' as a small boy and once having to walk 7 miles (11 kilometres) to go to the doctor after badly cutting his finger. While the doctor, Henny Fenner, tended to his wound, Bryce passed out from loss of blood and the doctor had to leave him to attend to an emergency. Feeling too weak to walk back to the orphanage, Bryce crawled under the house. He woke in the morning to discover he was sleeping against a chest full of books. Opening it, he found that the books were written in English, a language rarely read in this predominantly Afrikaner town. On top was a book bound in red leather with its pages edged with gold – quite the loveliest thing he had ever seen. Desperate to better his rudimentary English, he squirreled the book away and returned to the Boys Farm. The title of the book was *The Abolition of Slavery in the Cape Province of 1834*, and Bryce always said it allowed him to improve his English.

This story is expanded upon in *Whitethorn*, which Bryce always said was his most autobiographical novel. He wrote a lot about how a young temporary teacher taught him how to read in English, saying, 'Suddenly my life changed forever.' Apart from this he would have been able to study English from the Bible, which his mother ensured he saw plenty of. Bryce said she always spoke to her children in English, and in fact never mastered Afrikaans to the extent that he and Rosemary did.

Growing up in poverty and moving in and out of institutions weren't the only crosses the two young children had to bear. Duiwelskloof was largely an Afrikaner (Boer) town and Bryce and Rosemary were from an English background. This meant that the local kids regularly singled them out. South Africa's Boers had been defeated by the British in the Anglo–Boer War (Second Boer War) of 1899–1902. It had been a brutal conflict and the British continued to be viewed in Afrikaner towns with both suspicion and hostility. Bryce was still only a small boy but was nonetheless mercilessly bullied by the Afrikaner kids, who regarded the little *rooinek* (literally meaning 'red neck', perhaps because the British sunburned easily) as fair game. Peekay suffers the same racial taunts in *The Power of One*:

> I was the youngest child in the school by two years, and I spoke only English, the infected tongue that had spread like a plague into the sacred land and contaminated the pure, sweet waters of Afrikanerdom. To their barefoot sons, I was the first live example of the congenital hate they carried for my kind.

Bryce frequently told the story (incorporating a few Afrikaner words) of how he would defend himself by saying, 'Och man, please don't hit me. Don't hit me and I'll tell you a story.' And then he told his first story, 'but I didn't tell them the end. "Anybody who hits me before tomorrow doesn't get to hear the end of this story."' Sometimes he told me he managed to spin the story out for a week or more – and thus his storytelling life was born. As he said, 'I have in a sense been telling stories since I was six years old. My dream was to be a storyteller, and it saved my life. I also got to be a good boxer by the way, just in case.'

Even during the last few days of his life, Bryce told me how much he had hated being called *pisskop*, meaning 'pisshead' and *sprinkaan*, meaning 'grasshopper', while he was growing up. It was as though he still hadn't recovered from those ugly experiences in South Africa over seventy years earlier. I shudder to think that deep down Bryce still believed, as he wrote in *The Power of One*, that 'I was doomed to be a pisshead for the rest of my life.'

In 1941, in a surprise move, Paddy went to live with Ivy and Arthur, who had moved to the small coastal town of Winklespruit in Natal. It's unlikely at this stage Ivy was aware of Paddy and Arthur's relationship. It is likely she had gone there in desperation for a much-needed rest to try to restore her health. Her young children remained at the children's home in Duiwelskloof before they were reunited with her some weeks later. Bryce's half-sister Eirene Carroll (nee Ryder) wrote of their arrival: 'There you both stood when I got home from school, so quietly, and so obviously overawed by this change in your circumstances, and your new surroundings, that my heart went out to you both right away.' She described Bryce as 'not a handsome child, but you were the most lovable little boy, full of character and humour, traits which became increasingly evident after you had got over your initial shyness'.

Bryce and Rosemary still had no idea that Arthur was their real father: they were always told that he and Ivy were their godparents and they should refer to them as Uncle Arthur and Aunty Ivy. As they settled into a semblance of family life, they had the chance to get to know Arthur's six other children. It wasn't a particularly happy home as Arthur was wary of showing them much affection, and with money being scarce mealtimes were often frugal.

Arthur's children with Ivy were also completely unaware that Bryce and Rosemary were in fact their half-siblings. Eirene had stumbled upon the truth around 1950, but respected her mother's wishes to keep it a secret. Paddy also believed that Ivy and Arthur had eventually told their children, but in fact the truth had never been shared. This was confirmed in a letter I have dated 23 May 1991 from Tom Wallett, the husband of Arthur and Ivy's daughter Joan. He wrote from his home in Durban: 'Wow! Welcome back to the Ryder family circle. On her [Joan's] behalf I extend to you, Bryce and your families our true affection & to say that we are honoured to know of our relationship with you.'

In July 1991 Bryce and Rosemary arranged to meet up with several members of the Ryder family in KwaZulu-Natal, and what a special reunion it was! Contact was made with their half-siblings via advertisements Bryce paid to be placed in a Natal newspaper called *The Witness* in May 1991.

A letter from Eirene reveals her impressions of the nature of Paddy's relationship with Arthur:

> You once said you wondered why Dad had fallen in love with your mother. As I remember her first she was not pretty, but she had a sparkling wit, she had an admirable dress sense and a super figure. Above all perhaps, she had a keen intelligence that matched that of Dad's, and an understanding of the business world and its ups and downs, having been in business herself . . . She was also a wily young bird – she knew how to please men, to flatter them, and her total uncritical adoration of Dad had him hooked at a time in his life when he needed reassurance and a salve to his wounded pride.

Bryce was later told by Rosemary that their mother had got along well with Ivy and didn't have the heart to break up their marriage, and that they corresponded over the years. Rosemary recalled her mother even describing Ivy as 'my very dearest friend'. Eirene records a very different impression – perhaps in defence of her mother: 'She treated my Mom abominably, knowing that she had Dad's love and support and that my Mom had no redress and could do nothing about it. In those days Pat was a mighty unpleasant and ruthless woman, she had the upper hand and used that knowledge freely.'

At one point Ivy and Arthur offered to take on the two children full time, but Paddy ultimately refused, unable to hand her children over even in the face of such hardship. If she had relented, they may have been spared further years of living in institutions devoid of love and proper care. Within months of their arrival at Arthur and Ivy's, Rosemary and Bryce were unexpectedly removed and taken back to the boarding house at Duiwelskloof. Eirene provides an insight as to why they were taken away from the family: 'It transpired that the real reason for your sudden departure was that Pat & Dad planned to go away together, and Pat was to get a lift into Durban with Dad under pretext of looking for a job, so Mom wouldn't suspect.' Eirene claims that Ivy had confronted Arthur about his plans, and 'Dad could not endure the thought of telling his adult sons and daughters the truth, and reluctantly chose Mom.'

Soon after these volatile events Arthur moved with his family to Pietermaritzburg and settled into a job as a district manager with Colonial Mutual. He apparently became so well known in insurance circles that when the Traduna insurance company opened in South Africa they offered him the position of general manager. Eirene asserts that he was drinking quite heavily and would often take time off work, and so, 'With heavy heart, Dad had to refuse. He knew that he would not keep the job if they learnt of his drinking habits, whereas the Colonial Mutual did know & turned a blind eye.' She confirmed that in later years the general manager of Colonial Mutual in Cape Town said, 'He is the most brilliant man in his field in this country.' It is little wonder that the spectre of alcoholism arises in some of Bryce's later works. In *Matthew Flinders' Cat*: 'Billy wondered if indeed his brain *was* going, if he'd finally crossed over the line from the problem drinker he told himself he'd become to a blubbering, mumbling idiot.'

The children returned to live with Arthur and Ivy on a second occasion. Eirene wrote, 'She arrived in a car driven by a woman from her Church & left you kids with us. She apparently could not cope any longer & thought it time Dad had a turn.'

Eirene's final memory of Bryce and Rosemary staying with the family was in the family car on a Sunday afternoon drive:

> Dad was taking us for a Sunday drive – he and Mom in front, and Rosemary, Joan, you and I in the back. You suddenly sat forward & put your little hand on Mom's shoulder. Joan pushed your hand away, & said "Don't touch my mother"! The stricken, bewildered look on your face, & my intense anger at Joan. This time, Pat stayed with us for a couple of days, before the religious lady came to fetch you all in the car & you were to disappear from my life until I met you once again years and years later at Rocheberie Boarding House, when you had come to see Dad before you left for England.

Bryce often spoke about his mother as being someone who simply couldn't stay still, and it wasn't just due to her poverty and the need to constantly look for work. It was, he said, because 'She had an insatiable desire to keep moving around, probably linked to her ongoing mental health problems.' Rosemary and Bryce both spoke to me about their childhood cravings for security and their constant fear of being abandoned should anything happen to their mother. Her peripatetic nature meant that her two children stood little chance of having a stable place to call home. Looking back, he recalled that within the first ten years of their lives Paddy moved on at least twenty occasions. This played havoc with the children's education. It remains something of a miracle that both children continued to do so well in their studies, as reflected in some of their school reports I have.

Whenever Bryce and I moved house, which was twice, he was unusually out of sorts and only agreed to move to be closer to better medical services after he became unwell. He was a consummate homebody and always preferred to have meals at home rather than going out to restaurants. He was also fastidious about not wasting food and never threw out a single thing. I once saw him tucking into a piece of four-day-old steak, which he insisted on finishing, shared with our dog Timmy, who was lying as usual beside his chair.

Paddy sought refuge from her struggles by becoming increasingly engaged with religion, and eventually became a dedicated member of the Assemblies of God Church. This marked the beginning of her unwavering commitment to the Pentecostal faith. She had been raised as a Christian Scientist and sent her children to Sunday school as soon as they could walk. Bryce told me, 'We didn't have any say in the matter and were sometimes given a small treat, such as a handful of sweets.' I can understand why Paddy believed the church would offer her a kind of refuge and a sanctuary from her troubles. It was also her only chance to enjoy any kind of social life.

In an interview I recorded with Bryce at home in September 2012 he said, 'I never had what I would call a normal parent, because she was either down there having a bad time or she was up there talking to God with the Holy Spirit on her shoulder.' In other ways Bryce recognised that his mother forcing him to read the Bible gave him a great knowledge of the English language, especially as outside of home he mostly spoke Afrikaans. The Bible also overflows with stories and larger-than-life characters, which would have sparked his imagination and taken him away from the humdrum of daily life.

In our years together, Bryce never went to church other than to attend a funeral or a wedding. He would become slightly disconcerted when I told him that I sometimes took comfort from having been raised as an Anglican. Even so, on 20 November 2012 Bryce told me, 'I don't believe in God, but I believe what is in the Bible: 'A man reaps what he sows.' (Galations 6)

Paddy wouldn't tolerate any challenge to her reinvigorated religious fervour, and Bryce remembers being spanked without mercy by her if he couldn't recite lengthy passages from the Bible. He also said that she had a quick temper and he used to watch her closely to assess her mood. Perhaps as a result of this, he developed an uncanny sense of understanding what people were really like within minutes of meeting them. I am guessing that Bryce took the hidings in his stride, as he always remained positive regardless of what was going on. He said that Paddy would just as quickly pop him on her knee and sing him a song or tell him a story. He did, however, explain that the childhood beatings made him decide very early on that he would never lay a hand on his future children. He said that his three sons' only punishment if they misbehaved was that he would ask them to sit down and listen to him singing his favourite song, 'Summertime', by George Gershwin.

Bryce was a very patient and forgiving person who readily acknowledged the hardships Paddy had endured. He always admired her energy, resilience and sense of humour – interestingly, the qualities he himself had in abundance. In addition, he would reflect with fondness on her sense of style, her fascination with antiques, her love of nice clothes and her passion for reading and classical music. Occasionally she would write stories and poems, which he said were 'rather good'. Like Bryce, Paddy made friends wherever she went and maintained lifelong friendships. One of these was with Enda Murphy, whom Bryce honoured with a dedication in *The Power of One*, along with his mother.

Bryce's love of reading provided a treasured escape from the challenges he faced growing up. He told me he used to especially love reading cartoons whenever he could get his hands on them. Books including *Alice's Adventures in Wonderland* by Lewis Carroll, *The Wind in the Willows* by Kenneth Grahame and *Robinson Crusoe* by Daniel Defoe were favourites. I have no doubt that Paddy confiscated anything she thought 'inappropriate', which must have been exasperating for Bryce.

Bryce believed that few of us experience perfect childhoods, and he said in an interview at home in Canberra with journalist Roger Maynard on 8 May 2012, 'Remember we all have skeletons in our cupboards. I mean, if you shake any family cupboard it rattles like hell.' In his book *A Recipe for Dreaming* he asserted that 'The mental abuse of a child is the equivalent of spraying agent orange on virgin jungle', and he said of his childhood years, 'When I listen to the stories of what many people have gone through with their families, I am grateful that I never really had a family to speak of.'

The emotional deprivations Bryce experienced during childhood meant that he lived with a raft of insecurities from which he never fully recovered. As a child he must often have felt incredibly lonely, and he later said his greatest fear was 'not being loved'. This void in his soul was perhaps never filled, even when he in fact became greatly loved. Understandably, his childhood scars ran deep. As a coping mechanism he would compartmentalise events – and sometimes he would drink a little too much.

If Bryce was criticised by a journalist or hurt by a so-called friend or family member, he would cast his eyes downwards and say, 'However hard I work or however generous I am, I still seem to be viewed as the same old shitbag.' I found moments like this unbearably sad and would throw my arms around him and tell him how deeply I loved him and what a truly remarkable person he was. If I then said, 'Absoloodle' (from *The Power of One*), a smile would pass his lips and he'd say, 'Come here, kid, and give me a hug.'

Even the constant outpouring of love and affection he received from his family, publishing team and readers around the world was not sufficient to silence the demons that lurked within. Perhaps that is why he drove himself harder and harder to complete a book a year until the last three months of his life. Those close to Bryce often expressed regret that he hadn't taken more time to 'smell the roses'. We all ached to have more quality time with him.

Bryce firmly believed that his emotionally deprived childhood gave him a treasure trove of material for his fiction. Throughout his novels he tended to focus on shame, loneliness, love, hope and resilience.

These themes were drawn from his experiences as a child, but equally imagination and creativity played important roles in his work, and fuelled his passion to write. There is often a luminous and poetic dimension to his prose that was rarely acknowledged by critics – although loved by his readers.

Bryce featured strong female characters in his novels who carry on in the face of daunting circumstances, just as his mother had done. He never shied away from saying how much he loved women – he respected and admired them, and championed their stories. *Jessica* and *Sylvia* and the wives of husbands with PTSD in *Four Fires* and *The Story of Danny Dunn* are shining examples.

Bryce's female readers have always loved him for appreciating the contribution that women make in families, the workplace and in communities. *Jack of Diamonds* has its central character Jack Spayd reflect:

> It seems to me that happy families don't have to do a lot of thinking and planning and scheming. They don't have to leap at every opportunity that comes up. They don't have to learn from their mistakes because there's always someone to cover for them. But I grew up with a loving and determined mother fighting off a violent drunken husband, and having to support her son on a pittance . . . That brings you into the real world fast, makes you realise it's sink or swim and you have to grab every opportunity.

A respite from Bryce's early childhood woes arrived unexpectedly with a letter Paddy received from her father, Robert Bryce Greer, in 1941. As a result, Bryce and Rosemary embarked on a period that Bryce later described as 'the happiest four years of my life'.

2

HAPPY DAYS

'It seems to me that a child's past can be one of two things: a generally pleasant experience roughly summed up as childhood; or a graveyard of past happenings, the fatal emotional accidents that occur in the process of growing up without love.' – *Whitethorn*

WHEN BRYCE AND ROSEMARY wandered into their grandfather's garden in 1942 it must have felt like they were entering a dream, with the resplendent colours of the 'pride of De Kaap' (*Bauhinia galpinii*) to greet them, together with endemic proteas (*Protea curvata*) called Barberton sugarbush, and 10-metre stands of tree aloe (*Aloidendron barberae*) ablaze with rose-pink tubular flowers. The abundant orchard and well-stocked vegie patch would have heralded additional gasps of excitement.

They had arrived with their mother at Waverley House on Sheba Road in the town of Barberton to live with their grandfather Robert Bryce Greer, whom they barely knew. Robert Bryce had been born in 1870 and so would have been aged about seventy-two. The children, now aged nine and ten, were thrilled to finally be living as a family again.

Barberton lies in the beautiful De Kaap Valley in the southern part of the Eastern Transvaal (now Mpumalanga Province, meaning 'place where the sun rises') and is known as the 'Jewel of the Lowveld'.

Following in the footsteps of some earlier prospectors, Graham Hoare Barber discovered a gold-bearing reef there, and in 1884 the town was named after him. Barberton is ringed by mountains and with its hot tropical climate has been described as a veritable Garden of Eden. It is home to the Greenstone Belt, an ancient rock formation at least 3.5 billion years old. Hundreds of unique flower species thrive there, including the famous *Gerbera jamesonii*, commonly known as the Barberton daisy. Bryce said the family used to refer to Paddy as 'a true Barberton daisy' and he always made sure he planted gerberas in the garden of the homes we shared.

Bryce had great affection for his grandfather. In his interview with Diana Ritch he remembered him with great fondness:

> Quite a wonderful old guy. He was one of those Englishmen who sort of kept his mouth to himself but if you asked him he would tell you things. He read lots of books and he grew roses . . . that's all I needed to know about this splendid old man who completely minded his own business all his life.

Bryce described Robert as being a reserved and undemonstrative man but someone who had a passion for knowing what was going on. He never missed listening to the evening news on the BBC World Service with Derek Prentice announcing 'This is London calling'. Robert was the third-oldest of five sons and may well have lived in the shadow of his brothers' achievements. Frederick Arthur Greer, the second-eldest, was born in England in 1863; he was appointed as a judge of His Majesty's High Court of Justice in London in 1919, and in 1939 was raised to the peerage as Baron Fairfield. Another brother, Lawrence Greer, was made a commissioner in Rhodesia (now Zimbabwe) before relocating to New Zealand where he was a rector in the Anglican Church.

Paddy expected Bryce to follow in the exalted footsteps of her uncles as Bryce himself confirmed in the Diana Ritch interview:

So, anyway, here is this illustrious family and I'm going to grow up and be a famous lawyer, at least as famous as the Chief Justice of England, my grandfather's brother. So, in my mind's eye I could see that they really expected me to be Prime Minister of South Africa; nothing less would do because I now had this aspiration. But now, this sounds very enchanting but inside of this a fear started growing: was I good enough to be this, was I good enough to be Chief Justice of South Africa and then Prime Minister of who knows where? I had to now support this family, this antecedent that I was carrying for a thousand years and here I was – I only had one pair of boots and two pairs of khaki pants and I had to carry this family.

The weight of these expectations thrust upon Bryce would have been overwhelming given that he had grown up in an environment hardly ideal for nurturing a secure and confident child able to aspire to taking on the world. Years later he reflected on this with Diana Ritch:

Now, if you take this together with the Chief Justice of England, [my mother] managed to fabricate for me a quite awesomely wonderful family, to the point that consequently I spent my life really finding out the truth about this family, the Courtenays, and I discovered that they're the biggest bunch of blackguards you've ever met in your entire life and that they survived something like a thousand years of English history simply by being men for all seasons, and the reason they survived is because they always went on the side that was winning rather than the side that was right.

This is certainly a reference to the derring-do of Rob Roy MacGregor, whom Bryce said he and Rosemary were told by their mother was another of their ancestors. Lord Fairfield even used a crest with the motto *Hoc Securior*, which had been adopted by two of his Greer ancestors. I have a copy of the Greer arms, and it features a hand holding a shamrock, signifying that they had found safety in Ireland.

Robert Bryce Greer grew up in Liverpool and then trained as an engineer before serving with the Merchant Navy; later he joined the Union-Castle Line – a young man in search of adventure. Prior to this he was a stretcher-bearer for the Red Cross during the Anglo–Boer War before returning to South Africa and working as a ship's engineer. He fell in love on the voyage with Edith West, whom he later married. Edie tragically died in 1914 and Robert later married 'Mrs Jackson', his housekeeper who already had a child called Mary; Mary eventually left Barberton when middle-aged to be married. In her later years Mrs Jackson became incapacitated from the effects of what in those days was called senility, and Mary looked after her until she died.

Robert doesn't appear to have been very fond of Mary, saying in a letter to Paddy dated 2 July 1939, 'Mary Jackson is the problem and a problem that cannot be solved while her mother lives.' He does, however, acknowledge that he appreciated all she did for his wife (that is, Paddy's stepmother): 'She is the only one who can give her any companionship, the only one who can understand Mum's speech and whom Mum can understand.'

After his second wife's death, Grandfather Greer survived alone on a modest pension, and Bryce later understood that he asked Paddy to come back to Barberton to take care of him. Although she was fiercely independent, she may well have relished the invitation to offer her children a more stable home.

They found the house to be in a very dilapidated state, although Bryce told me it was crammed with antiques and its wide verandas gave it an air of grandeur. Their toilet was in an 'outhouse' at the end of the garden and before entering Bryce was always careful to check that a snake wasn't coiled up inside. It emitted a foul smell, and he said his mother used to hang up bunches of dried lavender to make 'sitting on the throne' more bearable.

Their grandfather's luxuriant 1-acre garden quickly became the children's sanctuary. It was home to hundreds of varieties of roses and supplied the family with abundant fruit, including mango, papaya, avocado, guava and all kinds of citrus – a contrast to the institutional grey food the children were used to. Bryce wrote in a letter from Barberton, 'We have been having afocartoe pear every supper and o'k I enjoyed it on my bread so much.'

It was while living with his grandfather at Waverley House that Bryce developed a great passion for growing things that was to stay with him throughout his life. He reflected in an interview recorded by Penguin Books Australia on 9 November 2009 that 'Gardening is what I discovered with my grandfather. Getting your hands dirty and watching things grow and seeing the miracle of plants rising from the earth. There is so much that nature gives you so generously, and the joy of it is that anyone can do it.' He later introduced his grandfather as 'Granpa' in his debut novel – a man who, like Robert Greer, spent his time growing roses in the memory of his late wife. Whenever we moved house, the first thing Bryce did was to go outside and start working on a new vegetable patch, and he would think about what else he could do to make the garden his own.

For a boy who was already devouring books, laying eyes on his grandfather's library filled with the classics must have set Bryce's heart racing. Quite fortuitously, Barberton had also once been home to the famous South African writer Sir Percy FitzPatrick, who wrote *Jock of the Bushveld*, published in 1907. It tells the story of FitzPatrick's travels with his dog Jock, a Staffordshire bull terrier cross. Bryce loved this book and told me he often read it while seated next to his grandfather on a bench in the garden. He always regarded Jock as one of his greatest fictional heroes. Bryce also discovered that his grandfather enjoyed telling stories, and learned later that his favourite book was Alan Paton's *Cry, the Beloved Country*, which was first published in 1948.

Most of us grow up with domestic pets, but for Bryce, in and out of institutional care, it was a childhood rite of passage he had never experienced. Within weeks of arriving at Barberton the family took in a few stray cats and a couple of dogs and purchased hens to supply the family with eggs. It could be that one of these chooks had a special place in Bryce's heart. I refer to his character 'Granpa' Chook, who was Peekay's only friend in the hostile boarding school in *The Power of One*: 'Granpa Chook was a survivor; how fortunate I was to have him as my friend.' These pets must have given Bryce and Rosemary a lot of pleasure as well as providing a source of comfort during troubled times.

Much later they were given a fox terrier they named 'Tinker'; readers of Bryce's first novel will recall how much Peekay loved him until his tragic death. According to Bryce, Tinker was an expert at killing the poisonous snakes that slithered into their garden. Bryce told me, 'I could never bear to have another dog called Tinker as I never got over losing him.' But while we were living in the Yarramalong Valley (inland from the New South Wales Central Coast), he rescued a dog he named Timmy who became Bryce's most loyal furred companion and would sit by his feet as he tapped away at his novels in his study.

Bryce reflected that their grandfather provided a foil to their often-forthright mother. Paddy dearly loved her children, but she had a sharp tongue and would not hesitate to put them over her knee and give them a sound spanking for misbehaviour. At this stage her religious fervour was in full flight, with her having become a Pentecostal Christian. Bryce elaborated on this with Diana Ritch:

She discovered God fairly early in the piece and I suffered mightily at the hands of the Lord because God became a partner with my mother in bringing me up and I found that they were spending a lot of time together – the Lord and my mother – and that most of it was about me and that I was getting an awful lot of Lord time thrust upon me . . . every time I did something half decent with myself the Lord got the credit and any time I did something for which I supposed I needed to be ashamed, I got the credit.

Bryce described the Assemblies of God as a charismatic Pentecostal faith: 'It believes very strongly that you have to confess to God and you have to be born again and you have to live a fairly cramped and restricted life.' He was increasingly at odds with his mother's religious ardour:

> I didn't quite see it that way because I went and examined all these people down at the Assemblies of God and even at 10 or 11 I could see that I didn't think I wanted to grow up much like them, in that the more blessed they became the more it seemed to me they were self-indulgent: they loved to talk about themselves and they liked to get involved with what dreadful sinners they'd been and how now they were all cured and they were going to be good but they just seemed to be ordinary shit-kickers to me.

Later in life, and in a letter written to Rosemary in late 2008, Bryce said that his mother's religious zeal had been damaging:

> I feel sure she was doing what became euphemistically known as 'the Lord's Will' fulfilling her duty as a charismatic Christian parent by constantly imposing a frightening and threatening, rather than enlightening, dogma upon us. It took years for me to undo the psychological damage and the burden of guilt it imposed until I was able to fully and finally exploit the potential of my own intellect.

He also expressed his scepticism through his character Peekay in *The Power of One*:

> All I know about the Bible is that wherever it goes there's trouble. The only time I ever heard of it being useful was when a stretcher bearer I was with at the battle of Dundee told me that he'd once gotten hit by a Mauser bullet in the heart, only he was carrying a Bible in his tunic pocket and the Bible saved his life.

Robert Greer's indifference to religion provided a stark contrast in approach for his grandchildren, but would have been a source of consternation for Paddy. The children were regularly dispatched to attend Sunday school at the local Apostolic Faith Mission as there wasn't a Pentecostal church in town.

He and Rosemary were enrolled at the local Barberton Public School, where their lessons were conducted in both English and Afrikaans. They were already fluent in Afrikaans, having learnt it while living in the boarding house at Duiwelskloof. The school motto was *Vincit Qui se Vincit*: 'He who conquers himself will win'. Bryce's school report confirms he received a merit certificate for Standard 5 (the last year of primary education) in 1946 for 'Conscientious work'. Another report dated 9 December 1942 states: 'Bryce has tried very hard and improved a great deal. He is interested in all the work.' He returned to the school in 1994 and was delighted to discover his name was registered in its honour rolls.

When not at school the children spent their days playing with the local kids, whose circumstances weren't much better than theirs, as described to Diana Ritch: 'Although we were very poor I never realised we were poor because in small towns like that everybody was poor. The doctor wasn't poor and the lawyer wasn't poor and the headmaster wasn't poor but most of the other people were. So you really didn't know you were poor.'

They loved exploring the mountains behind the house, and Bryce always referred to himself as a 'mountain man'. Long after he left Barberton he reflected in the Diana Ritch interview:

> As I've gone through life I've discovered that you can actually categorise people into three: there are mountain men, there are plains men and there are people who understand the sea. Mountain men understand that you can't tame the mountains – that the mountains are there and that you have to accept them on their terms . . . You can take nothing for granted and . . . life is really a

bigger process than you are and . . . you're not all that important in it . . . Really you're a human being and that is in itself quite a phenomenal gift.'

At school Bryce was able to indulge his love of Rugby, and he soon had plenty of friends given his cheerful and gregarious nature. Even so, the bullying and taunts from the Afrikaner kids continued. Fortunately, by then he was a seasoned fighter and had become adept at fending them off. *The Power of One* provides glimpses into Bryce's early school days. Readers will recall Geel Piet and the 'Barberton Blues' boxing squad who prize Peekay's fancy footwork to overcome his small size. But it must have been a frightening experience to run the gauntlet every day when walking home from school. He would have also felt the need to protect Rosemary and would have taken the brunt of the assaults being meted out.

Within a couple of years of their arrival at Waverley House, Bryce and Rosemary experienced further uncertainties arising from the Second World War. There was rationing of foodstuffs, and luxuries such as sugar and butter were in short supply. Bryce told me he always remembered the huge military camp situated not far from where they lived, which was strictly off limits. He would hear army vehicles in the dead of night as they rumbled along the road that ran beside the house. Many local men were sent off to fight, and South Africa went on to make a significant contribution to the Allied war effort. German nationals who lived in Barberton were interned, including a local music professor who appears in *The Power of One* as Karl von Vollensteen, a musician and botanist whom Peekay calls 'Doc':

'The good professor, who has lived in this town for fifteen years and has taught many of your young daughters to play the peeano, was born in Germany. It is for this alone that he is being put under my custody.' Several pockets of people in the crowd had started to boo and someone shouted, 'Once a Jerry, always a Jerry!'

During these years Bryce hardly saw his father, still only known to him as 'Uncle Arthur'. However, he told me they received an occasional letter from him and a very welcome gift of ten shillings every birthday. Their mother kept in touch with Arthur as well, but since she had become consumed with her Pentecostal beliefs her relationship with him had changed. This was confirmed in a letter written to Bryce by Eirene on 3 February 1994:

> Now that Pat was religious, she had changed completely. There was no longer any question of a love affair between them. Pat's religious principles precluded anything of that sort. The mother you remembered was a tired, disillusioned, religious woman. Religion had become her solace, and because she went overboard on the religious aspect, the person she once was, had become submerged.

Eirene then makes the point, 'There was an enduring love that remained, & you & Rosemary forged the bond even more strongly. He never stopped loving her, and I believe she continued to love him too.' Eirene also recalled Paddy once looking at her with a stern expression and saying, 'Eirene, always remember that only children of the Devil go to dances.' How fascinating it would be to know if Eirene's siblings shared her views on Paddy!

On several occasions Arthur pleaded with Paddy to hand over her children to him as he believed they would be better off. Apparently, Paddy contemplated this idea but couldn't go through with it, even though she did allow them to stay with Arthur and Ivy for short periods of time. And while Bryce and Rosemary got along well with their six half-brothers and half-sisters, Arthur's chronic drinking problem and constant house moves may not have provided them with much more stability. Bryce told me he faintly recalled how kind Ivy was to them although Arthur remained fairly aloof. Even though Bryce later always enjoyed a drink or two to relax after a day's writing, I think he remained for the most part conscious of not overdoing it, perhaps remembering the untold woes alcohol had caused his father.

Regardless of their dire circumstances, Paddy continued to lecture Bryce unabated about where his future lay as told to Diana Ritch:

'But it so happened that – again, possibly a figment of my mother's imagination – somewhere along the line the first born of this Courtenay family were always lawyers and I was the first born of the Courtenay family in South Africa and it was destined that I would become a lawyer.'

Perhaps, though, what Paddy did was teach Bryce to dream big, especially as her own childhood dreams had been thwarted by difficult circumstances and the dark shadows that shrouded people's lives during the Great Depression and two world wars. What Paddy had in store for Rosemary I cannot be sure of, but given the times I expect most of the career aspirations were directed onto Bryce.

Paddy's bold ambitions for her son did not, however, change the reality of their lives. The lack of money was a constant and relentless source of anxiety. Paddy found it difficult to secure good and reliable employment during such economically volatile times, and was hampered by her recurrent health problems. Taking in sewing provided a welcome supplement to her income and she taught Bryce how to use a needle and thread. I occasionally found him darning a sock or sewing on a button. Knowing that as a child I had loved sewing, he suggested we invest in a sewing machine, although we never did.

Paddy was a restless soul and after four happy years spent at Waverley House she began to contemplate moving again. Her nerves were continuing to play havoc on her health, and she knew she needed to go to a bigger city to find a better-paying job. Bryce's mother was a proud and stubborn person, and overtures to assist her may have been resisted. The children were also now teenagers and the local secondary schools were unlikely to have been of a particularly high standard. Paddy valued education greatly and never forgot the disadvantages she suffered from not having had the chance to acquire a professional qualification. Even so, it must have been a hard decision for her to make given that her children were settled into a real home and enjoyed living in Barberton so much.

In late 1947, she packed up their meagre belongings and moved them to Johannesburg, some 360 kilometres away. This unexpected move must have been a terrible shock for the children, and Bryce told me his mother later realised she had made a huge mistake. There was, however, no turning back, and Rosemary and Bryce were immediately packed off to boarding schools once more. Paddy took a job as a matron at an expensive girls' school and lived in one of its boarding houses. They would never live together as a family again. Eirene claimed that once Paddy returned to Johannesburg, Arthur sometimes paid her a visit. This may have been a factor that influenced Paddy to leave her father and their settled home in Barberton. It could also have been that she was tired of bickering with her father regarding the raising of her children.

Ivy suffered years of misery and humiliation following the discovery that Arthur was having a protracted relationship with Paddy. It became apparent to her after she found bundles of letters sent via poste restante, and became an enduring source of discord in their marriage. Even so, Arthur insisted that Ivy send postal orders to Paddy to help her out. Eirene wrote, 'So I do know that a bit of help was given – not enough, but then there was never enough of anything in our home!'

Grandfather Greer was unable to manage staying on at Waverley House and moved up to the Roan Antelope mine at Luanshya in Northern Rhodesia (now Zambia), where he was taken care of by Paddy's brothers Bryce and Jim, both of whom were there with their wives. Bryce Greer's son Errol wrote to me that he remembered both his grandfather and his father listening to the BBC news; if Winston Churchill was speaking, the children were not allowed to make a sound!

After leaving Barberton, Bryce never saw his grandfather again – a source of great sadness for him. Grandfather Greer passed away in 1956 at the age of eighty-six. Little did Robert know that his grandson who loved reading and gardening would one day become a world-famous author – and would plant roses and gerberas, as he had done, in each garden he created.

Bryce had done well enough at the Barberton Public School to secure a place at the exclusive King Edward VII School in Johannesburg, also known as KES. The school provided Paddy with some support to cover his fees. He was enrolled as 'Arthur Bryce Courtenay Roberts' and commenced his studies in what was called Standard 6. Rosemary was enrolled in the eighth grade at Johannesburg Girls' High School (now Barnato Park High School), the sister school to KES.

KES was named after the son of Queen Victoria and Prince Albert, and Bryce later described it as 'the Eton of South Africa'. The school's motto is *Strenue*, meaning 'Carry on', which must have held resonance for Bryce at that time and is an apt description of how he lived his life. He continues to be featured as one of their more illustrious alumni and I corresponded with KES while undertaking research for this book.

The school was founded in 1902 as the Johannesburg High School for Boys but was soon relocated to a mansion built for the mining millionaire Barney Barnato. Eventually, in 1911, the school was moved to the upmarket suburb of Houghton, and it was here that Bryce was enrolled. The century-old school buildings are set in magnificent grounds and are today regarded as national monuments. Nelson Mandela took up residence in the same suburb in the early 1990s, and I was driven past his magnificent estate when I travelled to South Africa in late September 2010.

On a visit to Australia in September 2006 Rosemary confirmed that she had won a scholarship to attend her girls' school and went on to do very well there. I recall Bryce saying, 'Rosemary was always much brighter than me. If she had wanted, she could have gone on to study medicine, but in the end her abiding religious faith shared with her beloved husband Esmund directed the course of her life.'

I well remember Rosemary confirming that from an early age Bryce was determined to achieve great things and always dreamt of one day becoming a successful writer. She remarked on how he made friends easily at school and was very popular with the girls! A letter from Eirene to Bryce written in 1994 stated: 'You did it the hard way, against all the odds, and I am so proud of you. I recognised that you were pretty special all those years ago, when you were a very young man.'

KES afforded Bryce an opportunity to secure a first-class secondary education. It was also his first real introduction to children from wealthy backgrounds. Seeing other parents roll up in shiny new motor cars, dressed in fancy clothes, must have been a confronting experience, as Bryce shared with Diana Ritch:

Here I was – the King of Jerusalem was on my back and the Count of Constantinople and the Chief Justice of England – and suddenly I was in an environment where everybody's father was a millionaire practically, and I couldn't even have my clothes dry-cleaned because I didn't have that kind of money . . . I discovered that suddenly here I was placed in this terribly posh school amongst hugely wealthy people and I had nothing . . . So I had to kind of devise a way of surviving this. I did very well at school and I was a brilliant sportsman and so I became sort of disguised . . . because this fear in me was growing that I really wasn't up to all the things that were happening to me. So I had to be better than everybody and so I grew up very carefully camouflaged, and now when I think back on it I was kind of beginning to live a lie. I was increasingly becoming afraid that people would find out the truth about my background, and so you can see a fairly complex sort of personality was sort of evolving here.

Peekay in *The Power of One* speaks as though he were Bryce himself: 'I had become an expert at camouflage. My precocity allowed me, chameleon-like, to be to each what they required me to be.'

Bryce quickly made friends, whom formed the basis of characters in *The Power of One* as Paul Atherton, Pissy Johnson, Hymie Levy and Cunning-Spider, who form a brotherhood called 'the Wooden Spoon Goons'. He was selected to become a winger in the firsts Rugby team, he told me, as although he wasn't tall he was very fast. This sporting prowess may have helped his chances of staying on at the school. I have no doubt he felt compelled to work harder and run faster than all the other kids to make sure he held on to his dreams.

How Bryce's time at the school was funded remains unclear, although from conversations I had with him and Rosemary it appears that his father may have contributed. By this time, according to Eirene, Arthur had gained some control over his drinking habits and was doing well in his job selling insurance. She confirmed that he had joined Alcoholics Anonymous and went on to assist other reformed alcoholics in their rehabilitation. Even so, Bryce's letters reveal that the payment of his school fees was an ongoing battle:

> Last Sunday night after we'd got back J.B. called me through and told me that there was no avialable fund which could help me. But that he and the Acting Head had dicided that for this term anyway there would be no fee. So that if you already have an account sent to you just dont take any notice of it. J.B. says that this may be continued next term depending on what our position is. But anyway we're clear for this term. 'I'st God wonderful' Honest mom when he told me I couldn't quiet grasp it.

I suspect that the school saw Bryce as an incredibly bright young boy who was brimming with potential, and the school's support of Bryce was commendable. It also nurtured other young students from difficult circumstances, including the great golfer Gary Player who, like Bryce, endured a terribly tough childhood.

The school holidays always posed a problem as Rosemary and Bryce no longer had a home to return to. In addition, not long after leaving Barberton their mother suffered a severe mental collapse, which in those days was described as a nervous breakdown, and according to Rosemary ended up at Tara Hospital in the Johannesburg suburb of Hurlingham. Bryce mentioned that Paddy had several of these throughout her life and used to tell me that he came to believe his mother was probably suffering from bipolar disorder. Certainly he witnessed her regular depressive episodes, and her mental health issues would have been exacerbated by the pressure of having to hold down a job. After being released from the hospital, Paddy bravely carried on working in a variety of jobs while living in a succession of modest lodgings throughout the city. This meant she did not have the ability to accommodate her children during their holidays.

Bryce was a popular boy and often received invitations to stay at the homes and farms of his wealthy schoolfriends, though finding the money to travel to their homes was a battle. He enjoyed these occasions, even though, as he told me, 'I used to feel like an orphan on the receiving end of charity.' In one letter to his mother he wrote, 'The Fordyas have invited me these Hols do you think it can be done. If not it's just tough luck.' An especially good friend was Jean Minnaar, and he used to go and stay with Jean's family near Nelspruit (now Mbombela).

Bryce told me about one holiday period when he simply had nowhere to go and ended up living among the homeless people in Joubert Park in the heart of Johannesburg. Although this posed considerable risks, he said it gave him an insight into the lives of people who existed a world away from the privileged students at KES. He was humbled by the kindness and generosity of those he met and found their tales of how they had ended up there deeply moving. Much later he wove aspects of these experiences into some of the stories in his novels. The scene featuring Tom Fitzaxby is painted vividly in *Whitethorn*:

> I suppose I could have afforded some sort of cheap boarding house or even the YMCA, but I continued to stay with this brotherhood of drunkards in what was referred to as the Starlight Hotel . . . In the winter we'd move over to the back of Johannesburg Central, or Park Station, as it was commonly called. We'd camp among the huge steam pipes pumping heating into the railway station.

Books continued to feature heavily in Bryce's time at KES regardless of him not having much money to buy them, as described in a letter to his mother:

> About some books Ma! I bought 15/- worth of books second hand – new they were about £3-10-0 worth. But of course I didn't have the money for them (School books). So mom if you have it, if you haven't it can wait it's not terribly urgent.

He was thrilled when he secured a part-time job at 'Mr Lights Bookstore', a position he maintained through most of his school years and through which he earned the pocket money he couldn't do without. He would have loved being surrounded by books, and told me the owner would give him new titles to take home and read so that he could then recommend them to customers.

Bryce had his share of ups and downs at KES. He wrote to his mother, 'Please pray for me – lots of things aren't going too smoothly. After all, I can't expect everything to go right – if it did there'd be something wrong.' However, his persistence with his studies paid off and it wasn't long before he reported:

I haven't done too well this form-order but so far the second half hasn't gone badly at all. This afternoon while watching some tennis J.B. came along and informed me he'd seen my marks. For a quarter of an hour afterwards I didn't see a scrap of tennis'.

Bryce spoke on a number of times about running classes for Africans, which began at KES, such as in a 2009 interview with Sheridan Voysey on Hope 103.2 FM. He was in a unique position to do this, as he'd learnt a fair bit of Zulu and Xhosa while in several institutions as a child:

I was able to communicate, whereas most white South Africans at the time couldn't speak an African language, and I started this school for Africans who worked at all the jobs that white people wouldn't do – and loved doing it, and they loved coming, and the police raided it and said it had to stop . . .

A Father Huddlestone, an Anglican minister in Soweto, then offered a space for the lessons to continue after his Sunday church services: 'So I'd take the bus out to Soweto and do this and the police burnt down the church hall.' I regret I didn't ask Bryce more about this seminal experience while he was alive, as it's one that clearly informed his crafting of *The Power of One*.

It was during these years at school in Johannesburg that Bryce and Rosemary finally discovered who their real father was. Their mother met up with them for a weekend outing and revealed that 'Uncle Arthur' (Arthur James Ryder) was their biological father. Bryce told me he had occasionally wondered about the true nature of their mother's relationship with Arthur, especially given his frequent visits to see her during their childhood. Even so, he said, 'It was a hell of a shock, although a relief to be finally told the truth.' Bryce had begged Paddy to tell him and never accepted why she held on to her secret for so long. Rosemary emailed me in 2013, saying, 'Hearing that we were illegitimate blew my mind – but Bryce seemed to be quite intrigued. We thought our father had died.' The revelation of being born out of wedlock evoked feelings of shame and humiliation especially I expect for Rosemary, given her strong religious convictions. They were also now faced with the daunting spectre of being half-siblings to Arthur's six other children, whom they didn't realise had not been told the true nature of their relationship to them. An altogether confronting set of revelations, and in a time when society's moral compass occupied centre stage.

Paddy had maintained the lie of being a widow, and the children would have felt caught up in her web of secrecy. They would also have known that the lie needed to be maintained. It could be that Paddy held off telling them in a desperate effort to afford them some protection from cruel jibes from other children, as well as to protect herself from unwelcome gossip and innuendo. Bryce provided reassurances to Paddy concerning his origins in a letter he wrote on 13 June 1956 while working in the mines in Northern Rhodesia:

> You're a silly little mother really, what on earth does it matter how I was born, the most important thing in the world to me is that I was born out of a love that was too great to know of any barriers and that the gift of life was given to me, I shall never try and justify my being born out of wedlock, but only endeavour to justify the life God was willing to breathe into me. Mother if anything I love you more than ever I could have conceived had you been socially obliged to bring me into the world. Please Mother never never feel any regrets that way.

I am not convinced Bryce ever got over not being told earlier about who their father really was. I even think he may have unconsciously carried a certain amount of shame connected to being born out of wedlock. In subsequent interviews throughout his life he offered various explanations about his tenuous relationships with his parents, noting that he grew up in an era where being born illegitimately was severely frowned upon.

Bryce and Rosemary didn't see much of each other during their years at secondary school and weren't especially close. Bryce told me that they squabbled constantly as children, even though they relied on each other a great deal due to their mother's frequent absence. Rosemary, he said, 'was much more of a goody-goody than I was and was more straitlaced – even though she was clever, kind and suffered just as much as I did during our childhood years'. Certainly, a letter he wrote to Rosemary in October 2008 confirms that he held a very different view of their upbringing than she did:

You appear to have seen our mother as almost saintlike, a beacon of moral rectitude and one of God's more remarkable servants. While I loved and respected her for the struggle she endured to bring us to adulthood, in hindsight I have come to see and abhor the bigoted and singular dogma and religious sect-isms she imposed on her children.

She inculcated guilt and punishment in our young lives while morally monitoring our actions and reactions in a constant imposition of a religious zeal that brooked no contradiction or discussion. In the process she made us smaller and lonelier, more isolated and fearful than children ought to be.

. . . While we share the same blood ties, quite different life experiences have caused us to choose intellectual and spiritual lives that differ vastly. I accept that your convictions are absolute and that mine are of an equal conviction, so I must and do respect your viewpoint but, alas, this comes at the emotional cost of familial closeness and affinity.

Bryce later reflected that being at KES was an exceptionally happy time in his life, and the friends he made there gave him the confidence to embrace the future with optimism. In late November 2012, a few days before he passed away, he mentioned one special schoolfriend in particular, a head boy called Fred Brodwick (I'm not certain of the spelling of his surname). At the same time, he told me how thrilled he was when Miss Bornstein – a teacher who inspired a character of the same name in *The Power of One* – arrived at KES to work there as a temporary teacher:

> In my tenth year a new teacher, Miss Bornstein, arrived at the school . . . [She] was the most beautiful person I had ever seen. At ten you are not supposed to be sexually attracted, but every nerve in my body cried out to be a closer part of this beautiful woman.

Bryce was now enjoying the benefits of being a teenager even though he had the maturity of a much older person, having navigated the trials of his upbringing. Not surprisingly, he began to have more adult insights into his background and his mother's view of the world, as he discussed with Diana Ritch:

> I had a fairly torrid time at my mother and the Lord's hands because they conspired mightily to bring me undone, but somehow I managed to evade them. I'd had about enough because everybody was guiding my life except me because I'd managed so skilfully to disguise myself and I was becoming exactly what all those mystical members of my family were proved to be later: men for all seasons. Boy, I could con anybody, I could bluff you into doing anything . . . somewhere along the line the mountain man got lost and so I had to go and re-find myself.

Consequently, even before leaving KES, Bryce decided he would thwart others' plans for him. He continued: 'I figured out that rather than try for all these huge scholarships and things I'd go and jolly well put myself through university.' This was a courageous, and even a naive decision, but he clearly wanted to forge his own path. He was also prepared to take on the responsibility of creating the means to do so. Regardless of these frustrations, he remained dutiful and loving towards his mother. It was as though since becoming a teenager he had become a kind of surrogate husband to her given the absence of a male breadwinner.

At the end of 1951, aged eighteen, Bryce graduated from KES with excellent academic results and a cache of prizes for his sporting achievements. However, he had no money and no home to go to. He therefore decided to hit the road with a rucksack on his back and look for work.

Before doing this, he set out on a journey he felt compelled to make: he hitchhiked to Pietermaritzburg to meet up with his father. He camped out in a small tent and caught up with Arthur each day after he had finished work. This was the first quality time he had ever spent with his dad and it gave him the opportunity to discover more about Arthur's life.

Bryce described this experience to me in November 2012, just four days before he died. He said he discovered his father was the only white man in Pietermaritzburg who was prepared to sell life insurance to black Africans, which meant their families would receive payments should something happen. Arthur was adored by the Africans for doing this, and they would say to him in Zulu (which Arthur spoke fluently), 'Uyasikhathalela', meaning 'He cares about us'. This story reminds me of the Africans in *The Power of One* who hailed Peekay as their 'Tadpole Angel' and as a chief who would one day free them from white oppression. Bryce said his father was persecuted by the white families for doing this, but he never gave up on the black Africans. He was also proud to learn that Arthur supported several social welfare groups in his community, and must have been relieved to discover for himself that his father was a thoroughly decent man even though he had faced a mighty battle with alcohol. It's quite possible that his father's example inspired Bryce's history of philanthropy once he had the means to do so.

Eirene wrote that during his final years Arthur became filled with remorse:

> He laboured tirelessly to help others, in an endeavour to make up for his lost years when he felt so keenly the fact that he had failed all of us. He became widely respected & admired, but he could never forgive himself for failing all of his children, & his grief and agony of mind over this fact during the time before he died was pitiful to see.

This was something Bryce could relate to. At times he also regretted missing out on a lot of time with his children both during his years working long hours in advertising, and later, due to his commitment to writing a book a year. This inevitable guilt is incurred by many people who forge stellar careers and embrace creative passions that are all-consuming. Looking back, I feel some of this myself having had a young son to raise and an all-consuming career firstly in adventure travel, and later when I was running my own strategic planning and marketing company.

To Bryce's delight he also discovered that Arthur was a natural storyteller known in his community as 'the raconteur of Natal'. It is tempting to think that Bryce may have had a talent for writing embedded into his DNA! Discovering that his father was a talented storyteller was undoubtedly a significant moment in his life and must have fed into his dreams of one day becoming a writer. The meeting is likely also to have emboldened him to make his own way and bypass the grand plans of his mother, in partnership with the Lord.

His father gave Bryce a special book he proudly displayed on his bookshelf where he wrote his novels: A Writer's Notebook by Somerset Maugham. Inside is written:

Bryce Arthur Courtenay,
With admiration & delight of your impeccable choice of good literature
From –
Uncle Arthur.

Few people are mathematicians, The vast majority are – Bookkeepers!

Arthur also included his address details: A. F. Ryder 'Rocheberi' No 165, Pietermaritzburg St., Pietermaritzburg, Natal (Rocheberi was a boarding house). In 2012 Bryce wrote in this book, 'Given to me the year I became aware my Godfather was in fact my biological parent. I was 15 years old.'

Even though Bryce had been named Arthur (with the second name of Bryce), he never liked the name and from a very young age preferred to be known as Bryce. In a playful tone I remember once saying to him, 'Darling, you are definitely a Bryce and not an Arthur.'

During their time together Arthur told Bryce about his younger brother 'Chummy' – who, as Eirene wrote, was 'a character among characters' who created football teams in the African schools of Newcastle where he and Arthur were born. Being a great sportsman himself, he was one of the few white people at that time who predicted, Eirene wrote, 'that one day the blacks would take their place as top achievers in the sporting field'. Sadly, Bryce never had the chance to meet Chummy.

Paddy didn't tell Bryce or his sister much about their father, which Bryce found equally exasperating and emotionally cruel, especially as he told me he begged her to do so. It may have been she didn't want them to know about the troubled periods in Arthur's life, particularly his battles with the bottle. I struggle to fathom why she didn't ultimately share more information with them, especially as they had grown up without a father present in their lives. Unfortunately, it is now impossible to resolve the true picture of this conundrum. When I commiserated with Bryce about the vicissitudes of his childhood, he wouldn't hear a word of it, and would say: 'Darling, you must understand I don't want you or anyone to ever feel sorry for me. Sure, my childhood was tough, but it made me the person I am. It also made me determined to really make something of my life. If my early life had been easy, I am certain I wouldn't have set the bar for myself so high.'

He said in the interview with Diana Ritch:

> I had quite an idyllic upbringing because I was a child who fell in love with life very early and because I'd been kicked in the bum fairly early and discovered that life was a fairly serious and tough affair, I kind of grew to enjoy things because I saw everything for what it was . . . I discovered fairly early in life that no matter how nasty things are they come to an end . . .
>
> So I think probably the greatest lesson of my life was taught to me very early: that if you endure, you actually win in the end. So I actually had quite a nice time growing up because there were good friends and nice people in this town and I used to love to roam the mountains and I became a mountain man.

Many people reflect to this day that Bryce was a complex person, and that is true. His childhood traumas undoubtedly sowed the seeds of this, just as they spurred him to reach for the stars. He and Rosemary suffered mightily in those appalling institutions and their childhood was a rollercoaster of uncertainty. Bryce, however, was always mindful of the dreadful circumstances Paddy went through to survive, even though he said to me, 'My mother's regular mood swings meant that being around her wasn't always very pleasant.' But he never failed to acknowledge the sacrifices she made, and ultimately believed she had done her best.

In late February 1953 Bryce made plans to travel to Nelspruit in South Africa's Lowveld, not far from the famous Kruger National Park. He was about to start his first full-time job, as a 'learner farmer' at the Crocodile Valley Citrus Estates. As far as he was concerned this meant he was stepping out to make his own way, and he couldn't have been more excited. Rosemary by this time had gone to work at the Johannesburg Standard Bank, a job she later told me she never liked.

Bryce never forgot the words said to him by Dr Henny Fenner, who drove him back to the orphanage in Duiwelskloof in his chocolate-brown 1939 Chevrolet Coupe, the one with the dicky seat, after Bryce badly cut his finger while gardening aged only five: 'In the end, lad, a man is responsible for himself. The best helping hands you will ever receive are what is attached at the end of your wrists. Take these hands, lad, and apply lots of "bum glue" and you will one day go on to achieve great things.' Two days before Bryce passed away, he confided, 'This was the single most important thing that anyone ever said to me.' Dr Henny reappears in *The Power of One* as Dr Henny Boshoff.

Bryce and I always planned to go to South Africa for a second visit to explore his childhood haunts, and I still have his KES school blazer hanging up in my wardrobe. Sadly, we ran out of time to go on that journey. However, returning to explore the places of his childhood was probably an unlikely scenario and may well have been too painful a journey for him to make. Bryce Courtenay was never a man who liked to look back. As Granpa said to Peekay in *The Power of One*: 'Sometimes it's best just to walk away from your memories, just put one memory in front of the other and walk them right out of your head.'

3

IN THE JAWS OF THE CROCODILE

It was sunset . . . A dangerous time in the bushveld, when
thirsty animals come to drink and hungry claws wait to tear
at bloody meat. – *The Night Country*

ON 1 MARCH 1953, not long after he had completed his matriculation
year at KES, Bryce arrived at the Crocodile Valley Citrus Estates, located
not far from Nelspruit, 110 kilometres by road west of the Mozambique
border. He arrived there with his schoolfriend Jean Minnaar who had
suggested they go farming, and it seemed like a good chance to earn
some money and leave the constraints of his childhood days behind.
Bryce was nineteen years old and farming was not exactly the life he
aspired to. However, with no money and few prospects he felt he had
little choice. He knew he had to get some money behind him to have
any chance of following his dreams.

Jean's parents, Dr Minnaar and his wife, Abigail, lived in a beautiful
home at Witbank about 4 kilometres away, and Bryce had often stayed
with them during his school holidays. The boys planned to secure
positions as 'learner farmers', a type of apprenticeship in farming with
on-the-job training. Crocodile Valley Citrus Estates, originally called the
SA Prudential Citrus Estates, had been transformed by Ivan Solomon
into one of the largest private citrus farms in South Africa. They shipped

Valencia oranges all over the world and cultivated several other varieties of citrus fruits.

The Minnaars were hoping that once the boys graduated from being learner farmers they could buy some land together and form a partnership. Dr and Mrs Minnaar drove them on the 360-kilometre journey from Johannesburg to reach the farm, and Paddy and Rosemary travelled with them. Along the way they marvelled at the majesty of the Drakensberg escarpment and were excited to know they would soon be passing near the Kruger National Park, South Africa's largest wildlife sanctuary. It was also a revelation for them to discover the Lowveld, a terrain named for its lower height above sea level, which they were told was 'the real Africa'. They marvelled at its broad valleys below 1000 metres and sweated in its subtropical climate as they passed lush plantations of tobacco, pawpaw, avocado, melon, lychee and citrus fruit.

The Minnaars explained that citrus fruits had first been brought to Africa by Arab traders during the first century CE. The explorer Vasco da Gama had taken on supplies of oranges when he docked at Mombasa in East Africa during his voyage from Portugal to the East Indies via the Cape of Good Hope in the fifteenth century. The early white settlers had also planted orange trees in Natal at the beginning of the nineteenth century and these were later propagated and brought across to the Lowveld.

On their approach into Nelspruit, the travellers were stunned by the beauty of the lilac-coloured blossoms of the jacaranda trees, and the magnificent bougainvillea that hugged roadside fences. They also saw whitethorn trees, an indigenous acacia species that left an indelible impression in Bryce's mind. That vibrant landscape must have felt like paradise after the urban sprawl of Johannesburg. Years later, when he was living in Sydney's eastern suburbs, Bryce always felt happy to see the jacarandas come into bloom in November.

Memories of this pleasant journey quickly evaporated once the realities of farm life unfolded. Bryce had signed a contract to stay there for two years, but after the first few days he wondered what he had got himself into. He realised he had been taken on more as a labourer than a learner farmer and that it was in reality a form of slave labour. The wages were pitiful, and he found the living conditions nothing short of deplorable. He slept with the other white workers in corrugated-iron huts that were stifling-hot, and they lived off greasy stews served with boiled maize. The only thing in abundance was endless supplies of oranges, which sometimes gave him hives.

From the outset it was a life of drudgery, which must have been especially onerous for a young man bursting with hopes and dreams. Bryce's first job at the estate was in the dreaded 'packhouse', overseeing a team of African workers who were expected to grade and sort thousands of barrels of oranges each day. Bryce wrote each week to his mother of his experiences. One letter said:

> I wake up once or twice each night or very early morning having dreamt of millions and millions of Valencia oranges floating in a thick almost downy carpet of air in front of me. I'm sweating and am done in, having lined up seemingly thousands of orange sizers to try and keep ever-overflowing bins from overflowing onto the floor.

Bryce's friend Jean wasn't faring much better: 'Jean has had a lot of bowel trouble due to nerves the doctor says, and it can only be the packhouse which is to blame.' The area was endemic with malaria, and many workers, including Jean, also succumbed to tick-bite fever.

After several weeks sorting fruit in the packhouse, Bryce was sent outside to work in the orchards. After two weeks of thinning out tangerine trees it was clear that the orchard would not provide the reprieve he had hoped for. He reflected that he had been thrown from the frypan into the fire: 'No human mind could think out a more boring, heartbreaking or unsatisfying job than this.' Another unwelcome task was to report on the yield of each tree:

> Today I started what surely can't be equaled in soul destroying
> jobs – equipped with a large three-ply board . . . my job, to gauge
> the yeald of every tree on behalf of the Estates, which means sixty
> thousand trees all need to be personally inspected and 'charted',
> entailing a walk of about fifteen miles [24 kilometres] a day. The job
> is expected to take me about twenty days working on an estimate of
> three thousand trees a day . . . however working hard all day today
> I completed a mere one thousand eight hundred – not at all up to
> expectations.

Bryce's love of books provided his only real solace, offering a way to
escape from the monotony and exhaustion of the farm work. He wrote
to his mother, 'Don't worry about my "Packhouse Phobia" . . . I've
started a nice but rather heavy novel and have become so absorbed
that during the day I spend a good deal of time digesting the previous
evening's reading.' He complained that the local library in nearby
Nelspruit 'Owns exactly four books which I care to read and I'm on
the last now, there is also little chance of them buying with their new
stuff anything decent . . . The remainder of the stuff range between
reading Zane Grey's *Blood on the Trail* and Peter Cheyney's *Lady with
a Motive*.' Zane Grey was one of the world's first millionaire authors,
and his success may have inspired other writers in waiting, including
Arthur Bryce Courtenay!

During this time Bryce's greatest aspiration was to own a
typewriter – much to the consternation of his highly practical sister,
who thought the idea was extravagant. Undeterred by her remarks,
Bryce borrowed the money and purchased a German-made 'Erika'
manual typewriter, which was the best model on the market. He set
about improving his typing skills and insisted that Rosemary post him
his leather-bound dictionary. He worried that having to speak Afrikaans
all day would further diminish his knowledge of English, and so he made
improving his vocabulary a priority.

*

A welcome respite from this purgatory arrived when Bryce and two friends, Mike and Chris, arranged to visit Kruger National Park. Paddy had never had sufficient spare money to take her children on a safari, so this was a new adventure for him. With great anticipation, after work one Saturday they set off in a barely roadworthy Hudson motor vehicle. They reached the gates of the reserve in about three quarters of an hour and were admitted after paying ten shillings each for permits. To their disappointment they realised there was nowhere to stay: all the campsites were already covered in a sea of mattresses. They drove deeper into the park and, just as the sun was setting, were pleasantly rewarded:

> A magnificent bull giraffe broke into the road and crossed slowly, not twenty yards [18 metres] ahead, and then with an ease seemingly impossible in so great and clumsy looking an animal, broke into an effortless and graceful run covering a bare strip of veld in a matter of seconds.

By sheer luck they managed to rent a small tent from a man called Jock, and the boys spent a cold night huddled together under blankets. Soon after dawn they drove out of the campsite and 'Impala began to appear immediately – and although they're as common as house flies, they never fail to give me a lift'.

Seeing the wildlife at close range cast a spell on Bryce, and he remained enchanted by seeking out Africa's wildlife throughout his life: 'There's something terribly thrilling about coming upon rare game all on your own. It gives one a personal sense of achievement – a feeling of intimacy that just isn't there when you come across game "second hand".'

The friends' game-park experience was further enhanced when on the second day they came across 'a beautiful young lioness not quite in her prime but nevertheless a rare sight, she kept coming at a trot neither looking to left or right and passing the side window – my window not six feet [1.8 metres] away'. Bryce managed to snap a photo of her with a borrowed camera, and then minutes later a large black-maned male emerged: 'he was in hot pursuit of the female, a young fellow also approaching his prime, the sun catching his mane and sleek powerful buttocks'. Bryce felt utterly thrilled, and with excitement wrote: 'he passed so closely that had I stretched out I could have touched him'. Unfortunately, after snapping the lion he realised he hadn't rolled the film back, and all his photographs were spoilt.

Feeling like wounded lions themselves, the boys drove on until they arrived at Skukuza, the administrative headquarters of the park situated on the southern banks of the Sabie River. Bryce prepared a feast of steak cooked over the coals, eggs and fried tomatoes, followed by tinned peaches and coffee. After devouring this meal, the boys kept on driving until they reached a more remote section of the park at a place called Tshokwane. Here they saw wildebeest, sable antelope and zebra, and came across an old hyena with a badly lacerated backside. Bryce said that Chris reckoned 'he'd probably come too close to a kill while the lions were still eating and had received a whack for doing so'. Soon after, 'we came across some bush pig who immediately gave me the impression of being perfectly dressed in a Victorian or rather Edwardian manner but being without their pants.'

All too soon they had to make their way back to Crocodile Valley. Resigned to not seeing an elephant on their visit to Kruger, just 32 kilometres from the park gates they were rewarded:

Suddenly, not twenty yards ahead and to the right hand side of the road, were three tremendous bull elephants – they were about thirty yards [27 metres] in and standing absolutely in the open. We moved right up to their sides and this time cap was carefully removed and camera turned back and we all got some lovely photographs of them.

Feeling 'Too happy for words, [the boys] moved on – this was our crowning point . . . The elephants were even more thrilling than the lion, and with only a few minutes to reach the gates we hurried.' It had been a memorable weekend – and then, within sight of the park gates, they were stunned to see five cheetahs bound across the road.

After arriving back at the estate Bryce wrote a long letter overflowing with a rare bout of happiness: 'We couldn't have done or seen more – a cheap and wonderful one and a half days, food, petrol and accommodation costing us £2-8-0 each.' This tiny amount always makes me smile, as in December 2000 Bryce departed Sydney to go on an African safari that cost a small fortune. However, this first one in 1953, and the experience of seeing game in the wild for the first time, left an indelible impression on him. One of my favourite stories Bryce later wrote appears in *The Night Country* with a beautiful scene inspired by this first encounter:

> And then, from a high thicket of whitethorn and wild palm a giraffe emerged, a ghost shape in the moonlight. It moved with great rocking strides up to the waterhole where it stood a moment, then collapsed its front legs like a folding chair. Its elegant neck, a slender stem darker than the night, craned down and over and sipped from the silver bowl of the moon.

Another break from the unrelenting drudgery of working among the citrus groves arrived when Bryce was invited by Jean to a party at a magnificent estate called Bill Buddy Farm in Plaston. It was home to the Saunders family, and the occasion was to celebrate the coronation of Queen Elizabeth II on 2 June 1953 following the death of her father, King George V1.

After a lavish supper with drinks served in crystal glasses, Bryce and the other guests gathered around the television to watch *A Queen is Crowned*, broadcast by the BBC live from Westminster Abbey. On the same day the news broke that Mount Everest had been summited for the first time by Edmund Hillary and Tenzing Norgay, who were members of the 1953 British Mount Everest Expedition led by Colonel John Hunt. They had summited on 29 May and the news was relayed to Base Camp on 30 May, but the story written for *The Times* by the journalist James Morris (who became Jan Morris) was deliberately put on hold until Coronation Day.

Bryce had been told by Jean that the Saunders family were real-life millionaires, and he had never seen such opulence on display. He wrote to Paddy, 'They were all extremely charming people and not at all conscious of the gap between £13-12-3 all found and three quarters of a million.' Bryce was especially enamoured by their magnificent garden: 'Probably the prettiest and most spacious in the Lowveld, wide spacious lawns which almost ramble and are certainly without better, lots of ponds and running water and with everything that be in bloom at this time of the year making a rather breathtaking show'.

Bryce also discovered that Mrs Saunders worked tirelessly on behalf of the Red Cross and was impressed that she had raised over £100 000 for the charity. In a lighter moment he observed a rather haughty woman from Rhodesia, a Mrs Skien, whom he said looked 'like wool wound around a chair . . . rather well dressed except for her shoes, which were black and open at toe and heal. I couldn't keep my eyes off them they were without a doubt the most ghastly footwere I've ever seen and if they cost more than nineteen and six at Edworks, I'll buy her a bunch of bananas.'

Bryce's visit to Bill Buddy Farm may have planted a dream in his mind to one day create a water garden of his own, something he finally achieved nearly fifty years later at our home in the Yarramalong Valley. Featuring large boulders from the nearby Wyong River and dense with tropical plants, its centrepiece was a waterfall that flowed into a lily pond, just as he told me he had seen at the Saunders home all those years before.

*

The next job Bryce was assigned at the citrus farm was spraying the endemic red ants in the orchard. Typical of agricultural farm production at the time, no protective clothing was provided and there was no escape from being drenched in parathion, the highly toxic chemical sold under the brand name of Thiophos. Bryce already had a delicate chest from illness he had suffered as a baby, and the new job played havoc with his lungs. The chemicals he inhaled soon caused blurred vision, headaches, vomiting and bouts of excessive sweating. Many of his fellow workers also fell ill due to exposure to the chemical, and there were rumours some even suffered cardiac arrests. Bryce complained to his superiors about the danger but his protests fell on deaf ears. There was probably a limited understanding of the extreme dangers these pesticides posed back then, and he may well have been warned to back down or risk having his employment terminated. It was another moment of humiliation not dissimilar to many he had experienced during his childhood.

Bryce told me that he became even more conscious of the injustices of apartheid during his latter childhood years, and in this ostensibly beautiful place he felt an increasing sense of unease. On the farm, beyond the cushioned environment of KES, he became increasingly mindful of the vast disparity in treatment, opportunity and experience between the white workers and workers of colour. The injustices presented by entrenched racism were palpable but in those days went largely unchallenged. Eventually Bryce was asked to supervise a 'spray gang' of local African workers, and he tried his best to help them. On 24 October 1952, he wrote to his mother about a very unsettling incident:

I had a rather nasty row with the assistant manager. After having badly beaten one of the spray-gang boys in a contiguous orchard, he came over to where I was working, elated still with his bravado, and without even a greeting made directly for a 'Spambaan boy' (Spray boy who holds a spray gun), his fist already clenched. Anticipating what was going to happen I shouted to him to keep his hands off the boy or I'd hit him. I have to admit I nearly passed out when I realized the true content of what I'd said. I could however almost hear the soft dead note of deflated air as it oozed out of the balloon, and to my utter surprise and confusion, for I had anticipated a dreadful row, he merely opened his mouth once or twice and without a word strode up to his car, jumped in and accelerated.

This kind of intervention from a white employee would have been extremely rare, and from then on Bryce found himself to be quietly looked up to by the black workers. They could see that he was someone who didn't condone the culture of racism and bullying.

Bryce was also troubled by the living conditions and lower wages paid to his black co-workers but had no authority to do anything about it, and his letters reveal that he was flat out surviving there himself. By then the multiracial political mobilisation against apartheid laws was well underway, although largely confined to South Africa's larger cities. Black leaders such as Nelson Mandela, Walter Sisulu and Oliver Tambo had formed the African National Congress (ANC), and by 1950 had started promoting demonstrations, mass action, boycotts and strikes demanding better conditions and more freedoms. On 26 June 1952 the Defiance Campaign was launched, which saw mass protests take place across South Africa. The winds of change were gathering pace and the regime's day of reckoning was on the radar.

His dismay regarding the treatment of workers of colour at the farm only increased when he discovered that nearly all of them were illiterate. He knew that most had never been given the chance to go to school: this was a familiar set of circumstances he had witnessed growing up, and it had motivated him to start lessons for Africans when he was a student at KES. I expect he contemplated raising a similar idea with his current bosses but knew it would probably be met with resistance and they would most likely have seen him as a potential troublemaker. However, the situation continued to gnaw away at Bryce's sense of what was right, and deep down he probably knew that staying on in South

Africa was an unlikely scenario. For now, he had little choice but to keep his head down and keep his job. He needed to earn enough money to survive and to help his mother. Thankfully there were interludes that raised his spirits. For example, he wrote:

> Three days ago, while spraying in one of the orchards for red spider, I spied a movement in a giant marula tree at the foot of a rockface some 200 yards [180 metres] away . . . seeing the opportunity for a break from a most tedious job I left the boss boy in charge . . . I saw tiny grey monkeys with jet black faces and white extremely fluffy rear ends.

The whole troop took off except for one 'little fellow either too frightened or inquisitive to leave [who] hid only his head behind a branch . . . I guess he was working on the ostrich principle'. These would have been vervet monkeys, commonly found in this part of the Lowveld.

His delight in seeing these creatures provides an insight into Bryce's capacity to feel a sense of wonder in nature, and never give up hope even in the most trying of circumstances. Connecting with the natural world always gave him more pleasure than any material item (other than books!) and was a big reason why he escaped Sydney to spend his later years in rural areas far removed from the 'concrete jungle'. He wouldn't countenance any creature that strayed into the house being killed, be it a rat one of the cats had brought in, or a praying mantis clinging onto a blind.

In late November and to progress their business plans, Bryce and Jean hitchhiked up to Witbank in the Highveld to meet with Dr Minnaar to discuss their idea of entering a farming partnership and buying some land. Although wary about the concept, Bryce wrote to his mother: 'I can hardly wait until I can discuss everything, in the clear light of day, with you.' Following the meeting his concerns had not been laid to rest: 'I began to see the numerous, yea countless, misunderstandings that will have to be cleared up before ever we set foot on a farm in partnership. I have insisted that when the time comes, a contract be drawn up, legalized by a lawyer and sanctioned by yourself and doctor.'

The idea of the partnership with Jean did not ultimately progress. At the time Bryce and Jean were working there, the prices for South African fruit were dropping and uncertainty was brewing about the future of citrus farming. Countries such as Italy and Spain were providing stiff competition, and Bryce worried that he might be getting himself entangled in a losing proposition and a significant amount of debt. He worried that all the effort and hard work required could eventually come to nothing.

He sought advice from his mother, whom he dutifully wrote to every week. It troubled him that he had so few pennies left over each month to send her. Paddy continued to have regular bouts of ill health but battled on alone, and Bryce felt responsible for taking care of her in any way he could. He loved receiving her letters, as letters from Rosemary were few and far between; he once wrote: 'Please give Rosemary my love, with it you might add that she didn't receive a new pen for nothing.'

While at Crocodile Valley Bryce tried to stay in touch with Arthur Ryder, telling his mother:

> Should you contact Uncle Arthur, please let me know how they are for I wrote him some time ago, and also sent him half a dozen hankies for his birthday and quite recently some fruit. He hasn't acknowledged anything and I've wondered whether he has received such as had been sent.

Deep down I think the absence of a father during most of his childhood left Bryce with a feeling of profound loss, and a sense of abandonment and rejection. His close relationship with his grandfather at Barberton had been his only experience of a male authority figure and mentor in his life, and even that had been cut short when his mother decided to move her children back to Johannesburg. I used to wonder if Bryce thought that in some way he was partly to blame, even though of course he'd had no say in the matter whatsoever.

To his immense surprise, one of the farm managers asked him to create labels for the estate's jars of jam. Perhaps this was an early indication of Bryce's aptitude for marketing! He had always loved drawing and was known among his family for his love of comics and for creating cartoon characters. He used to often make cartoon-like drawings of our pets, especially when writing cards to me laden with words of devotion from them. Now, he plucked up the courage to ask to be paid for designing the labels and to his astonishment the manager agreed, but then Bryce found himself in a quandary as he had no idea what price he should quote. Nor did he have the materials he needed to make the labels. Without delay he dashed off a letter to his mother: 'Please mother if you can possibly get to getting a paintbox send it down as soon as you have the opportunity.' He was relieved when his mother dispatched examples of fruit labels to him along with the art materials he had been hoping for. She was a woman with an entrepreneurial flair, so I expect she would also have counselled Bryce on how to conduct the business negotiations.

The labels proved to be a great success and Bryce was talked about for having created 'those legendary labels'. For him, this was an unexpected glimpse into the world of marketing. Overall, though, his experience working at Crocodile Valley Estates was unremarkable. He lived a parochial life with his days soured by drudgery, backbreaking work and exasperation over the injustices that played out. There were few parties and no girls to go out with, and the whole situation just didn't sit well with his youthful, fun-loving disposition. Furthermore, he was bored witless and desperate for intellectual stimulation. Thoughts of going to university in England began to swirl in his mind – not that he had a bean to pay for it.

In the end Bryce came to realise that he didn't have the money to contribute to the farming partnership with Jean, and that it was too risky a proposition. He was also certain that being a fruit farmer wasn't for him. Unlike Jean he had no prospects of inheriting a farm, and he was far too ambitious to settle for a life spent counting the proceeds from sales of oranges and lemons. Understandably, he felt he was about to let both Jean and Dr Minnaar down. He wrote to his mother:

> I have written to Doctor, indeed it took me all day, and then some two hours back when I started the final draft (enclosed for your approval) it turned out not a bit the way I had made it sound in preparation. I spoke also to Jean today, I must take back all I might have said with regard to his expected attitude, for he couldn't have been more understanding and apart from the original dismay was soon reconciled to the matter. I can only hope that his parents are equally considerate.

Regarding his friend's plans, Bryce wrote: 'Jean thinks he'll stay here another year and after that perhaps a couple of years with an uncle in the Free State, but of course everything is still undecided.'

After ten-and-a-half months at the estates Bryce was desperate to leave, and on 15 January 1954 he resigned. This must have made him heave a huge sigh of relief, but his escape didn't prove to be straightforward: 'it seems they do not normally accept a mid-monthly resignation and in doing so for me, it was clearly stipulated that I would be relinquished as soon as it was to their convenience after the 13th February'.

Bryce dreamt of a bigger life. Like many young men in South Africa he knew there was good money to be made at the mines on the Copperbelt in Northern Rhodesia and was soon making plans to go there. He was eager to return to Johannesburg to complete the necessary paperwork and needed to find enough money to cover the cost of the journey up to Luanshya, where the Roan Antelope mine was located. In addition, he was required to sit an exam to secure a 'red ticket'. His plans were temporarily delayed as he wrote to Paddy, 'it cannot be this month for I am dead broke'.

Because he was leaving the company early, he already knew he couldn't afford to take his mother on a planned holiday to Portuguese East Africa (now Mozambique). While this was disappointing, he went ahead and completed the 'Position required' form for a job at the mines. To progress his application, he drew on help from his Uncle Bryce. Bryce and his Uncle Jim were already working as hoist drivers at Roan Antelope, and this was probably another reason why Bryce chose this mine over others. Once there he looked forward to spending time with his Uncle Bryce and his wife Mavis, as well as his Uncle Jim and his wife Marie, and his cousins Errol, Wendy, Courtenay, Robyn, Glen and Pamela.

To his relief, Bryce's final bout of work at Crocodile Valley turned out to be surprisingly pleasant:

> Pest Control was a dreadful period of purgatory, however it has formalised into a rather nice compensation: I'm in charge of the nursery for the month while the regular nurseryman takes leave, it's a stagnicolious type of existence and for this very fact a most enjoyable one, thus I terminate my services on a high note, or rather a low-high note, repairing my blistered hands, i.e. pruning prior to the Nursery, under the shade of a tree with a good book for company, for there is very little to do at this time of the year and thus there is no need to seek appeasement for my conscience after a little lying around.

Bryce had of course already been introduced to the pleasures of gardening by his grandfather in Barberton, and so came to discover that being in the nursery was in fact rather interesting: 'There's quite a deal of valuable knowledge to be gleaned, and the routine is easygoing and restful.'

Bryce never sprayed any of the trees or plants in our garden, regardless of how much a professional gardener implored him to do so. He was well and truly done with spraying after his youthful stint 'in the jaws of the crocodile', as he called it. He was also never a fan of marmalade or jam and preferred to have peanut butter (the crunchy variety) on toast each morning after tucking into a serving of two soft-poached eggs. Planting citrus trees was never a priority either, although at our home in the Yarramalong Valley he did grow some kaffir lime, cumquat and lemon trees after I told him I needed the leaves and fruit for cooking. He would grow other fruits and vegetables wherever he lived and even did so on the tiny balcony on his flat in Rose Bay where we began our unlikely courtship. I prevailed upon him to make me some utterly delicious cumquat jam from the plants he had growing in pots there.

Finally, and to his immense relief, the Crocodile Valley Estates 'released' him from his contract. Bryce was more than ready to get the hell out of there and earn some decent money to enable him to go to university in England and carve out a better life for himself. On 12 February 1954, the estate manager handed him a letter that read:

This is to certify that Mr A.B.C. Roberts joined our staff on the 1st March, 1953, as a learner and was to have stayed with us for a period of two years. He is now being released at his own request before completion of this period. Whilst in our service he spent some time on general orchard work, pest control including spraying of trees with Thiophos and Copper, scale survey, and also in our nursery and our packhouse. Mr Roberts proved himself a willing worker and his conduct has always been exemplary.

After leaving Crocodile Valley, Bryce returned to Johannesburg. His elation at being free was shortlived: he was exhausted and still recovering from the effects of the toxic fumes, but there was no time to rest as he had already spent his meagre savings. Within days of arriving he began looking for work, and with the help of his mother secured a sales position in a department store called Polliacks. He worked there for several weeks serving customers who came in to purchase men's underpants, shirts, ties and suits.

Rosemary later told me that although Bryce had hated the job at the farm, it had not been a complete waste of time. He had continued to fall in love with books and told her that he wanted to become a writer one day. Rosemary also told me that during his teens Bryce was sensitive and intellectual and valued books, music and writing above all else. It was little wonder that he must have felt like a fish out of water doing the long days of repetitive manual labour in the citrus groves.

During these years Bryce appeared to some extent to go along with his mother's and Rosemary's embrace of the Assemblies of God church. Paddy had been helped by the church following her series of nervous breakdowns in the late 1940s and now, back home in Johannesburg, Bryce was actively involved in the church's youth group even though this flurry of religious activity was by no means a long-term commitment. I think he may have become involved to please his mother and sister. Involvement in the church would have been the family's only opportunity to enjoy a social life as well: they didn't have the money to do anything else, such as attend a movie or go out for a meal, which other families could look forward to. Paddy retained an unwavering commitment to the church, and while Bryce was at the citrus farm, she reassured him not to worry and to instead put his trust in God's plan to chart the course for his future.

Working at the department store allowed Bryce to pay off some of his debts, including the loan for the purchase of his prized typewriter. He had more time to write up his diary, type letters to his father, and even draft a few short stories. How I wish copies of those precious stories were still in existence but, with Bryce leaving South Africa and travelling the world, they became scattered to the four winds. It's likely that working at the department store reignited his dream to go to university as the first step in a new career. He had already contemplated journalism – a profession that would allow him to write – and set his heart on eventually securing a tertiary qualification to make that dream possible. But for now he simply didn't have the funds to even make a start on elevating his educational prospects.

With a mind to progressing his plans it wasn't long before Bryce applied for a passport, which he needed to cross the border from South Africa on the long journey up to Ndola, the railway head close to the mines. Having completed all the paperwork, it was soon time for him to pack his bags, leave Paddy and start work in a new job – a job where he needed to head hundreds of metres underground and face unimaginable dangers. His dream of studying and then one day becoming a writer, which he had been mulling over amid that sea of oranges 'in the jaws of the crocodile' up at Nelspruit, was still a hell of a long way off.

4

DOWN THE MINES

The detritus of the world washed up there, ex-Nazi SS troops and officers, the scum of the earth. It was a dangerous job, but I needed the money for university in England. And it gave me an enormous lust for life; every night I faced the prospect of not coming out alive. – *The Silver Moon*

BRYCE DIDN'T SEE THE explosion coming, and it nearly cost him his life.

It was 15 July 1955, and the day started like every other in Luanshya. Each day at the Roan Antelope mine began early, and often went on long into the night. Bryce would emerge from his rondavel, a round hut with a thatched roof and a veranda covered in mesh to keep out mosquitoes, furnished with a wire-framed bed, a small table and a few hooks to hang up his clothes. After a cup of coffee and some bread and jam he would pull on his overalls, lace up his boots and strap a miner's lamp to his helmet.

He would then head out to begin another nine-hour shift 6000 feet (1800 metres) below the surface, and would return from his underground lair just as the sun was setting. Before bedtime, he was careful to place his boots on the rafters to keep out the scorpions that came in under the door. His body would be covered in dust and particles of copper ore that would irritate his sensitive chest, causing bouts of coughing that kept him up at night.

Despite these hardships Bryce was certain that working at the mines was the right decision. He wanted to make as much money as he could so that he could go to London and attend university. He was determined to make something of his life and understood that furthering his education was essential.

As ever, he wrote home to Paddy of his experience. The chance to forge a new direction had emerged – as Bryce explained to Diana Ritch – during a train trip he took while working at the Crocodile Valley Citrus Estates: 'I heard two men talking about the copper mines in Northern Rhodesia and how you could make these fabulous sums of money underground, and I couldn't believe this . . . I realised that in a couple of years I could actually make enough money to put myself through university.' It must have felt for him like the way out. He was determined to make something of his life and understood that furthering his education was essential.

Back in June 1954, aged twenty-one, Bryce took the 2000-kilometre train journey to Ndola. The route took him through Southern Rhodesia (now Zimbabwe) via Bulawayo, not far from the legendary Victoria Falls, Livingstone and Lusaka. From Ndola he travelled by bus to Luanshya, close to the Roan Antelope mine. In a letter to his mother he wrote: 'The trip up was really not terribly unpleasant, right at the start I met a very charming young girl (Rhodesian) . . . no need to get any ideas she's three years older than I . . . I had a bath at Bulawayo . . . I cannot remember when I enjoyed anything quite as much.'

The mine was one of many on the Copperbelt, which stretches for 450 kilometres from Northern Rhodesia to the Belgian Congo (now the Democratic Republic of the Congo). 'Luanshya' means 'a river of antelopes'. The Africans called it 'the valley of death' as they believed it was home to a dangerous 'snake spirit' that lurked in the nearby river and was a harbinger of bad luck.

After his arrival Bryce was intrigued to discover that Roan Antelope was the first copper mine to be pegged in Northern Rhodesia. It was said to be named after a prospector called William Collier, who in 1902 had shot and killed a roan antelope beside the Luanshya River. Apparently when Collier went to bag his kill, the beast's head was lying on a deposit of green malachite copper ore. Some claimed the deposits had been known about for centuries; indeed, the British missionary and explorer David Livingstone had mentioned the ore in his journals. The Roan Antelope mines were finally incorporated under the British Companies Act in 1927 by the Rhodesian Selection Trust, and production commenced in 1931, even though copper prices had slumped and no dividend was able to be declared until 1935. As operations commenced many Africans began to die of malaria and blackwater fever, and rumours of this danger made it difficult to secure workers. The British ran and dominated all facets of life here, although challenges to their authority were already smouldering when Bryce arrived. Coincidentally, Luanshya was the birthplace of the celebrated author and philosopher A.C. Grayling in 1949.

Bryce's initial impressions were that Luanshya was a pretty town with streets lined with flame trees and jacarandas covered in blossoms. Even so, he lamented to his mother:

> I'm afraid the five months at home has spoilt me, for my home sickness isn't wearing off and I miss you both more and more each day . . . Yes Mother, I do often wish I were back at Polliacks, but am learning slowly the futility of looking back or digging in the past, and for the next four years or maybe longer it's Central Africa or 'Bust'.

The sunrises were magnificent, and Bryce marvelled at their beauty: 'Early Rhodesian mornings are too wonderful, and for an hour or so each day my soul really expands, making me feel a new creature.' For the rest of the day this magical scene was extinguished from his mind:

> I have been working three days now, each day a little worse than the one before, however tis not unbearable, for after an hour at work mere physical exhaustion is merely an indication that now you're about ready to start some real work, after a couple of hours 'real work' you're long past the stage where you're physically conscious of your plight . . .

Bryce was initially housed in the cramped single men's quarters not far from where his Uncle Jim and Uncle Bryce were living with their families. Bryce's arrival gave him the opportunity to get to know his mother's side of the family, as he had rarely spent time with them during his childhood. His letters indicate that his dealings with his relatives were mixed at first, but later he really appreciated being around them and got along famously with his Uncle Bryce's twin girls, Robyn and Wendy. He must have enjoyed being in real homes full of love and far away from the memories of his own fractured childhood, which the girls said in an interview he never mentioned. They however already knew from their parents that their 'Aunty Patty' had gone through a very tough time raising her two children.

Before long, Uncle Bryce tried to coerce young Bryce into joining the Masonic lodge:

> I told him that it would proberbly be incompatible with the way I believe, he is however very adamant and insists that it couldent possibly be, I have said nothing further about it, but have been praying as also searching the scriptures, however I have had little satisfaction.

He was thrilled when his uncle arranged for him to get a boxer puppy, but wrote:

It won't however be for some time, which suits me better as then I shall be on eighteen months night shift, repeat, eighteen months night shift, and will thus be able to train the puppy really well as I shall have a good deal of each day free . . . it will be wonderful having a dog once more . . .

Bryce was required to attend the School of Mines for a period of six months, where the lectures were conducted underground. He and the other trainees spent their days going up and down the mine shafts in a steel cage and were taught how to set explosives to release the copper from the malachite ore. To do this, machinery was used to drill holes into the hard rock and then explosives were inserted into the drill holes to blast and break up the rock. The 'grizzly' was a large grate made of logs or steel that was placed near the end of the fall of rocks to slow the flow of ore. Because the grizzly was a grid of squares each roughly 30 centimetres wide, larger rocks would get caught and eventually block the flow of ore. Bryce and his fellow trainee miners were taught how to keep the grizzly free and to dislodge rocks that became stuck in the chute. They were also trained to be on the lookout for gold seams and deposits of diamonds, as the mine owners used the sale of these to cover much of their overheads.

Over time Bryce came to quite like working on the grizzlies: 'Although a dangerous job it is one that keeps the hours flying by, and is most interesting and requires a mind on the alert.' In an interview years later he reflected on the danger of his experience:

It is a very, very dangerous job . . . of the thirteen people who joined with me, a year later six of them were dead and a couple of them had been very badly maimed . . . A lot of people got killed doing this, and to be a grizzlyman you had to be under the age of twenty-three because after that they figured your reactions were going to be too slow.

One of the first things the students learnt was 'lashing', which consisted of shovelling rock and muck into barrows in a shift that lasted for six-and-a-half hours. They were given forty-five minutes' break but were forbidden to lie down, sleep or read a newspaper. Bryce was also given one of the beginner's jobs of pipefitting, which he wrote to Paddy was the hardest and grimmest work a miner could do: 'I am actually so tired that after three hours of it my whole body is numb, and after that it's easy for you to drop a bomb on me and I wouldent even notice, and three hundred pounds [136 kilograms] of pipe across my shoulder might as well be a fishing rod for all I care.'

Bryce quickly learnt to keep his head down and his mouth shut, as he described in another letter: 'I very foolishly objected to something today . . . I came off the poorer for having done so and shall henceforth continue to have my face pushed into the mud without objecting, for it's the only way of getting through each day.' In his letters he endeavoured to reassure his mother, who must have been worried: 'Don't worry however, it's not impossible and I am gradually getting used to it, each day a little better than the one before – after all, it's not inconceivable when a man is earning £94 a month they are expecting something out of him.' Bryce also told her that he was keeping up with his commitments to the church:

> I am determined to try all the Churches here until I find one a little less 'Rigor Mortis' than the rest. Next Sunday it's going to be the Dutch Reformed, for the Free Church is simply awful and I cannot imagine four years of it . . . worse even I think than the thought of being underground for that period . . . I think of you all each night long after your thinking of me has ceased, remember you've someone praying for you even at the darkest hour of night.

Rosemary had by now become smitten with Esmund Anderson, whom she'd met in 1953 at a church youth-group cricket match. Esmund's parents were of Swedish descent. They had been Assemblies of God missionaries and it was already clear that the young couple were destined to follow a religious vocation. Rosemary told me that for her it was a case of love at first sight, even though for some time she struggled with the fact that 'Es' was three-and-a-half years younger than her. Bryce wrote to his mother: 'Should Rosemary go into the Lord's work full time this may be God's plan for her support – however I have speculated enough; from now on it's prayer by us all that will decide.'

The food at the mine was only a slight improvement on the fare he had consumed at Crocodile Valley the previous year: 'I do however miss milk up here . . . and they will insist on having Cabbage on the Menu as the main "green", also the Coffee has almost a forty-five percent acorn content and tastes at first taste like very poor Coca.' Aside from this, he wrote: 'I was most disillusioned to find that I have gained weight consistently and am only five pounds short of Croc Valley, being at the moment weighing 145 pounds [66 kilograms].'

Bryce soon began to play a bit of squash and 'rugger' and even arranged lessons in Latin, although he couldn't make a start on them until he had graduated from the School of Mines. To his delight he discovered that the Roan Antelope Rugby Club held the record for having the world's tallest goalposts, which stood at 110 feet and 6 inches high (about 34 metres).

With so much physical exertion in and above the mines, Bryce quickly noticed dramatic changes in his physique: 'I certainly have started to bulge with all sorts of muscles I didn't even know I owned and my legs from climbing miles and miles of chain ladders, begin to look like lengths of knotted rope . . .' Sleep had become his most treasured desire: 'I dream of sleep these days and my ambitions have dwindeled to an inner spring matterass, a cool breeze and lashings and lashing of lashing of almost eternal sleep.'

Bryce described the regular letters from his mother as 'cool and soothing balm', but what really urged him to persevere was the thought of being able to secure 'my Blasting ticket Exam, and thereafter I shall be a bonafide fully fledged miner earning £115 a month'. However, by late October 1954 the strain was taking its toll:

> It's the usual sticky afternoon and I feel like a stale bun with pink icing on it. How I long for the rains, due late in November, and until they arrive I shall survive: certainly no more . . . How I wish I could drive this ambition fanatic away, everything I touch becomes a challenge and always a worry until my nerves are like banjo strings and the three and a bit years up here seem like eternity itself.

Being hundreds of metres underground felt claustrophobic, and there was the constant noise of ore being detonated, the thunder of jackhammers and the sound of fellow miners cursing. Bryce developed a ringing in his ears that he never fully recovered from. He knew that becoming 'a grizzly man' was a potential death sentence but tried to put this out of his mind as he was consumed with the burning ambition of making as much money as he could. He later wrote of this in his final novel, *Jack of Diamonds*:

> These guys, usually no older than twenty-three, couldn't wait to get onto a grizzly with a box of gelignite, a roll of cortex and a box of fuses and start making money. Next to the true professionals, the diamond drillers, engineers and shift bosses, working a grizzly was the highest-paid job in the mine and a young guy could earn some serious money.

Bryce discovered that the depths of the mines wasn't the only place to fear. Even taking a shower in the communal facilities had its risks. He never entered the showers to scrape off the dust without keeping a sharpened knife in his trousers to defend himself: he had heard rumours of men being raped in there, and never lingered. People came to work in the mines from all over the world and some arrived with highly dubious reputations, as he described in his novel *Whitethorn*:

A great many of the men who found themselves in Central Africa had left other parts of the world in an unseemly hurry. I was to discover that the truth was a very rare commodity among the men who lived in the single quarters and that a simple rule prevailed: you never asked a man anything about his past . . . If a man talked about his past history, this invariably proved to be an elaborate fabrication told during the course of a bout of heavy drinking. In this manner, ex-German SS officers turned into Polish Jews who had survived Hitler's concentration camps.

The same kind of Afrikaners who had bullied him at school in South Africa were also there, and as an Englishman he endured the brunt of their grudges that still smouldered from the Anglo–Boer War.

Music and books provided Bryce with a source of solace during these days of wretched sweat and toil. Like Tom Fitzsaxby in *Whitethorn*, Bryce always felt like an outsider, and he knew it was safer to keep to himself. Fortunately, he was able to take great comfort in reading, as his character Tom did: 'Books are like that, you know. When you haven't got a friend they can be your best friends and one thing is for sure, they'll never let you down or leave you in the lurch.'

Bryce later discovered that the celebrated author Wilbur Smith was also born in 1933 and grew up on a cattle ranch only a few hours' drive from Luanshya. Wilbur passed away on 13 November 2021 at the age of eighty-eight, having written forty-nine books. Their paths never crossed, which is a pity as I am sure they would have had a lot to talk about!

As the training progressed, the recruits were moved on from lashing duties to commencing night shifts. Bryce understood that this would elevate the risks to an entirely new level. The conditions were deplorable, with scant lighting for setting up the explosives, and when fatigue would set in during the early hours of the morning the chances of making a catastrophic error increased. Bryce's exhaustion levels were escalating. He had toyed with the idea of teaching Sunday school, but night shift put an end to that:

Sunday school becomes a different problem now, for a Saturday night shift when many of the boys are a little drunk is always a trial and I seldom get to bed before four thirty, and to be up at eight again is no mean problem and tis a very bleary eyed me giving out the lesson on Sunday morning.

However, there were times when working night shift delivered some compensation:

The days have been lovely now the rains are here, and if there are no compensations to night shift barring this, it is indeed something, and when I have learnt not to sleep so much I shall feel as if I'm always on holiday . . . Three in the morning is a lovely hour, and coming off shift is more of a pleasure than ever. A steaming cup of coffee and a hot shower, hours after you're all asleep.

Now and then his indomitable spirit was crushed:

One is soaked to the skin imediately on comencing each morning, and the day is spent thus, with muck and mud and water and oil fumes and compressed air shooting back at you, from the top bottom and sides, one stands in water a foot deep and by the end of each day the terrible vibrations from the 'Jack hammer' and later on the 'Pom Pom' drills coupled with there noise . . . one is left dazed and weary enough to just curl over and die, if it wasn't for the sodden clothes which are far to uncomfortable to die in . . . I have however giving up the prospect of ever having a cushy job and am getting so used to earning my bread the hard way that I cannot even conjur up in wildest imagination a normal six-and-a-half-hour day worked in daylight.

Further trouble lay ahead as in the mid-1950s the prospect of rolling strikes at the mines materialised. The Africans outnumbered the white workers tenfold but were paid far less. They also sustained much higher death rates and tended to leave after just a few months to escape the punishing conditions. The transitory nature of their tenure was one reason why the mine owners were sluggish about improving their conditions. The only improvements were that the swamps had been drained and better sanitary conditions provided to keep the mosquitoes and subsequent malaria at bay.

The first strike took place in 1935 and resulted in the police shooting at random into a crowd of Bemba miners and their supporters. Six people were killed and twenty-two were wounded. The Northern Rhodesian African Mineworkers' Union was formed in 1949, and some gains were made following a strike in 1952, with pay increases awarded and the company beginning a new policy of promoting Africans into low-level supervisory positions. The mine was then reorganised under the Northern Rhodesia Mining Ordinance on 1 July 1954, and during the ensuing years several strikes took place that did not cease until September 1956.

Bryce worked underground with gangs of black African workers who were required to refer to him and his superiors as 'bwana ('master')', and were mostly referred to by the white workers as 'boys', or 'boss boys' if they held a more senior position. The mining fraternity throughout Africa had developed a pidgin called Fanagalo or Cikabanga, which was influenced by the local Bantu language and included Zulu words, many of which Bryce was familiar with. He told me he became quite fluent in this vernacular within a matter of weeks and this contributed to him being a popular leader of his gang, and he enjoyed their company just as he had done during his childhood in South Africa.

On one occasion Bryce recalled a rookie who had recently arrived from England who, to Bryce's disgust, insisted on referring to a young African worker as 'you bloody savage'. He went on to unintentionally call him 'a sweet violet' as he had not yet fully grasped Cikabanga and this caused everyone to roar with laughter, including Bryce and the worker who was the target of the abuse.

By October 1954 the goal of securing his blasting licence finally drew near:

> I've been glad of being able to get in four hours sleep a day, really it's been rather dreadful. The grand climax to the past six months – on Saturday I go to Kitwe [about 50 kilometres from Luanshya] to be examined by the Inspector of Mines for my Blasting Licence. Should I pass – and indeed it would be too ghastly if I did not, which is by no means impossible – I will be at last a fully fledged Underground Operator with a rise of three shillings a day and the 'inexperienced' tag will be removed from my name.

However, the school delayed issuing the licence for several weeks due to the strikes, and Bryce was feeling exasperated:

> The school has the pleasure of my company yet another week, this is the third anti-climax and it was a terrible disappointment not to be leaving, how glad I will be to see the last of it, night shift with all its drawbacks is going to be perfect bliss . . . if I do not pass I shall sit down in the middle of the haulage and sob my heart out.

Bryce finally secured his licence in late November 1954. It was issued by the Government of Northern Rhodesia and reads: 'The Explosives Regulations (Regulation 57). Blasting Licence (Not Transferable) No 6746 C. This is to certify that Arthur Bryce Courtenay of Luanshya the undersigned is licensed to carry out blasting operations in Northern Rhodesia.' The certificate was signed (but undated) and handed over after Bryce paid the sum of two shillings and sixpence. He was now eligible to be paid a copper bonus, which doubled his monthly wages and must have felt like a king's ransom.

The prospect of further strikes gained momentum and he was encouraged to join workers from across the spectrum who were demanding better pay and safer working conditions. Fellow church members were convinced that the pathway to better conditions instead lay in the workers embracing the word of God, but Bryce remained unconvinced by their rhetoric. Indeed, continuing with his childhood faith was increasingly gnawing at his intellect. He had come across a novel called *Elmer Gantry* by Sinclair Lewis, published in 1927, and reading it had a life-changing effect on him. It tells the story of an unrepentant con man, the Reverend Dr Elmer Gantry, and the revelations in it contributed to extinguishing Bryce's Pentecostal beliefs and changing his views on the church forever.

Rosemary and his mother remained in the bosom of the church throughout their lives. At one stage Bryce had to beg his mother not to cancel a specialist medical consultation, the prospect of which appears to have conflicted with her beliefs:

I'm sad that I should write a letter like this on an Easter weekend, but it seems a little incongruous that Pentecostal missionaries are crying out for nurses and Doctors, and yet we spurn directly what aid medical science can give us. Please Mother see a specialist.

He also continuously reassured her that he would keep sending money: 'If needs be I could support you both, my ambition to go to university you must never forget will always come second to your own welfare . . .'

Bryce began to develop a business idea he was very excited about:

I have had an idea on my mind ever since I've been up here . . . of starting a small 'Contemporary' Furnature shop . . . contemporary furnature isn't hard to make and would I think be tremendously in demand, for there isn't a single place on the 'Copper Belt' . . . we could also stock curtains and perhaps later carpets . . . but there's money crying out to be made up here . . .

He hoped that his mother would relocate to Luanshya and run the business while he continued to work in the mines. He had discussed securing financial help to progress the idea with his Uncle Bryce: 'He thinks the idea a good one, and would I think, be very willing in with financial help . . . for with your business and salesmanship, our ideas and Bryce's drive and financial help, we could sell a Fridge to an Eskimo.'

He further urged Paddy to send him a diary as though he knew instinctively it would be useful for his later writings:

> I should however love a Diary as I feel that this phase of my life might in the light of future years be well worth recalling (there's my ego raising its ugly head once more) . . . I have had some very original if not terribly interesting [ideas] personally, down the mine. I'm afraid my spelling is its awful self in this letter, indeed I begin to despair . . . as looking up a word takes me twice a long as it does most people.

Paddy did a bit of writing too, which Bryce encouraged her to continue with: 'You have virtually every qualification needed and certainly a varied and pretty full life to write about. Looks like we'll both be famous, all of us yet.' He was equally impressed by his cousin Wendy's writing efforts: 'Wendy has been writing some very clever Fairy Stories with Rhodesian backgrounds. I would almost be bold enough to say that should she persivere she has the makings of a most original writer the first one since Enid Blyton made her debut.' Wendy's younger sister Pamela, whom they always called Sam, later also wrote several acclaimed historical novels under the name Luanshya Greer.

Aside from these positive ideas, Bryce continued to suffer from the heat as well as a raft of injuries he sustained underground:

> 'Indeed t'is terribly hot, even the trees, which only a few weeks ago were shimmering fresh and bright, are limp and tired, and all Rhodesia is aching for the first rains, only the Cicada beetles enveloped in a sort of heat rapture revel in the baking sun, Oh to be a Cicada beetle . . .'

He also suffered recurrent nightmares, which only subsided when the rains finally arrived in November of that year: 'How wonderful to be able to sleep and not to wake, sticky and bathed in perspiration. Even the dreadful nightmares I've been having most nightly have vanished into unadulterated sleep, and morning finds me fresh and wonderfully cool.'

In December 1954 Bryce was thrilled to move into a new hut of his own: 'I moved on Saturday into a hut with veranda and inbuilt cupboard all freshly painted and an absolute paridise in comparison to the former "Dump". There is even place in the front for a small bed of Nasturtiums and perhaps a Hydrainja bush.'

He began to think that he might have the means to purchase a house for him and his mother back in South Africa:

> I came up to the Copperbelt because I wanted us to have a home, a real home not a compromise, this will indeed be the first home we've really ever had for on your part Barberton was too much of a battle to really have been a home, and I should like this to be everything that a home should be like, which belonged to us. I haven't come up to Rhodesia to enjoy myself and I have no intention to be consumed with self-pity should I have to stay here a little longer than I normally would have had to. Getting our flat the way we want it is as much an ambition as going on to study so that until this is accomplised the reason for my being down the mine is just as materialistic as that.

However, by the New Year of 1955 the strikes were escalating. Bryce described them as 'a bubling cauldron of trouble . . . and we all hold our breath':

> Tonight, my first on Grizzlies, I start work 11pm and continue through until 7am tomorrow morning – not a pleasant shift, however I'm grateful to be able to work it, for it may be the last for

some time. So it looks as if we are going to spend a great hunk of time like birds in a wilderness, doing nothing.

It wasn't long before the mine compound was surrounded by police patrols armed with machine guns. Africans were not permitted to leave without a pass and all comings and goings were strictly controlled. This must have been a very confronting development. Bryce observed: 'Everything is fast mounting up into an enormously poppible balloon.' In a somewhat gloomy letter he wrote, 'There is to be no reconciliation after this strike, only a great deal lost and nothing, absolutely nothing gained.' Even worse, his hopes of saving a lot of money hadn't come to fruition:

> I've saved nothing but have worked out my saving requirements if there is to be any chance of my leaving here in three years as from now, £200 is the minimum endeavor and that includes this year, that is I must save on my own £200 a year in order to leave here with two thousand pounds.

A welcome distraction arrived on 8 June 1955, when Rosemary and Paddy arrived for a visit. It was Paddy's birthday, and their visit was timed so that they could celebrate together with Bryce and her brothers and their families, with whom they stayed.

Paddy had been born at the Geduld gold mine in Springs, where her father worked as an engineer. Being back at a mining town would have been something she was very familiar with. Bryce was working from dawn to dusk or on night shift, but he managed to see his mother and sister as often as he could. Rosemary had not been to a mine before and would have no doubt been alarmed to discover the dangerous conditions Bryce was faced with on a daily basis. Some such incidents were recorded in *Jack of Diamonds*, such as when Jack helped in the rescue of an African 'grizzly' worker:

I'd been underground about six months when one night, at about 2 a.m., a call came to attend an accident on a grizzly on the eleven hundred level . . . When we got there, the grizzly man's leg was trapped between the bars, jammed between rocks. The grizzly man's name was Karel Pretorius, and while he was pretty stoic, it was, of necessity, a crude procedure and he screamed in agony as I finally pulled his leg free . . . Black medics were forbidden to perform some of these procedures, of course, but fuck it, Karel Pretorius wasn't going to be allowed to die . . .

Once Paddy and Rosemary departed Bryce was once again left alone with his thoughts, and his dreams of one day getting out of there:

It seems so long to even the beginning of the road; I'm learning slowly however, but so very slowly, that one must decide and having made up one's mind close one's eyes and stumble on, there is an end to everything even I suppose Latin and the Copper Mines (Not to be confused with the Salt Mines) and I guess it's a privalige to be earning this sort of salary – though the Lord only knows it's not given away.

There would soon be time to ponder his future. In July 1955 Bryce received a letter confirming that he would soon be wearing a military uniform: he had been called up to serve four-and-a-half months as an army conscript in the Rhodesian Army, and there was no getting out of it. He was required to make his way to Kitwe to be medically examined, and while there was told to expect to be drafted into the army towards the end of the year. He wrote: 'What a prospect, Christmas with a drill pack on my back. I'm just waiting for the sky to fall down and then the process will be complete.'

He felt somewhat galled to learn that his cousins Courtenay and Glen had both been rejected for being unfit: 'I who would give almost my right arm to be certified unfit gets two taps on the chest by an army doctor, get told I'm just what the armies looking for, and these two who were simply dying to go to camp get thrown out on their ears.'

On 15 July 1955, Bryce survived a serious accident underground that reminded him that it was only a matter of time before his luck would run out. It was not the first accident he had survived but certainly the most harrowing. On 19 July he described to his mother what had happened:

I imagine you're itching to know what the 'unpleasant experience' was, I mentioned. Really it was quite amazing and has made me thank God for a God . . . It was exactly six o'clock the following morning, I'd taken out my watch just prior to lighting up a big mud blast I'd put on a rock, the last blast of the night I thought and called to my boy to bring a lighted cheesa stick, he blew the warning whistle and I could hear the igniter flare up as it toched the burning rope used for lighting these up. He brought it to me and I was standing on the bars and I was amazed at the brightness of this particular stick, a great ball of white terribly beautiful I'd never seen one quite just as startling as this one and held it in the air just befor toching it to the fuse, thankfully that the day or rather night was all but spent.

I bent down and put the cheesa stick to the fuse sticking out of the mud, but nothing happened, no tiny flare to denote the fuse was alight, this is infallible and I held the burning stick right on top of the fuse until even the top began to melt, still no flare or even a tiny jet of smoke. A grizzly fuse is ten seconds long and they were passing quickly, I fought back the panic and streached out to feel the fuse it was soft and warm and alight and burning I had about three seconds to get away, I turned and took a headlong dive into the lead in drive [and] as I did so the blast went off the concusion throwing me against the wall . . . unharmed but very very shaken . . . I've told you all this so that you will stop worrying and realize that there is a guiding hand and that you have nothing to fear.

It is testament to Bryce's maturity and resilience that such incidents didn't shatter his nerves – and he didn't have a girlfriend or close friends to console him. He did, however, continue to enjoy catching up with his cousins Wendy and Robyn when he had a few hours to himself. They simply adored him, and apart from thinking he was very handsome, said, 'He opened the doors for us, because this confined world in Luanshya was a cocoon – and he opened that cocoon and said, "You can be butterflies" and "reach for the stars."' Bryce introduced the girls to jazz and classical music, the first composition being Tchaikovsky's *Piano Concerto No.1*. Even back then, when Bryce was still only twenty-one, they said he had something special about him and displayed an inner strength and confidence. They said he had already set himself the goal of becoming a writer, telling them, 'I am going to be a world-famous author'. I expect they felt pleased and amused when they discovered their father Bryce was written up as 'Fats Greer' in *The Power of One*!

Bryce was also very relieved when a welcome distraction from his inner demons of working underground turned up in August 1955. It came with the arrival of two Australian travellers who had come to Luanshya looking for work. Iain Finlay and his best mate, Noel White, had been working their way around the world since leaving Melbourne in 1954 after completing their national service. They had originally met at Torquay Surf Life Saving Club, about 100 kilometres south-west of Melbourne. When Noel had told Iain he wanted to get the hell out of Melbourne, Iain had replied 'I'm coming with you'.

They travelled by ship to Italy and hitchhiked north through Europe, eventually running out of money in Norway, where they took on jobs as lumberjacks. At the end of the year they headed to London, where Iain found himself work first selling toys at the famous Hamleys store on Regent Street, then cleaning lavatories at the Pyrene Fire Extinguisher Factory on the Great West Road, and lastly at Thomas Cook tours in

Berkeley Street. Noel meanwhile was working in a vinegar factory. They worked until the beginning of spring when they had enough money to move on, hitchhiking to southern France, sometimes sleeping in barns or on benches at railway stations. 'On the road' romances were often a factor that determined how long they would stay in the one place!

By the summer of 1955 their money had almost run out again and so they travelled from southern France to the Italian port of Genoa. From there they managed to secure jobs as deckhands aboard a Danish freighter, *Tekla Torm*, bound for New York via Casablanca. On 24 June 1955 they stepped ashore, both of them blind drunk, and hitchhiked through northern Africa. Their adventures are recorded in Iain's compelling book *A Hitch in Time*, published in 2016.

Iain and Noel had heard about the Copperbelt being the place to make some decent money from a couple of Rhodesians who had given them a lift while they were hitchhiking in Europe. They caught a ride to Luanshya with a mining engineer called Frank Partridge on the afternoon of 1 August 1955. He reassured them, 'You can live a pretty good life here, if you want to stay. The money is fantastic, depending on where you're working. And you can save a hell of a lot.'

Soon afterwards Frank introduced the boys to Syd Hall, the club manager, and let him know that they were looking for work. As Iain described it, 'A slim young man in his early twenties had walked up to our table, and Frank said, "This is Bryce Courtenay. Bryce is one of our local squash champs." Bryce responded, "I'm . . . well, I'm just a miner really," in an accent that sounded very English and free of South African gutturals.' Frank told them that Bryce was a supervisor, and Bryce explained that he worked underground with around twenty-five African miners in his team.

Before long Martin O'Brien, the *Mine Magazine* editor, turned up and was enthralled with the story of Iain and Noel having travelled all the way from Cairo across North Africa. Syd said he had an administrative job going at the club and tossed a coin. Iain scored that job, and then Bryce suggested they meet with Wattie Watson, one of the club managers who ran the swimming pool and bar. After Wattie learnt of the boys having acquired bronze, silver and gold lifesaving medallions at Torquay Beach, he told Noel he was hired. Both were due to earn £54 a month, which was lower than the wage for working down the mines, and they were ineligible for the lucrative copper bonus. Iain and Noel were undeterred: they regarded the wages and conditions on offer as 'a big step up on our previous situation'.

Like Bryce, they were told in no uncertain terms of the risks of fraternising with the local women, black or white. Everyone working there had been warned to steer clear as being caught was punishable with instant dismissal. Not that there were many women around – and those who were there were usually the wives of the white mine managers. Iain recalls that most of the white women were 'on the whole pretty stuck-up and standoffish, which made it very difficult to score'. Bryce draws upon this situation in *Jack of Diamonds*:

> Noel White was being pretty open with me and so I thought I'd ask him about the opposite sex. 'Noel, what does a guy do about, you know . . . sex?'
>
> He threw back his head and laughed uproarously and in the process nearly drove off the road.
>
> 'Mate, your donger's a goner! No naughties for free unless you want ya balls danglin' from the nearest tree.'

The two Aussie boys settled in well: 'Our extensive travel stories had made us something of a sensation amongst the crowd, which gathered around the bar of the club each evening.' Bryce listened to their adventures wistfully, and they must have nurtured his own burgeoning wanderlust. His friendship with Iain and Noel, which lasted a lifetime, also ignited a great fondness for Australians and the Australian way of life and may have influenced him eventually deciding to live there.

Iain recalls that Bryce was rather shy and quiet in those days, and that he was well read, well educated and seemingly unflappable:

'Even so, his conversations were usually peppered with a fair amount of "bullshit".' But he found him to be a far cry from the brash advertising man he met up with years later at Caltex House in North Sydney when Bryce was employed as a copywriter with the advertising agency McCann Erickson. During his days at the mine, Iain further remembered that Bryce rarely smoked or drank and would instead prefer to go off with Noel or him and play a game of squash. Together the three of them also ended up as members of the Luanshya Dodgers baseball team.

Their friendship blossomed and Bryce told me he didn't know what he would have done without their companionship. Prior to their arrival he had kept largely to himself, and Iain observed in his book that Bryce 'seemed in a way to latch on to us . . . not, I thought, because we were the newest arrivals in Luanshya, but in a genuine need for real friendship'. Their easygoing Aussie manner and readiness to have a good time undoubtedly cheered Bryce up, and both Iain and Noel were also hugely bright. It must have been with a feeling of sheer relief that Bryce was finally able to engage in stimulating conversations.

Iain clearly remembers that even back then Bryce had worked out a life plan that he was certain was going to unfold:

Bryce envisaged the first phase being earning a lot of money here in the mines, and after this he would take off and do some travelling. The second stage would involve him going to London to study journalism so that he could learn how to improve his writing. During the third stage of his life Bryce planned on becoming a full-time writer and a successful and famous one at that.

Several weeks later, Noel managed with another toss of a coin to score a job supervising the pool gang of mine workers and this meant he was immediately earning double the wages Iain was being paid. Noel's role was to supervise a gang of Africans who were paid on an hourly basis to carry out a variety of tasks above ground at the mine; he was now eligible to receive the sought-after copper bonus.

In October 1955, after spending a few months at the mines, Iain decided it was time to move on as he wanted to see more of Africa. He was also thinking about either returning to Australia in time for the 1956 Melbourne Olympic Games or returning to Europe to rekindle his romance with a Norwegian girl called Lise, whom he had met in Cannes. Parting ways with Noel was a difficult decision, as the two had originally planned to do a lot more travelling together. However, Noel was not yet ready to give up the good wages he was earning.

The friendship between Noel and Bryce grew, and it was Noel who began to impress upon Bryce the risks presented by the dramatic accidents he witnessed deep below on a daily basis. Bryce began to question more why he was risking life and limb for a fortune that was increasingly feeling like an illusion. In addition, he had been nursing a nasty acid burn on his buttocks as a result of sulphuric acid leaking from his miner's lamp. The pain was excruciating and made working underground almost impossible: 'Woe is me . . . I have sustained . . . a rather nasty rash which burns like hades, so that I go round plucking at and with my hand fanning the seat of my pants, most embarrassing, but I'm long past the stage were I care . . .'

Bryce had by now received definite confirmation that he would be leaving Luanshya: 'Yes indeed I've been called into the army and will be spending Christmas (proberbly on guard duty with my luck) at Heany, an army Barracks fifteen miles [24 kilometres] from Bulawayo.' He was scheduled to commence this training in mid-November and was required to stay there for four-and-a-half months, which meant he would be free to return to the mines on 31 March 1956. He reassured his mother of the financial implications: 'The mine has decided to give us a subsidized pay while we're training and thus you will receive as ever your monies with the one exception that you'll get it on time as the mine will be sending it to you directly.'

In some ways Bryce's weary constitution began to look forward to going: 'I'm so tired of being underground, and so weary of nightshift, that I've come almost to welcome the idea of at least a dayshift job army or otherwise. It's a new experience and any new experience is something, and couldn't be worse than working underground.'

By October 1955 Bryce was attempting to swap or sell his battered Ford Motor car before he headed off to camp:

I was unable to get any price at all for it, as it wasn't in running condition . . . I thought it my duty however to offer it to Courtenay as he is saving up as well as selling his motorbike for a new car, mine patched up would at least get him £80 towards his goal. I offered it to him, and he accepted with a 'Right'o I'll take it', no mention even of a thank you . . . Believe you me it's harder yet harder to live down my family and I shan't be sad to leave Luanshya permanently.

In a letter dated 4 November Bryce was still battling to recover from the acid burn: 'I have instead of the battery burn on my tail a severe rash caused by the ointment they attempted to use in an effort to relieve the original burn, I'm not working today, having had to go to hospital for a morning treatment . . .' He also asked his mother to do him a favour, something he rarely did:

Mother, an Australian friend of mine who has been hitch hiking around the world will be arriving in Johannesburg any time after you receive this letter, he has spent almost four months up here having arrived with a friend who is staying on a little longer, they've been quite a stimulent to me and I've grown to like them greatly. Would you prepare the spare bedroom and put him up for as long as he cares to stay . . . I shall endeavor to arrange for a little extra on your November cheque to cover this. I know it will be a little inconveinant, for which I'm sorry, but I know he'd do it for me and I'd rather like it if he met you. His name is Iain Finlay.

Today, Noel resides in the United States and Iain writes at his home in northern New South Wales, having enjoyed a stellar career as a television journalist. He has written over twenty books, some of them co-authored by Trish Clark, his partner of over fifty years.

Before departing Luanshya to commence his army training Bryce wrote to his mother:

> I shall proberbly be coming down next June, but only if I can get a car, for I should like to take you to the coast for a couple of weeks so that you can come back fit and well and can start work rejuvinated a little . . . I leave for camp on Sunday next and my next letter will proberbly from there, I am hoping by then this rash of mine has cleared up, I shall work for two months in order to square what I owe the mine after I return from camp. No Christmas presents at Christmas I'm afraid, perhaps when I get out of camp, for there'll be niether time nor money until I get back the army pay being ten shillings a day. I have come to look forward to it, for mining is driving me steadily crazy. I shall be sending only Post Cards from camp as writing is going to be inconveiniant so that this is the last real letter I am going to promise.

Bryce must have felt frustrated in his efforts to forge a better future for himself. I suspect it was with a heavy heart that on 13 November 1955 he departed Luanshya with nothing more than a rucksack on his back. He would soon be trading his miner's overalls for battle fatigues and military boots, and he must have wondered if this was going to be another miserable chapter in his still-difficult life.

5

BATTLE FATIGUE

The major premise behind training a man to fight hasn't
changed much since Alexander the Great and probably
even predates that: do as you're told and never question a
superior. – *Brother Fish*

BRYCE HAD NEVER HAD the slightest interest in joining the Rhodesian
Army, but the army had him firmly in its sights. He felt frustrated at
having to leave behind the well-paying job at the mines. As he wrote
to Paddy, 'This feels so unfair Mother, as I have worked so hard risking
life and limb and I must now accept being shipped off for months
earning wages that shall be barely worth spitting at.'

On 13 November 1955, he found himself travelling along a
winding dirt road that eventually reached Llewellin Barracks at
Heany Junction, about 1000 kilometres from Bulawayo in the south-
west of Rhodesia (Zimbabwe). It had been a Royal Air Force training
base during the Second World War but was now a conscript training
centre for the Rhodesia Regiment (RR), one of the oldest and largest
units in the Rhodesian Army. The barracks were deliberately sited
away from the temptations of Bulawayo, and Bryce had heard the
place was boiling hot in summer and freezing cold during the dry
winter months.

He quickly realised the experience would be far different from the wonders of the world-famous Victoria Falls some 450 kilometres away, which he hoped to one day visit. Arriving at Llewellin confirmed that he had been caught up in the power plays of the British Empire, which needed army 'fodder' to protect its African territories. Bulawayo's nickname is the 'City of Kings', but Bryce instinctively understood that he was not about to enjoy a right royal experience. National service had only been introduced in 1955 and the regiment had been initially mobilised for the Korean War in 1951 but never made it there. Bryce soon realised that some of the conscripts were spoiling for a fight and the chance to spill some blood. However, as he wrote years later in *Brother Fish*, the reality of being deployed in an actual combat zone was a far more frightening proposition:

> I've suddenly gone flat, like someone has punched me hard in the gut, taken the wind out of me. I can't see too clearly and then I just sort of collapse, sink to my knees and throw up.

After passing through the boom gate at the main entrance he saw lines of corrugated-iron huts bordered by white painted stones and devoid of any gardens. This must have made his heart sink, and he told me he felt like his world was falling apart. Bryce had only just restored his confidence following the near-fatal accident down the mines earlier that year. He had also been saving like mad to fund his dream of going to London to study. Now he found himself facing four-and-a-half months of training far away from the lucrative Copperbelt. As an army conscript he was set to earn a pitiful wage of only £3.50s a month, whereas at the mines he was earning over £150 per month. At the time this felt like a small fortune, although much later Bryce realised it really wasn't, given the significant risks he confronted daily.

He was inducted into the regiment as recruit number 54001, Rifleman Courtenay A.B. in No. 6 Platoon, B Company; his rank of rifleman was equivalent to that of a private. Upon arrival his 'civvy' clothes were confiscated; whenever the conscripts left the barracks they were required to wear their uniform. There was little time to dwell on his new set of circumstances. Days at the barracks were crammed with endless drill parades and bayonet training, and hours spent crawling through the bush without being detected by a would-be assailant. They were also required to fire off rounds at the rifle range and were given tear-gas training, including being plied with 'puke gas' to test if their masks were fitted correctly. Bryce was certain that their superiors screamed 'Fix gas masks!' a moment too late as a form of torture and then watched with sadistic pleasure as their charges gasped for breath.

The conscripts were required to be in bed by 10 p.m., but they usually rose again at 2.00 a.m. in a frantic effort to apply lots of 'spit and polish' to their shoes and brass buttons. They would then scrub the green concrete floors of their quarters in time for roll call and inspection. Their bedding consisted of a mattress and a greatcoat, three blankets, and some sheets and pillowcases. There seemed barely enough time to go to the lavatory, and with Bryce and his fellow conscripts surviving on only four hours' sleep a night, rest was the most coveted of luxuries: 'Since we've been here, it's just been rush, and shoot and panic . . . I guess I'm just about the tiredest man in the Federation at the moment.' It wasn't long before the situation began to take its toll: 'Thus far life has been perfect misery – 16 hrs of work, more in fact, with everyone shouting and screaming and making sure that you don't have even ten minutes a day to yourself.'

From the outset it was clear that humiliation was part of the course, and Bryce discovered it was ingrained in the culture of the regiment. He also saw that his superiors had an uncanny capacity to uncover the fears of their charges, and showed no mercy in demanding obedience:

I do grow somewhat used to life here though and shall become more so, once I become used to being daily and hourly humiliated by youngsters both younger and certainly far less intelligent than I cowering behind two stripes . . . I've never realized before how dreadfully proud I am, and IF nothing else this camp will certainly be good for that.

Declaring that you felt unwell came with consequences, as did any unfortunate 'slip in the showers':

> Sick Parade is yet another fall in and fall out, yet another session of shouting and bellowing from Hospital orderlies and in particular the doctor, all who treat you like the dregs. Nobody dares try and 'shoot a line' – sick parade is almost a punishment, and we all try and stay away until we're ready to drop.

Bryce once told me about the time he suffered a severe bout of diarrhoea that made jogging back and forth at fifteen-minute intervals over a couple of hours an incredibly daunting experience! His spirits during training regularly dropped very low, largely due to exhaustion.

Bryce sometimes felt in fear of his life, especially following the occasion when a particularly malicious sergeant seemed intent on killing him with a bayonet. The details of this incident are patchy, but he alludes to them in a letter to his mother: 'I'm yet alive – life continues to graduate between miserable and absolutely miserable . . .' His experience as a conscript informed his writing on war in many of his novels, and it's tempting to think this particular incident contributed to a perspective offered in *Brother Fish*:

> History is redolent with fools in command, field marshals, generals and brigadiers who have managed to send legions of men to their deaths on the principle that the greater force knows better than the individual soldier, and that dying needlessly is a peculiar privilege granted to the lower ranks.

At least the food supplied at the barracks was good, even though there was never enough of it. A typical meal was a mound of boiled bully beef served with mashed potatoes and gravy, and for dessert a steaming plate of pudding sloshed with lumpy custard. Doubly important, mealtime was the only part of the day when Bryce had some time to himself – that is, after being quick-marched at double time into the canteen. He wrote, 'Most of us eat more than we need just to remain a little longer.'

Quite unexpectedly Bryce and his fellow conscripts were offered a chance to go home for Christmas. This prospect raised Bryce's spirits enormously, and he wrote to Paddy, 'I am however keeping my head above water . . . the thought of being with you in just over two weeks keeps me going . . . I shall be coming home, for even if I've to hitchhike . . . Christmas with you seems almost unbelievable!' The opportunity to enjoy ten days off for Christmas made Bryce heave a huge sigh of relief, as the recruits were normally only allowed out once every six weeks to go into town, and even this was granted purely on merit. This extended leave was an exceptional treat as the conscripts were usually required to complete their training without having any home-leave periods whatsoever.

He thoroughly enjoyed the precious days back home in Johannesburg, even though he fretted that he only had £5 to buy his mother and Rosemary a few treats, including ice-cream sundaes. I used to say to him, 'Even at this young age you had taken on the role of both breadwinner and confidant for your mother and sister.' He would shrug in response and say, 'Well, darling, that's what men do.'

As usual, Bryce thought little of himself. When asked by his mother whether he wanted an electric shaver for Christmas, he responded, 'No mother my skin has blistered from the sun out here and an electric shaver would be agony. Instead I'd like a sleeping bag. It would cost you far less and be far more useful. If not a sleeping bag, a Diary once again.' I so wish he had kept a diary for the rest of his life as I understand Paddy did.

During the Christmas leave period Bryce had the chance to meet Rosemary's fiancé, Esmund David Harry Anderson, for the first time. Bryce discovered that like him, Esmund loved sport – especially cricket and Rugby, as well as athletics. Esmund was one of five children born to his mother, an American from Minnesota, and his father's parents had been missionaries in Natal, having come from Sweden; they later went on to join the Church of the Assemblies of God and, and like his parents, Es (as he was usually called) was very committed to his faith. Bryce liked him immediately and subsequently wrote to his mother, 'I think Esmund is a wonderful fellow and right for Rosemary.' This turned out to be true, and by early May 1956 they had announced their engagement, and then on 6 October they were married. Rosemary and Es continue to enjoy a blissfully happy marriage, well into their senior years, and on 5 April 2022, Rosemary celebrated her 90th birthday.

Leaving the two women in his life to return to the barracks must have been hard, but with a big sigh Bryce was soon making the long journey back with fellow conscript Eddie Wentzel. It proved to be a perilous two-day trip through rain, mud and unsealed roads, as he later recounted to Paddy:

I'd had as you know no experience of bad weather driving. The clutch plate had broken earlier on which meant we couldent do over 35 [56 kilometres an hour] nor go any slower as the clutch was slipping both ways. It was the most ghastly hundred miles [160 kilometres] I've ever known – indeed we seemed to skid across most of it sideways and even on occasion backwards . . . Once an ox jumped out in front of the car. I was skidding and he came from nowhere just ten yards [9 metres] in front of the car. Thank God I didn't slam on my brakes, for we would have most certainly turned over; instead I swung wildly into the bush and out again just scraping its side as I went past. It happened so quickly it couldent have just been me reacting. I guess you must have prayed . . . We arrived at 4.15, four hours late, the military cop wouldn't hear of an excuse and proceeded to remonstrate. We were all so weary I couldent even see him properly, only the blur of his red cap.

This chap took the boys' names and numbers and proceeded to lay charges before allowing them to head to their bunks. Within an hour they were out of bed and another army day had begun. In a small show of mercy, the charges didn't go through: the commanding officer must have been satisfied with their excuses.

Procuring a leave pass on the weekends could never be taken for granted. Soon after returning from the Christmas break, the holiday euphoria was snuffed out:

I've been breathing double time since our arrival back. I had hoped to have this evening all to myself, we'd been granted a weekend leave and most all were going out on the town this evening, however as usual under some typical Army pretence it was cancelled at the eleventh hour. Thus a minor riot is going on around me.

Having the bright lights of Bulawayo once again out of reach would have been another blow for Bryce. He always had a strong sense of fair play and was not about to forgive the army bullies for being so mean-spirited. It's likely that life in the Rhodesian Army reminded him of the raft of rules he had endured as a child moving from one boarding house or institution to another. The total lack of emotional sustenance must have been an added burden, but then Bryce was used to being alone and coping with feelings of abandonment. He would have just carried on hoping that things would improve. It is little wonder that he barely mentioned this period of his life in later media interviews or in conversations we had during our years together. Instead, he chose to relay fragments of his experience in the army in his novels, including *The Power of One*, *Whitethorn*, *Brother Fish*, *Jack of Diamonds* and *Smoky Joe's Cafe*.

There were some upsides. Writing in his diary provided him with moments of solace, as did working his way through a pile of books by authors including Dickens, Kipling, Camus and Goethe. He wrote, 'I do agree with you Doctor frieinds. I'll be fit when I leave here – fit for nothing. Enough, enough, I'm in a poor mood this evening and as usual very tired. Indeed writing is the only relaxation I have, and you know how much I love writing.'

Despite the harsh regimen, Bryce would have relished being in the outdoors again after having spent months underground at the mines. And he would have enjoyed becoming fit again, even though he would have preferred to be playing Rugby rather than running up and down hills carrying a heavy pack!

By the end of January 1956 Bryce had graduated to another unit and his life became easier: 'My change of rank gives me a break from the usual training, and regularly unarming a "fanatic" whose purpose is to ram me with a bayonet.' He began to learn about unarmed combat while seated in a lecture room, and how to fight a war by gazing at diagrams. He found this phase a great deal better than the first, and it came with additional privileges, such as not being bawled out quite so often by his superiors. There was, however, no escape from guard duty, as he was now appointed as a guard commander and 'was obliged to remain awake from six on Saturday morning until I was relieved at six thirty on Sunday evening'.

The unwelcome and miserable stint of army training finally concluded, and on 9 April 1956 Bryce returned to the Roan Antelope copper mine just shy of four-and-a-half months after he had departed. He expressed his unfettered joy in a letter to his mother:

> Freedom is like a wild free bird you don't appreciate it until its wings are clipped and then it becomes very, very important . . . It's certainly

good to be a civilian again and to wear my hair a little longer and muddy boots to work and sloppy comfortable clothes, not to smell of brasso and stale cigarette smoke first thing in the morning and have greasy baked beans and bacon for breakfast and most important not to have somebody yelling at me most of the time.

He returned to the mines feeling lean and fit and was desperate to have the higher wages rolling back in. The transition wasn't easy, however: 'Coming back has been a rush and a worry and even yet I'm far from being back to even keel.' The burden of debt and money worries returned to haunt him, and he wrote to his mother in a despondent tone: 'I'm afraid there's no chance really of my being able to get away from here for quite a while yet, for being in camp has left me rather badly in debt.'

His stint in the army had left him stony broke – a bitter blow as he had worked so hard at the mines during the previous two years. The mining camp had paid part of his salary but had subtracted his army pay and taken out another £15 as a food allowance. This meant that in the end, and with some lingering debts, he was about £100 short and was obliged to repay his debt at a rate of £25 per month.

However, he was determined to make up for lost time and even considered taking on extra shifts. This didn't happen: fellow miners warned him it could lead to certain death as working down a shaft when you were overtired was a recipe for disaster. Bryce tried to reassure his mother regardless of his financial woes:

Please mother don't think that I consider having been able to support you is or has been a drudge – very much the converse in fact. It's just that I know that if I give up my job and immediately dig into my savings the two years almost that I've already spent here will have been completely futile and I'm more determined than ever, that this should not be so.

Bryce got back into the swing of life at the mines, even though he wrote, 'I've become the slowest old dodger in the world, mostly on principle, for being last out of the change rooms in the afternoons is in many ways quite a triumph, a bit warped I'm afraid but nevertheless so, for it sort of reminds me that the military system didn't radically affect me.' His cousin Courtenay also worked at the mines and was soon due to head off to the army himself. Bryce wrote, 'Poor little begger I wouldent even wish it on my cousin. I hope he sticks it out however for I think his is the type that the army does radically remould. Lord, what a concieted little prig I must sound.'

Getting back to playing Rugby really cheered Bryce up. He had arrived back just in time for the start of the season and predictably ended up a bit the worse for wear after a few games:

> I seem to have bumped into every sort of trouble this season all the
> biggest forwards seem to make me their special target and I have a
> nose the size of a small melon, small peeled melon, where a huge
> blond full-back punched me, nevertheless thus far it has been my
> best season for a long time.

This aside, he was hopeful he would keep his place on the firsts team.

Bryce often closed his letters to Paddy by saying, 'Time for bed and as a final bombshell "Grizzlies" in the morning. Nevermind Mother, it's not forever – I guess I just have to be philosophical. Others do it too.'

Indeed, it wasn't to be forever, even though his exit plan turned out to be anything but straightforward. Bryce's departure from the mines came sooner than he had planned. He confirmed his decision to make a clean break to his mother: 'I've finally decided for better or for worse I can't take any more mining or I shall bust.' As it turned out, his timing was pretty good as the boom in the Copperbelt was beginning to end.

Bryce had loved hearing about the adventures of his Aussie friends Iain Finlay and Noel White and was eager to do some travelling himself. Making travel plans must have provided a welcome distraction while he spent his final days working as a grizzly in the dangerous underground shafts. He and Noel had discussed doing a bit of travelling together, as he told Paddy in a letter:

We plan to hitch-hike throughout the Union and then back through Central Africa overland to the Continent and England. I hope I haven't startled you by doing it that way I shall save at least £100 and at the same time see the whole of Africa [and] have an experience which is by no means commonplace.

Finally, in mid-August 1956 and after Bryce had been at Luanshya for three years, he and Noel left the mines, their pockets rattling with money. They travelled north for about 60 kilometres until they arrived at Elisabethville (now Lubumbashi) on their way into the Belgian Congo. They then continued for another 1000 kilometres before reaching the legendary Mountains of the Moon – the Ruwenzori range, north of Lake Edward in Uganda on the Congo border. Both boys were tired, and a storm was brewing, but they gasped in awe at the mountains before them: 'They're very beautiful but appear very dark and ominous and capped with snow. The Belgian Congo is indeed the most fantastic country I've ever seen and indeed without compare in Africa. I'm afraid patriotic as I am, for sheer beauty South Africa cannot compare.'

Clearly they were enjoying themselves enormously, and Bryce wrote a letter to Paddy from Elisabethville filled with rapture:

Already well into the swing of things, thus far we really have been on the pigs back . . . Folk up here have showered us with hospitality and we've been staying in a luxury flat with the most charming folk imaginable and have lacked for nothing, paid for nothing and crammed ourselves full of Continental food . . . please not to worry, this couldent be better and I'm having the time of my life . . . No more there isn't any time as we're going out to supper in borrowed suits and an American convertible.

For a boy from South Africa who had grown up in harsh circumstances, this exciting trip and first taste of freedom must have made him feel like he was on the set of a Hollywood movie.

In search of adventure and good times, Bryce and Noel travelled into East Africa and arrived at Malindi, a town on Malindi Bay in south-eastern Kenya. On 17 August 1956, Bryce wrote a letter that he posted from the office of the local district commissioner:

Well at present I'm a fully-fledged bloned [blond] in this glass beach corner with nothing all day to do but spear fish swim and hours and hours to think. How lovely these last two weeks have been, perhaps the nicest in my life and I begin to feel much a new man with the memories of the mines slowly pulsing out of my system. How good it is to feel clean and free again, like some nasty skin disease slowly fading.

Bryce and Noel boarded a ferry to travel to the ancient trading island of Zanzibar, 250 kilometres from Mombasa. On arrival there, more good times beckoned. They explored the island's ancient alleyways, which crisscrossed between white stone houses and the minarets of local mosques. They haggled for souvenirs and carpets and Bryce said he especially loved the intricately carved wooden doors, even though they were far too expensive and heavy to contemplate buying. While sipping beers at sunset they watched Arab dhows glide across aqua seas to the reefs beyond. This magical scene was surely as far away from the mines as it was possible to get. The whole experience must have felt like a dream: apart from going up to Luanshya and then to Bulawayo, Bryce had never travelled outside of South Africa. While he was growing up holidays had been practically unheard of and the family's social life had revolved entirely around the Church, apart from occasional visits to his mother's relatives or friends.

It was with a very deep sigh that Bryce eventually had to prepare to return to South Africa. He had faithfully promised his mother he would be home in time to attend Rosemary's wedding on 6 October 1956. However, getting back to reality proved difficult:

> I don't know whether I shall arrive in time. Please try and forgive me if I don't – I know it to have been very selfish of me to linger here when really I should have made an earlier start home, ensuring a certain arrival. But I needed this mother, more indeed than I have needed anything for a long, long while, so do both of you try to understand should I arrive too late.

As it turned out, he needed to head back to Johannesburg as soon as he could to prepare to leave for London. He finished this letter with reassurances about sending further funds: 'I'm enclosing your cheque, hopelessly late I'm afraid but there hasn't been a Post Office open for weeks.' He had also made a backup plan, something he seemed to need to do throughout his life: 'If there's been any difficulty, ask Enda [a childhood friend of his mother] to substitute until I arrive, whereapon I shall reimburse them.'

I expect Bryce didn't fully realise how exhausted he had been, and was clinging to the chance of taking more time to rejuvenate. What he had come to appreciate from working down the mines was to value his life and not to throw it away. This experience also reaffirmed his decision to leave Africa and go directly to London to study – his chosen course commenced in early October and he barely had time to get himself organised to depart.

Rosemary was understandably very disappointed when she learnt that Bryce would not be attending her October wedding. However, she completely understood and was happy that he was going off to do something to advance his life. During a visit to stay with us in September

2006, Rosemary told me that, like her mother, she felt hugely relieved that Bryce survived the mines. I have sometimes wondered if she ever regretted not undertaking further studies too, despite always conveying a sense of absolute joy in the path she followed with Es and their shared abiding commitments to their faith.

It was very unlike Bryce not to fulfil a commitment as important as attending his only sibling's wedding – but he had little choice with his course starting so soon, and needed time there to get himself set up before his course commenced. During the years we were together he nearly always put the needs of others before his own – except, that is, when there was a game of Rugby on. Nothing ever got in the way of that!

After nearly a month spent travelling with Noel, Bryce began to feel he was himself again. It was time to part ways so that they could each get on with their lives. He made it back to Johannesburg by mid-September 1956 and was reunited with his mother and the soon-to-be-married Rosemary. Both women would have been overjoyed to welcome him home. Over the years Rosemary compiled an (unpublished) family memoir she called *Rosemary's Story*, and in this she recalls that they could see he still wasn't his usual cheerful self. One afternoon their mother found Bryce curled up in a ball on the floor, whimpering, his head in his hands. That near-fatal fall through the grizzly bars continued to haunt him. Years later, any story about a mine accident broadcast on the news had him heading for another glass of wine to settle his nerves.

After resting up at home Bryce was ready to embrace the next chapter of his life. He was now aged twenty-three and buzzing with dreams and hopes for his future. While his precise plans were still being formed, what was clear was that he saw no future living under the dark clouds of the apartheid regime. The protest movement was gathering strength and Bryce knew perfectly well that if he stayed in South Africa he would almost certainly be arrested and end up in jail. He wanted no part of the ruling regime's charter, which consistently meant crushing the hopes and dreams of the predominantly black population, and he was about to become one of many young white South Africans who chose to get out while they could.

Before leaving for London, Bryce travelled to Pietermaritzburg to spend a few days with his father, who was living at the Rocheberie Boarding House. It was the last time they ever met. Bryce had missed out on having a normal father-and-son relationship and those years could never be reclaimed. Arthur Ryder passed away from heart failure in Natal on 8 December 1966, at the age of seventy-eight. Like Bryce's grandfather, he didn't live long enough to see Bryce become an internationally acclaimed author.

On 26 September 1956, Paddy saw Bryce off at Johannesburg Airport for his flight to England, not knowing when or where she would see him again. London was calling him, and he couldn't wait to arrive.

6

LONDON CALLING

———————

For we feast on the words of the storyteller and, if words can make a stomach contented, by journey's end we will all be plump as partridges. – *The Family Frying Pan*

ON 27 SEPTEMBER 1956, Bryce sat on a bench in London's Hyde Park surer than ever that he didn't want to become a lawyer as his mother had hoped. He also knew he had no future back in South Africa, as he described to Diana Ritch in her 1991 interview:

All these expectations I suddenly realised had absolutely nothing to do with Bryce Courtenay . . . I had the money to go to university and I was sitting there and I tried to see into my future and this is what I saw: I saw myself becoming a lawyer and I saw myself going back to Africa . . . Now instead of climbing this ladder of success I had realised that at school more and more I was getting into serious trouble for asking the most simple single question, and the question was: 'Why are the black people different to the white people? Why is one inferior and the other superior?' . . . I would have spent my life trying to answer the question and I knew I couldn't answer it because I knew it was a lie. I saw myself in jail and I actually saw myself being hanged . . . I couldn't bear it and I decided I couldn't be a lawyer and I also decided I couldn't go back because if I went back I would destroy my life . . .

For the first time Bryce felt free to chart his own course, and set his heart on journalism. He would have realised that once he graduated from his studies in journalism, he would be able to secure a job with a newspaper or work as a scriptwriter in the emerging field of television. Having arrived, his spirits were high: 'I am sure I shall like London, England indeed is a "Green and pleasant land", and I look forward to seeing as much of it as possible.'

However, London in 1956 was a far cry from the comparative opulence on display today, and it didn't take long for the stark realities of life to sink in. The Second World War had only ended a decade earlier and piles of rubble caused by the bombing raids still scarred the city's landscape. There were also shortages of foodstuffs even though rationing had officially ended in 1954. Bryce rarely spoke about his time in London, but he wove some of his experiences and perceptions into his novels, including in *Jack of Diamonds*:

> To my surprise, there was still a lot of bomb damage, and Londoners, generally speaking, looked drab and disconsolate in the late winter gloom. Perhaps it was the food rationing, which continued to make their lives joyless. They'd been required to show their stiff upper lips for way too long, and I couldn't help wondering whether winning the war was all we'd thought it would be.

Being in London would have been both exciting and overwhelming for Bryce. Apart from being at boarding school in Johannesburg he had never lived in a big city. In 2006 he reflected on *Talking Heads*, 'I came from the boondocks so to speak and suddenly I found myself in this huge cosmopolitan city. I'd come from a high African sky, and I was now in a place where the sky sat on my shoulders, and everything was always damp.'

Bryce's first task was more prosaic: just like Oliver Twist, he needed to find lodgings. This proved to be difficult. He walked the streets carrying a battered suitcase containing his clothes, some books and his prized Erika typewriter. On 2 October 1956 he wrote: 'Well here I am at last, certainly in England but as yet far from settled, accommodation is almost impossible and finally after much trying have a room, bed and breakfast, at £3.11s. per week . . .' This was a hostel at 47 Barkston Gardens in Earl's Court with no bathroom or heating. It was the first of a series of temporary lodgings he stayed in during his time in London.

After the Second World War the district of Earl's Court in West London became known as 'the Polish Corridor' because Polish officers who had fought alongside the Allied forces but were unable to return home began opening shops there. By the late 1950s South Africans like Bryce as well as Australians and New Zealanders had started to move into the area as its rows of stuccoed terraces had been converted into studio flats and hostels, and in the 1960s it become affectionately known as 'Bedsitter Land' or 'Kangaroo Valley' (it still is). Bryce instructed his mother to write to him c/o 'The Overseas Visitors Club' and described how he spent each day:

I awake each morning at a quarter to seven, wash and have a shave, that is sometimes have a shave, though I always wash. Put on the kettle and whilst it is boiling, dress. Having dressed, an old pair of khaki trousers, two sweaters and your warm slippers, I make a cup of coffee. Breakfast is invariably two coughs a splutter and a cup of coffee, in that essential order.

After breakfast I sit down and type for three hours, whereupon if I have no lecture to go to I go out for half an hour, which is usually spent in a little coffee bar around the corner. All coffee bars have Indian rubber plants in the windows, onions hanging from the ceiling, fishnet draped across the walls, dim lighting, and a shiny machine used for making perfectly vile Italian espresso coffee. The one I frequent is no different, so that instead of creating a Left Bank atmosphere, they take on the uniformity of a large Company canteen ...

Over a cup of chocolate, I usually meet a few familiar faces, actors, writers, linguists and students, most of them 'resting' a term which translated, usually means, they are too lazy to work, haven't got a job or are hoping the purity of their art will pull them through.

Given that Bryce's ambition was to become a writer, the sight of these impoverished artists may have sent a shiver down his spine. He continued:

The time before lunch is usually spent washing and ironing and perhaps reading for an hour or so. Lunch is mostly a couple of eggs, bread and butter, fruit and a glass of milk. After lunch I once again get behind my typewriter and work until six in the evening ... After supper I usually work until about eleven, make a cup of coffee and crawl into bed, very thankfully into bed. I seldom go out in the evenings as this puts me behind with my work ...

Nothing could have prepared him for London's bitter cold, with afternoons enveloped in darkness by 4 p.m. It always seemed to be raining, and the damp seeped into his bones. Like Jack Spayd in *Jack of Diamonds*, 'At one stage on the crossing from America I'd toyed with the idea of "disappearing" in England, but the dull weariness of London had left me depressed ...' Bryce wasn't a fan of the food, either. It reminded him of the tasteless stodge he had forced down in institutions during his childhood: 'I have grown incidentally to eat – even almost, to enjoy – cabbage, for normal civilized greens are almost impossible to get.'

Within a month of his arrival, the Suez Crisis was dominating the news and the Conservative Party leader, Prime Minister Anthony Eden, was weathering the storm from its fallout. Despite this, the British public continued to be enchanted with the beautiful young Queen Elizabeth II. Bryce's mother was a huge fan of the Queen and he said she used to daydream that one day he would have the opportunity to meet her. In fact, he never did meet Her Majesty, but in May 2018 I received an invitation to attend a garden party at Buckingham Palace. We were offered sandwiches, slices of Battenberg cake and, naturally, a cup of tea! I would have adored to have shared this special occasion with Bryce and knew he would have loved exploring the immaculate 17 hectares of gardens.

Bryce felt some excitement to be in the land of his much-lauded Scottish ancestors, the MacGregors – one of Scotland's most famous clans, claiming royal descent form Grigor, the son of King Alpin, who flourished in the 8th century. As a result of their lawlessness, their name and part of their lands were proscribed. The MacGregor chief supported Prince Charlie and fought at the Battle of Culloden in 1746.

And England was the country his mother had always referred to as 'home', and she was as British as a cup of freshly brewed tea. Bryce was thrilled to know she planned on joining him there: 'How you will love London, so big, the city of Johannesburg would be quite lost in just one of the forty or fifty postal districts in any part of London.' He did, however, suggest she consider delaying her arrival until the weather became warmer.

On 3 October 1956, Bryce commenced his studies at the London School of Journalism. This institution was founded by Sir Max Pemberton in 1920 and is still a magnet for aspiring journalists. Bryce wrote to Paddy: 'My course starts tomorrow, a course in pure journalism which carries a diploma as there is no degree in journalism and in addition a short story course, if after a year I have progressed sufficiently I can take a job on any one of the papers as a reporter.'

I was disappointed to be told that almost all the school's records of those years have been 'responsibly disposed of'. Sadly, those records that were kept and digitally archived do not include any information about Bryce's time there, but letters to his mother reveal that he threw himself into the course even though he found it hard going:

> Being rather slow, writing to me means mostly slow drudgery and very hard work . . . [It] is quite the most mentally exhausting thing I've ever done and terribly humiliating when I realize how long it will be before I even reach a mediocre standard, and I've been mediocre for so long in everything.

Growing up in places where Afrikaans was the predominant language meant that Bryce had to work hard on polishing his English even though his mother always spoke to him in English. Bryce had problems with his spelling and used to believe he was 'somewhat dyslexic'. He more than made up for this, though, with his unbridled creativity and astonishingly large vocabulary, acquired from decades of reading and writing.

I don't think Bryce ever fully embraced the sentiments of the famous quote by Samuel Johnson: 'When a man is tired of London, he is tired of life; for there is in London all that life can afford.' He became tired of London on many occasions, as did many other new arrivals. As he wrote to Paddy, 'It is little wonder that the cream of the British youth immigrate as soon as they are able – there just is nothing here for them.' He realised early on that his staying in London long-term was unlikely, and even then he toyed with the idea of building a future on the other side of the world: 'As soon as my course is over I shall have to leave, perhaps to Canada or to Australia.' He was also exasperated that he was so hard up, especially having worked in the dangerous job at the mines to cover the cost of his studies, and he began to think about how he could earn a living from writing:

> I shall have to start selling stories soon as my financial status is fast becoming critical. So that soon it will mean either selling stories or a job during the day. Still it will all be worth it, for for the first time

in my life I am doing something I really need to do and must at any cost continue doing.

To shore up his funds, he decided to take on a variety of part-time jobs: 'Things have been a little rough for a while, I start a job packing parcels at one of the big departmental shops. They take on extra staff over the Christmas rush and the pay is extremely good . . . I shall make about £50 a month, which for Britain is more than good.' Taking on such jobs was an added pressure as it meant he could focus on his studies only after work or in the daytime hours following a night shift.

Bryce moved to another bedsit, this time in Chelsea, where he became very unwell: 'I am sorry not to have written sooner, however, I've been pretty well on my back for the last month or so, first with a brace of crushed ribs (Rugger) and thereafter with a severe dose of Asian flu complicated with bronchitis.' Like most people living in England, the gloomy weather continued to be a preoccupation for him:

'It's nearing winter over here and already folk are beginning to wear top coats and mufflers, tho England slides into winter so gracefully that I think it's perhaps for me the nicest part of the year, though I dread the prospect of winter ahead.'

Despite this, he remained cheerful as he always did in the face of difficulties:

'There is a lovely garden outside my window, Chelsea is quite the nicest part of London to live in . . . so old life seems to breathe softly frowning on all the hurrying and worrying people . . . I realize how happy I am to be here, almost despite the pretty continual battle to make ends meet.'

The prospect of celebrating his first Christmas in London additionally raised his spirits:

> Christmas in London is really an occasion, the shops have done their best to wash the wet pavements in a swirl of colour and the Christmas shopper into a hysteria of spending. There are coloured lights and giant fairy lanterns everywhere and the shop windows are splendid . . . there's a continual snowstorm in some of the windows and laughing Father Christmas's of every shape and size.

He described to his mother how even a local busker had polished up his act for the festive season:

> The little old man who plays the violin on the corner is wearing a sprig of holly in his shabby buttonhole and appears even to have the cap he uses for gathering pennies cleaned for the occation . . . When I asked him, he replied: 'No Gov'nur, me special festive season cap it is.' I left him two pennies and he scraped out 'Silent Night' in a manner guaranteed to break the silence of any night in history.

A similar character pops up in *The Family Frying Pan*:

> People would stop and watch in wonder and most would leave a coin in the old felt hat which lay at the professor's feet. In fact, so popular a tourist attraction did the old man become that the hat filled with coins several times a day and the professor was forced to take a taxi to Barclay's Bank every evening and then home to where he lived under Chelsea Bridge.

His being ill meant that Christmas did not end up delivering Bryce much festive cheer:

> Well I have just spent a month in bed but feel quite fit again . . . I spent the week over Christmas in bed but did however write you all for Christmas and gave the letter to the Char woman to

post . . . I had a dose of Asian flu, the second this winter, and I guess I must have got up too soon, for I was down again in January the second with complicated Broncitus and that has laid me up ever since.

Before long he was down to his last pennies, but his family back in South Africa came to the rescue. Throughout his life it was rare for Bryce to accept help from others, and he wrote: 'Please thank Rosemary and Esmund for a very acceptable pound, more so as I have not been able to work and have only had sick benefit coming in, hardly enough to cover the rent of my room . . .' The prospect of his mother's arrival to England raised his spirits: 'Thank goodness you will be arriving in the sort of Spring . . . It's grand to see a patch of green grass when you look out of the window even if the trees do look a little like disused garden brooms.'

By March 1957 Bryce had moved to another location in Chelsea, which he wrote was 'more a matter of economy than anything else, though I liked it very much at Earl's Court my funds are very, very low and even £3 for a room is too much . . .' In those days Chelsea wasn't the chic, high-end borough it is today. When I am visiting London, I generally stay at the Sloane Club in Chelsea, which was founded in 1922 as the Service Women's Club; I always feel quite emotional knowing that I am close to where Bryce once lived.

He was looking forward to concluding his journalism course so that he would be able to secure a better job: 'I have finished all my lectures during the day and the remainder of the course is merely by correspondence with an occational night lecture, this has happened none too soon as I have very little savings left and am looking quite desperately about for a job . . .'

Hardships aside, Bryce was enchanted to be living in the land of his favourite author, Charles Dickens. The great works of English literature had made a big impression on him when he was growing up in South Africa. In *Whitethorn* he includes a long list of other stories by English authors close to his heart, including *Peter Pan* by

J. M. Barrie, *The Voyages of Doctor Dolittle* by Hugh Lofting, *Treasure Island* by Robert Louis Stevenson, *Twenty Thousand Leagues Under the Sea* by Jules Verne, *Tom Brown's School Days* by Thomas Hughes, *Kim* by Rudyard Kipling, *Robin Hood* by J. Walker McSpadden, *King Solomon's Mines* by H. Rider Haggard and *Gulliver's Travels* by Jonathan Swift. Just as it had been true for Dickens, those bleak and dark days in London provided precious material that Bryce squirreled away (just like the squirrels you still see scurrying through London's parks!) for books already spawning in his subconscious. Years later he conjured the London he knew in a range of his novels, perhaps most memorably in *The Potato Factory*:

> Ikey Solomon was so entirely a Londoner that he was a human part of the great metropolis, a jigsawed brick that fitted into no other place. He was mixed into that mouldy mortar, an ingredient in the slime and smutch of its rat-infested dockside hovels and verminous netherkens.

You can just about smell the city's stench from the page! 'This was one of the vilest slums in London, and the mist lay thick on the river, and the streets were dimmed to near blindness by the sulphurous-coloured smog from the first of the winter fires.'

None of Bryce's letters record him visiting London's famous landmarks, such as the Tower of London, Westminster Abbey, or the gates of Buckingham Palace, although I am certain he would have done so. The glittering shops on Regent Street, the theatres of Soho and taking tea at the Ritz were indulgences he couldn't savour until decades later. The odd game of Rugby was about the extent of his recreational activities. However, if he had a few spare hours, he enjoyed walking through London's parks, including Kensington Gardens, Regent's Park and Battersea Park, like Jack Spayd in *Jack of Diamonds*: 'I'd walked the streets and parks of London, and increased my knowledge of water birds and much else besides.'

The 'besides' included the chance to attend some concerts – a rare treat, but one Bryce was determined not to miss out on. Jack Spayd in *Jack of Diamonds* shares his sentiment:

One of the best things about living in London was the wonderful variety of classical music concerts on offer. I'd never lost my love of classical music, but my life had led me to places where it was rarely played. Now I was in one of the classical music capitals of the world, and I took full advantage of it.

Browsing through the antique shops in Mayfair and St James's and along Portobello Road was another favourite pastime. He also visited bookstores, including Hatchards in Piccadilly, founded in 1797, and Foyles, founded by brothers William and Gilbert Foyle in 1903. Bryce made sure his chief protagonist in *Jack of Diamonds* shared his passion for London's bookstores: 'Almost the sole purpose of my trip to London was to visit Foyles Bookshop to stock up on Penguins, the famous paperbacks that had been popularised in the 1930s, and were orange for fiction, green for crime fiction, blue for biographies, and so on.' Bryce couldn't have imagined that some of his own novels would one day end up in the Popular Penguin classic paperbacks! He treasured books above anything else and our house was jammed to the rafters with them. We ended up with over 4000 titles believing in the famous quote attributed to Cicero: 'A room without books is like a body without a soul.' In Bryce's study, though, where he undertook his writing, the only books on display were those he had written himself.

I'm sure Bryce felt lonely at times in London as he was someone who made friends easily, just as his mother did. There are hints of this in *Whitethorn*: 'I spent the university vacations alone, walking through various parts of Europe, and made very few friends at Oxford where I was seen as a loner, always polite but seldom engaged in any activity or discussion other than those involving my studies.' Bryce was well aware that at this stage in his life his mother would have been happier if he was studying law at Oxford, just like Tom Fitzsaxby did in *Whitethorn*. Certainly, Bryce would have adored browsing the shelves of the magnificent Bodleian Library, as Tom did, and which I explored several years ago.

Bryce told me that even though he didn't have much time to socialise, he did forge a few lasting friendships in London. Mostly, however, his social interactions were confined to exchanging pleasantries with his charlady or waitresses in cafes. The letters he received from his mother were a lifeline but would have been intermittent, with each one taking weeks to arrive by ship from South Africa. Phoning Paddy was prohibitively expensive and meant venturing outside in the bitter cold in search of a red K2 telephone box, the ones that first appeared on London's streets in 1926.

There is no mention in Bryce's letters of any girls on the scene – not that he would have felt inclined to share details of romantic interludes with his mother! However, while studying at the London School of Journalism Bryce did meet a beautiful and sophisticated Australian woman called Benita Solomon. Bryce had been introduced to Benita on a night out in Chelsea by one of his London friends, Ron Kneebone. Like Bryce, Benita was passionate about music, art and literature, and in fact he acknowledged that from the start he was 'outclassed' by her. The couple quickly fell in love, and it was a match made in heaven. Their romance blossomed over visits to London's galleries and museums, which Benita so loved, and late-night chats in small cafes. There were occasional visits to the theatre, but Bryce's meagre funds and workload would have limited the time they could spend together.

In 1995 Ron Kneebone appeared as a surprise guest on Channel Nine's, 'Bryce Courtenay', *This Is Your Life* hosted by Mike Munro, and revealed that Bryce 'was a bit wet behind the ears – and boy, was he shy with the girls'. Ron's comment may have surprised the viewers, but I would hazard a guess that Bryce had had very little experience of women prior to arriving in London. He had led a tough but sheltered life while growing up, and after leaving school he had worked in environments where romantic liaisons were difficult to pursue. In *Whitethorn* he fictionalised this hesitancy when it came to girls:

> The university campus was full of young female students, many of them gorgeous enough to render one trembling at the knees . . . In those days before the pill, getting a nice girl to part with her knickers was a very difficult process, even for the Casanovas of this world. While my imagination ran to lurid detail, in reality my wildest hope extended to a chaste kiss on the lips (nevermind tongues becoming involved), and a bit of a fumble at the front of a straining sweater.

On *This Is Your Life*, Benita confirmed that she had met the man of her dreams while in London and that she married for love. Bryce always credited her with introducing him to the world of art and culture he had always hungered for. In an interview with Steve Meacham for *The Sun-Herald* published on 29 November 2009, he said, 'Benita was wonderful for me . . . She was Jewish with a wonderful cultured background. In a sense, she educated me.' Much later, their mutual love of stories and books was passed on to their children. In *April Fool's Day*, Damon is quoted talking about the role stories and books played in their lives: 'I can't really remember when my dad wasn't telling me stories because he was just always telling them. With my mum it was books. They lay in stacks beside my bed, I'm sure she must have tucked them up with me in my cot.'

Benita had grown up reading the English magazines of the day, introduced to her as a child by her mother Aida and inspiring a lifelong love of all things British, as revealed in *April Fool's Day*:

I'd be given all the English magazines to read – *Tatler*, *Town &
Country*, the *London Illustrated News* and *Punch* . . . There were
Girl's Own and *Girls' Crystal*, which I loved with every breath of
my body . . . I feel quite sure that my consequent love of Britain
and the things of England, which has been so much a part of my
life, was born at this time.

Benita and her brother Victor (much later affectionately known by all
the family as 'Uncle Victor') had been raised in Sydney's eastern suburbs.
Like many young Australians of the time, Benita had sailed to England
to see the world:

When at twenty, like so many of my generation, I sailed on the
P&O line *Arcadia* for London for the mandatory two-year working
visit to Britain I had already acquired a knowledge of the English
nation and its history and culture which, I now realise, was well
beyond what most Australians knew and which I still maintain
with a fierce loyalty and unabashed love.

Benita shares much of her background in *April Fool's Day* – that her
father, Jacques Solomon, but always known as Jack, was English, from
the East End, and had been orphaned at birth and brought up in a
home for boys. He had two brothers and a sister, each raised in separate
orphanages and so having no common upbringing. At the age of just
fourteen he had joined the Royal Navy during the First World War.
He didn't share much about his early life with his children, and Benita
reflected that this must have been because growing up in an orphanage
in Edwardian England was so hard.

She also explained how she became interested in art:

What I didn't know about my daddy's background I filled in from
the things I read . . . For instance, at the age of eight he'd won a
prize for art which had been presented to him by Queen Alexandra,

no doubt on a visit to the orphanage. But in my eyes this amounted practically to being a famous artist patronised by royalty and so I began to study English artists, Whistler and Constable and Turner, hoping that some day I might stumble across an early Jack Solomon. He'd also been middle-weight boxing champion of the Royal Navy Mediterranean Fleet and, while stationed at Gibraltar, had won a medal in the fleet marathon.

Interestingly, Benita's father had been raised in an orphanage, joined the military, run marathons and was also a boxer – just like the man she had met in London who would later become her husband.

At some stage Benita made the decision to return to Australia, and Bryce confirmed they had discussed that he would eventually follow her there. He told me that he was sorely tempted to accompany her but realised he should stay on and complete his studies. He also said that he couldn't get Benita out of his mind: meeting her had given him a beacon of hope during those cold and dark days in London. I can only assume their courtship continued in letter form and via phone calls, though I have not discovered any of these letters.

It is important to remember that Bryce was accustomed to living alone, having been in and out of boarding houses and hostels during his childhood. Even as an adult he remained something of a loner, which is perhaps the lot of any writer. He needed time to himself to mull over his next novel, free of distractions and the idle chatter of daily life.

By January 1957, Bryce had managed to fit in a short trip abroad: 'I am quite well settled in this new place and . . . after my trip to Norway am feeling just fine', even though 'London, after the Christmas splash, has put on its working clothes once more and has settled shabbily back into Winter mourning'. But his studies were proceeding well: 'I seem finally to be breaking the back of the Writing course and seem to be making fairly consistent progress, though my spelling, alas, seems to have remained stationary.'

While in London Bryce took some time out to visit his relative Louise Mary Greer, whom everyone called 'Lulu'. She was the only daughter of Paddy's uncle Lord Fairfield (Sir Arthur Greer) and his first wife Katherine Van Noorden. Following his first wife's death he went on to marry Mabel Lily Fraser in 1939.

Bryce's cousin Errol Greer confirmed to me that Lulu was a successful magistrate who married Goronwy 'Ronw' Moelwyn Hughes (known simply as 'Moelwyn Hughes'), a Welsh lawyer who became a member of parliament and who died in 1955. This was the first contact Bryce had made with any of his English relatives, and he didn't appear overly impressed:

> Yes indeed I've been to see Lulu, very ordinary I thought, but as it was only a short visit I perhaps got the wrong impression. The entire family are rather plain looking and I am afraid we found little in common to talk about, so that the whole visit was rather a painful experience.

Bryce also had two elderly unmarried aunts living in England, Anne and Jess Greer, who resided in West Kirby in Cheshire. According to Bryce they had been supported for most of their lives by their brother Frederick Arthur Greer, Lord Fairfield. It appears that Bryce never visited his aunts, perhaps because he was too caught up with his studies and part-time jobs.

During 2021 I received further information from Errol. Prior to his retirement, he enjoyed a successful career in Johannesburg managing an aerial surveying company. He had gone to the United Kingdom aged seventeen in 1953 to study aerial surveying at Loughborough College in Leicestershire and was there until 1956, but may well have left before or soon after Bryce arrived in the United Kingdom. After Bryce became a published author, they reconnected on two occasions when Bryce was in

South Africa on book tours. It was Errol who told me that Bryce was the spitting image of his beloved grandfather Robert Bryce Greer.

As the spring of 1957 approached, Paddy still hadn't arrived in England and Bryce began to feel ambivalent about her coming. This is confirmed in a letter dated 22 March 1957:

> If I didn't know you were determined to come over here to England I should try to put you off – for even I am beginning to feel new and bitter pains in all sorts of unknown joints, all most certainly caused by the damp and cold – even though the past winter is supposed to have been the mildest for a hundred and fifty years . . .

By 2 May, Bryce had even more reasons to worry about his mother. He had long ago moved on from the clutches of the Pentecostal church, but Paddy had moved to a mission station to live with an American woman called Ruth who was an affluent and devout Pentecostal missionary. As children, Bryce and Rosemary had once lived in her house with Paddy, and they had been required to address her as 'Aunt Ruth'. It was clear that Paddy's stay there now was not going well, and Bryce must have felt helpless to do much about it: 'I am sorry to hear that things are not so good at the Mission . . . I had hoped that you would at least have got the long rest your body so badly needed.'

By 3 June he had moved to yet another address in Chelsea, this time in Colville Gardens. In his wildest dreams he could never have imagined that nearly forty years later he would purchase a beautiful flat on Chelsea's Pimlico Road, directly above a bespoke furniture shop called Linley founded in 1985 by David Armstrong-Jones, the 2nd Earl of Snowden.

Bryce felt bereft at not being able to afford to send Paddy a gift to celebrate her fifty-second birthday on 8 June:

> I am sorry mother not to be sending you a small something . . . however next year perhaps, there are such lovely things in the shops over here, that being unable to shop for something

seems almost unfair . . . moving seems almost to be in the blood, yours and mine anyway. This time to a much nicer little flat shared with an Australian friend . . . though the bath is in the kitchen with a hinged hard board top to act as a table when not otherwise used . . .

While working in the mines Bryce had of course become firm friends with Iain Finlay and Noel White, and now here he was sharing a flat with another Australian. The company must have felt welcome, and the experience likely encouraged him to travel to Australia after he graduated.

Life was now going well for him, and his determination to become a writer was increasing: 'Writing is becoming a real joy, how I wish I were able to do it all the time. Perhaps, however, that day may yet come.' His desire to travel was also burgeoning:

'There is as yet so much to see, so very many places as yet to visit, that I grow impatient lest I grow old too soon and have to settle down. What a terrible thing it is to have a wanderlust, when you should be doing the sensible thing, looking to a life of security in the future.'

Finally, the conclusion of his studies came into view, allowing him to plan the next big steps in his life:

My course, though progressing slowly, is going quite well and I hope in another four or five months to have it completed as living conditions are impossible in this country and I want to get out and somewhere more reasonable where there is a dab of sunshine occasionally . . . I've learnt an awful lot, but I guess it will be a long while yet before I shall know very much at all. Perhaps, at the end of the month I shall send you some of my exercises, would you like that? Work is pretty awful, and if I didn't have a bit of writing to relax on each evening I think I should go crazy. Still, anything and everything this time is worthwhile, and the harder things seem to become, the more worthwhile. I shall have changed quite a lot when next we meet, not quite so impossible to get on with I hope.

You can see from his letters that Bryce's writing skills were developing and he was displaying the cinematic qualities that featured in his later novels. On 22 November 1957, he reported some exciting news to his mother: 'First, a snippet of good news. I have sold my first story. Not a very good story to not a very good magazine – and certainly for not a very good price. Still, it does make these last twelve months seem of some avail.' Before long he confirmed some further great news: 'Had another story published just before I was ill, this time quite a good one in a very respectable magazine so things are beginning to look a little cheery . . .'

Alas, I have not been able to locate either of these stories, nor the names of the publications in which they appeared, but it must have been an unbelievably exciting moment to see his first stories in print. I am certain Bryce would have decided then and there that they would be only two of dozens of stories he planned on writing. In the meantime, he continued to work hard: 'I am working evenings as well as during the day and also endeavouring to keep ahead of my course, so that at the moment I am pretty tired, but after Christmas it should be better.'

The long days and nights were beginning to take their toll, and for a young man he had a lot to cope with:

'I begin to feel like an old man, your every letter seems to mention yet another wedding. Though I think it will be a long time yet before you are likely to be a "Male Grandmother". So many long, tired years ahead of me I'm afraid before I shall be able to settle down.'

No doubt he would have also felt disheartened by Benita's departure – but the prospect of his annual Christmas hamper from South Africa offered some comfort:

> I hope I shall be able to send you all something for Christmas . . . If you are sending a hamper . . . I should prefer tinned meat. Meat is very hard to get and terribly expensive and I grow daily tired of eggs. Meat and perhaps a tin of sweetcorn, which I haven't tasted since being over here. The jersey. Navy blue or midnight blue, very warm and sloppy. Then I shall never have to wash it, no ribs except around the cuffs and collar. One plain one pearl etc and the thickest wool you can get.

When it came to clothes, Bryce always knew precisely what he wanted – he never held back telling me what to wear, either! His first cousins Robyn and Wendy confirmed in an interview that he did just the same with them during his years working down the mines at Luanshya.

He was thrilled to receive a further gift of a few pounds in the post from his mother, and his father, 'Uncle Arthur', which allowed him to do some travelling around England: 'I've been away almost a month, having a look at England. I arrived back two weeks ago, having not quite seen all I'd intended to, but I started with no funds and after a couple weeks without a penny just couldn't go on, so made my way home.'

Before long he was off on another trip. This time he travelled to Scotland, where, he had been told by his mother, his ancestor the legendary Rob Roy MacGregor and his brothers had come from before fleeing to Ireland, where they had changed their name to Greer. Rosemary referred to this connection in her family story, and I would love Bryce to have set a novel around this legendary clan. Bryce wrote to Paddy:

Your letter was waiting for me with strict instructions as to how I should spend the money, as I knew how hard it must have been for you to send the £5, I felt I had to do it justice. Uncle Arthur had also sent me a fiver, so with £10 in my pocket I set off the very next day for Scotland, expecting it as the country I thought you would most care to see. My pack or rather rucksack was heavier but my heart a great deal lighter as there was sufficient food for days packed in with my sleeping bag.

Scotland made a big impression on Bryce, not only as the country of his forebears: he fell in love with its wild landscapes:

Scotland was wonderful, wild, completely untamed, with even a touch of Afrika in a sulky mood about it. The weather too was wonderful and I'm brown as a nut and feeling very well. I kept to the 'wilder' remoter parts of Scotland just glimpsing the cities of Glasgow and Edinburgh. The Scots are fine generous people, the cream of the British Isles. I have never spent a couple of fivers in a better manner and must thank you for the suggestion.

Being back in a beautiful natural environment must have felt great, especially having fresh air once again pumping through his delicate lungs.

Bryce also travelled to France with an Australian friend, most likely the friend with whom he had previously shared a flat. They had barely a few pounds between them and ended up sleeping rough. Bryce described this journey in a letter dated 2 May 1957:

We had enough in common to go together, though I should still have preferred to go alone. We flew over the channel, cheaper that way, only £2 and takes only twenty minutes to a small town called Le Touquet on the coast of Picardy, and from there we hitch hiked to Paris.

They arrived in Paris at two in the morning to find that the rooms they had booked had been given away when they did not arrive by midnight:

> We only had £4 each and trudged from dingy establishment to dingy establishment, to find them all full, thus my first night in Paris until the following morning at ten thirty when we found an unbelievably dirty little pension in the Artists quarter . . . We lived on dry bread and coffee for the three days. But nevertheless Paris is a wonderful city and I should much like to go again. The poor are really poor and I was shocked on the first night to find men and women fast asleep on the pavement, main throughfare or not, quite unpreturbed by the passing crowd who in there turn just stepped over or around them.

Bryce likened the streets of Paris to the cities of Dickens' novels: 'It was like stepping into the pages of Dickens. I can see now why a Social State in Europe is a good thing. Britain no doubt would be much the same, were it not for Government aid.'

Dickens' nineteenth-century novels were a great influence on Bryce's writing and showed him that strong characters were the key ingredient of stories that readers couldn't put down. There were also parallels in the two men's lives, with both Bryce and Dickens having endured tough childhoods before going on to become successful writers. Bryce's publisher at Penguin, Robert (Bob) Sessions, observed that Dickens, like Bryce, had drawn on his tough upbringing when writing *Oliver Twist*, *Bleak House* and *Hard Times*. After Bryce passed away, Bob reflected, 'If you believe in serendipity, you might find something symbolic in Bryce's death coinciding with the bicentenary of the birth of Charles Dickens . . . I just hope they're happy swapping stories, wherever they are.'

Bryce's letter continues:

We visited all the famous places of course and spent much of the nights in the back streets, where the real Paris lives. A strange city, beautiful as well as incredibly vile. We hitch hiked back from Paris, but there was little traffic on the roads and were unable to make the return trip in a day, and were resigned to spending the night in a wood, quite in the middle of nowhere, in fact had already settled down, when a peasant farmer seeing us, invited us back home, gave us a meal and a room, both wonderful, the room spotless, his wife so house proud we were obliged to take off our shoes before entering the home. We slept between clean sheets on a feather bed . . . We were given breakfast, a huge pudding bowl of coffee and French bread and butter . . . delicious. And were back on the road about nine and back home in London before evening.

Bryce's accommodation on that first trip to Paris was a far cry from the luxury apartment we stayed in, in the Marais district not far from Place des Vosges in January 2012.

After returning to England, it was back to work for Bryce, but in a new job:

Yes, I have a job or rather a better paying job, office work with a Greek shipping line, the salary is poor but better than most and I should just about be able to live on it. Prior to this job, I was working as a labourer, though I thought not to tell you at the time as you would no doubt have worried, still the pick and shovel did me no harm, and I'm back to a white collar again. I don't like it very much, I mean going back to office work, but beggars can't be choosers and I was grateful for it, so no complaints.

Paddy finally arrived in England in the spring of 1958. She was there primarily to support her Aunt Jess, whose sister Anne had passed away.

Even so, Paddy needed to find a job and, although she could have worked as a typist, Bryce told me she ended up working for a short while as a cleaner. This must have been a shock for a white South African woman who was used to occasional household help – back then, even people in the humblest of circumstances were able to engage home help now and then.

Bryce told me that Paddy found it hard settling in even though she loved the English countryside, the stone-walled villages and the company of her aunt. Perhaps England did not live up to her wistful imaginings of it. She went home to South Africa two years later and never returned to England again. As it had been for Bryce, it was most likely the weather and her lack of funds that extinguished any residual desire on her part to return.

By the end of September 1958, Bryce had completed his Diploma of Journalism. Without any prior experience he quickly realised that his chances of landing a job as a journalist in London were slim. He made the decision to leave England in search of adventure, and almost certainly to pursue his romance with Benita. I haven't been able to establish precisely how he funded his passage by ship to Australia, but I suspect it was paid for from his meagre savings and was supplemented by contributions from Paddy and Benita. He may have even been able to secure a bit of casual work once aboard the ship.

Curiously, it appears that he didn't meet up with Paddy in London until a week before he was due to leave – so much for his initial hopes of their spending a lot of time together. These plans were probably dashed due to their mutual workloads and him not having the means to treat her to an earlier visit. Bryce wrote a letter to his mother thanking her for the week they spent together and recording his final days in England: 'I had a good send off and arrived at the boat a little tired, a little sad at leaving England. London turned on a foggy rain soaked day as a send off, I didn't mind though, for I remember it best like that. And in retrospect, I shall no doubt long for it just like that . . .'

It must have been difficult for Paddy to farewell her only son again, not knowing when or where they'd next meet. Bryce was aware of the gravity of the situation for her:

> How nice it was to have a mother again. I too felt a little heart sore at leaving you, it always seems to be a train pulling out of a station with you and I. You looked so very small and tired standing at the end of the platform. I want you to know, though I haven't always shown it, I love you very much.

After farewelling Paddy, Bryce travelled by train to the historic port of Tilbury in Essex. He appears to have felt ambivalent about his imminent departure: on the one hand he had found the weather and his financial situation unbearable, but on the other he had come to like living in England very much. However, he had missed the big skies of Africa, and if he hadn't chosen to board a ship bound for Australia, I am certain he would have gone somewhere else warm. Returning to South Africa certainly wasn't an option as his support for black African freedoms would not have been tolerated.

On 10 October 1958, he departed England aboard the RMS *Strathaird*, belonging to the Peninsular and Oriental line (P&O). The good ship *Strathaird* had been refurbished as a one-class vessel, meaning it was engaged only for long international voyages. On the ship's outgoing passenger schedule, he is listed as Arthur Bryce Courtenay of 16 Sloane Gardens SW 5, occupation 'Writer'. The Australian government's post-war catchcry was 'Populate or perish' and the ship was used to transport migrants to Australia from Italy, Greece, Malta, Croatia and Turkey, many of whom were displaced persons (known as DPs). The proposed route was scheduled to take forty-eight days via the Suez Canal and would include stops in the ports of Piraeus (near Athens), Aden, Bombay (now Mumbai) and Colombo.

Bryce relished the voyage almost from the moment he stepped aboard, despite a lingering virus. He posted a letter to Paddy at the second port of call as he had been too unwell to disembark at the first: 'I had a dose of flu, the tail end of a London existence.' He shared colourful portraits of the men with whom he shared his cabin – an Australian government official, a Polish head waiter and a Cockney house painter – and provided a description of the voyage:

I have been sleeping on deck lately. I'd almost forgotten how wonderful a cloudless sky and a tropical star filled night can be. I am awakened in the morning by the seamen swabbing down the decks, about six thirty. I wander wearily down to my cabin where the steward has a cup of tea waiting for me. After tea I slip into a pair of trunks and go for a swim and then lie in the sun until breakfast at nine. It's the best part of the day and already I'm turning a good travel poster brown. Wish you could see me as I am. It's quite surprising what a sun tan can do to the human wreck. I look like a person again and even the blue rings under my eyes have gone a crisp brown.

Each port offered a new experience, and Bryce, ever the passionate traveller, relished discovering each one:

Port Said [in Egypt] was very dirty and smelled more evil than even the dirtiest kraal . . . though it was very colourful and it was good to see Jacaranda, flame trees, bluegums and bougainvillea again. The inhabitants will sell you anything from a shoe-shine to a grand piano, and seem very hurt when you accept the shoe-shine but reject the piano.

You bargain for everything, even the price of a cold drink. Aden with its tax free law is a buyers paradise, with everything so ridiculously cheap it hurts. All I was able to buy though was a box of Kleenex tissues, my money having all gone on doctors bills, which at five shillings a treatment soon mounts up.

Aden has a magnificent setting, in truly the grand manner.

It nestles in a scoop of sheer granite mountains, without a tree or even a small shrub bush to be seen. Almost like the last station before reaching hell. Bombay tomorrow, where this will be posted, we have twelve hours so will have time to wander about a bit. In another two days Colombo and there-after the next port will be in Australia.

After arriving in Bombay, Bryce wrote a further letter:

I wore your suit a couple of evenings ago, and a very 'Pukka Sahib' come across to me and enquired as to where I had my clothes cut! I looked quite un-surprised and answered somewhat pertinently: 'As a matter of fact, Old Chap I have a marvellous tailor, though unfortunately only private work is undertaken.' He looked rather sorry and I felt marvellous.

At just twenty-five years of age, for Bryce this voyage would have been an incredible experience – especially after having lived amid the grey skies and grimy streets of London. Even though he had grown up in Africa, the ports must have felt exotic and exciting.

Eventually the ship made its way into Australian waters. Bryce's first glimpse of Sydney as *Strathaird* sailed through the Heads was unforgettable and emotional, and the connection he felt to Australia was instant and binding, as told to Diana Ritch:

Australians who are born here you don't realise what an absolutely wonderful gift Sydney is: if God had to create a special wrap, somehow I think he'd probably end up making it Sydney.

I came up from below decks and I came on to the deck just as the boat was coming through the heads and it was one of those unbelievable early summer days and it was about 7 o'clock in the morning and the harbour was like a mirror. It was almost as though the whole thing was taking place in the interior of a polished goblet; the air was absolutely crystal, the water was totally still and clear and beautiful.

As we passed through the Heads I looked to my left – I think that's port – and there was this tiny beach and on the beach was a white house and over the white house was magnificent purple bougainvillea and the sun was shining and the sky was absolutely flawless. Of course, this reminded me of Africa and I started to weep because in a way I'd come home. Although here was a mountain man who didn't know the sea, this town felt right – and I knew instantly. Though I'd travelled all over the world I knew instantly that I'd come home, that I'd come to some place where I could settle.

In an interview recorded at home in 2012 by Michael Dillon, Bryce said, 'It was almost as though I had been born in the wrong place, that I really should have been born in Australia. I had come home.'

He could not have known that when he stepped ashore at Sydney's Circular Quay he would one day write a novel called *The Potato Factory*, the first book in his Australian trilogy, whose two main characters, Mary Abacus and Ikey Solomon, would dock in Australia in far less comfortable circumstances, having been transported from England to Van Diemen's Land as convicts aboard the *Destiny II*.

It is possible that someone as adventurous in spirit as Bryce had an inkling on the day of his arrival that he would make this country home for the rest of his life, just like Ikey Solomon: 'Until I returns to London to live, my dear, though I daresay that be never.' What Bryce couldn't have known was that he would go on to make history in his adopted home.

7

A LONG WAY FROM
DUIWELSKLOOF

Any fool knows that to sell a cause, you have to have a
proposition. Words gather around a good proposition like
bees around mimosa blossom. – *The Pitch*

BRYCE ARRIVED IN SYDNEY on a glorious day in late November 1958 and
it was love at first sight, as Bryce described in *The Silver Moon*:

Everything about Australia was right; the sky was high, the land
and people felt familiar. From day one I felt like an Australian.
I remember we came through the Heads and that was it. Then
we could see land and I noticed a white house with a splash
of bougainvillea. I immediately thought, I want to own that
house . . .

He arrived in Australia carrying only one suitcase and with barely enough
money to stay at a local youth hostel: 'The whole world fell about my
ears almost on arrival. I had to spend the £20 on my first month's rent
as it's monthly in advance over here. It left me absolutely nothing and
I started looking for a job on the afternoon of my arrival.' He managed
to get a job as a labourer in a paint factory at Botany Bay, not far from

where Captain James Cook had dropped anchor aboard HMS *Endeavour* in 1770.

Bryce worked twelve hours a day, from five in the morning until five at night, and with fifteen minutes for breakfast and twenty minutes for lunch. He wrote to his mother of his new circumstances: 'I've never been so glad of a job in my life and although it was hard work, most backbreaking, I think it's done me good and the debts I've incurred are all but payed for.'

After work Bryce used to relax by watching television, which had begun broadcasting in Australia not quite two years prior to his arrival, on 16 September 1956. On that day Bruce Gyngell from TCN Channel 9 famously announced to viewers across the country, 'Welcome to television.' For amusement he began rewriting the TV advertisements he saw, telling me, 'I knew I could write better ones.'

Bryce's initial impressions of Australians as conveyed to Paddy were positive: 'The people, though a little brash, are all bursting with enthusiasm for their country, and everyone appears to be working with the knowledge that the future is a great one.' Having come from South Africa and then London, he was struck by the relative absence of class distinctions:

This is quite the most snobless country I have ever been in, the dustman calls the Director 'Mate' or by his Christian name if he's been introduced. There are no social barriers of any kind and the idea of referring to anyone short of the prime minister as 'Sir' would be about as alien to the average Australian as a cloudless sky is to an Englishman.

He also noted wryly that 'The Upper Average Australian thinks "Culture" is a growth on a jam jar lid . . .'

One thing he found disturbing was the existence of the White Australia policy, which he learnt had been introduced in 1901 (it was not rescinded until 1973). This onerous law restricted the arrival of non-white immigrants and smacked of the very reason Bryce had left South

Africa. For a while he wondered if in fact he shouldn't have moved to New Zealand!

Having decided to stay on, Bryce didn't at first have the opportunity to explore his true potential career-wise. He worked in a succession of low-paying jobs, from digging ditches to selling goods door to door. With his natural charm he did very well at the latter, but after several months he was desperate to find something more fulfilling. Bryce did write two plays but was offered only £10 for each of them, which provided little encouragement. He also secured several interviews as a prospective scriptwriter, which offered him some hope for his professional future, as he confirmed to Paddy: 'If I could get something like this, the future would be a lot easier as there is a dearth of good scriptwriters and the job is very well paid, could take me anywhere and leaves enough time over for serious writing. So, you'd best pray.' He contacted several local newspapers, but no one wanted to hire him. Although he had studied journalism, he had no experience in the field and therefore never managed to secure a position.

Despite these hardships and frustrations, Bryce felt it was a great time to be alive. He was madly in love with Benita, the beautiful, accomplished Australian woman he had met while studying in London. He told me it didn't occur to him to begin living with her after he arrived in Sydney: back then it wouldn't have been seen as the right thing to do – and certainly Paddy, his deeply religious mother, would not have approved. So, in early 1959 he moved into a shabby share-flat in an inner-city suburb. He soon discovered that his flatmate was suffering from schizophrenia and that living around him was intolerable. It appears that Bryce was in fact helping this vulnerable young man to write a book, as recorded in a letter dated 27 April 1959: 'Afraid what work has been done on the book will have to go by the wayside, he'll benefit, but that can't be helped. Will work on my own in future.'

Bryce then moved into a place of his own in Birrell Street, Waverley, twenty minutes from Sydney's spectacular Bondi Beach, where he'd go to catch a few waves and lie in the sun.

Benita was working as a senior radio manager at the McCann Erickson advertising agency and earning considerably more money than Bryce. She would have been quite a trailblazer as a young woman occupying such a senior position in a leading firm. Bryce told me that she always had great faith in him and was certain that he too would end up doing very well. What Bryce was more certain of was that Benita was the woman for him. He confirmed this in a letter to Paddy in 1959:

> She has an enormous capacity for love, which sometimes completely overwhelms my rather stilted and difficult Anglo-Saxon nature, we're almost diametrically opposed in nature, Benita being very flambouyant and startling both as a looker and in nature, completely spontaneous in her every expression in both anger and love, with a tremendous sense of loyalty . . . Like every real woman she is a bundle of contradictions . . .

Benita's love and support and her belief in Bryce would have been invaluable given he was so far away from his homeland and still struggling to find his way. He was very much aware of this, and very much in love:

> She believes absolutely in me and has, in fact, been responsible for a great deal of what little success I have had in Australia. It's almost as though you can't believe that a woman can exist who is so naturally and easily the other half of a complete unity, and is still so much of a woman you could love her if she were deaf, dumb and blind.

It was Benita who first suggested that Bryce consider applying for a job in advertising, and at McCann Erickson where she was working. McCanns was by then a huge international agency that in 1959 had taken over

Hansen Rubensohn, a local agency founded by the South African–born Solomon Rubensohn, known as 'Sim'. Bryce took Benita's advice and with her help secured an interview with Bill Lockley, who gave him his first job in advertising. Bill had attended school in Sydney's Canterbury and then Summer Hill, delivering newspapers to help make ends meet for his family during the Depression. Money was tight: it was reported after Bill passed away in 2008 that his mother, Charlotte, sold her jewellery so that her son could learn the violin. Music was Bill's lifelong passion, but to everyone's surprise he ended up getting a job in advertising at Hansen Rubensohn after reaching the rank of flight lieutenant as a test pilot for the Royal Australian Air Force during the Second World War. He stayed on when the company became Hansen Rubensohn–McCann Erickson and evolved his love of music to creating jingles for several legendary television ads. There must have been something about Bryce that told Bill that together they might be able to make some 'music' by working together. And indeed they did!

Bill initially engaged Bryce as a junior copywriter for a wage of £12 a week, which was the same rate they were paying their dispatch boys. Bryce couldn't have cared less. With the emergence of television and good writers being in short supply, he knew he was in the box seat to make his mark, as recorded with Diana Ritch in 1991: 'Sometimes you just stumble into things which are right for you. I instinctively seemed to know how to do it.' In an interview recorded at our home in Canberra in September 2012, he said, 'Advertising seemed almost natural to me because it was a business where you had to inform, persuade, and educate.'

After his first week in the job, Bryce reflected on the excitement he felt about having secured a job with so much potential:

The firm I work for has been taken over by the biggest and perhaps the most famous Advertising firm in the world – McCann Erickson of New York. This makes me an employee with a great deal of potential, and besides anything else will enable me to get a job anywhere in the world as the name is an international password. There is also just a chance, and I repeat a slim one, that I might be sent to America for further training.

Things were blossoming on the romantic front as well. On 11 August 1959, three days shy of Bryce's twenty-fifth birthday, he and Benita announced their engagement. Bryce told me he had saved up furiously for the ring, an emerald set in a square of eight diamonds with baguette shoulders.

Just two months later, on 2 October 1959, Bryce and Benita were married at Sydney's Queens Square registry office. Benita wore a stunning, simple gown featuring adornments by Dior. Their reception for two dozen guests took place at the iconic Bondi Hotel Astra, overlooking the southern end of Bondi Beach. Bryce told me that he felt so excited he was a bundle of nerves, whereas Benita was a picture of grace and elegance.

Paddy and Rosemary were unable to attend but both sent gifts, which included a set of bed linen and some towels. The team from McCann Erikson gave them a Sunbeam Steam & Dry iron: in those days these appliances were keenly sought after and were perceived as the latest 'must have' items for aspiring couples. Bryce and Benita spent their entire savings on the wedding, which meant their honeymoon was spent at home in the Waverley flat. They made frequent trips to the beach, and Bryce's skin turned beetroot in colour. Not that he complained – he was delirious with happiness.

The newlyweds wrote to Paddy with ongoing concerns for her delicate constitution, which Bryce had witnessed from early childhood. At that time she was still living in England looking after her Aunt Jess, but after Bryce's wedding she returned to South Africa, feeling dreadfully homesick and desperate to escape England's bitter cold. Organising a date for Paddy to visit Australia proved to be difficult and it was to be many years before she would set foot in Australia.

Benita's and Bryce's careers in the advertising industry remained a core focus of their lives for several years, and following their wedding Benita received a big promotion to radio manager. Bryce wrote: 'Benita . . . is probably the youngest Radio Manager in the country, and this is no mean position. It makes me quite humble to think that, not only do I have beauty, but also brains to contend with. We ought have impossible little swots for children.'

A mix of work ethic and raw talent meant that Bryce's career also flourished. At McCanns he worked on a range of campaigns that Sim oversaw, including Mortein, Caltex oil, Nestlé, Philips electrical supplies, Victa lawn mowers and Trans Australia Airlines (TAA). Years later he told me that working under Sim was a baptism of fire. He painted a fearsome but colourful picture of Sim's character in *April Fool's Day*:

> Despite his small, lopsided size, Rubensohn was tough, an ex-alcoholic and ex-gambler who, when forced to give up both vices, fell into a foul mood from which he never recovered . . . Sim ran his ill-tempered life at top speed and expected everyone working with him to fit into his time schedule, which was to start at 7 a.m. each morning . . . he left work promptly at 4 p.m. . . . leaving behind sufficient work to keep his minions working back, often until late at night.

Sim's agency later became famous for running the legendary 'It's Time' campaign for the Australian Labor Party, which saw Gough Whitlam sworn into office as Prime Minister on 5 December 1972: 'Sim was a great tactician with a brilliant, political brain . . . [He] told the party what to say, how to say it and when to say it . . . Sim could move upwards or downwards or sideways in the party room; in broad terms, he was a Labor Godfather.' Much later Bryce was involved with several federal election campaigns for both sides of politics, but these experiences led to a lifelong scepticism about that world. He never once contemplated a foray into politics, which was suggested to him now and then as something he should consider.

Bryce embraced his new career head-on and with an almost evangelical zeal to succeed. After the trials of his childhood and the dangers of working down the mines, the world of advertising probably felt like a piece of cake. In fact, he once quipped, 'If you start at the bottom, you're not scared.' He could not have known then that he would stay in the business for nearly thirty-four years and that it would offer him the best training ground any writer could wish for. He was constantly drawn upon to scour his imagination and come up with slogans, which inevitably danced off the page. He was also required to meet rigorous deadlines and had to learn how to market products to consumers whether they wanted them or not.

From the outset he showed great promise: 'Work is going very well, and my television projects have not gone without comment, though it will take months before the results show good or otherwise. In the meantime I breathe freely and continue to work hard and keep my nose clean.' He quickly made a name for himself within the industry. The job was demanding, but after eighteen months his salary had trebled and within two years one of his advertisements was showcased at the Venice Film Festival, something that had never happened for anyone from the Australian advertising industry.

Indeed, Australia was good to Bryce, and on 1 June 1960 he made the decision to take out Australian citizenship. In a letter to his mother dated 29 June he explained:

Australia has been wonderful to me and the past 18 months almost unbelievable. Don't get a shock, I became an Australian citizen on the 1 June, firstly because I deemed it my duty to do so, but just as important, should there ever be any trouble in South Africa and this appears from here anyway inevitable, I shall be able to get you into Australia without any trouble.

The Sharpeville massacre had taken place on 21 March in the Transvaal close to where Bryce had grown up, and had shocked the world.

What started as a demonstration against pass laws outside the local police station resulted in the police opening fire on the crowd, killing sixty-nine civilians and injuring 180. (The Pass Laws Act of 1952 were a form of internal passport system designed to segregate the population, and the movement of black African citizens in South Africa.) It is possible that this terrible event motivated Bryce to shore up his Australian residency and make it easier for his family to leave South Africa in the future.

The days of living hand to mouth were soon over, and in the ensuing years Bryce and Benita moved into several lovely apartments and houses in Sydney's exclusive eastern suburbs. After leaving Waverley they moved to a beautiful flat in Double Bay, in a building called Gladswood. They both yearned for children, and it wasn't long before their family began to grow just as they had hoped. Bryce alluded to this prospect even before he was married: 'Her conversations run something like this: "Shall we have four or . . . please, Darling let's be rash and have six – maybe five of our own and then we'll adopt a little Korean child."'

On 20 November 1961, their first child, a son named Brett, was born weighing 7 pounds 9½ ounces (3.4 kilograms). In a letter dated 27 December Bryce described the pride he felt at becoming a father:

All my life I have wondered why women fill their letters with quite insignificant details concerning baby's first burp, smile, pooh, tooth, yawn, rate of growth, word, sentence, rash and weight (always weight) . . . And now at last I know! . . . I have developed into the most impossible baby bore. Of course, there's no doubt about it, Brett is a genius.

In December the family moved again, this time to a flat overlooking the harbour in The Crescent, an exclusive street in Vaucluse. Vaucluse was the suburb where Benita had been raised.

Baby Brett was the pride and joy of both parents – so much so that he was cast in a TV commercial Bryce created that called for a baby of around Brett's age. It wasn't to be the first time Bryce engaged his family to be the centrepiece of advertisements, no doubt to their amusement and, at times, consternation.

All the while, Bryce begged Paddy to consider relocating to Australia and hoped that Rosemary and Esmund would do the same. The turbulent winds of change were well and truly blowing, and he feared his mother and sister had no future in South Africa. On 13 August 1962, he wrote to Paddy:

> It certainly isn't everybody's pioneer country and to the average South African not an easy land to settle in. I would do almost anything to have you all over here, but I'd want you to come with your eyes fully open. Australia is like living in tomorrowland with many of the disadvantages of not having it today and all the excitement of building the future with your own hands. Sydney is streets ahead of Johannesburg as an urban, sophisticated city yet it retains the excitment of being young, growing and vigorous.

Paddy's relocation to Australia was, however, unlikely, as she had lived in South Africa for almost her entire life, and Rosemary and Esmund had also been born and bred there and remained committed to their Christian ministries within their local communities. The financial realities of making such a big move may also have influenced their decision to stay on. Rosemary and Es were also now busy raising their children: a son called Owen Esmond was born on 14 June 1959, and their only daughter, Dorrin Joan was born on 10 September 1961. Their third child Trevor Bryce was born several years later on 4 October 1967.

On 19 August 1963 Bryce and Benita's second son, Adam, was born, bringing the family additional joy. Soon after, they moved into their first house, in Bellevue Hill. Life with two very young boys was no doubt busy as well as immensely rewarding. It was around this time that Benita left her job and became a full-time mother and homemaker.

Bryce told me he had from the outset felt totally committed to providing for his wife and family. In a sense he had been a breadwinner for as long as he could remember, having always contributed whatever he could to help his mother make ends meet. A family of his own meant everything to him, especially after his chaotic childhood. He used to say, 'All I had ever wanted was to have a family of my own,' and he was intent on working until he dropped to make sure they had everything they could possibly want. In fact, throughout Bryce's life his immediate family and close circle of friends were the cornerstone of his existence.

A cartoon character called Louie the Fly ensured that Bryce's advertising career became the stuff of legend. Not long after joining McCanns he was handed a brief for Mortein, the pest spray company then owned by Samuel Taylor Pty Ltd, and tasked with convincing Australians that no home should be without a can of it.

As we know, every great ad campaign has many people involved who go on to claim the credit. However, Bryce's close friend and advertising colleague Alex Hamill asserted unequivocally that Bryce was the brains behind the iconic Mortein advertisement. He wrote to me, 'The simple fact is that it was Bryce's idea. He conceived it. He fought for it. He sold it!!.' A team of others were naturally involved in aspects of the campaign, but it is, I believe, widely accepted that Bryce dreamt up the concept for the advertisement, which he said was 'a fluke idea that became a legend'. The man credited with the original lyrics and music of the 'Louie the Fly' song was the composer and pianist James Joseph White, known as 'Jimmy', and the character of Louie the Fly first emerged in 1957. The advertising concept Bryce worked on was released in 1962.

Bryce said that the idea for the advertisement came to him during a fifteen-minute taxi ride across the Sydney Harbour Bridge with a driver named Louie, as described to Larissa Dubecki in *The Age* in 2007. He scribbled a drawing of Louie onto his notepad before presenting the concept to the Mortein company's managing director, 'a man named Bob Graham, who was answerable only to God'. Bob had earlier rejected the concept, but Bryce continued to press his case for 'the lovable rogue who broke the mould' and who was 'the archetypal symbol of the little man who keeps coming back despite the knockdowns and the frustrations of life'. Sound familiar? Perhaps Louie was something of a metaphor for the life of the ad's creator!

The other people who have been credited with playing a role in the success of this campaign include Neil Williams, who sang the original jingle, Bob Gibson, Brian Henderson, Norman Godbold, Geoff Pike, Jean Tych, the actor Ross Higgins, and singers Jimmy Parkinson and Ted Hamilton. The advertisement featuring the jingle recorded by Williams was released by McCanns in 1962 and went on to become the longest-running ad in Australian television history. In 2006 it was named by the Advertising Federation of Australia as the fifth-best ad of all time. 'Louie' lived a long and eventful life and was retired by Mortein in 2011 – but following a public outcry he was reinstated.

Bryce once said: 'Some people are more impressed that I invented Louie the Fly than by the fact that I've written seventeen books . . . I often wonder if my epitaph is not going to be Bryce Courtenay, author, but Bryce Courtenay, inventor of Louie the Fly.' I still have an original transparency of Louie hanging on my kitchen wall proudly asserting his longevity as 'Louie the fly, I'm Louie the fly, straight from rubbish tip to you'. Years later, when Bryce was heading for the finish line in the New York City Marathon, someone must have spotted him: he told me they held up a handwritten sign that read 'Louie the Fly for Prime Minister'.

While working on the Nestlé account, Bryce created the original 'Milkybar Kid' commercial, which was released in 1961. The first Milkybar Kid, a blond bespectacled boy dressed as a cowboy whose catchphrase was 'The Milkybars are on me!', was played by Terry Brooks. Milkybar is credited with being the first white-chocolate bar on the market. It was created by Nestlé as Nestrovit but was later launched as a confectionery item. I once asked Bryce if he had ever eaten a Milkybar and he responded sheepishly, 'I can't say I ever really liked them, but I sure as hell knew how to sell them.'

It's important to remember that these successes were taking place during the 1960s when an explosion of sex, drugs and rock'n'roll was striking the world like a meteorite arriving from outer space. Songs by The Beatles, Led Zeppelin, Bob Dylan, the Bee Gees and the Rolling Stones were blaring across the airwaves. Long hair, flared pants and miniskirts were all the rage and young people were embracing newfound freedoms that spawned a 'hippie' revolution called 'flower power'.

Passionate opposition to Australia (and America's) involvement in the Vietnam War was also gathering pace. In November 1964 Prime Minister Robert Menzies had introduced a selective conscription known as national service with the aim of creating an army of 40 000 full-time soldiers. Bryce wasn't required to enter the ballot, which became known as 'the draft', and always said that apart from having to be a conscript in Rhodesia, he was fortunate to have missed having to go to war by a whisker.

In 1964 Bryce's successes in advertising were rewarded when he was appointed as both a board member and creative director at McCanns. He was the youngest-ever creative director appointed to an Australian advertising agency and was to stay on there for ten years. These elevated roles meant he needed to travel regularly to South-East Asia, the United States and Europe. His growing family must have missed his absences but were beginning to reap the benefits of his hard work, living the Australian dream. By 1965 they had put down a deposit on a larger home, in Jesmond Avenue, Vaucluse. Bryce reflected on this time in his life in his interview with Diana Ritch: 'Life prospered and I mortgaged myself to the hilt and we dreamt of the pool and the big house, and the double garage and all the other unbelievable nonsense people carry on with in life . . .' I sometimes pass by this house when walking down to Watsons Bay and try to imagine what it must have been like for Bryce to live in such a beautiful place and with a loving family, so far away from South Africa and the memories of his tough childhood where life's necessities were always in short supply. I expect he didn't think too much about it as he was 'flat out like a lizard drinking' being a husband, father, advertising executive and writer-in-waiting.

In 1966 Bryce made the big decision to leave McCann Erikson to take up a lucrative job offer with rival firm J. Walter Thompson (JWT). He was appointed as both creative director and chair of South-East Asia. He stayed in this job until 1971, and along the way won a further slew of advertising awards. I still have most of them, and there are enough to fill the walls of several houses. During his time at McCanns and JWT, both became Australia's most-awarded advertising agencies, no doubt with Bryce having made a significant contribution.

Perhaps inevitably, Bryce decided to start his own agency. He did this in 1972 by creating Courtenay Keane & Bernstein but quickly became aware of the pressures of running a small private company without the backup of the big organisations he had worked in before, recorded in the Diana Ritch interview:

> You can work for large multi-national organisations but when you have to go out on your own it's very lonely, it's very difficult and all those people who seemed so friendly and so full of admiration for you before you went out on your own suddenly don't want to know who you are. So it's a very lonely business starting something . . . Nevertheless, I started and of course I didn't suddenly build up a huge organisation; it got built like all organisations, brick by brick, until finally you ended up with something.

Years later he wrote about this experience in a letter to his mother postmarked 30 March 1978. He confirmed that the partnership had not worked out and he had sold his interest in the company: 'When I brought the situation to a head by offering to buy them out at the original ingoing fee they refused and in turn made a counter-offer.' In the Diana Ritch interview he said, 'Partners tend, even if they're really nice people, to make life hell for you, and so I guess on the other side they probably thought I made life hell for them.'

Following this disappointing foray into owning his own business, in 1972 he was invited to join a small agency as an equal partner in a firm that came to be called Black Courtenay:

> Without the finance to start my own I was obliged to accept, though a little reluctantly, having had my fill of partner-ships and the anxiety that goes with them . . . it all seemed rather good . . . My new partners though far from ideal at least appeared to do a day's work and that was enough.

Bryce entered this deal on a six-month trial basis and later confirmed to his mother that during that time he tripled both the size and the income of the agency. In those heady days partnerships came and went, and Bryce, like many talented creatives, was always keeping an eye out for a better opportunity.

On 15 July 1974, Harrison Robinson Courtenay Advertising Pty Ltd (HRC) was registered, the other partners being Phil Harris, Michael Robinson (known as 'Robbo') and Vincent Tesoriero. An earlier company, Harris Robinson & Associates, had been founded by Michael, who was known for his warm-heartedness and flamboyance and for being outrageously talented and occasionally fiery. He and Phil had started the later company that Bryce joined and where he stayed until late 1987. It was hugely successful even though it must have been a bit of a juggling act residing in the base camp of such opinionated and ambitious creatives. One newspaper article recorded that the company ended up with billings of about $85 million. It was recognised internationally for a brilliant series of TV advertisements made for Lego, created by Phil and the small team at HRC; some were awarded the Mobius Award, and the Lion d'Or in New York.

Bryce reflected on these heady years in advertising in his interview with Diana Ritch:

> I mean, when you look at the huge tycoons in the world, don't think that they're special. They've learnt one particular secret and that is that at the top there's no competition . . . It's very hard at the bottom, it's very easy at the top. But it's also a bit boring because nothing is more boring than something that's easy, or so I find it.

From junior copywriter to creative director and partner, Bryce had enjoyed a rollercoaster ride – and in doing so had become a star in an industry that was on fire and that he had worked devilishly hard to make his own. According to him, the sense of style, beautiful clothes, sex, drugs, drinking and rock'n'roll as portrayed in the 2007–15 TV series *Mad Men* indeed went on, but what the series missed was portraying the absolutely gruelling work ethic that the top advertising executives revelled in. Fourteen- to sixteen-hour days were the norm and 'Work hard, play hard' was their motto. He spoke of how exhilarating it was to work with some of the sharpest minds he ever met, who, at the same time, were shaping the way society looked at things.

In 1986 Bryce became a columnist for *The Australian* newspaper, providing weekly content inspired by his career in advertising. He was required to file 50 000 words a year, and the expertise garnered from his London journalism course was firmly on show, with headings such as: 'Stuff the panda – how about a cute koala', 'A bird on the ground is worth more as PM' and 'Our cult of failure is the biggest obstacle to success'. The column headings alone reveal the breadth in subject matter of Bryce's columns, his readiness to make political comments and his all-round versatility as a writer. The columns were collated into a book called *The Pitch*, published in 1992 by my sister Margaret's company,

Margaret Gee Publishing. Of course, by that point Bryce had become a famous author of a very different kind of book.

These glorious days of unrivalled success were dealt a devastating blow not long after the birth on 4 November 1966 of his and Benita's third son, Damon. Bryce told me the family were overjoyed and he wrote, 'He was a lovely baby with a fright of soft blond hair that stood up like a long brush cut from the very beginning' – but not long after his birth something didn't feel right. Early on, a doctor at the hospital told Bryce and Benita that Damon was 'a bit bruised, but that will soon pass. He's pale, so we've given him a blood transfusion.' This would have caused understandable feelings of grave concern as no medical intervention of this gravity had been necessary following the birth of their other two boys.

Damon was soon diagnosed as having the genetically acquired condition of classic haemophilia. This blood disorder occurs when there is no factor VIII protein, which prevents the blood from clotting. The smallest bleed can be life-threatening and require a transfusion. From the moment they received the first diagnosis Bryce and Benita devoted most of their days and nights to caring for Damon, which often meant taking him to hospital to be treated for bleeds. Bryce remembered the emotional toll on the family but said that all that mattered was making sure that Damon was taken care of and felt safe and loved. Over time, they became aware that this focus on caring for Damon impinged on the time they were able to spend with Brett and Adam, but he said he and Benita were delighted and grateful that both boys continued to thrive.

It was a punishing schedule for all the family. Bryce would work twelve-hour days at the agency and just get to sleep to be awoken by Damon crying and the need to rush him to the hospital. He would return home in the early hours of the morning, have a shower and head off to work. It was this regime, Bryce said, that taught him how to work ninety hours a week while surviving on very little sleep. He could function quite well on four-and-a-half hours' sleep a night; just as British prime minister Margaret Thatcher apparently did.

Bryce and Benita enrolled their boys at Cranbrook, an exclusive school in Sydney's Eastern suburbs that my son Nima attended many years later. Their three children were clever and diligent students and Benita and Bryce always reflected on how proud they were of them. The family took holidays when they could for much-needed time together, but it was rare for Bryce and Benita to be able to get away together. On 12 April 1979, Bryce wrote to his mother from Christchurch, New Zealand, where he had been on business, saying: 'Benita and I have booked to go on a holiday in June to Western Samoa, our first holiday of any kind for 7 years. Naturally we're rather excited.' He further explained, 'We had arranged to put Brett & Adam into boarding school for the three weeks with Damon staying with a friend.'

Bryce and Benita were occasionally even able to travel to Europe, where Benita was able to indulge her passion for art, music and the theatre. A dedicated Anglophile, she always dreamt of going back to England, and if you wanted to bring a glow to her face you only had to engage her in conversation about London's art galleries and museums, which she loved to explore.

From time to time Bryce was offered highly paid jobs in advertising agencies overseas, but he never accepted them. He told me this exasperated Benita, especially if an opportunity arose to move to her beloved London. In other ways, he said, they both realised that moving abroad would have been far too difficult, given Damon's health.

A big milestone in Bryce's advertising career arrived in 1973 when he founded the Caxton Awards, which continue to this day. They are named after William Caxton, the English merchant, diplomat and writer who is credited as the first person to bring a printing press to England, in 1476. Being a printer, he went on to be the first English retailer of printed books. On 13 December 2012, Bryce's close friend Ray Black reflected on this part of Bryce's legacy in trade publication *Campaign Brief*:

Bryce was a tough but generous creative director, fostering many talented creatives who benefited from his mentoring. In presentations of all kinds he was the master showman. I think Bryce's lasting legacy was he was the dynamo behind the Caxton Awards weekends. In the early 1970s each capital city had their own creative culture, like groups of tribes, with their own styles. These differences were jealously guarded, vividly demonstrated by the different styles and cultures between Sydney and Melbourne.

With a decision worthy of the United Nations, in 1973 the first Caxton as we know it was not held in Sydney, it was held at Australia's Panmunjong, Albury-Wodonga, straddling the mighty Murray River.

Would the Melbourne and Sydney creative tribes metaphorically gather on the river's edge and continue to throw rocks at each other from their side of the river?

No they didn't, this first awards show and speakers were very encouraging as a model.

It was a creative master stroke. Caxton was born as our first real national creative idea exchange presenting the best creative talent sharing their knowledge with their peers. Caxton was the child of Bryce, a great industry visionary.

Ray Black followed Bryce as the Caxton Awards chairman, a role he fulfilled for sixteen years – one more than Bryce.

Founding the Caxtons was yet another example of Bryce continuing to drive himself forward. The family moved into a larger house with a swimming pool in Hopetoun Avenue, Vaucluse, which Bryce once took me to see many years after it had been sold. He said, 'We now had a beautiful home [and] two fancy cars, and I wore a gold Rolex watch.'

Even for Bryce, who had arrived in Australia as an immigrant with nothing, the life he had created would have felt like a dream. His success did not come without its costs, and by the early 1970s cracks were beginning to emerge. His drinking, heavy smoking and fast-paced lifestyle were taking their toll, as reflected in the Diana Ritch interview:

> As I prospered and became somewhat famous in the process, I had also acquired all the bad habits that went with it. I became one of those brash creative types in advertising who seemed able to do no wrong. As my salary went up so did my conspicuous lifestyle. Remember the big white house with Bougainvillea, well I bought it.

Besides the time he was able to spend with Benita and the boys, his most treasured activity each day was getting up early just as the currawongs were calling and going outside to work in his garden. The love of gardening nurtured by his grandfather Robert Bryce Greer wasn't enough, however, to stem the fractures beginning to appear both physically and mentally.

The deprivations of his childhood enabled Bryce to be resilient, but he retained a mortal dread of being poor: 'I always felt the wind up my back and never dared to stop.' It was a fear shared by many people of his generation who had grown up during the Depression and the Second World War. Bryce had fallen headlong into the swirling waters of the world of advertising during the 1960s and '70s – an era that became renowned for its flashy clothes, fast cars and long, liquid lunches – with little thought of the consequences. Although not materialistic by nature, he was ultimately seduced by the glitz and glamour of that world.

Alex Hamill, at the time managing director of George Patterson in Australia and Asia, was a great mate of Bryce's. Their friendship was born of advertising but extended far beyond and over many years. Alex's own career in advertising spanned forty-four years, thirty-four of those with George Patterson, which was then Australia's biggest agency. He went on to be appointed chairman of the group, a position he held for ten years until his retirement in 2001 – not bad for someone who left school at fourteen and grew up in the then working-class suburb of Balmain. Alex also made a sterling contribution to the Olympic movement and has taken a hands-on role in several charitable organisations. It's fair to say that few others knew the game of advertising in Bryce's time like Alex. His reflection on Bryce's career is telling, which he shared in *Family Confidential*, 'The Courtenays', ABC Television, recorded late 2011 and broadcast February 2012:

> Bryce Courtenay was a star, and everyone knew Bryce Courtenay in advertising . . . The advertising world back then was probably money for nothing and chicks for free, and going to lunch for a living. It was about hard drinking, pretty hard working, and was a highly competitive business. A lot of the stuff you see in *Mad Men* – despite the fact that it was almost a satire – was actually true. Bryce walked into this world and he was a hard drinker, and I can tell you Bryce drank with the best of them.

He had come a long way from Duiwelskloof, but fame and fortune were to end up exacting a heavy price – one that even Bryce Courtenay was not able to talk his way out of.

8

THINGS FALL APART*

Always take the spoon out of the sink before you turn on the tap. – *Four Fires*

BY 1976, BRYCE HAD reached the pinnacle of success in advertising and was a partner in the ad agency Harris Robinson Courtenay, but other aspects of his life had begun to crumble. He reflected poignantly years later in his interview with Diana Ritch, 'I had everything going for me except in the end I had absolutely nothing going for me.'

Like most calamities in life, this one was unexpected. At around midnight, while waiting for a bus home from work, as his car was in for a service, Bryce was randomly attacked by a gang of bikies. They brought him to the ground and kicked him in the kidneys and base of his spine so hard he was coughing up blood. After eventually struggling to his feet he returned home feeling very sore and sorry for himself, but nothing more than that. However, the pain in his back increased and he began to suffer severe muscle spasms that locked up his entire body. Regular injections of diazepam (Valium) provided temporary relief but his doctor

---

* The title of this chapter is a nod to the Nigerian writer Chinua Achebe, a Man Booker Prize winner and author of *Things Fall Apart*, published in 1958. He has been called the 'father of African literature' and I had the great privilege of meeting him in 1973 when I was a student at the Australian National University in Canberra.

subsequently sent him to see a neurosurgeon, who ordered a series of tests. The results showed that the bottom five vertebrae in Bryce's back had been badly damaged and five of his discs had worn through. The prognosis he was given was sobering, as described to his mother on 13 March 1978: 'I asked him what the chances of my walking again [were] and he said that as the sciatic nerve was almost severed things didn't look good but that there was a chance.'

The chance the doctor alluded to involved Bryce undergoing a complicated ten-hour operation where the five damaged vertebrae would be fused with bone grafted from his hip onto his spine. He would then be required to lie down in a plaster cast from head to toe for three months. The alternative was to go through a series of operations over a period of eighteen months. Either way, Bryce was told, 'You won't really walk properly for the rest of your life – you'll probably need a stick.' This news was a shock and he took it badly: 'I told him to go forth and multiply.'

Bryce told me he went home and sat down with his family to discuss the options, and everyone agreed that he should undergo the one big procedure. In a matter of weeks he was admitted to hospital for surgery. After he had served his sentence entombed in the cast, he still didn't have any feeling in his legs. He confided to me that the whole ordeal was 'in many respects the worst six months of his life: 'Here was a guy who'd spent his entire life working sixteen hours a day and who was frequently up most of the night looking after Damon, and now I was completely immobilised. I couldn't use my hands, I couldn't use my arms, I couldn't do anything.'

It was a grave situation and Bryce realised he had only a slim chance of fighting his way out of it. He told me it reminded him of the challenges he had faced while growing up, and he began to wonder if his entire life was destined to be an unrelenting test of endurance.

After several weeks of doing nothing but gaze at the ceiling, Bryce began to feel a tiny twitch in his left big toe. He figured that if he could get movement in his other leg too, he would walk again; if he had movement in only one leg, he'd simply walk with one stiff leg. To his immense relief, three weeks later he felt some movement in the other side of his body. His medical team gathered around his bed and declared that his recovery was miraculous. During the operation they had seen that the sciatic nerve was in fact severed. They also saw evidence of the injury he had sustained while playing Rugby when he was a student at KES in Johannesburg, when four vertebrae were damaged. The doctors concluded that the breakthrough had been achieved as a result of the daily massages on Bryce's legs that were made possible after the nurses had broken open the bottom of the plaster cast. From then on, and for the rest of his life, Bryce had regular massages as he always remembered the miraculous result they had delivered.

But Bryce wasn't out of the woods yet. One night while still in hospital he began to experience severe pain in his back. It felt like it was too high up to be related to the operation. The deeply concerned nurse called the doctor rather than administering further painkillers, and fortuitously a senior surgeon from the emergency room quickly arrived and his diagnosis was that Bryce had suffered a massive thrombosis. The thrombosis had already entered one of his lungs and was moving so fast that the doctor had only minutes to act. Bryce said that even while the surgeon was examining him, 'I was coughing up large pieces of lung while they seemed to be pouring dozens of bottles of drip into me via every artery I possessed.' He confirmed the results of their efforts in a letter to his mother dated 30 March 1978: 'Anyway, they stopped the thrombosis reaching the brain and some ten days later I was good as new.'

After this dramatic turn of events, Bryce returned to a routine of daily massages and the results continued to be encouraging. But most importantly, having survived this life-threatening ordeal, he committed to changing the course of his life. While lying flat on his back encased in plaster, he had a lot of time – probably for the first time in years – to reflect on where his life was headed, as described to Diana Ritch: 'One morning I woke up and looked at the ceiling and thought, that's an A4 piece of paper, and so I started to write. I wrote on the ceiling and in three months I wrote the outlines for seventeen novels, and I knew exactly what I was going to do with my life.'

Bryce had always wanted to be a writer, but that ambition had lain dormant. Now it was roaring back to life and he couldn't wait to begin. Not that he was ever sorry about having carved out a career in advertising, which had provided well for his family and covered the significant costs of Damon's medical care. Bryce believed that these years had also given him a lot of life experience that he felt would contribute to him becoming a better writer. He also said often, 'The joy of advertising was that I was writing every day, and every advertisement is a story.'

Bryce's plan involved him accelerating the fortunes of his advertising agency and staying on there for several more years before selling the company to some unsuspecting multinational that would pay them a fortune and enable him to leave the industry and become a full-time writer. Then, he said, 'I would start writing all of these seventeen books – and of course I'd become a world-famous writer and live happily ever after.'

However, like many grand plans forged when the mind is distracted by hospital painkillers, things didn't immediately run to plan.

Upon returning home from his long stint in hospital, he relished being reunited with his family while implementing this ambitious plan, and there was little choice left but to resume his punishing work schedule. Not long afterwards, Bryce would be up well into the night working on a new business pitch. He would then slump into bed to grab a few hours' sleep. By 5 a.m. he was awakened by the calls of currawongs and, as was his habit, got up and did some work in the garden before another long day began. While standing on one leg to pull on his trousers he glanced in the mirror and didn't like what he saw: a rather funny little man with a large paunch, bloodshot eyes and a double chin. He elaborated in an interview with the *Sydney Weekly* in 1997: 'I looked down at a thirteen-and-a-half-stone [86-kilogram] slob and said, "You're going to be dead in five years – that's not what you set out to do, you set out to be a writer."'

Looking around, he saw a carton of Dunhill cigarettes and five empty packets strewn on the table along with several empty cans of beer. He had also polished off a couple of bottles of wine the previous evening and was barely able to string two words together before 10 a.m. Years later Bryce confessed to me that during those roller-coaster years he had also engaged in a few marital indiscretions – another indication that his life was veering out of control.

Then and there he decided to give up smoking and stop drinking as the first steps in getting his life back on track. I suspect he realised he also needed to focus more on his family and pull back from some aspects of his indulgent lifestyle, which was placing at risk everything he had worked so hard for. In defiance of his doctors, he headed off to the nearest swimming pool, and began swimming slow laps. He swam every day until he could swim a mile (1.6 kilometres), but thought swimming was the most boring thing a human being could do. During the years we were together I only saw him jump into a pool a couple of times. He would climb out and with a pained expression on his face say to me, 'I now know why I haven't wanted to swim since my spinal fusion.' I, on the other hand, love swimming, and always wanted to install a pool in our own backyard; we never did.

After a year Bryce stopped swimming, fitter and trimmer than when he'd started, and pulled on a pair of sandshoes. He began to run instead, saying to himself: 'If I can recover from this back operation and run a marathon, that means I can do anything.' Completing a marathon (42.195 kilometres) became a major personal goal, and the following year he did it – I have the medal to prove it. Not that he found it easy. In fact, far from it. He described the experience in the Diana Ritch interview:

After 30 kilometres you run out of blood sugar and . . . in effect your muscles are eating themselves – that's the best description of what actually happens – so that you're running on empty. It's like a car running without petrol . . . So a marathon kind of sorts the men from the boys for the very simple reason that sheer character gets you through, and in the end you arrive more exhausted than it's possible for a human being to actually be.

Much of the credit for Bryce's foray into running goes to Alex Hamill, his best mate and advertising colleague and the person who inspired him to strap on his running shoes. Alex elaborated on this as quoted in both *The Australian* in 2011 and the *Australian Financial Review* in 2016:

I watched the guys around me and thought, 'They won't make fifty.' I was a young man in the ad business at the *Mad Men* time in Australia, when most of the executives went to lunch for a living almost every day, and often stayed out for dinner. I had left school at fourteen, so by the time I was in my early thirties, I had a very senior job and decided that exercise would always beat excess . . . I saw the combination of workload, stress and entertainment as potentially lethal.

Alex was bitten by the running bug in the 1970s and quickly set up a lunchtime running group that included Bryce and the likes of well-known ad men Wayne McCarthy and John Singleton. Alex explained further:

We had ten or twelve guys who would turn up at a lunchtime. It proved to be the antidote to the stress, huge workloads, and excesses of those times . . . It all grew from there and we finished up running marathons all over the place. Bryce and I ran Hawaii and then the New York City Marathon twice . . . I have not stopped since.

*

Alex gave Bryce the nickname of 'Lucky Legs', because 'His legs were so skinny he was lucky they didn't break off and jam up his bum.' He shared a story with me of when he and his wife Brenda ran the Honolulu Marathon with Bryce in 1982 that provides some insight into Bryce's tenacity and determined spirit:

> The holy grail of marathoners is to break the three hours. Bryce came to running late in life and therefore was not expecting to crack that barrier, but he never stopped trying. We agreed that the difficult Honolulu course was not the place to attempt this. However, as we were huddled together at the starting line with the temperature already in the thirties I noticed all this writing in biro on Bryce's arm. He had written the exact time he needed to be at each 5-kilometre mark to break three hours. So off he set, leaving us in his wake. We did not see him after that and when I finished in a respectable three hours and eighteen minutes and hadn't passed him, I assumed he had finally got in under the three hours.
>
> We'd agreed to meet up for a beer that afternoon, so we went back to our hotel to shower and change. I turned on the midday news and to my astonishment the bulletin opened with vision of Bryce, who had collapsed from sheer effort and exhaustion about 1 kilometre from the finish line and then crawled on all fours to complete the 42.195 kilometres. Unbeknown to us he then spent two hours in the medical tent. Bryce's dramatic finish led every news bulletin that evening. By the way, he didn't break the three hours, but as in everything he ever did, he gave it a damn good shot.

For Bryce, this achievement provided an electrifying symbol of hope after all his suffering, as described to Diana Ritch: 'The philosophy of life is: he who endures wins. It's based on the fact that there isn't such a thing as a goal, there isn't such a thing as arriving first in a race – the prize goes to the guy or the girl who hangs in longest.'

Alex told me another great story of when he and Bryce ran their first marathon in New York in 1983:

> Bryce and I ran a number of marathons together, including Sydney's first in 1978, and we had always talked about doing New York. We got our chance in 1983 and stood together on a very cold November morning waiting for the event to start. A huge African American man came up to stand close by and Bryce recognised him immediately. It was Floyd Patterson, the famous ex-world heavyweight boxing champion. Bryce introduced himself, telling Patterson that he'd done a bit of boxing in his younger days in South Africa, and Patterson started asking him questions about his life in Africa. Well, the start gun went off and the two of them ran together for about four kilometres chatting like old friends. We had vowed to stay together for the whole race, but I didn't catch Bryce again until well into the race. He was fifty at the time and had hardly trained so it was no surprise that he fell into a heap with about ten ks to go. I stayed with him as he staggered slowly forward, helping him with his water. He was really struggling at the end and I had to support him as we sighted the finish line. As promised we finished together and Bryce fell to the ground in exhaustion, unable to regain his feet for some time. Next morning he knocked on the door of my room at the Plaza Hotel where we were both staying, with a copy of the *New York Times* under his arm. 'Matey, I've got the marathon result. Great news – I beat you by four seconds.'

In some respects, Bryce taking up swimming and running wasn't all that surprising. He had loved sport since he was a small boy and played Rugby and, to a lesser extent, cricket while at school, and while working down the mines at Luanshya, he used to enjoy playing squash and regularly Rugby. For him, the challenge was as much mental as physical, as he explained in *The Power of One*: 'The mind is the athlete; the body is simply the means it uses to run faster or longer, jump higher, shoot straighter, kick better, swim harder, hit further, or box better.'

Bryce went on to appreciate the benefits exercise delivered to his writing. In an interview with Peter Thompson on ABC TV in 2006, he elaborated on the role it played in his creative process: 'The reason I walk for an hour-and-a-half each day, apart from the exercise, is that it's brain food. That's when you do your homework, and you think about what might happen and could happen and where the writing is going'. Bryce smiled in surprise when I once told him that his literary hero, Charles Dickens, felt the same way: I'd read that every afternoon without fail Dickens would take a long walk to clear his head and dream of what to write about next.

On 6 May 1979, Paddy arrived from South Africa for her first visit to Australia, which filled the family with joyful expectations after all that they had been dealing with. Bryce wrote in a letter prior to her arrival: 'You are, and always have been, known as "Our African Nana" and very misterious at that!' This was also the first time Paddy had met Benita and her three grandchildren, and there would have been huge excitement all round. The family took her on a whirlwind of activities, including ferry rides on the Harbour, a trip to Taronga Zoo and walks on Bondi Beach followed by seafood barbecues at home. During the visit Paddy witnessed what Damon went through, and Bryce said she was deeply moved to observe how Damon never complained and was always so patient and cheerful.

Bryce was exasperated that due to his busy work schedule he couldn't spend as much time with his mother as he had hoped. Quite early on it was also clear that Paddy wasn't the least bit interested in moving to Australia on a permanent basis. Prior to her visit Bryce had written, 'Perhaps you are meant to come out as the vanguard for the rest of the family?' Bryce told me that although she loved being in Australia, and meeting Benita and her grandchildren that she was quite happy when it was time to go back home to South Africa, and she never returned. Bryce never took his family to visit her, either, although it was necessary for him to make several trips back there to promote his books. The ongoing security concerns in South Africa may have been a deterrent to travelling over with the family, although I can't be sure of this. I am sure his boys would have loved to have gone and would have made sure Bryce scheduled a safari for them as well!

In 1985 Bryce went to China to lecture on advertising and marketing. In a letter to his mother dated 16 December he wrote, 'Lectures and talks took around ten hours every day and the remainder was eating! One Chinese banquet can be up to thirty courses over a period of three hours with fare both exquisite and quite atrocious.' The best part was 'a three hour visit to the Great Wall and an hour or two snatched to see the Forbidden City and the Empress's Summer Palace'. I have a photo of Bryce running along the Great Wall displaying an ebullient smile of a man in his prime. In the same letter he explained to Paddy that his son Adam was now living in Europe and Brett was working at George Patterson (still then being run by Alex Hamill) and both boys were doing extremely well. Bryce also confirmed some devastating news about his youngest son:

> Damon, as you would know, has been constantly receiving blood since birth now shows that he is AIDS Positive from having recieved AIDS contaminated blood. This doesn't mean he has AIDS, it only means that he has the AIDS virus [HIV] in his blood. This can of course develop into AIDS in the next couple of years or he may develop an immunity. It is all terribly sad and so very unfair and we need your prayers.

The story of Damon's life, and his courageous battle to survive, was the subject of Bryce's most poignant book, *April Fool's Day*, published in 1993. The recollections recorded by Bryce, his wife Benita, their son Damon and his partner Celeste Coucke, as well as other family members and friends, is the most moving, eloquent and dignified tribute to Damon's life. I wholeheartedly agree with the comment, 'This life-affirming book will change the way you think'. And that of a reviewer who wrote in the *Weekend Australian*: '*April Fool's Day* is one of those rare, wholly beautiful books that lets life speak for itself without any attempt at artifice . . . yet stands as a powerful work of literature . . . Damon certainly lives in the pages of this vital book.' Damon's remarkable life story continues to provide us all with a powerful message of hope, and faith in love, when all else appears out of reach. Bryce's great friend Alex Hamill offered insight into *April Fool's Day* on the ABC's *Family Confidential*:

> It's a soul baring story about the death of his son. He wrote *April Fool's Day* for Damon. He lives it every day and doesn't need to read the book again. I cannot comprehend what the loss of a child would do to you. The shock would have been extreme but Bryce realised that life has to go on. He moved on gracefully and with enormous dignity.

In addition to this heartbreaking news of Damon's devastating diagnosis, Bryce was worried about the deterioration of the political situation in South Africa:

> We grow very concerned about you all, in Australia, the news of South Africa is constant and not good. I think you have to prepare for the beginning of the end of the South Africa as you know it. The abhorrence the rest of the world shows towards Apartheid may seem hipocritical to you, but it's nevertheless very real. I know how hard it is, but shouldn't you all be thinking about getting out?

That same year, for some reprieve, Bryce ran the London Marathon and afterwards he and Benita went on a trip to France and Italy, where Benita was able to explore several world-famous art galleries and museums. Bryce told his mother that it was wonderful, but 'I long for a quiet holiday where I don't have to do a thing'.

Bryce had boundless energy, but the goals he set for himself meant there was little time to rest. In a letter dated 8 June 1985, which was his mother's eightieth birthday, he wrote: 'How very much I wish my life would just slow down a little, despite the very best planning and hours that stretch from dawn to midnight I never seem to have any time for the important things like writing letters to dear friends . . .'

Like Alex, Bryce ended up completing many marathons, including the Comrades ultramarathon of approximately 89 kilometres in South Africa in May 1993 at the age of sixty. He and Alex met up with some friends there who were fellow members of the Sydney Striders Running Club. The Comrades is the world's largest and oldest ultramarathon and is convened every year in KwaZulu-Natal where Bryce spent much of his childhood. It was such a punishing experience that it took him weeks to recover. After returning to Sydney, he wrote a piece about it called 'Blood, Sweat & Tears' for the *Sydney Morning Herald* that included:

> I returned to South Africa recently to run the Comrades Marathon, arguably the world's toughest road race, which this year started in Pietermaritzburg [where his father, Arthur Ryder, had lived for much of his life] and ended in Durban, about a thousand hills and 90 km down the road . . . I completed the race in 11 hours and 18 minutes, poured the blood out of my shoes, and discovered that long-distance running had made me taller, until I realised that I was standing on a platform of plump blisters. They didn't give me a medal because I should have completed the run in 11 hours or less. At least that hasn't changed. South Africa still loves rules.

Prior to the race he spent time with his mother and Rosemary and her family, showering them with thoughtful gifts and spending precious hours together. Bryce recorded in the same article his complicated feelings about his homeland:

> Africa has always had an ugly side, a heart of darkness where white men have, from the beginning, largely disgraced themselves, though they are by no means alone. In Africa, white, Arab and black all have blood on their hands. But my childhood remembered another Africa – the far horizons, smoky with distance, the stillness of the bush at noon, the animals at dawn and dusk coming to the waterholes to drink . . . My family have been in southern Africa for 170 years, about half the time it has been dominated by the white tribe of Africa.

I treasure the bunch of Bryce's prized running medals that sits on my office bookshelf. It is a reminder for me to keep exercising just as Bryce always did, although completing a marathon is not on my radar!

Despite Bryce's challenges, there could be no looking back. He had fallen apart on several fronts but had slowly built himself back up by adopting a healthier lifestyle and running hundreds of kilometres. Our experiences of course shape our character, and in Bryce's case surviving the tough years of overwork, stress and physical breakdown may have been helped by recalling the wisdom he had learnt from the people he shared park benches with during those secondary school holidays when he had nowhere else to go: 'In the winters we slept behind Johannesburg Station and I learnt that all people are wise and good and all human beings are marvellous if you give them half a chance.' Lofty, an alcoholic and ex-miner, told him one day: 'Always take the spoon out of the sink before you turn on the tap.' Bryce used to explain to people that this meant that we are usually the architects of our own dilemmas.

Bryce believed this, and elaborated on the subject in an interview with US photographer and filmmaker Andrew Zuckerman for a spectacular book called *Wisdom*, published in 2008:

> Life is about climbing a cliff, not about running a race. Failure is an absolute essential in life. You dare your genius to walk the wildest, unknown way. Of course you're going to fall down. Of course you're going to. But it's your way, and when you get to the end you'll know something.

The small boy from South Africa was now a man on a mission, fighting hard to maintain his career and provide for his family to care for a very sick son while at the same time holding on to his lifelong dream of one day becoming a writer. 'Lucky Courtenay', as Bryce would call himself, had once again survived. But, as he later evoked in *Smokey Joe's Cafe*, 'You've made it one more time, but there was always a next time, the hole in your guts never gets filled, the fear never stops.'

Perhaps, with little self-awareness, he was a shining example of what it means to overcome great adversity. Bryce was about to create a story that encapsulated that spirit, called *The Power of One*.

9

THE POWER OF ONE

Mystery, not logic, is what gives us hope and keeps us
believing in a force greater than our own insignificance.
– *The Power of One*

BRYCE COURTENAY WILL ALWAYS be remembered as the writer who
created *The Power of One*. It was first published on 21 February 1989 by
Heinemann in Australia and, soon after, in the United Kingdom, and
by Random House in the United States – and it took the world by storm.
Its success launched a spectacular literary career that yielded twenty-one
bestsellers over twenty-three years.

Bryce had waited his whole life to write this book. He finally sat
down to commence it on 8 June 1986, his mother's eighty-first birthday.
While it's essentially fiction, there can be little doubt that Bryce drew
from his own life story to write it. He recalled the day he began writing
his first novel in *The Silver Moon*:

> I climbed out of bed early one morning in 1986, headed to my
> study and began what was to become *The Power of One*. 'This is
> what happened' seemed a good place to start, and I wrote about
> what I knew – growing up in South Africa.

Bryce was then aged fifty-two, and had been in the advertising industry for nearly twenty-eight years. Reinventing himself as a fiction writer was to realise a childhood dream, and he had no illusions as to how difficult it might be. He believed he would need to write at least four books before he would be good enough to secure a publisher – he had undertaken some research into bestselling writers and discovered that most of them had not become successful until their fourth book was completed, as he reflected in *The Silver Moon*:

> I gave myself five years in which to write four novels. The first three would be practice books I'd complete in exactly a year each (you have to have a deadline); the fourth novel, the one that would hopefully be published, I'd lavish with attention over a period of two years. Cheeky, I know, but there you go – you have to have a dream.

Bryce was a born storyteller. The people who knew him from childhood all recall that he wanted to become a writer from an early age and was convinced he would become a world-famous one. But starting to write fiction so late in his life meant that Bryce was in a tearing hurry. He already had over a dozen novels in his mind, planned while recovering from his back surgery several years before, and was hungry to move them from his head to the page.

Few people realise that Bryce's first published book was not actually *The Power of One*. It was called *Words* and was published in 1981 by Smith & Miles Ltd. I have a letter written to Bryce from the house's managing director, Andrew Smith, which confirms that 600 copies were printed. *Words* is based on a collection of papers Bryce presented in Hobart at the 1980 Caxton Awards, in which he implored the audience to be proud of and embrace the language spoken by everyday Australians: 'Our language is laconic and often recalcitrant but it has a blunt vigour, a lust for life that is not being included in much of our work.' As Alex Hamill recalled at Bryce's memorial service, Bryce demonstrated this point – larrikin as he sometimes was – by proclaiming, 'An advertisement without a promise is like a fart without a smell. It passes into the environment unnoticed, causing no reaction whatsoever and serving only as relief to the fartee that he got away with it.'

Bryce's remarkable debut novel, *The Power of One*, is written in the first person and records the story of Peekay, a boy growing up in South Africa during the 1930s and '40s, including the early years of the apartheid regime. It's a quintessential coming-of-age tale where a brave young boy survives the school of hard knocks while managing to keep hope in his heart. It unfolds in a rollercoaster of action and catapults the reader into the heart of Peekay's world. The book is dense with characters that embody the universal themes of isolation, racial injustice, resilience and hope. Ultimately, it demonstrates that love and kindness are what all human beings crave and in the end they are all that matters. Comprising over 500 pages, *The Power of One* delivers a message of inspiration, and with inclusion on school lists, a young readers' edition and the popularity of the film, a new generation of readers are now embracing it.

Peekay, who is five years old when the story starts, negotiates a minefield of deprivation and abuse after he is torn from the breast of his Zulu nanny and banished to an orphanage. Later he makes regular visits to a prison full of Afrikaners determined to take down the 'little Rooinek' they call 'Pisskop'. His friendships with Granpa Chook, Professor Karl von Vollensteen (known as 'Doc'), Giel Peet and Hoppie Groenewald, among others, secure his pathway to salvation – but only after he survives a childhood devoid of compassion. Peekay's mother, a born-again Christian zealot, provides precious little succour for a small boy thrust into a world of adults with only animals and a precious few trusted friends for company. The brutality meted out by the characters Bormann, Rasputin and the Judge is a baptism of fire for the innocent souls caught up in a web of injustice, cruelty and poverty.

Bryce had originally thought of making his hero a chess player, but in an interview for *Book of the Month Club News* published in the United States in August 1989, he explained his decision to make Peekay a boxer: 'Boxing has more action. I was a boxer, and I still think of myself that way. Life is a lot like boxing.' Peekay often finds himself in the boxing ring, where he learns profound lessons from Hoppie Groenewald, who tells him, 'First with the head and then with the heart, that way small can beat big.'

As Peekay's life evolves so does his name, which becomes Peekay, the Tadpole Angel and Onoshobishobi Ingelosi. The story is steeped in mythology arising from the traditions of Africa, which play a big role in transforming Peekay's life. As Bryce often said, 'The only people who were really kind to me were the Africans'; from them he learnt about their beliefs, myths and legends.

The story unfolds in a stream of consciousness, inviting the reader to inhabit Peekay's world. Peekay's childhood sense of irony and humour subsides as he matures into manhood: 'Parting, losing the things we love the most, that's the whole business of life, that's what it's mostly about.' The tone shifts, and he grows to become less forgiving as his life is marred by tragedy, bitterness and heartache. Finally, in the closing stages of the novel, he achieves a level of redemption when he realises that 'The power of one was the courage to remain separate, to think through to the truth and not to be beguiled by convention or the plausible arguments of those who expect to maintain power whatever the cost.'

Make no mistake: while *The Power of One* is an inspirational coming-of-age adventure story about overcoming adversity, it is also a direct indictment of the inequity and brutality of the apartheid regime that Bryce witnessed growing up. On 5 April 1988, he wrote to Paddy: 'Thirty years in a world bigger than the boot of Africa have shown me that any form of racism is repulsive and counterproductive and cannot ever be condoned, whatever the circumstances which bring it about.' In an interview with the *Los Angeles Times* in 1989 he clarified his intention in creating *The Power of One*: 'I thought, I'm going to write about apartheid, not as a statement and not as a flaming sword. I am going to write it so that people feel it.'

The Power of One is rich in dialogue, as are all the novels that followed. In his interview with Roger Maynard in April 2012, Bryce said, 'When I am writing, a conversation is going on. I am talking to my characters. It is exactly as if they are in the room. It's a movie.' *The Power of One* is also a work of historical fiction – a genre that applies to most of Bryce's books. Apartheid was the historical background underlying the plot and the themes in this first story.

Bryce may have been influenced by Alan Paton's powerful novel *Cry, the Beloved Country* set just prior to apartheid in South Africa (it is cited in *Whitethorn*). Bryce always said he was profoundly influenced by conversations with his grandfather about this book. And it was Bryce's grandfather, in fact, who was the source of the advice Bryce often quoted, that a good story must have 'a bucketful of tears and a bellyful of laughs', as disclosed on *Family Confidential*. This became so much a part of Bryce's brand, and his mantra for writing:

> My grandfather, who I didn't have enough time with, but occasionally I spent time with my mother and my grandfather, and he once asked me what I wanted to be in life, and I said, 'I want to be a storyteller.' And he said, 'Do you know what the ingredients of a good story are?' And I said at that stage, I would have been ten or something, 'Probably a spitfire pilot and lots of Germans being killed,' and he said, 'Oh no, no lad – the elements of a good story are, a bucketful of tears and a bellyful of laughs.'
>
> I wish I'd thought of that but he did, and whenever I sit down to write a book, the first thing I write on the page is 'A bucketful of tears and a bellyful of laughs.' It's my mantra.

The Power of One is character-driven, as Bryce believed passionately that 'character is plot'. He often said he came to understand the power of character by reading the novels of Charles Dickens, his literary hero. In an ABC radio interview for *Book Club* on 9 February 2011, he described Dickens as 'the consummate, total, complete storyteller'.

Reading for Bryce from a young age was a lifeline. As a boy he was excited by Daniel Defoe's *Robinson Crusoe* and *Toad of Toad Hall* by A.A. Milne (a dramatisation of Kenneth Grahame's *The Wind in the Willows*). Then, as an adult, he loved *The Grapes of Wrath* by John Steinbeck, Ernest Hemingway's *The Snows of Kilimanjaro*, and *Catch-22* by Joseph Heller, which he said was 'a book . . . which absolutely totally shook me to my foundations'. *Robinson Crusoe* especially thrilled him: 'I loved that book because it was my first metaphoric book. It is about a man stranded on an island, but I saw it as a metaphor for how my life was at the age of eight. I said, "This is me, this is me!"'

Bryce said of these authors, 'Always they were all great storytellers, and always their characters were paramount.' Their influence, along with that of Dickens, shaped Bryce into a character-driven writer. He believed that 'What the characters feels and thinks and does decides what the plot will do. I mean, that's how it works in life so why wouldn't it work in fiction?' Years later, in 1997, and now with several bestselling novels to his name, he reflected in an interview with *The Mercury* (Tasmania): 'I'm a character-driven novelist and I'm fascinated by the human persona and the travails and troubles and angst and adventures that we human beings manage to create for ourselves . . . I'm driven to tell stories.'

Bryce wrote *The Power of One* at a desk in the spare room of a flat in Rose Bay he had rented while the family home in Vaucluse was being renovated. He explained in his interview with Diana Ritch that he wanted to write something different from the contemporary works he had been reading, which he thought fell flat: 'What I need in my life is a really good adventure story where people don't feel sorry for themselves and they don't tell you about their operations – spiritual, mental and actual – and everything isn't inward-looking.'

Each day he would pull on a grey *Canberra Times* promotional sweatshirt, regardless of the weather (he also wore this when writing each of his subsequent novels). As the book grew in length, so did the number of drafts stored in boxes on the floor. In the end, he told me, the room barely had any light coming through the windows as there were so many boxes rammed up against them. He first called the book *The Tadpole Angel*, which Peekay explains to his school friend Hymie is 'a symbol, a symbol of hope'. Geel Piet tells Peekay why the Zulus have given him this name:

> 'It is like this, small baas. The professor is known as *Amasele* (the Frog), because he plays his peeano at night when the prison is quiet. To the Zulus the frog makes always the loudest music at night, much louder than the cricket or the owl. So it is simple, you see. You are the small boy of the frog, which makes you a Tadpole.'

In writing his debut Bryce instinctively knew that recalling aspects of his own life was the best place to start, even though this process must have roused demons from his past. He also didn't have the luxury of sitting around in a dreamlike state waiting for inspiration to arrive as he was still working full time at Harris Robinson Courtenay. Bryce explained how he found the time to write in his interview with Diana Ritch:

> I wrote religiously, getting up at around 4.15 a.m. and by 4.30 I was at the word processor, every day for a year, Saturdays and Sundays, every day. I just cut myself off: I didn't watch a television program, I didn't go to a movie, I didn't go to a dinner party . . . I just wrote and wrote and wrote, and when I wasn't writing I was back at [advertising] work.

In short, his writing had to take place whenever he could snatch a few spare hours, and he needed to apply liberal quantities of what he called 'bum glue'. Even though Bryce was undoubtedly born with a storytelling gift, he was always adamant that the cornerstones of his success were hard work and discipline as captured in *The Power of One* by Singe 'n Burn:

> Let me conclude by saying, in my experience the glittering prizes in life come more to those who persevere despite setback and disappointment than they do to the exceptionally gifted who, with the confidence of the talents bestowed upon them, often pursue the tasks leading to success with less determination.

The huge workload Bryce had sustained throughout his advertising career meant he had learnt to get by on four-and-a-half to five hours' sleep a night, a regimen he maintained for the rest of his life. He explained the need to balance his dream of becoming a novelist with his advertising career in an interview with the BBC's Michael Peschardt in 2010:

> I had to postpone everything. I thought by the time I reached thirty-five, I'd have enough maturity to write a book. I've always wanted to be a storyteller, that's the only thing I've ever wanted to be. I thought I'd get some life experience and then at thirty-five I'll start writing, but my youngest son was born a classic haemophiliac, and he required a great deal more money than I could ever hope to make as a young writer. So, I had a career in advertising and postponed it.

In another interview with Peter Thompson, he said:

> I didn't grow up in the fortunate situation of being nicely cushioned in a middle-class spectrum. Writing was always going to be my life, but things just got out of hand as they do in everyone's life. Every morning of my life I would wake up and say 'There's another day of not being what I want to be.'

Bryce would frequently have to rush Damon to the hospital when he suffered a bleed and spent many nights keeping a bedside vigil while Damon slept. He told me he would balance an old Remington typewriter on his knees and tap away through the night to ensure he achieved his daily quota of words. But he told me that caring for Damon was a routine he never resented for a moment: 'Damon's dignity and courage were always so extraordinary, and his trials so much greater than anything I was going through.'

Challenges and hardship form a part of every life, and Bryce believed in the importance of experience to writing. He believed that at fifty-two he was in the prime of his life and couldn't have written a book that good earlier anyway. He used to say to me, 'Life needs to kick you in the guts before you have enough in your tank to be able to write properly.' Through the decades of working in advertising he had also learnt a lot about what makes people tick, as he reflected in his interview with Peter Thompson: 'I think I learnt to understand what made people laugh, what made people cry or feel hurt and why they did things.'

Bryce often used to talk to me about his beliefs surrounding the power of the mind. He was fascinated with differing conscious states, which he regarded as integral to his writing. He also had a lifelong fascination with hypnosis and once tried to hypnotise me out of my fear of snakes, which was entirely unsuccessful! He wrote in *April Fool's Day*: 'I have never completely lost the ability of childhood to become totally lost, going so deeply down into my subconscious that I forget where I am and the dreaming becomes more real than the reality around me.' He explored this state of mind, this headspace, in *The Night Country*:

> You may come back here to the Night Country whenever you wish by closing your eyes and sitting very still, and by the counting of ten, frontways and backways . . . This place will always be yours, little white boy who has tears enough for a black man's mourning.

In the 1991 Diana Ritch interview he elaborated on how his state of mind summoned his creative process:

> I believe that writing, for me anyway, takes place in a state of daydream . . . So, in writing *The Power of One*, I spent a great deal of time in quite deep hypnosis but I actually regressed my memory quite deliberately until I was five years old, until I was six and seven, and I wrote the book in the actual state of mind which took place when I was that age.

Bryce's sense of story and the mythical power of stories had roots in his childhood in Africa:

> All stories are the same story and they all begin like this: they begin at nightfall when hunter-gatherers have been out and the women have been out and they've dug for roots and wild yams and they've brought them in well before the sun has set so they can prepare the fires. And the hunters have circled the grasslands and they've come through and they've brought in the hunt and it is getting dark, it's a danger time, and so they're all sitting in the mouth of a large cave which they can protect which looks over the grasslands.
>
> They hear the cough of the lion and the call of the jackal and the fire is snapping in the semi-darkness as the darkness grows and they can smell the roasted meat and the women's chatter becomes quiet as the meal is eaten. Then finally it is finished and children gather into the arms of their parents and they hold them tightly and then there is the voice as the old man comes and he sits in the quiet and he says, 'This is what happened', and that is the beginning of all stories.

In some respects, writing *The Power of One* was a lonely road. Bryce had no publishing contract to provide a deadline and no editors on hand to refine his copy, encourage his efforts or help with the research. However, what mattered most was that he was fulfilling his lifelong dream of sitting down and writing a book. He was driven to write it and didn't give a damn if he ever made a cent out of it.

On 8 June 1986, Bryce provided his mother with an update:

> I have also just about completed my first novel, a rather big book (it's already 350 pages with a fair way to go yet) . . . It is the story of a small boy very loosely based on my life, beginning at the age of five and is concerned with the Afrikaner/English confrontation and the gradually dominating Afrikaner element, though seen through the unknowing eyes of a small boy.
>
> Writing it has been incredibly hard work, working often through until dawn, all weekend from dawn to midnight, while at the same time running a company . . . But it's also been very gratifying to be able to use the skill acquired over a lifetime to do something original . . . How wonderful it is to do something truly difficult which makes you reach further and dig deeper than you thought possible.

By early 1987 the manuscript was evolving well, as Bryce confirmed to Paddy on 19 January:

> The book goes well, and I passed page 500 this weekend, so its back is well and truly broken. Perhaps another 300 pages and then the hard work of subbing it begins . . . I look forward to the first commentary from a South African reader. I keep reminding myself that I have been away longer than ever I stayed and may well have lost the idiom entirely.

It was a huge undertaking but one he was committed to finishing:

> It's not hard to see how writers can be consumed by their work. Finding an extra forty hours a week on top of a seventy-hour

working week isn't easy, but I'll get there. As the Chinese say: "Each book of a million words begins with one word, each journey of a thousand miles with one step."

He asked his mother to help him with some research:

If you can get any literature at all on Barberton when you visit, a street map, local sights, mines, farming industries and anything that would have related to my childhood I would be enormously grateful as there is much that I have forgotten. Duiwelskloof as well.

Bryce became filled with momentary despair when his book wasn't completed, as he had planned, by midnight on his mother's next birthday, 8 June 1987. However, 365 days and several minutes after he had started it, he declared his book *The Tadpole Angel* finished. He said he cried happy tears and was really impressed that he had written such a big book: the stack of pages – which he tied together with a piece of string – stood 22 centimetres high and weighed over 2.5 kilograms.

A very dear friend, Albert 'Albe' Falzon, director of the internationally acclaimed classic surfing film *Morning of the Earth* released in 1972, remembers the day in 1987 when he had arrived for a meeting in HRC's office: 'Bryce arrived with reams of paper a foot high and he placed them onto a desk and declared, "I've just finished my first book!"' That 'first book' was of course *The Power of One*, and outside of Bryce's family, Albe and Michael were the first people to see it.

Bryce placed the bundle in a plastic box with the words 'Practice Book One' scrawled across the lid. The kitchen screen door had been banging all year, so he decided to use the tub as a doorstop. Remember, he was convinced this was just a practice book and said he hadn't shown it to anyone. As he said during *Family Confidential*, one of his final interviews in 2012, 'I wrote it very freely, because it's never going to get read. I mean, Benita never read it until it was published. I didn't show it to anybody.'

I still have a signed copy of all of the pages of that first manuscript, which Bryce gave me on my fifty-eighth birthday, along with a tiny green frog he had specially made to be from 'the tadpole angel'.

Before long, the book stopping the screen door from banging was picked up and read by Ann Barrett, who was engaged to Bryce's eldest son, Brett. Bryce used to tell me that after reading it Ann said to him 'This is one of the best books I have ever read!' However, his immediate plans involved getting back into daily life. This meant helping Benita to take care of the boys, doing his daily runs to Bondi Beach, and working in the agency to support the family, pay the mortgage and cover the costs of Damon's medical treatment. Bryce told me he had made a deal with Benita that he would set aside three further years for writing, and if he wasn't successful in that time he would stay working in advertising.

As it turned out, Bryce had to change jobs anyway. In 1986, while still writing *The Power of One*, Harris Robinson Courtenay was sold to Clemenger and became the Sydney arm of Harvie HRC. His interview with Diana Ritch reveals he did not make much from the deal, which must have been a setback for his plans: 'So, I said to my wife, "We're in trouble. I've sold the company. I haven't got any money. We've just about got enough, I think, to probably live for nine months if I scrape all of our assets together."'

This situation was arrested when his old friend Alex Hamill phoned. George Patterson's chairman and CEO Geoff Cousins had been told that Bryce was unhappy balancing his writing and the demands of a small company with few support staff. George Patterson was still Australia's biggest agency and Alex said to Bryce, 'For fifteen years I've wanted to hire you. Will you come over here and be our creative director? You simply write better than anybody I've ever known.'

Bryce was relieved to land this job and thrilled to be working for Alex. He said in an interview published in *The Australian* at the time, 'It's time to get back to writing good advertising.' He also said that before landing this job he had been wondering if he wasn't beginning to 'look like a bit of an old fart in a young man's game'. He was very grateful that Alex and Geoff had worked out a way to utilise his talent while giving him time to continue his writing. I suspect he probably wasn't ready to lead the solitary life of a writer and actually looked forward to still being part of a team.

Alex confirmed that before long, 'Bryce was of course the star that all the clients wanted to meet.' He explained, 'Agencies go to an enormous amount of effort to try and win an account. It can be a real dog and pony show, with all the glitz you'd expect from a stage show.' Alex told me about the time he and Bryce went to pitch for a lucrative campaign with the Roads & Traffic Authority of New South Wales:

I had decided that we needed Bryce to make our pitch and offered him as their creative director if we won the account. Wanting to appear different to all the other agencies, only the two of us would present. I would do the usual intro and Bryce would reveal the campaign idea. The day before our presentation Bryce had not shown me even one campaign idea. As much as I believed in him, I began to worry. On the appointed day I still had not seen anything and I knew he had not commissioned any artwork or television story to present his campaign. As we walked to our boardroom all I had from Bryce was 'Don't worry, matey [he always called me matey when I was stressed], I've got this.' So we walked into the boardroom to meet six bureaucrats and Bryce didn't even have a sheet of paper with him.

I said nice things about how great Patts was and gave Bryce a glowing introduction, not having any idea what he was going to present. I will never forget what he said, because nobody else could have got away with it. He commenced his pitch as follows:

'As Alex knows, and I also know, this is a tough idea to communicate – trying to tell motorists to actually stop driving and rest is almost impossible. As of midnight last night I had no answer either. Then I woke up at 4.46 this morning and it came to me, and the answer to the biggest problem is often the simplest. So, I give you in three words the way to get this very important safety issue across – three strong words that every motorist will remember the first time they hear them.'

He walked up to the whiteboard and wrote slowly in capitals: 'STOP. REVIVE. SURVIVE.' There was a hush and then a spontaneous round of applause and I knew we had won the business. It was the shortest presentation we ever did, and it won us one of our biggest accounts, and the campaign became the stuff of legend.

Afterwards I asked Bryce if the idea had really come to him in the early hours of that morning. He answered, 'Matey, of course not – I thought of it weeks ago. I just wanted to add some theatre and drama to our pitch.' That brilliant campaign launched in 1990 continues to be a feature of the Australian Government's road safety initiatives today.

There will always be debate as to precisely how *The Power of One* came to be published. Bryce recorded his own recollections in his extensive interview with Diana Ritch:

Some weeks [after I had finished] I was running with a friend and he said, 'How's the book going?', because I must admit I bored everybody to tears talking about the fact that I was writing this 'practice book'. I said, 'I've finished.' He said, 'Well, why don't you send it to a publisher?' I said, 'What for? It's a practice book.' He said, 'No, no, you've got to send it to a publisher because that's how you learn the tricks of the trade.' So I said, 'Do you know any publishers?' He said, 'Oh well, you could send it to Bantam Books, they're the biggest in the world' . . . I thought, that's great, I'll send it to Bantam Books.

Bryce did just that, and a week later he received a letter of rejection. Following this rebuff he was told by another of his running mates he needed to engage a literary agent – not that he knew what literary agents did, or where to find one. Eventually he was introduced to Jill Hickson, who in 1983 had formed Hickson Associates. She represented a stable of highly successful authors, including Kathy Lette and Thomas Keneally, and was married to Neville Wran, the former Premier of New South Wales. She had probably never heard of Bryce and is likely to have been sceptical at first, but knowing he was a copywriter she must have held a glimmer of hope that he had a flair for words, and she asked to see the manuscript. He explained that it was just a practice book he was using as a doorstop and said he would instead send her the real book down the track, but she asked for the doorstop: 'Can you send me the manuscript just as it is?' A short time later he received a phone call from Jill, who told him, 'You have written a marvellous book.' His reaction, she claims to this day, was 'Shit, have I?'

Jill sent a copy of the manuscript to Mic Cheetham at Anthony Sheil Associates, her counterpart in England, who also loved it. Mic had previously had a young assistant named Laura Longrigg, who had come straight from Oxford into this entry-level position as a way to break into the publishing industry in the UK. She had recently left to take up a position as a junior editor at Heinemann, and as a parting gift Mic passed on Bryce's manuscript for her to pitch in-house: 'This was a gift of an author, in a sense, and if it worked, then she would have her own first author.'

The story goes that on her first day at her new job, Laura reported at the editorial meeting that she'd been up all night reading a manuscript she couldn't put down by an author from Australia. Everybody looked at her in astonishment as she said, 'I've got the next bestseller for Heinemann . . . There is this Australian writer. He's fifty-four years old and he has written the most marvellous book about Africa.' She was apparently told that apart from Wilbur Smith they didn't 'do' books about Africa because no one read them.

Nevertheless, legend has it that Heinemann publisher Helen Fraser found herself reading right through that night and didn't go to work the next day, instead finishing the book. She too was convinced they had a bestseller on their hands. The very next week she had to go to New York on business, and word spread of the new Australian author on Heinemann's list. Riding the wave of the buzz, Jill decided to auction the book in New York to American publishers. According to Bryce, 'It had never been done before, absolutely never been done before – and suddenly an unknown author is going to have his book auctioned.' He continued:

> So, out went the manuscript and at a quarter past four the phone rang on the allotted day . . . and it was Jill Hickson and she said, 'Are you sitting down?' I said, 'No, but I will.' She said, 'Listen to this. Bantam Books of New York have bid $320 000 US for your book. How about that?' and I said, 'Jill, tell them to go to buggery.' She said, 'You can't mean that.' I said, 'They rejected my book. Tell them to go to buggery. I'm not accepting.' She said, 'Bryce, that's the highest price ever paid for a new novel for an Australian author. I can't tell them that.' I said, 'Jill, I absolutely insist.' Two days later a bid came for three times that amount from another publisher, Random House, and we became the highest amount of money ever paid for a first novel by an Australian.

Bryce claimed it was 'one of the nicest moments of my life' and affirmed that 'there is some justice in the world'. He remembers that to celebrate he went out the next day and ordered himself a mixed grill – an 'extravagance' he had believed years before would signal he had made it! It's a story – also recorded in the Diana Ritch interview – that always brings a smile to my face:

> When I was nine there was a little cafe in town and it used to have the menu pinned to the checked window . . . and it said 'Mixed

grill: one and sixpence' – one and sixpence in today's language is fifteen cents. And in my head one and sixpence seemed to be about like a \$250 meal might be today; I couldn't imagine anybody ever having one and sixpence for a meal. So I imagined that a mixed grill had to be the most sumptuous thing a human being could possibly ever eat and I used to dream of one day being old enough to have a mixed grill and that would suddenly establish in life that I'd really, really made it.

I can't be sure who decided to change the title from *The Tadpole Angel* to *The Power of One*, but I am certain it wouldn't have been changed if Bryce hadn't agreed the new one was better. Laura Longrigg went on to edit the book – quite possibly the only time one of Bryce's editors had a complete manuscript to start with, as Bryce later notoriously delivered his manuscripts chapter by chapter, with the final chapter hitting the editor's desk days before the whole was due at the printers.

I have a letter from Mic Cheetham to Bryce dated 13 February 1989 citing the pre-publication buzz:

Well things are certainly hotting up around here and we await your arrival. I expect that Laura has already told you that Heinemann are re-printing now before publication. The quantity is likely to be between three and five thousand copies and the buzz about the book is becoming very intense. This is just what we wanted. Talking to Laura last week it seems that Heinemann are really going to be working you hard from the 20th until 24th [of March] when I gather you go to Venice, and then you will come back here for the London Book Fair which is very good indeed because I know that a lot of your foreign publishers will be here . . .

I have a further letter from Anthony Sheil's dated 16 March 1989 and signed by both Bryce and William Heinemann Ltd, confirming details of the financial deal for the paperback edition.

Bryce told his mother of the international interest in his book in a letter on 5 April 1988 (Rosemary's birthday):

> My book has been received in New York and London with some fuss, as you can see from the clipping attached, which appears on the front page of *The Australian*, to my acute embarrassment. Both publishers, Random House in the USA and Heinemann in the UK, are positioning it as a bestseller and talk of it being the book in both countries for 1989 when it will be published early in the year.

The Power of One was released in hardcover editions in March 1989, and in the same year a junior edition was published for young readers. The official launch event in Australia was held at George Patterson's office in North Sydney on 6 March, and I have a copy of the original invitation. As ever, in the pages Bryce warmly acknowledged the people whose support made writing his first novel possible: 'First, my wife, Benita, who went without a husband for the year it took me to write this book.' Among others, he also thanked his son Adam; his friends Peter Keeble and Owen Denmeade; and Alex Hamill, Jill Hickson, Laura Longrigg and Kate Medina.

Plans were soon underway to publish a softcover edition, as Bryce confirmed in a letter on 3 January 1989: 'So, I guess we'd all better fasten our seat belts because when the paperback comes out at the end of the year the sales will really rocket! The rest, as they say, is history.' Almost overnight, Bryce became a household name.

Reviews of *The Power of One* were mixed, with some of the least favourable emanating from critics in the country Bryce had adopted as his own some thirty years earlier. Some went so far as to suggest it was just the kind of book a man from advertising would write. This kind of rebuff was something Bryce had to learn to take on the chin. With a rare note of indignation, he once said to me, 'I'd far rather speak to a room full of schoolchildren than a room full of literati.' He wrote for his readers and no one else, and used to spend hours personally answering fan mail. When a new book came out, he would regularly receive hundreds of letters a week.

Some reviews of *The Power of One* were effusively positive. The *Sunday Times* (London) stated: 'Bryce Courtenay's first novel is a triumph . . . an epic of survival . . . (and) a portrait of evil . . . It is also infected with a mischievous sense of comedy', while Christopher Lehmann-Haupt of the *New York Times* wrote, 'If a shrewdly programmed computer were to design the ultimate international best seller, it couldn't do much better than this first novel. On almost any scale of measurement *The Power of One* has everything . . .' The *Canberra Times* stated that it was 'that rare phenomenon, a novel actually as good as it is cracked up to be'. The British-American author Barbara Taylor Bradford wrote in her endorsement, 'This first novel by a strong new voice in fiction has such integrity, force and power it left me breathless.'

Later, Penguin Books Australia described *The Power of One* as follows: 'Bryce Courtenay's classic bestseller is a story of the triumph of the human spirit – a spellbinding tale for all ages.' It won Newcomer of the Year at the 1990 British Book Awards and was celebrated globally by bookstores and book groups, with Bryce giving speeches at hundreds of literary lunches and dinners. Business organisations also clamoured to have him deliver keynote addresses, and he quickly became one of the world's most sought-after speakers. His preference, though, was always to give speeches to raise funds for the many charities he was proud to support.

Even with all these accolades, Bryce is quoted online in *Better Reading* (11 June 2019), which hosts Australia's largest online reading community, as saying, 'I was absolutely staggered when somebody wanted to publish it in the first place' and 'Its worldwide success and the fact that it's available in twelve languages still amazes me'. *The Power of One* has been published in nearly twenty languages worldwide, from Hebrew to Finnish, Mandarin to Spanish, Italian to Japanese and more. An audio version (with an introduction from Bryce) lasting

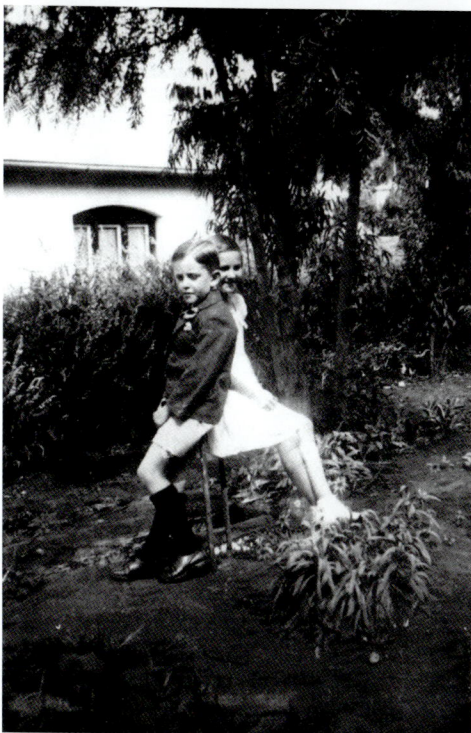

Top Left: Bryce's father, Arthur James Ryder.
Photograph from Rosemary Anderson's collection, published with her kind permission.

Top Right: Bryce's mother, Maud Jessamine Greer, known to her family as 'Paddy'.
Photograph from Rosemary Anderson's collection, published with her kind permission.

Left: Bryce and his sister Rosemary at Duiwelskloof, now Modjadjiskloof, South Africa – a challenging time during their childhood.
Photograph from the author's collection.

Bryce, Rosemary, Paddy and Bryce's beloved grandfather, Robert Bryce Greer, during four happy years living together in Barberton, Mpumalanga Province, in around 1942.

Photograph from Rosemary Anderson's collection, published with her kind permission.

Working as a 'grizzly' at the Roan Antelope copper mine in Luanshya, 1955. Photograph from the author's collection.

Enjoying a day off from working in the mines: Bryce shouldering his friend Iain Finlay, with another miner leading the trio down a water slide.

Photograph from Iain Finlay's collection, published with his kind permission.

Bryce paid his way to London in September 1956 to study journalism. He's pictured here at Trafalgar Square.

Photograph from Owen Anderson's collection, published with his kind permission.

While in London Bryce met and fell in love with Benita Solomon. They reunited in Australia in late 1958 and married on 2 October 1959.

Photograph from Brett Courtenay's collection, published with his kind permission.

Family was everything to Bryce, and he was so proud of his three sons, (from left to right) Adam, Damon and Brett.

Photograph from Brett Courtenay's collection, published with his kind permission.

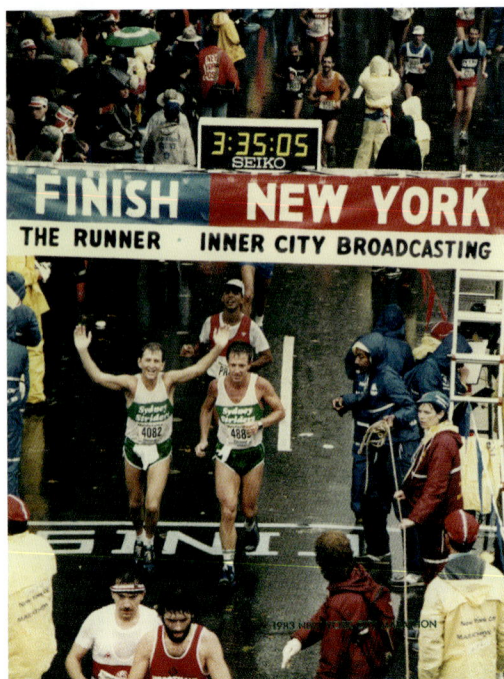

Top: Bryce took up running to keep in shape during his demanding career in advertising, and completed several marathons – including Honolulu in 1982. Photograph from the author's collection.

Left: Bryce and his great friend and advertising colleague Alex Hamill crossing the finish line of the New York Marathon in 1983. Photograph from Alex Hamill's collection, published with his kind permission.

As a talented advertising creative, Bryce perfected storytelling of a different kind. His 'Stop Revive Survive' campaign was one of his most successful and enduring. He is pictured here with Graeme Cox, account director at George Patterson.

Photography by Penny Wright, from the author's collection.

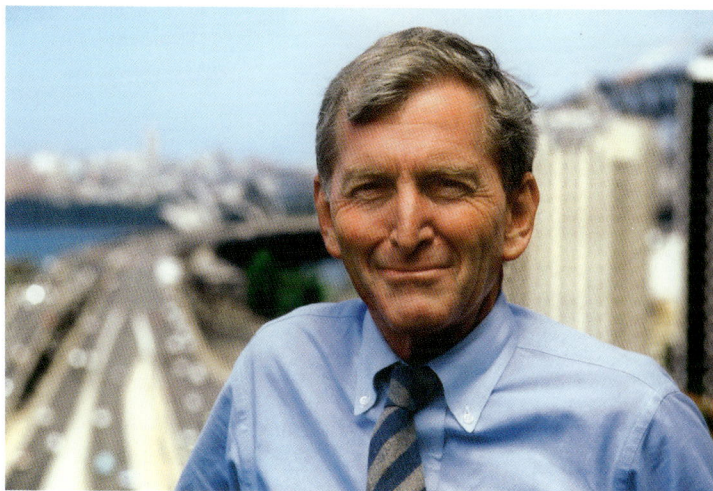

Bryce's dazzling advertising career took him to the top of that world. This portrait by Heide Smith was taken while he was at George Patterson.

Photography by Heide Smith, from the author's collection.

The publication of *The Power of One* in 1989 changed the course of Bryce's life. He returned to South Africa in 1989 to celebrate its publication with Paddy and Rosemary in Port Shepstone, as covered by the local paper.

Photograph courtesy of David Rush, editor, *South Coast Herald*, Port Shepstone, South Africa.

Bryce's advertising running mates donned T-shirts to celebrate the publication of *The Power of One*. From left to right, a visiting colleague, Hugh Spencer, Bryce, Alex Hamill, Tony Crosby, Peter Keeble, John Ayliffe and Michael Mooney.

Photography by Penny Wright, from the author's collection.

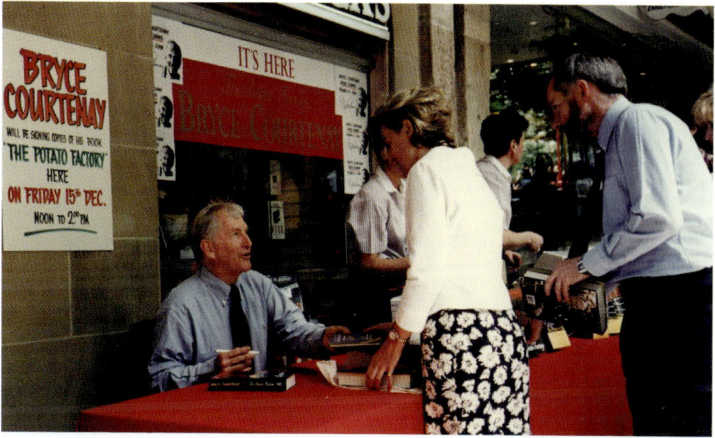

Bryce wrote a succession of bestselling books. With each release he would spend hours signing books for loyal readers – including in North Sydney for the publication of *The Potato Factory*, 1995.

Bryce's portrait, painted in 1998 by Paul Newton, now has pride of place in my study.

In 1997 Bryce signed up to Penguin Books Australia, which began a long-term partnership with publishing director Robert Sessions, known affectionately to Bryce as 'Uncle Bob'. *Photograph from the author's collection.*

In November 2000 Bryce travelled by ship to Antarctica and South Georgia to run a writing workshop on board. He got a laugh sending this shot back home to the Penguins in Melbourne. *Photograph from the author's collection.*

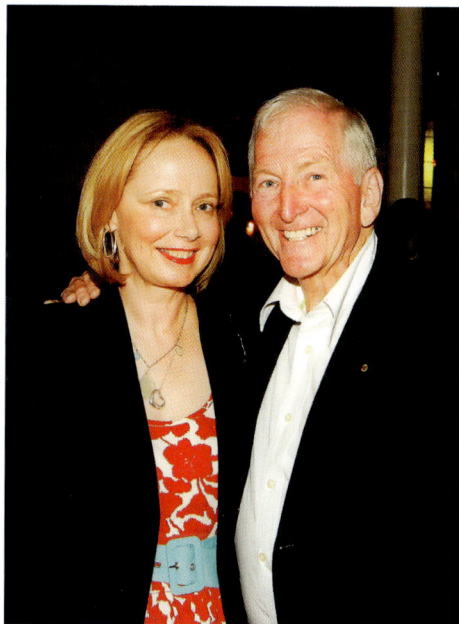

In 2005 – and much to my surprise – Bryce and I came together as a couple. We are pictured here at the launch of *Sylvia* in 2006. Photograph from the author's collection.

The marketing campaigns for Bryce's books were always exciting and innovative. To mark the launch of *Brother Fish*, the cover was splashed upon the sails of a yacht that crossed Sydney Harbour. Photograph from the author's collection.

Top: Bryce and I loved exploring wild and beautiful places together. In 2007 we embarked on a journey to Patagonia.

Photograph from the author's collection.

Left: Africa always resided in Bryce's soul. He returned to Kenya with friends in October 2010 and they completed the Great Walk of Africa guided by Iain Allan, founder of Tropical Ice. Bryce is pictured wearing the green shirt.

Photography by Kerry Freeman.

On 21 October 2011 we celebrated
the joyous occasion of our marriage.
Our special day was shared with family
and friends – including Bryce's beloved
grandchildren, Jake, Marcus and Ben –
at Point Piper's Royal Motor Yacht Club.
Photography by Autumn Mooney.

Bryce at home in Canberra with
Timmy, our dog, and Ophelia, now the
only surviving pet.
Photography of Bryce and Timmy by Tim Bauer:
timbauerphoto.myportfolio.com; photograph of
Ophelia from the author's collection.

Left: When not behind his desk, Bryce was happiest in his garden. We are pictured here under the cherry blossom in our front garden in Canberra.
Photography by Tim Bauer: timbauerphoto.myportfolio.com.

Below: Ben, Bryce, Brett and me at Parliament House, Canberra, where Bryce was awarded an Honorary Doctorate by the University of Canberra – becoming Dr Bryce Courtenay AM on 28 September 2012.
Photography by Michelle McAulay.

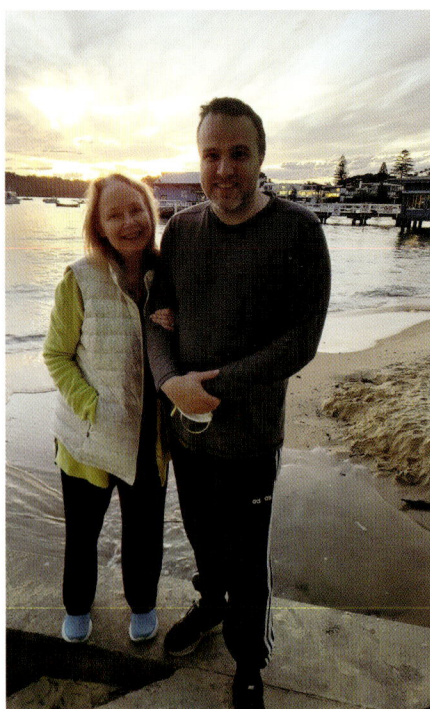

Top: Inside Bryce's study in Canberra, where he wrote his final novel, *Jack of Diamonds*. Photograph from the author's collection.

Left: Enjoying a harbourside walk at Watsons Bay with my son Nima, May 2022. Photography by a family friend.

twenty-one hours and thirty-three minutes was narrated by Australian actor Humphrey Bower, who went on to narrate most of Bryce's books in a masterly fashion. Estimates vary, but sales of *The Power of One* now number well into the millions.

Bryce saw himself as a storyteller and an entertainer, and that sat very well in his skin for every book he wrote, but being popular did not come without its costs. Throughout his writing life he had to wrestle with criticism of the literary merit of his work. He wrote for his readers and no one else, and valued their opinions above others. He was bewildered as to why any writer wouldn't want to be popular as he explained to Roger Maynard: 'The opposite was to be unpopular, and what was the point of that?' The director of book-lovers' organisation Better Reading, Cheryl Akle, a renowned reading and writing champion, met Bryce on several occasions and said, 'He was one of the first authors to understand the connection with the readers.'

Indeed, his success was testament to the masterpiece his novel was subsequently called. He deservedly secured his place in literary history for having written a classic book that has survived the passage of time. I believe Bryce was a consummate storyteller whose books' literary qualities were often undervalued. In August 1998, critic Ramona Koval commented in *The Age*, 'He's a good ad man: he knows what touches people. He's a salesman who can sell a story.' Acclaimed publisher Louise Adler took her praise a step further, also published in *The Age*: 'I think he's a very good popular fiction writer. I want book review pages to take him seriously and review him seriously.'

Bryce was understandably concerned as to how *The Power of One* would be received in South Africa. On 5 April 1988 he wrote to Paddy:

> I am already well into the sequel [*Tandia*], which involves the same characters, but this time as adults. This could well involve

my coming over to do research for a few weeks. In the event of my book being banned, I too would be banned from entering the country, so may have to do so some time this year. Although, I can't think when.

He needn't have worried, as by 3 January 1989 he was able to tell Paddy about the intense anticipation for his book in the region: 'The Power of One has been received in South Africa by Heinemann with great enthusiasm and the CNA [bookstore chain] has slotted it for the major new release this year.' The book continues to be cited as the most popular novel read in South Africa, which is a remarkable achievement; I gather it is still often listed as a set text in the school curriculum.

Bryce travelled to South Africa in 1989 for a promotional book tour. Upon arrival he announced he would be donating all the South African royalties to provide educational bursaries for a charity called Ziphakamise, co-founded by his sister, Rosemary. It was based in KwaZulu-Natal, where they had largely grown up, and Bryce went on to become its major benefactor. He took great joy in seeing the positive outcomes of his support, and both Rosemary and Esmund stayed working at 'Z' for twenty years.

Bryce also spent time in Johannesburg with his dear friend Lydia Blumberg, whom he called 'the Duchess' and who was the primary force behind his book becoming such a monumental success in South Africa. In early 2022 her daughter, Barbara Goldin, told me the remarkable story of how her mother had been committed to making sure The Power of One was read by as many people as possible. Although Lydia's father died when she was twelve and she left school at sixteen, reading was her passion and she ended up working for Joseph's Bookstore founded in Johannesburg in 1951 (this later became Exclusive Books, which now has forty branches). She oversaw the book club orders and made sure that every one of them embraced Bryce's book, which in turn created a sales tsunami. Lydia and her husband, Harry, and Bryce were kindred spirits. They met for the last time in September 2010. Sadly, Harry passed away in 2012, while Lydia passed away in Johannesburg on 22 December 2021 at the age of ninety-four. I treasure a little red box of Krugerrand (gold coins) they once sent us as a special gift.

While still on tour Bryce met up with Rosemary and Paddy, who was now living in a residential home at the Flower Foundation in Port Shepstone in KwaZulu-Natal. He had dedicated *The Power of One* to her as 'Maude Jasmine Greer' and to her best friend, Enda Murphy, writing 'Here is the book I promised you so long ago'. However, this wasn't enough to deter his mother and Rosemary from having misgivings about the book. Bryce came to understand that they never entirely accepted that it was a work of fiction. Possibly not helped with his reference to a character with the surname of Cunningham-Ryder in the novel! Maybe they were upset with him for including aspects of his upbringing that in their eyes cast shame on the family. The family went on to benefit from its spectacular success, however, and they always warmly acknowledged and appreciated Bryce's unfailing generosity and kindness towards them.

Bryce had tried to appease their concerns in a letter to Paddy on 19 January 1987: 'I do hope you are not expecting an autobiographical novel, for while location and some incidents will be familiar to you, the characters are, and the action is, fiction.' On 3 January 1989 he wrote:

Peekay's mother is a somewhat neurotic woman, which is important within the scheme of things. However, I feel sure that you would not wish to be identified as the character in the book, which would plainly be unjust and untrue. You are advised, right from the outset, to say that the book is a work of <u>fiction</u>, who's author happens to be your son.

Long after his mother had passed away, Bryce felt bound to debate the nature of the novel with Rosemary – a situation he found tedious and unsettling. On 29 October 2008, he sent her a forthright email in a final attempt to resolve her concerns:

As an example of this ongoing moral judgement imposed on me by our mother when I wrote *The Power of One*, a book that has since become a classic in the country in which we were born and in the two countries we have chosen to spend the remainder of our lives . . . her only comment was, 'One day you will write a decent book.' In saying this she was exercising the same bigotry and censure she had imposed on us as a child, but while the remark hurt me, it did no further damage and simply confirmed what I already knew and had long since rejected . . .

I have never asserted that *The Power of One* was an autobiography and always presented it as a novel in which I used some of the experiences of my childhood . . . It is printed, presented and sold as a work of fiction and I have never pretended otherwise. You on the other hand have clearly decided that the woman in the story was our mother upon whom I was passing judgement and the major character PK was meant to be a vainglorious version of myself. This thought had never occurred to me. If it had, why then would I have dedicated the novel to our mother?

Despite these tensions surrounding the book, Bryce was always fiercely loyal and supportive of his mother and sister, and I am certain that they felt hugely proud of his novel *The Power of One*, and the books that followed. Their extended family share this pride in all that Bryce achieved both in life and in writing. In September 2012 Bryce said in an interview at our home in Canberra that *Whitethorn*, published in 2005, was in fact far more autobiographical than his debut novel.

What makes the creation of his first novel even more remarkable is that Bryce had spent most of his early childhood speaking Afrikaans and some Zulu, far more often than he had spoken 'the infected tongue of English'. He only spoke English during the fragmented periods in his life when he was at home living with his mother or spending time with his relatives. Even then, Bryce told me, he and Rosemary often spoke to each other in Afrikaans to conceal their childhood 'adventures'. His secondary-school studies at KES were conducted in English, but after leaving school Bryce had to work hard to improve his English skills. He was constantly poring over dictionaries and fretted constantly about how long it was taking him to make any progress. After reading the letters he wrote to his mother I noticed that his grammar and spelling were indeed deficient. I even wondered if he suffered from a level of dyslexia, which he discussed with me but whatever it was it didn't hold him back one bit! There is little doubt that Bryce's editors over the years have had their work cut out for them.

My friend Sherri Reginato, who did an incredible job transcribing Bryce's letters for this book, wrote to me in March 2022, 'How Bryce ever became a bestselling author is in some ways amazing given that his letters confirm he had big issues with his spelling and grammar.' His deficiencies in English were clearly overcome over time, and certainly he had the largest vocabulary of anyone I have known.

The year 1989, when *The Power of One* was published, was marked by a number of significant events. The 14th Dalai Lama, whom Bryce and I had the honour of meeting at Canberra's Parliament House in 2011, won the Nobel Prize; China brutally suppressed the pro-democracy rallies in Tiananmen Square; and devastation was unleashed when a magnitude 6.9 earthquake hit the San Francisco Bay area, killing sixty-seven people. In literary terms, Kazuo Ishiguro's *The Remains of the Day* claimed the Booker Prize, and *Caribbean* by James A. Michener and *The Russia House* by John le Carré were topping the bestseller lists. A year later, on 11 February 1990, South Africa's greatest national hero, Nelson Mandela, was released after serving twenty-seven years in prison.

In a professional sense, the success of *The Power of One* was the best thing that ever happened to Bryce. His lifelong dream of becoming a writer had been realised and his very first book was an international bestseller. The phrase 'the power of one' was absorbed into the vernacular and continues to be liberally used in reference to people achieving great things. Bryce used to say to me playfully that he and I were 'the power of two'! People often asked him what he meant by 'the power of one'; he responded with several different answers, but each related to the individual triumphing over adversity. One answer he gave – on both *Talking Heads* with Peter Thompson on the ABC in 2006 and *A Current Affair* with Tracy Grimshaw on Channel 9 in 2012, was that it was 'the power to be able to say "Och man don't hit me and I'll tell you a story" and I learnt never to tell them the end'. In the former interview he said:

> People read my book *The Power of One* and they think it's all about individual character and they discover this wonderful mantra, the power of one, but . . . I named it . . . after a Miss Bornstein, this power of one teacher who lifted this child out of an impossible environment and allowed him to have an education and escape and discover whatever he was capable of becoming.

Bryce repeated this in an interview with journalist Tim Ayliffe published after Bryce died: 'Miss Bornstein was the inspiration for *The Power of One*, a story [Bryce] told me was about one person's ability to touch another and empower them to help themselves.'

Bryce's long-time publisher, Penguin Books Australia, recorded an extensive interview with him towards the end of his life in which he talked of Miss Bornstein and her significance in his life's journey:

> It was the first time I'd been shown any kindness. I asked her to teach me to read. By the time I was twelve I had memorised that book. The point is I fell in love with words – the power of words, what words could actually do to a person. After she left, Miss Bornstein wrote to me every month and sent me three books and a little exam paper on what was in them. When I was eleven, Miss Bornstein said I should sit for a scholarship for a very posh

school in Johannesburg. She said it was unlikely I would pass but it would be good practice for the following year. Well I sat the exam and passed. I won the scholarship. Without her I wouldn't be here today; she changed everything for me.

Following the book's success Bryce's material fortunes rose significantly and he was able to make a living from being a writer of fiction. He had always fervently believed that the harder you worked, the luckier you became, although he would occasionally refer to himself as 'Lucky Courtenay' when the stars aligned in his favour. He continued to wholeheartedly believe that it was a miracle *The Power of One* had ever been published, describing it as 'a spontaneous outpouring that I didn't think would be seen by anyone'. He reaffirmed this in the ABC *Family Confidential* interview, saying, 'When *Power of One* became big time I was caught completely off guard, and I thought it was a fluke, and I just went on working and writing till midnight.' He would also lament how many well-written books, far better than his, never saw the light of day. It is testament to his self-belief that he made his own publishing success happen, as the odds were surely stacked against him from the moment he was born. In his interview with Peter Thompson, Bryce reflected on the unlikelihood of his success:

Remember I was from the boondocks and the dizzy heights of ambition for me and the other kids in the orphanage were to end up being a railway fettler or a road worker or a tractor driver. Then this tiny crack opens for you and suddenly you see the world from a different perspective. Looking down, you see that people aren't there simply because they were born like that but because of their circumstances, and I was there because of circumstances.

He lived his life always believing, as he wrote in his novel, 'Pride is holding your head up when everyone around you has theirs bowed. Courage is what makes you do it.'

Regardless of the fortune he made (and sometimes lost), Bryce never seemed to stop feeling stalked by the threat of impoverishment. He dreaded ending up alone and homeless like the people he had befriended in the parks of Johannesburg during his school holidays so many years before. This drove him to keep writing until he could write no more, which seems rather a shame, but I believe he wouldn't have wanted it any other way.

I also believe that *The Power of One* was the ultimate expression of him overcoming his own tough beginnings and becoming the person that deep down he always believed he could be. While working down the mines, he said to Peter Thompson, 'I realised how cheap my life was but also how precious it was. I learnt to value my life and not to throw it away.' Years later, on *Family Confidential*, he claimed that *The Power of One* was 'an exaggerated version of my own life'. In the Foreword to the commemorative edition of *The Power of One* published in 2012 (also included in *The Silver Moon*), Bryce wrote:

> I'd had to pull myself up by the bootstraps, so I believe in the capacity of every human being to triumph and to achieve anything . . . But remember Peekay is larger than life, as fictional characters need to be. So think of it as the things that happened to me but with a character better than I ever was.

No doubt his millions of readers around the world will have come to their own conclusions as to what 'the power of one' means to them, and surely the true test of a novel is its power to speak and connect in different ways to different readers. I have the privilege of regularly liaising with over 60 000 of Bryce's devoted readers on the 'Bryce Courtenay' Facebook page, and their loyalty and continuing passion for his books is truly remarkable. Most of us only read a book once, but I believe *The Power of One* is a novel that deserves to be re-read. Many of Bryce's readers tell me they have read it more than twenty times – some even claim they go back and re-read it every single year. Not a bad outcome for a middle-aged man who sat down and wrote his first novel believing it was going to be nothing more than a practice book!

Bryce's greatest wish was that we never give up on finding our own power of one, just as he didn't in overcoming the travails of an early life often filled with loneliness, abandonment, shame and fear. In the ABC interview for *Family Confidential* he shared that:

> The mantra behind *The Power of One* is 'First with the head then with the heart'. Whatever happens you can overcome. Almost every one of us has a mountain to climb. This is a book that says, 'You can do it, kid.' It gave the readers hope and took them some way up the mountain.

A quote from another interview – this time from an article by Paul Dean published in the *Los Angeles Times*, 3 August 1989 – sheds further light on his understanding of the phrase:

> The power of one is that thing that makes all people who have a tendency to succeed, succeed. It is the highest level of personal survival. I really believe that life is a question of letdowns and broken contracts. We can exist within that situation or we can prevail. The power of one is the person who insists he will prevail.

As to whom Bryce thought was the embodiment of the power of one, the answer, he told me in September 2012, was Mahatma Gandhi. He said Gandhi was an astonishing character whom he admired enormously for achieving freedom for his people from British colonial rule by nonviolent means. On another occasion Bryce told me his greatest respect was reserved for wives and mothers and single fathers and grandparents bringing up children. He never forgot how they tended to their children, often after being at work all day and then arriving home dog-tired, and making sure everyone is fed and washed, and feels safe. In the end Bryce believed that these were the people who truly embodied the power of one, and he wrote for them. He said many times, 'My only aspiration has ever been that someone will put aside twenty minutes at night to read one of my books before going to sleep and think "gee, I want to read a bit more."'

'Absoloodle!'

Writing the book proved to be a cathartic process for Bryce and a vehicle by which he could confront the trials of his childhood, which he had kept a lid on for over fifty years. As it was a work of fiction, he did not have to directly confront the anguish of that time but instead was free to indulge his imagination and allow the story to travel wherever his subconscious and creativity took him.

I think back to the 'loneliness birds' who appear throughout the novel and how they are central to understanding who Bryce was. Their symbolic presence records the innate loneliness that I believe he continued to feel to some extent throughout his life. Bryce shed some light on this in his interview with Peter Thompson: 'C.S. Lewis said people read so they know they are not alone and in a sense that's why I'm writing, so I know I'm not alone.' I am always very moved to read the end of Chapter 8, where Peekay realises that he has grown up, because the loneliness birds have stopped laying stone eggs inside him. I hope that in the end those loneliness birds were banished from Bryce's life as well.

Certainly, he was adamant he would never write an autobiography. As he said to me in September 2012, 'The significant thing is that I am a storyteller, and that these stories are significant. An autobiography? It's a bit too grand, to be honest, for someone like me.' Bryce told me he knew that one day a biography of his life would probably be written, but during his lifetime he was more than happy to be tap-tapping away on another novel, digging in the garden or watching a game of Rugby with Timmy snoring at his feet.

But Bryce knew better than anyone that life is full of unexpected turns. Within two years of his experiencing the stratospheric success of his debut novel, he found himself having to draw on his own power of one to endure the greatest tragedy of his life.

10

FAME AND FORTUNE

Remember. whatever the dream, no matter how daring or grand, somebody will eventually achieve it. It might as well be you. – A Recipe for Dreaming

FAME AND FORTUNE FOLLOWED the phenomenal success of *The Power of One*, and Bryce took to both like a duck to water. He had already achieved a level of fame in the world of advertising, but with the publication of his remarkable debut novel he rapidly became famous the world over. He had earlier felt reticent about the prospect of celebrity status, writing to his mother in early 1989: 'I must confess to being somewhat bemused by the whole thing and I am not much looking forward to the celebrity status which seems inevitable for the writer of a successful novel.'

The advance Bryce received for *The Power of One* was significant for a debut novel, and in the years that followed Bryce became one of the few Australian writers who could make a living from writing – and he did this by writing a book each year. Yet money wasn't the driving factor that motivated Bryce: 'Money doesn't interest me in the slightest. Life isn't about having things – it's about doing things.' In *A Recipe for Dreaming* he wrote, 'You either make more money than you need without being bored in the process, or you discover that you don't really need all that fiscal security to live happily ever after. You also die smiling.'

Most people don't realise that following the success of *The Power of One* Bryce stayed on working as a creative director at George Patterson. His eldest son, Brett, had also started working at Patts, in the account services division (he later took up an executive role in a company based in South-East Asia).

It wasn't long before Bryce couldn't go into a supermarket or travel on a plane without being stopped by fans requesting autographs and photos. He never refused, regarding obliging each request as a small gesture of gratitude. The interaction allowed Bryce to understand his readers better, and before long he could describe what they ate for breakfast, the kind of car they drove and whether or not they were happy in their marriage! He would say, 'Give me half an hour with anyone and I can almost tell you their life story.'

Funnily enough, at one time as a young boy it was music and not writing that he believed would lead him to fame and fortune: 'I had this burning desire as a kid to play the mouth organ. I'd bring crowds of people to a hall, but I couldn't play – never got past "God Save the Queen!"'

Bryce's relationship with his readers was a key component of his success. He possessed an instinct for knowing how to connect with them, and they couldn't wait to buy a new book by him the moment it was released. Like Enid Blyton, one of his childhood literary heroes, he wrote for them and no one else. He worked to the mantra 'The reader is always right' and referred to the reader as 'the fourth protagonist'. The dynamism of this relationship fuelled a tornado of excitement and allowed him to take the publishing world by storm. As he explained in an interview with Neil Shoebridge for the *Australian Financial Review*, 'The best advertising for any product is two women talking about it over the back fence. That is what I want for my books.' It was an approach that reframed how publishing went about its business selling books.

Within a year of *The Power of One* being released, an option for the movie was taken up by Village Roadshow Pictures. The subsequent film was directed by John G. Avildsen and shot in Zimbabwe. Bryce travelled to the set and met the cast, including Stephen Dorff (who played Peekay), John Gielgud, Morgan Freeman and Daniel Craig. The movie was released on 27 March 1992, distributed by Warner Brothers and Roadshow Entertainment, but it received mixed reviews. I rather liked it when I saw it at a cinema in Sydney a year before I met Bryce, and the very next day I bought and began to read the book and couldn't put it down.

Bryce wasn't a big fan of the film. He said it was an impressive production but offered a simplistic portrayal of his story. However, he loved the musical score created by Hans Zimmer and also felt honoured that so many distinguished actors had roles. Bryce was also thrilled that an Australian, Dean Semler, was responsible for the cinematography. The movie undoubtedly increased sales of the book and brought Bryce's work to a wider, international audience.

Bryce's marketing instincts were finely tuned from his decades in the advertising industry, and he unashamedly applied them to the marketing of his books, insisting on being closely involved with the marketing plans for each one. This was important as *The Power of One* was initially only released in the United States, Australia and the United Kingdom and he hankered for it to reach the rest of the world. He needn't have worried: soon, literary agents were queuing up to secure territorial rights and have it published in their home countries. Alex Hamill told me that Bryce even wrote the copy for the Australian television advertisement for *The Power of One*.

He worked hard to persuade his publisher at that time to perceive the marketing of books just as he did, and at first he was frustrated by their approach, as quoted in the *Australian Financial Review*: 'Most publishing directors read literature, not popular fiction, yet they set themselves up as the arbiters of what people want to read. It is unbelievably stupid.' As far as Bryce was concerned, books should be sold wherever people went about their daily lives – in petrol stations and supermarkets, and big retail stores such as Kmart and Big W. At the time this was a radical idea as the industry was used to readers only buying books from bookstores.

Bryce also wholeheartedly subscribed to the old marketing adage 'There is no point inventing a better mousetrap if no one knows about it'. That was never going to be a problem for him. He said, 'A book should be promoted in the same way as a can of baked beans. Both are consumer goods.' He was ahead of the curve with the marketing thinking behind his books, always looking for the new technology, new ways of doing things, finding new channels and platforms through which he could reach his readers.

As part of the marketing campaigns for his books, cover designs were splashed across the sails of yachts skimming across Sydney Harbour, in sky writing spun by planes across the sky, and on motorway signboards, airport lightwalls, tram and bus stops and cinema screens. Sample chapters of his latest release were handed out to commuters at railway stations, and he insisted his publisher organise focus groups so that readers could select their favourite cover designs. In his own way he was spearheading a revolution in the way books were marketed, and today's writers are reaping the rewards.

He took a similar approach to publicity. From the outset Bryce participated in hundreds of media interviews, often doing up to twenty a day during a book tour. He also believed that doing interviews when a book came out wasn't enough and made himself available to talk to journalists nearly 365 days a year!

The bookstore owners loved him too, as they knew that when a new Bryce Courtenay book hit the shelves, their tills would run hot. Importantly, a new Bryce book brought in consumers and they often went on to purchase other titles. Bryce's books also brought focus to the possibilities of selling books to chain stores, and thereby connected a whole new audience to books. Bryce also appreciated how hard booksellers worked and went out of his way to do booksignings and events as part of his publicity tours. With each new release Bryce would sign thousands of books at bookstores and shopping centres. Bryce said he was bewildered by writers reluctant to go out on the hustings and sell their book and talk about it. In addition, he delivered keynote speeches at literary lunches and dinners in a packed schedule that writers half his age would have struggled to keep up with. After each speech, he would stay until every person in line had had their book personally signed.

Alex Hamill later said in an interview in the *Sydney Morning Herald*, 'Bryce is, beyond anything else, a *promoter*. There are some great authors in Australia, and I know many of them, who won't get off their bums and sign books in shopping centres.' Another of Bryce's much-loved advertising mates, the late Owen Denmeade, joked, 'We used to say, if you've got an unsigned copy of a Bryce Courtenay book, it's worth a lot of money!' Owen amassed a huge collection of Bryce memorabilia, some of which gave me precious insights for this memoir. He adored Bryce, whom he called 'Peekay'. In 1997 Jennifer Byrne, who was then publishing director at Reed, commented on the phenomenon that was Bryce:

> [Bryce] really, really wants the readers and forms an intensely strong relationship with them. He will do almost anything short of jumping up and down in a clown suit outside David Jones. He is also very serious about his writing. That's why there is only one Bryce Courtenay.

Bryce was mindful of the role of each person involved in the successful publication of his books. In the Acknowledgements section of each title, he was careful to personally thank individuals who had had direct involvement. He also never forgot the important role of the publishing sales reps and made sure they were invited to marketing planning sessions. Even the typesetters and printers were not forgotten, and each Christmas Bryce would pay for their teams to enjoy a barbecue and drinks for their incredible efforts in getting his books printed on time.

With publication scheduled each November, Christmas was the time when Bryce's book sales really took off. He always said, 'I belong with the socks and the chocolates under the Christmas tree, and that's just fine by me.' Thousands of his readers still tell me, 'I so miss having Bryce's latest book waiting to be opened under my tree.' With this memoir, I hope their prayers will be at least partially answered!

These early years awash with success as a bestselling author following the publication of *The Power of One* were tempered by the heartbreaking reality of Bryce and Benita's youngest son Damon's increasingly desperate battle to survive. At the most successful time in Bryce's life, his family – and especially Damon and his partner, Celeste – were going through an unimaginably difficult time. Bryce wrote about this in a letter to Rosemary on 29 June 1990:

> Damon has been through a very tough time and on one or two occasions I've felt he was about to go, but he's always rallied and pulled through . . . Sometimes, when he can't find the strength to continue he feels that 'it comes to him out of the air'. His expression, not mine.

Even with this anguish and heartache swirling around him, Bryce was bound by the pressure of a contract to finish writing his second novel, *Tandia*. He had begun it within weeks of finishing *The Power of One*, and by the middle of 1990 it was nearly complete. He knew that if it was successful he might be able to leave his job in advertising and become a full-time writer. In doing so he would be relieved of the punishing regimen of working up to eighty hours a week, which even he must have known couldn't be sustained.

Bryce enjoyed writing the sequel, while quietly trembling that he might end up being known as a one-book wonder. He knew the critics would be baying for blood, and this weighed on his mind, as told to Diana Ritch: 'All the sharks are standing by and they're standing on the edge of the feeding ground, and they've had a good hunk out of you in your first book . . . in the first book it was easy, you sat down, you had nothing to lose, you went for broke and you got lucky.'

He ended up completing *Tandia* while he was in London with the family, including Celeste and Damon. It was a desperate time for them all as Damon was so unwell, and finishing the manuscript on time became an almost impossible undertaking. As Benita confirmed in *April Fool's Day*: 'Bryce was forced to remain in London for a further three weeks to complete his novel *Tandia*, which was behind deadline, and we returned the morning after he completed writing the last page and we delivered it on the way to the airport to Laura Longrigg, his editor.'

Now, in the clutches of medically contracted HIV, and to the unimaginable heartache of his beloved family and friends, Damon's health continued to decline. Tragically he eventually lost the battle and passed away on 1 April 1991, aged twenty-four. All those close to him were understandably devastated, with Bryce saying in his interview with Diana Ritch, 'He made life such a joy for all of us that really he was an absolutely special gift.'

Tandia was published internationally in the same year. The dedication in the first edition published by William Heinemann reads: 'For Damon Courtenay my son. Who through all the bad years never once asked, "Why me?"' The opening words of the novel are both confronting and compelling: 'On the morning she was raped Tandia had risen just before dawn and come back to the graveside to pay her proper respects to Patel.' The story is told in the third person, in an adult's voice, unlike the child's voice of Peekay in *The Power of One*. It's a tale of impossible odds set in a South Africa struggling to find hope. Bryce was sometimes bothered by this, as he revealed in the Diana Ritch interview:

> I often wonder why I should write a book of hope for South Africa when the reality says to you that there is none . . . The only way that you could ever solve problems with people is to understand them and if I talk about the fusing of two bodies in perfect love, as I did, and I said *Tandia*'s a love story, in a sense the metaphor continues for a country.

Tandia was well received and became a number-one bestseller, even though it wasn't liked by all his readers, some of whom couldn't forgive Bryce for killing off Peekay in the book: 'Peekay launched himself into the silver air. This time he seemed to float and the old witchdoctor's voice came to him again, but from a distance. "You are wearing the skirt of the lion tail as you face into the setting sun."'

Bryce began writing *April Fool's Day* – his first major work of non-fiction – not long after Damon passed away. Following this profound loss Bryce began to withdraw from working in advertising, both to grieve and to support his family. Damon had begged him to write a book about him, and in one of many interviews Bryce quoted his son saying, 'Dad, you've got to tell the world that AIDS isn't a punishment from God. It's just a virus and you've got to tell them.' No doubt writing Damon's story was inevitably a way of processing his own loss and managing his own grief was a heartwrenching process. He confided to Rosemary on 14 February 1992 the toll of writing the book:

> *April Fool's Day*, the writing of, has simply been the most difficult thing I have ever attempted, and I shall be glad when I can put my grief to rest. I think 1991/2 have been the two most difficult years of my life. I sometimes fear I shall never stop grieving for my son.

Bryce was an incredibly versatile writer, attested in the first instance by his long career in advertising. He demonstrated a seemingly effortless capacity to shift genres and embrace new readers. This was reinforced with the publication in 1992 of *A Recipe for Dreaming*, which contains beautiful illustrations by Ann Williams. In the introduction he wrote:

> One of the nicest things to happen to me after I'd written *The Power of One* is that it has become a book which young people seem to enjoy a lot. They write to me or they come to see me and the question I am most often asked is: 'Can you help me to decide what to do with my life?' So I wrote this little book and quite a lot

of people – not only young people – seemed to like it, even take courage from it.

As if Bryce wasn't busy enough, in 1992 The Pitch was also released, which comprised a collection of newspaper columns he had written over several years for the The Australian. As for leaving the world of advertising, he began to consider heeding the advice he had once given an industry colleague, as published in the Campaign Brief: 'Advertising is great at preparing you to succeed at whatever you decide to do with your life. Just don't stay in it too long, otherwise you'll become one of those grumpy old farts in the corner office.'

So in 1992, after thirty-four years in the industry, Bryce left advertising to focus on writing books full time. He was following in the wake of others who had left advertising to pursue their creative passions beyond writing ads for breakfast cereal, including the American writer James Patterson and the Australian writers Peter Carey and Phillip Adams. Bryce's close friends Derek Hansen, Paul Wilson, Geoff Pike and the artist Ken Done also left and became highly successful authors, and in Ken's case, a visual artist.

Bryce completed April Fool's Day late that year and it was published by William Heinemann Australia in 1993. The moving dedication reads: 'This is Damon's book and it is for Benita and Celeste, whom he loved with all his heart. To his love and gratitude I add my own.' Bryce told me that he was determined to make the book a story of hope and inspiration as well as a love story, which indeed it is. An important motivation in writing it was to lobby the medical profession and relevant authorities to install better blood screening, and to urge more understanding and compassion in the community for those living with HIV and AIDS. This did happen, with many doctors and nurses confirming it to Bryce after the book was released. Damon, along with other HIV and AIDS sufferers, had endured a lot of stigma surrounding his illness.

April Fool's Day was the only work of autobiographical nonfiction Bryce ever wrote. Following its publication he visited twenty-nine

Australian country towns in twenty-seven days, signing books and giving talks to local communities. The response was overwhelming, and he told me later that emotionally this publicity tour was one of the most harrowing experiences of his life. Sometimes in the early mornings years later, he would wake up sobbing and I would ask him how he was able to go on after Damon died. The loss of Damon was something he'd never get over as he described in an interview at home in 2012:

> You don't move on. You pack it into a little private room in your brain where only you have the key. And you can go in and unlock the door and visit the room and visit the tragedy and visit your son. I suppose at least once a month, perhaps even more, I wake up with tears in my eyes and I take the key and I open the door and say, 'Good morning, Damon, how are you today?' You never, ever, ever get over it. Nobody does. We all share tragedy just as much as we share joy, and it is a part of life, and we can't avoid it. Life is like that and the whole of it is a beautiful process.

In February 1994 Bryce returned to South Africa to take part in a television documentary. This was two months before the 27 April elections that saw Nelson Mandela inaugurated as the nation's first black president on 10 May 1994. Being in the midst of a tidal wave of long-dreamt-of hope, Bryce said, was 'a phenomenal and moving experience' and a situation he couldn't have imagined coming to pass after what he had witnessed growing up. He travelled with the film crew to Limpopo Province and they visited his former primary school in Barberton. He said he was thrilled when they found his name recorded in the student enrolment books. They then went to see Paddy, who was now aged eighty-eight and living in Port Shepstone at the Villa Bruno Care Centre with Bryce happily funding all her expenses, just as he had done from when he was a young man.

Tom Krause, the documentary's director, wrote a story about this trip called 'Bryce Courtenay: Hamburgers on the road to Apartheid':

> On day 10 of the shoot, we went to King Edward School (known locally as KES) in Johannesburg, and Bryce addressed a class of sixth formers about his life and his most famous novel, *The Power of One*, partly set in KES. He told them how emotional he felt, returning to his old school and finding it was integrated. He even got a bit teary, and we put a radio microphone on him, and sure enough he got teary again. You could say it was manufactured the second time around (shades of *Broadcast News*), but there was no doubt: they were real tears. The students didn't seem to mind; they loved him. And there was a voter education class for the upcoming elections going on in the same hall where Bryce had started a weekend school for Africans, which the principal and the South African Police had closed.

In 1995 Bryce was honoured by being appointed a Member of the Order of Australia (AM) in recognition of his service to advertising and marketing to the community, and as an author. He was hugely proud to receive this but seemed even more excited when he learnt in 2012 that I was also going to be awarded an AM, in recognition of my efforts as a founding board member of the Australian Himalayan Foundation, and for progressing relations between Australia and Nepal during my tenure as honorary consul-general to Nepal for over twenty years.

Also in 1995, Bryce, along with his mate and fellow author Geoff Pike, played an instrumental role in a new venture. The Yowies were a collection of cartoon characters based around the idea of educating children about native wildlife conservation. The boys dreamt up a series of names around Australian native animals, including Boof the Bottlebrush, Crag the Mangrove, Rumble the Redgum, Squish the Fiddlewood, Ditty the Lillipilli and Nap the Honeygum. Cadbury produced a confectionary item for each character and they were a monumental success, with a million chocolate Yowies being sold across Australia every week. The characters later appeared in a series of children's books that have now become collector's items.

Also published in 1995 was a book that Bryce co-authored with marketing expert Ian Kennedy called *The Power of One to One*, which was essentially a textbook about direct marketing. On 12 October that year, he was a guest on the Nine Network's *This Is Your Life* program, hosted by Mike Munro. Bryce was overcome with emotion and gratitude to his family and all the guests who were interviewed. Not surprisingly, the program rated its socks off.

Bryce used to talk about how as a small boy he learnt about camouflage and that the best way of staying hidden was to lead from the front. Staying out in front as an author was always uppermost in his mind. 1995 also marked the year he began work on a series of books he called the Australian Trilogy, the first being *The Potato Factory*. He said, 'I was teethed on Dickens', and there is no question that he chose Ikey Solomon to be his central character just as Dickens chose the mean-spirited Fagin, 'the receiver of stolen goods', to star in *Oliver Twist*. The first book in the trilogy, *The Potato Factory*, was published by William Heinemann Australia in 1995.

The Australian Trilogy charted the arrival of convicts to Van Diemen's Land, the Māori Wars in New Zealand, and Australia's coming-of-age story with the Gallipoli campaign. Bryce travelled to Turkey and walked along the beach at Anzac Cove where the Gallipoli campaign had taken place. It was a seminal experience for him, and he found the scale of the losses there almost impossible to take in. I still have a small stone on my desk that he collected on that beach. These huge sagas were vintage Bryce Courtenay, with larger-than-life characters and adventures written in the context of significant historical events. They are dense with dialogue, which Bryce always said was critical, and, like nearly all of his books, they include a good dose of romance.

In some ways, writing the trilogy was an unusual choice for Bryce given that he had grown up in South Africa, but he felt it was a way of giving back to the country that had taken him to its bosom. He also believed that he was able to bring an outsider's perspective to Australian history, as he shared in an ABC TV news breakfast interview: 'When people read one of my stories, they are actually reading history that is correct. The only thing that is invented is my characters, who are invented within that landscape and I take a great deal of trouble to get it right.' Many Australian readers have said that reading the trilogy was the first time they learnt about their own country's history.

Later in his career, and as a way of giving back, Bryce turned to teaching the art of writing to aspiring authors. He was always mindful of the times he was writing about and would say, 'When you are writing a book, you have to know what was going on in the years you are writing about and then place your narrative into the times your characters are inhabiting.' He explained in his interview with Roger Maynard that his writing students were also instructed to be aware that 'Every story takes place somewhere, and wherever that is you must make sure you know the location, historical period and culture accurately. Don't guess . . . You owe it to your reader or fourth protagonist to take her into a world that truly existed.'

In 1997 William Heinemann published *The Family Frying Pan*, a delightful book complete with recipes and illustrated by Ann Williams, based on the story of Benita's great-grandmother, who walked across Russia carrying a large cast-iron frying pan! It was an edition treasured by Bryce's family – as well as his readers.

That year brought further change for Bryce. After the adult book division of Reed Books, which published the Heinemann imprint, was sold to Random House, he made the big decision to change publisher. This can't have been easy, as he enjoyed working with the team at Reed and felt great admiration for Adrian Collette, Reed's managing director. He landed at Penguin Books Australia, which was a huge coup for Penguin as by then Bryce had become Australia's biggest-selling author. Journalist Neil Shoebridge confirmed some of the details in the *Australian Financial Review*: 'The bidding for Courtenay . . . was intense: Penguin won with a rumoured $2 million advance and a promise to improve the way Courtenay's books are distributed and marketed.'

Publishing Director Bob Sessions expanded on how Penguin won Bryce over in an interview with Caroline Baum:

> One publisher sent in the big guns from overseas – well, that didn't impress him . . . Some others had not even read his books. In the end, it was a beauty contest between us and Pan Macmillan and minor things tipped the balance in our favour . . . I interviewed his friends and colleagues, asked what his favourite restaurant was. So we took him to Lucio's in Sydney, and there our publisher, Julie Gibbs, noted which was his favourite wine. When he came to see us in Melbourne, she ordered that wine and he noticed.

As part of Penguin's pitch to Bryce, the company invited him to visit its head office and adjoining warehouse, then in Ringwood in Melbourne's outer east. He insisted on meeting each person in every department, and was most excited about visiting the expansive warehouse and meeting the dedicated staff there who facilitated orders and the challenging task of distribution. In the years that followed he would send gifts to those he worked closely with, and always to the warehouse.

Bob became Bryce's long-term publisher, and from the outset it was a very happy partnership. Bryce called him 'Uncle Bob' and used to refer to 'the Penguins' as 'my writing family'. Bob said of Bryce, 'He was a born storyteller, and I would tell him he was a latter-day Charles Dickens with his strong and complex plots, larger-than-life characters and his ability to appeal to a large number of readers.'

Bryce never failed to recognise the support he had from the entire team at Penguin who rode the Bryce Courtenay publishing rollercoaster, including managing director Peter Field and (later) CEO Gabrielle Coyne; publishing director Bob Sessions, publishers Julie Gibbs and Clare Forster; in-house editors Anne Rogan, Rachel Scully and Saskia Adams, freelance copyeditors Kay Ronai and Nan McNab, and a host of proofreaders; Carmen de la Rue, Nicole Brown and Tracey Jarrett in production; marketing directors Dan Ruffino and Sally Bateman; marketing manager Sharlene Vinall; publicity manager Anyez Lindop; and sales director Peter Blake and sales manager Lou Ryan. Peg McColl looked after Bryce's contracts, in consultation with Bryce's own legal advisors, including with Frankel Lawyers, which became his preferred firm. A team of designers from the inhouse design team – including Tony Palmer, Adam Laszczuk and Cathy Larsen – would design a number of cover concepts for each book, which would be taken to marketing focus groups for input. How happy I am that Rachel Scully, who was a member of that team and knew Bryce very well, has worked closely with me on this book, with assistance in the copyedit from former Penguin senior editors Katie Purvis and Saskia Adams. Rachel worked closely with Bob and Nan on a handful of titles towards the end of Bryce's career, including his last book, *Jack of Diamonds*, when he was so desperately ill.

Year on year, a Bryce Courtenay book was published by Penguin to unparallelled success. After Bryce passed away, Bob reflected on the success of Bryce's books:

> No other author has even come close to Courtenay's book sales . . . For many, many years, we all in Australian publishing knew that 100 000 copies were a huge bestseller and some big names from overseas like Wilbur Smith would sell that many at Christmas time. Bryce sold 200 000. He is a phenomenon . . . He outsells any other writer by an enormous margin and has done ever since *The Power of One*.

I'm told Bryce's books played an important role in what has been described as a 'golden age' in Australian publishing at Penguin Books

Australia, enabling a period of highly innovative publishing and championing of Australian talent – something Bryce himself was very much aware of.

A remarkable factor in Bryce's success was that he wrote a book a year. Very few writers could match this output, with many taking years to finish one book. Equally remarkable was the way in which he delivered his work and the way the books were edited and produced. Most authors spend a year or more writing their books and submit the entire manuscript at once, at least several months before the book's scheduled publication date. Bryce always started writing on 1 February, aiming to deliver one chapter each week, and handed the final chapter to Penguin on 31 August, just a week or so before the book was due at the printer. He would send each chapter to Bob and the in-house editor on a Monday, and they would read and discuss it that morning. The editor would provide structural feedback and Bryce would work it up and resubmit for edit by a small team, always including a freelance copyeditor – for many years both Kay and Nan. At no point was any member of the team provided with a summary of the plot or an outline of where Bryce intended to take the story – which made the editorial process challenging! The only time any editor got to see the whole was just before the manuscript was sent to print. The team implored Bryce to deliver a manuscript in full so it could undergo an edit in its entirety rather than chapter by chapter, but he told them many times that he never knew exactly where the story was headed – it unfolded for him week by week, as it did for them.

The first of Bryce's books published by Penguin Books Australia was the sequel to *The Potato Factory*, *Tommo & Hawk*, in 1997. It was an instant bestseller, and won an Australian Publishers Association Reader's Choice Award. *Solomon's Song*, released in 1999, completed the triology. *The Potato Factory* ended up being produced as a television miniseries in 2000, starring Ben Cross and Lisa McCune.

Penguin followed the success of *Tommo & Hawk* in April 1998 with *The Night Country*, which is more a short story than an ambitious saga.

It is a beautifully crafted though confronting story that returns to many of the themes in Bryce's other books set in Africa. Sadly it is now out of print and has also become something of a collector's item.

At the end of 1998 *Jessica* was published, and many readers declared it their favourite of Bryce's novels. In a departure from Bryce's usual approach, it was based on the true story of a woman called Jessica Bergman who suffered a raft of grave injustices. These included her child being taken from her and the loss of 'Jack', the love of her life, who said to her, 'Look after yourself and if you're still there when the war is over, me and some of my mates will break down the walls and rescue you. I love you, Tea Leaf, with all my heart, and will be thinking of you as we go into battle.' Apart from her beloved Jack, the only people who showed Jessica kindness were her friends in the local Indigenous community – reminiscent of Bryce's own childhood, when his closest friends were the black Africans working at the many institutions he lived in.

Jessica's real-life descendants were from the Riverina in south-western New South Wales, and they had contacted Bryce in the hope that he would write her story. He accepted the challenge with a fair amount of trepidation but was passionate about Jessica's story and putting it in print. The family were delighted with the book, and it was later adapted into a highly successful television miniseries that won a string of awards. It also won the Australian Publishers Association Reader's Choice Award in 1999 and 2000. As a gesture of thanks, Jessica's family presented Bryce with a handpainted didgeridoo, which continues to have pride of place in my hallway. Bryce was very touched when years later Taylor Swift, the American singer-songwriter superstar, posted on her website: 'I've always loved reading his books. He's a brilliant author and I'm saddened by the news of his illness. His book *Jessica* I read a couple years back, and it's one of my all-time favourite books. I cried, a lot, while reading it. It was heartbreakingly beautiful.'

Given the changed times and sensitivities of today, I sometimes wonder if Bryce's narratives would now pass the test of political correctness and the current 'woke' environment. He wrote from the heart and was never in fear of what others might say, even though occasionally his editors would attempt to rein him in ('You can't say that!' and 'That section should be toned down'). He would consider backing down if they insisted, but didn't always comply – especially when it came to the passionate love scenes, which he knew his readers loved. He always said they were difficult to write well, as he recorded in *The Persimmon Tree*: 'The trouble with writing about making love – I don't want to call it sex because to me it was much more – is that all the words are worn out.'

On the home front, by the end of the 1990s big life changes were on the horizon for Bryce and Rosemary. In 1997 Rosemary and Esmund moved from South Africa to live in America. Other family members were already there, including their wonderful and devoted daughter, Dorrie. I gather from chatting with Rosemary that while this was a difficult decision, staying on in South Africa had become untenable. While mother and daughter were always very close, Paddy was too frail to contemplate leaving and I understand she never seriously countenanced the idea of doing so.

On 24 May 1999, Bryce's mother, Maud Jessamine Roberts (nee Greer), passed away in South Africa at the age of ninety-three, just days away from her ninety-fourth birthday. Bryce told me he spoke to her by phone just before she died and it was heartbreaking to be so far away, as it would have been for Rosemary too. Paddy had been an enduring link in their lives and, although she was now free of suffering, a feeling of great loss and emptiness descended on Bryce following her passing.

During that same year, after forty-one years of marriage, Bryce and Benita separated. Their divorce was finalised the following year and Bryce described this time as one of the most miserable years of his life. After their separation he moved into the small apartment he owned in Rose Bay, about ten minutes' walk from where Benita was living in Bellevue Hill. Bryce told me that he believed they never really recovered from the loss of Damon, but as with any relationship the reasons may have been more complex. Having been divorced myself I know that even years later you sometimes wonder what you could have done differently, and there is a residual feeling of sadness or even guilt that never completely goes away. Having a family had meant more than anything on earth to Bryce, and the breakdown of his marriage, he said, gave him a feeling of having failed utterly, even though he said he had always done everything he could to support them. It was rather sad to hear him say on *Family Confidential* in 2012: 'I loved being a father . . . I don't know that I was a great father, but I loved being one.'

Bryce told me he left his marriage with a canteen of silver cutlery and a few artworks, books and personal possessions. He was determined that Benita be well provided for and also knew he needed to write further books to get himself back on track financially – something he wasn't fazed by. Following their divorce Bryce and Benita remained on very good terms, and he was loyal and supportive of her. He always felt immense gratitude for her loyalty and love and the enormous contribution she had made to his life, their children and his career.

After the publication of *Jessica*, Bryce returned to historical fiction and wrote *Smoky Joe's Cafe* in 2001, which honours Australia's Vietnam veterans. He received thanks from many who were very grateful to him for telling their story as they had felt shunned upon their return to Australia. Bryce also wrote about the struggle they had (and continue to have) with the effects of the use of Agent Orange in the combat zones where they served: 'There wasn't only Agent Orange, but Agent Blue, Green, Purple, White, you name it, they had a colour for everything and every colour killed something. They sprayed this shit over the jungle like the monsoon rains had come early.'

Four Fires, a saga of a rural small-town Australian family and the triumph of love over adversity, was published the same year. I did a lot of the primary research for this book, which was fascinating. Many readers cite it as their favourite and, given the recurrence of bushfires that ravage our land, often write and tell me it should be on every school's curriculum. Bryce followed this novel with the very different *Matthew Flinders' Cat*, published in 2002, which tells the story of Flinders' circumnavigation of Australia through the eyes of his cat, Trim. Next was *Brother Fish* in 2004, a book of mateship set against the backdrop of the Korean War that was so long Bryce said it should have run to two books. Rachel tells me he called her after it was printed to say, 'You were right, kid – this book would have been better if I'd submitted you the whole thing from the start. It really *did* need more cutting!' Rachel was pregnant when she edited it and luckily delivered late, finishing the final chapter just a few weeks before she gave birth.

In 2005 Bryce began writing another book set in Africa called *Whitethorn*, which he claimed was his most autobiographical novel. I used to drop over for a cup of coffee and a natter and could see the narrative was pouring out of him. I suspect his dedicated editors barely needed to change a thing! The book stars Tom Fitzsaxby, who is growing up in the mountains of Africa on the cusp of the Second World War and learns to survive racial hatred and strive for justice and love. Bryce repeatedly said *Whitethorn* and *Four Fires* were his two best books, and I agree with him.

Bryce ended up writing twenty-one books in twenty-three years, and many of them shot to number one on the bestseller lists. They were all released in Australia, the United Kingdom, New Zealand and Canada, and some were released in South Africa, France, Germany, Japan, China, Taiwan and Italy as well. Only two of his books have been published in the United States, being *The Power of One* and *Tandia*: Bryce realised that to have a chance of making it in America back then he would need to relocate there, and this was something he never contemplated.

*

When interviewer Roger Maynard asked Bryce, 'What are your tips for the trade?' he answered:

> Well first of all it's called 'bum glue' – you have to put in the hours . . . I work twelve hours a day . . . six days a week. I spend four or five months just thinking about characters constantly, constantly, constantly . . . It's pick and shovel stuff . . . the muse doesn't suddenly emerge from heaven and sit on your shoulders . . . this is a shovel and this is a pick, and this is hard ground . . . You have to dig the ditches, the verbal ditches.

When asked if it got any easier with age, Bryce remarked: 'Like all professionals, the words don't get in the way any more – they're just a medium, you just know how to use them.'

Bryce firmly believed that he had learnt a lot about the human condition from having endured his fair share of desperate times during his life. He had always kept going, with little or no backup, and when he came across people who were suffering he felt enormous empathy for them. His capacity for empathy is key in understanding Bryce's stories and is also why his readers loved him. From a writer's point of view, he never regretted his own challenges as described to Roger Maynard: 'Life experiences which are desperately sad are also wonderful experiences in terms of the writer's persona. I understand what you've been through; read the story, it will help, it will be good for you. We are in this together.' I am certain his readers could feel that he genuinely cared about and understood them, and they still do.

Despite the fame and fortune that came his way, Bryce remained grounded and egalitarian. Indeed, he never lost sight of his roots and believed his background actually contributed to his success. He elaborated in the Roger Maynard interview:

> I have no sense of being special. I haven't met the queen, but I have met people as important almost, and I have met ditch

diggers . . . and I make absolutely no differential because I come from the bottom and that's the best place to have come from. If I'd been born into a nice middle-class family I would have been lost.

Bryce wrote in his inspirational life guide A *Recipe for Dreaming*, 'There is nothing in this world that is more compulsive than a dreamer, someone who says "Despite where I come from, I can".'

Staying fit was another essential ingredient he attributed to his success. There wasn't a day that I was with him when he didn't go out for at least an hour of vigorous exercise. Once he could afford it, he engaged a personal trainer and come hail or shine – even if he had been up all night writing – he submitted to a gruelling workout. As explained to Roger Maynard, 'If you are going to write for long hours, if you are going to practise "bum glue", you had better be very fit.'

He was also unashamedly confident, and this was true even when he was writing his first couple of books. He approached the whole thing as though he knew what he was doing and used to say to himself, 'I am a writer' – a mantra he later implored his students to say too at the start of each writing day. I confess I even occasionally did this myself to harness the determination and dedication I needed to finish this memoir.

Sometimes, as I watched him tending our garden, I could see his mind was deep in thought and detached from everyday life. There was a fundamental link between his working in the garden and his writing stories. He confirmed this to Roger Maynard: 'I could be a gardener too. The idea of growing stuff for me is a miracle and I can't separate it from writing. Writing is growing stuff, it's growing stories . . .' He was aware that gardening offered a counterbalance to the hours he spent at the desk writing: 'Gardening is exactly the opposite to what I'm doing. The one is sitting down there going tap, tap, tap and the other is getting involved and getting your hands dirty and watching things grow.' For all of his adult life Bryce worked hard to carve out time each day or each week to spend in his garden. It fuelled his creativity and provided him with precious and much-needed relaxation.

Bryce acknowledged that writing was a long and lonely road and would sometimes concede that each book took its toll. He said in an interview with Penguin TV in 2009, 'A writer's life is a lonely one. You learn to spend a lot of time with yourself, and whatever is happening in what is laughingly known as your head.'

Bryce was able to connect with readers like no other Australian author before him. But not everyone was pleased about the advertising guru who had become a bestselling author. Bryce was in line to be cut down to size, which he usually shrugged off but which now and then clearly hurt and irritated him, as he confided in the Diana Ritch interview:

> Here is a book [*The Power of One*] about Africa, which Australians have taken to heart enormously but I discovered . . . the tall poppy syndrome. God help us, an advertising man has written a bestseller . . . I'd written potentially the biggest novel for years and years and years and years. And the literati didn't like it.

He tried to brush it off, claiming 'When we chop down the tall poppies, only the weeds remain' and 'Celebrity is no more than the first step away from anonymity'. There is no doubt Bryce fell victim to the tall poppy syndrome, seemingly embedded in Australian culture at the time when he was writing (and perhaps still). Not long before he died, he told me he hoped the next generation would not tolerate this lamentable syndrome. It was the only thing he really disliked about living in Australia, and I wholeheartedly share his view.

In *A Recipe for Dreaming*, published in 1994, he offers further insights about having success:

> It isn't hard at the top. It's easy. It isn't crowded and it's really quite civilised. What's hard is the bottom – down there you'll find one

hundred times more competition. Down there is where people stand on your teeth so they can get a firmer foothold on the first rung of the ladder out of hell.

Bob Ellis, another former advertising man who went on to become a successful journalist and author, wrote soon after Bryce's death:

> You could buy his books at Woolworths, and he was the first writer to try this on; and he became not so much a name as a brand name, and a Christmas gift the under-informed would give to their relatives who, not having read a book since high school, would gulp down on Boxing Day out of gratitude, family feeling and curiosity.

On 11 May 2010, Bryce appeared on ABC TV's *The Book Club* program, hosted by his former publisher Jennifer Byrne. The episode was called 'Bestsellers & Blockbusters' and the other writers present were Lee Child, Di Morrissey and Matthew Reilly. Lee said of their critics, 'They know in their hearts we could write their books, but they cannot write our books . . . They are jealous . . . The rivalry doesn't come from us.'

We used to run into people who would say to Bryce, 'I know you've sold millions of books, but I don't read books like yours.' He would politely respond, 'I can only say that I can't write any better than I am doing, and if you don't like my books, it's very simple – you can always read something else.' Even though he brushed off the criticism, it was hurtful – a sentiment perhaps reflected in *Whitethorn*: 'Did they not see that my punishment forever was the harsh cruel words, the never-ceasing hurtfulness that cut deeper into my soul than any *sjambok* [leather whip] ever could my flesh.' It was also a predicament that he never overcame during his lifetime, and things haven't changed in this respect since he passed away. I still bristle if someone talks about Bryce's books as though they were churned out in a matter of hours.

During our years together I often wished Bryce would take more breaks from writing as it exacted such a physical and mental toll on him.

He didn't need the money, and the fame he had come to enjoy was firmly established. Perhaps he needed his books to reach number one and the adulation that followed more than money – the fame and recognition being a salve to soothe those self-esteem cobwebs still lingering in his soul. I doubt he would have agreed with this, as writing was also at the core of his being: 'When you are a storyteller – and that's all I am – the stories just have to come out.'

Having started writing books so late in life, he felt there was a lot of catching up to do and was in a hurry to get down all the stories swirling in his head. In an interview recorded by Penguin in 2012, he said, 'Storytellers are the keepers – we are the timekeepers, the continuity keepers. We are the people who tell us who we are, where we've come from, and maybe even where we're going.'

Eventually, a new romantic partner for Bryce arrived on the scene and in 2002 she and Bryce had moved out of Sydney to live together. Their dream was to build a house in the beautiful Yarramalong Valley, located two hours north of the city. I was working with Bryce at this point as his publicist, and he told me it felt like a big step but he was looking forward to it and to once again becoming a 'mountain man'.

Being a writer, Bryce was never concerned about being isolated from shops or the conveniences of city life. There was no mobile phone reception in the Yarramalong Valley and the internet only became available after he installed a satellite dish in the front garden (and even then it was troublesome). Bryce was then in excellent health, and together they set about overseeing the build of their dream house. The site boasted beautiful views down the valley and had a creek running through it, while the nearby steep hills were covered in native trees and low-growing scrub. I think Bryce's sons and grandchildren as well as his friends may have been sorry to have him living so far away, even though they loved going up there to visit. Despite the picturesque setting, there were times, Bryce confessed to me, when he missed being able to see those close to him more often. He was never particularly interested in making new friends, but he was devoted to his group of old friends he had spent time with over decades.

Bryce was also a bowerbird, constantly collecting minutiae from whatever was going on in his life and storing it to include in a later book. He didn't miss a thing. Sometimes he would overhear a conversation while we were in a taxi or at an airport check-in counter and he would say, 'Write that down, darling. One day it's going into a book.'

As it turned out, Bryce's relationship came to an end, and he found himself occupying the big house with only Timmy, his dog, for company. Extracting himself from this relationship took a toll, as it does for anyone going through a break-up. He was in low spirits and told me he thought he was becoming depressed. He also admitted that he was drinking too much during that time. Those loneliness birds were once again perching on his shoulders, and the fear of what lay ahead loomed like cattle gathering at a gate after smelling the smoke of a bushfire.

Fame and fortune had come to Bryce, but the price he had paid in an emotional sense had been high. It was once again time for him to visit the 'Night Country' and return to a place where he could revive his spirits, just like the giraffe who came to drink from the silver bowl of the moon. He wrote in *The Power of One*: 'Sometimes the slightest things change the directions of our lives, the merest breath of a circumstance, a random moment that connects like a meteorite striking the earth.' One such meteorite hit several months later when Bryce and I came together as a couple. If you had told me this was going to happen, I would never have believed you!

11

OUR FIRST CHAPTER

A strong woman must be like the willow tree – while
she bends to the wild and wicked winds of life she will
endure. – *Sylvia*

IN 1992 I WATCHED the movie *The Power of One* in a Sydney cinema and
was moved to tears. I hadn't read the book and certainly had never met
Bryce Courtenay, the man who would eventually become my husband.
The film triggered memories of the anti-apartheid demonstrations I
had seen on television in 1971 while a student at Beechworth High
School in north-eastern Victoria. Those protests were focused on the
controversial Springboks Rugby tour of Australia to highlight the
plight of disenfranchised Africans, the same people Bryce wrote about
in *The Power of One*.

In early 1993 I was invited to attend a meeting of Writers' Bloc,
a group of advertising executives who had decided to become full-time
writers. They included, among others, Alan Gold, Derek Hansen, Paul
Wilson, Geoff Pike and Bryce Courtenay. I went along as I owned my
own marketing and public relations company – Christine Gee Strategic
Communications – and was hoping to secure more clients.

It was already dark when I parked my car outside the host's house
in the upmarket suburb of Bellevue Hill. I noticed a bright-yellow

Porsche in the driveway and remember thinking, that's just the kind of car I bet someone like Bryce Courtenay would drive. I recall feeling a little nervous after pressing the doorbell. I had met the Dalai Lama, several world-renowned mountaineers, and a distinguished British polar explorer, but never an author as famous as Bryce.

On entering the house, I noticed a rather short man with bright-blue eyes. He was wearing grey flannel pants and a navy sports jacket and was leaping around the room like a grasshopper on steroids. There was no doubt in my mind that this was Bryce, and I could see he was the leader of the pack. He walked towards me and said, 'Hello, I'm Bryce – and you must be Christine.'

I spluttered back, 'Yes, that's right, and I'm very honoured to meet you, Mr Courtenay.'

'Call me Bryce,' he said. 'Just think of me as "Mr Tap Tap", the person who sits down and applies heaps of "bum glue" to finish a book.' He then clapped his hands and said, 'OK kids, let's sit down and get this meeting started.'

From the outset it was clear Bryce was a force of nature. I imagined that the others seated at the table were surely itching to achieve his success. You could see this by the looks on their faces. 'I write better than the short man,' one of them whispered with an air of certainty before swallowing another mouthful of red wine. Over several glasses, enthusiastic discussion ensued. I was made very welcome, and that night we heard Paul Wilson's advertising-style pitch for his new book about teaching people how to be calm. This book later became hugely successful, as did many others he wrote.

About a year later I was given the opportunity to be Bryce's publicist, and I was very excited to work for him. Later I joked with him that I had gone to that meeting in Bellevue Hill to secure some more clients and years later had come away with a husband!

Our first work meeting took place in early 1994 in an office he was allocated at George Patterson in North Sydney, even though writing was now his major focus. *April Fool's Day* had been published in 1993 and he was writing *The Potato Factory*, the first in the trilogy he had planned. The desk and floor of the office were covered with papers, and advertising awards lined the walls. The phone never stopped ringing and Bryce appeared to be juggling a thousand things at once – a sign, I thought, of what was in store for me as his publicist.

He instructed me to 'run my own race' and from the outset was receptive to my efforts to ensure that his books were never out of the public's gaze. I told him I believed his readers would also love to know more about him and to understand what he stood for outside of his books. I once organised a campaign around him pleading with parents to read stories to their children and he discussed the shameful state of literacy levels, especially among Australia's Indigenous communities. Literacy was a subject close to his heart as in South Africa he had seen many children denied the opportunity of going to school. Bryce later went on to join Hazel Hawke in signing the 'Sorry Book' on 28 January, 1998, a decade before prime minister Kevin Rudd's formal apology to the Stolen Generations in Australia.

Bryce was a natural talent when it came to the media, and on-air presenters and journalists couldn't get enough of him. He was a popular guest on top-rating shows such as *Midday* on Channel 9 and the John Laws breakfast program on radio station 2UE.

I don't think Reed Books, his publisher at the time, were overjoyed about my appointment as his publicist as they had their own in-house publicity team, but I certainly appreciated having him as a client, and over time the team at Reed were impressed with my efforts. It was just Bryce and me working together one on one, and from the very beginning we got along like a house on fire. He was warm and funny and bursting with enthusiasm, and unlike me wasn't fussed if an interview didn't go to plan or a journalist said something cutting and tinged with envy about 'the ad man' who had reinvented himself as a bestselling author.

Bryce was thrilled I was on board as he understood that his publisher could not fund someone waking up each day with the purpose of having him in the media 24/7. The concept of achieving this with a local author was new for some publishers, and it wasn't until Bryce came along that literature and mass marketing joined forces with the aim of creating 'brand loyalty' between an Australian writer and their readers. As Bryce said in an interview with Sheryle Bagwell in the *Australian Financial Review*:

> We are creating a popular fiction genre in Australia for the first time in 50 years, maybe even 100 years . . . The Lawsons and the Patersons were the last really popular genre that was created here. And I think we can make an impact as Australian popular writers all over the world.

Regardless of the eyebrows this comment raised in certain quarters, Bryce took his writing seriously and his commitment to it was absolute. He was like a man possessed and nothing and nobody would stand in the way of him finishing a book on time. *April Fool's Day* had sold more than 195 000 copies the previous year, but Bryce was a man in a hurry and never forgot the impoverishment of his childhood.

In addition to carving out his career as a bestselling author, Bryce was involved in a dizzying range of activities, from still doing a bit of work for George Patterson to delivering corporate lectures, supporting charities and regularly turning up at shops to sign books for his readers. The schedule was gruelling, nevertheless he would rise at dawn each day to go for a run on Bondi Beach, make time to be with his family and close friends, and tend to his garden. He possessed a zest for life and an insatiable curiosity that was mesmerising and occasionally exhausting to be around!

He was also astonishingly generous. Bryce loved shoes and beautiful classic clothes and one day asked me to meet him at David Jones in the CBD. I thought he wanted us to meet for a working lunch, but instead we scooted upstairs and he insisted on buying me a Burberry handbag, an Armani jacket and a pair of Yves Saint Laurent high-heeled shoes! He would grab something from a rack and say, 'This will look great on you.' I was a bit overcome and embarrassed, but he beamed with delight and said, 'Now, kid, we are ready to take on the world!'

He could also be bossy and slightly controlling. One day he told me I needed to lose weight and suggested I change my hairstyle. I shot him back a rare grimace of disapproval and was tempted to suggest that he shouldn't drink so much. Even then I think he was getting the idea that he had met his match and this woman was ready to stand her ground! I came to understand that he loved and respected strong women as long as they were also decent and kind, just as he was. His books are dense with strong and resolute women who even in the most trying of circumstances stand up to bullies and fight for justice – Mercy B. Lord, Mrs Moses, Mary Abacus, Jessica, Maggie, Anna and Helen to name a few. In *Sylvia* Bryce crafted a chief protagonist who endures against overwhelming odds: 'Hold your head high, my lovely child, let no one bring you down. A strong woman must be like the willow tree – while she bends to the wild and wicked winds of life she will endure.'

Bryce and I had an entirely professional relationship, but he took a keen interest in my life and was supportive when, say, my latest romantic liaison came unstuck. He was also wonderfully kind towards my young son, Nima; soon after we started working together, he gave him a signed copy of the junior edition of *The Power of One*. Nima loved sport and he and Bryce used to enjoy chatting about the cricket scores or a recent game of Rugby. Bryce was also candid about what was going on in his own life, and sometimes it was a case of too much information!

Sometimes Bryce's publisher asked me to accompany him on interstate publicity tours, during which he might be required to give a talk at a literary lunch or dinner in a city hotel and then visit several bookshops, where he would sign copies of his books. The line usually stretched around an entire block and readers arrived with piles of volumes for him to sign. Bryce never refused, even if he was asked to sign one for Auntie Wilma and Uncle Allan as well as for the person's children and three grandchildren. I have never seen a writer before or since who respected and cherished their readers as he did.

Bryce suffered from arthritis in his hands – a legacy of childhood beatings and sporting injuries – and after a long day signing he needed to plunge his hands into a bucket of ice to ease the pain. He never complained or cancelled the next day's appointments even when he looked grey with exhaustion, instead saying, 'The reader has spent their hard-earned money on buying my book, so the least I can do is show up and sign it for them.'

He always went the extra mile, personally answering his fan mail as well as talking to anyone who came up to him on a flight or in a cafe. Even if we were in the supermarket buying a bottle of milk he would tell me, 'Darling' [he called everyone 'darling'], now don't forget to get their address and make sure you post them a signed book.' His signature resembled characters you might see in Chinese calligraphy and took him nearly a minute to write. I always made sure I had the correct Artline calligraphy felt pen in my handbag ready to whip out.

These years were heady for Bryce, who by this time had written four bestselling books, and his prowess as a marketer of books was getting as much attention as his place at the top of the bestseller lists. In October 1995 Neil Shoebridge wrote a story in the *Australian Financial Review* titled 'An Author Sells His Book as a Cereal' about how Bryce was changing the way books were sold:

Five years ago Bryce Courtenay was unpublished. Today he has worldwide sales of four million books . . . Critics dismiss books by Courtenay as pulp fiction. Retailers and many consumers disagree . . . The plans for his latest work (*The Potato Factory*) owe a lot to mass marketing . . . The publisher, Reed Books, expects to sell all 125,000 copies in the seven weeks before Christmas. To achieve that budget, Reed needs to sell almost 18,000 books a week in an industry that regards a book that sells 30,000 copies in a year as a best-seller . . . [Courtenay] believes that the recent success of popular, as opposed to literary, local fiction writers has broken the hold that the literati have had on the Australian fiction market.

When *The Potato Factory* and *Tommo & Hawk* were released, the beer, wine and spirits company Tucker Seabrook launched Tomahawk ale, produced by Coopers Brewery, and a sea shanty was recorded and played prior to interviews with Bryce going to air. As Sheryle Bagwell wrote on 1 December 1995:

> In just three weeks, *The Potato Factory*, the first in a Courtenay trilogy which will follow the travails of an English criminal in 19th-century Van Diemen's Land, has sold 155,000 copies into bookstores to date, with its publisher Reed Books confident 200,000 will walk out their doors by Christmas.

Not bad in what had been a tough sales environment on all fronts. Adrian Collette, Reed's managing director, told Sheryle, 'One author can't change a year, but an author like Bryce can be extremely helpful.' *Tommo & Hawk* was the first book published by Penguin Books Australia following Bryce's decision to jump ship in 1997. Penguin printed 260 000 copies, which at the time was the largest-ever print run of a new Australian title.

Indeed, his fans loved him and he always felt a great sense of gratitude for their loyalty, as he expressed in another interview with Neil Shoebridge:

> To be a good writer, you have to care about people . . . Most writers live in ivory towers and don't give a bugger about people. I don't want to be Australia's best writer; I want to be Australia's best storyteller. To do that, you have to like and nurture people.

Neil also noted, 'Courtenay employs a public relations consultant, Christine Gee, to ensure, he says, "I am somewhere in the media every day of the year.'" While I worked hard to achieve this, I was always mindful that going to the media can be fraught with danger: you never know when someone is going to come out of the woodwork and try to take you down. Someone once wisely told me that 'Envy is the Australian disease'. Bryce survived his media journey while we worked together, but that didn't end up always being the case.

During the mid-1990s I was the marketing manager for Aurora Expeditions, an innovative polar cruising company co-founded by my friend the legendary Australian mountaineer Greg Mortimer OAM and his extraordinary wife, Margaret. Greg was the first Australian to climb both Mount Everest and the impossibly difficult K2, and it was wonderful working with them. I was always trying to come up with original ideas so that we could sign up more passengers. Bryce had commenced hosting workshops for aspiring writers within a few years of becoming a successful writer himself, generously sharing what he'd learnt of the writing and publishing process. So in the middle of 2000, I suggested to Greg that we invite Bryce to conduct a writing workshop on one of the voyages to Antarctica.

Greg loved the idea and before the trip departed Bryce presented a lecture in a hall not far from Greg's office in Sydney's Rocks. He gave a brilliant address and spoke about the importance of 'going to places of unspoilt natural beauty such as in Africa or Antarctica, topping up the emotional capital which we lose by living in cities'.

In early November Bryce and I left Sydney for Buenos Aires, the capital of Argentina, accompanied by my brother, Bruce. I had always dreamed of going to South Georgia, having already been to the Antarctic Peninsula in 1999, and was thrilled that Greg had asked me to go with Bryce. I almost had to withdraw from the voyage as I became unwell in the northern Patagonian town of Puerto Madryn a day before our embarkation. Bryce was very understanding when I told him I had booked to fly home the next day, even though he looked disappointed. Thankfully, I rallied just in time and am so pleased I did, as we both went on to say this was the greatest journey of our lives. Bryce commented in an interview filmed at our home in Canberra in 2012 that 'It was like being born in the world before humans had any say in it.'

I shall never forget being pelted by sea spray as we made our way to shore in a rubber Zodiac at Salisbury Plain, home to around 300 000 king penguins – the ones that stand nearly a metre high and appear to be wearing waistcoats and bow ties. The scene before us was straight out of a spectacular David Attenborough documentary. I suggested to Bryce that he use a photo of him among the penguins as his Christmas card, which thrilled the Penguin Books team back in Melbourne. While still on 'South G' we visited the grave of the legendary explorer Sir Ernest Shackleton at the former whaling station of Grytviken. At the church there, Bryce stood in the pulpit and told everyone present the story of how Shackleton's twenty-two crewmen survived being stranded on Elephant Island for fourteen months by eating penguins, seals and seaweed. Their rescue on 30 August 1916, with not one man lost, is one of the greatest survival stories of all time. I quipped that if Bryce ever wanted to give up writing he could always become a man of the cloth!

We bathed in the heated waters flowing from a volcano on Deception Island having sailed to the Antarctic Peninsula. We took to the Zodiacs and gazed in awe at a pod of humpback whales who playfully flicked their pectoral fins as they dived beneath us, leaving an oily residue on the surface from their having fed on tiny krill and other small marine creatures. Another highlight was walking among the giant nests of the wandering albatrosses on Albatross Island. They have the largest wingspan of any flying bird and we felt deeply humbled to be there; later, in 2004, the island was closed to visitors. The experience had a deep impact on Bryce: 'For the first time in my life I appreciate how insignificant we as humans are. We must return as ambassadors to tell people that we must do all that we can to protect these beautiful creatures, and their fragile habitat.'

Bryce was thrown from his bunk and broke four ribs during the force 10 gale we encountered while sailing from Port Stanley, the capital of the Falkland Islands. Being Bryce, he didn't complain even though he was clearly in a lot of pain. Another passenger, the famous Australian Antarctic explorer Dr Phillip Law, then aged eighty-eight, was similarly thrown to the floor and sustained a nasty bump to his head. Bryce and I loved being together on that voyage, and he later confided that each night he had thought about knocking on my cabin door!

The writing workshop was a great success even though it was conducted in uncertain conditions as the vessel crossed the infamous Drake Passage, known colloquially as 'the Shaky Drakey'. I had already attended one of Bryce's writing courses so was ready for his first 'trick' writing question. He asked the group of around thirty-five (out of the thirty-seven passengers on board) to write 350 words describing the day they had left home to come to Antarctica, and then called on them each to stand up and read out what they had written. After listening patiently, he nodded before leaping to his feet and saying, 'OK, kids, now I want you to write down what really happened.' That was Bryce – everyone roared with laughter before knuckling down to write the truth.

Bryce said during that voyage that he would be forever grateful to me for bringing along freshly ground coffee beans and a coffee plunger. He was addicted to coffee and couldn't abide what was being served on the ship: it tasted like burnt chestnuts and he was certain it could only have been sourced from a prison in a Siberian gulag! One fateful morning I managed to break the glass plunger in the handbasin in my cabin, and Bryce declared that surviving without my coffee was too ghastly to contemplate. I dug into my holdall for the spare one I had packed and plonked it onto the breakfast table, and Bryce announced in front of everyone that at that precise moment he had fallen truly, madly and deeply in love with me. Years later I told him I always knew I came a close second to good coffee and a game of Rugby! To be honest I did notice how well we were getting along, but it felt innocent enough and

I just enjoyed being in his company, together with Bruce, in one of the most magnificent places on earth.

After rounding Cape Horn in mercifully calm conditions, we disembarked from the good ship *Polar Pioneer* at Ushuaia, the world's most southern city, located at the bottom tip of Argentina. We spent a few days together at Iguazu Falls on the Brazilian border, which together make up the biggest waterfall system in the world and is where the movie *The Mission* was filmed. Over dinner one night at the gorgeous Hotel das Cataratas, we heard someone say, 'Oh my, that's Bryce Courtenay who wrote *The Power of One*.' Sure enough, a couple of fans came over and couldn't believe they were meeting him in such a remote location. We couldn't either, and although Bryce was unfailingly warm he remarked quietly to me how lovely it had been to be among the penguins and whales in Antarctica where he could remain invisible.

After returning to Sydney we went happily back to our respective partners, but the experience of being together on that journey formed a bond that we always cherished – not that it ever occurred to me, even once, that anything would happen in a romantic sense. I was thrilled to be home in Bronte and reunited with my fiancé, Duncan Thomas, who had forgone his chance to join us on the voyage to look after a small information publishing business we had recently purchased. Duncan was an accomplished professional mountaineer and polar guide whom I had met while working for Aurora, and I had helped him secure sponsorship for an expedition he led to climb Mount Français, which at 2760 metres is the highest peak on the Antarctic Peninsula. In February 1998 he and Dave Adams achieved an Australian first by reaching its summit.

In 2001 Bryce asked me to be chief researcher for his novel *Four Fires*. It was an intense but fascinating experience, and I will always remember the fax he sent me at 3 a.m. on the day his manuscript was submitted: 'The Mole has risen. Thank you, dearest Christine, for all that you did. I have loved working with you. Yours, Bryce.'

In September 2012 Bryce revealed in his interview with Michael Dillon that *Four Fires* was a tribute to Australia: 'This is my love story to the country which was kind enough to take me in.' The back-cover blurb states that the book is about 'The fire of passion, the fire of religion, the fire of war, and fire itself – with love the brightest flame of all' and he wrote, 'Not since writing *The Power of One* have I felt this close to a book.' Bryce was thrilled when General (now Sir) Peter Cosgrove agreed to launch it in Melbourne, and afterwards we joined the Penguin team for lunch at Donovans restaurant overlooking Port Phillip Bay in St Kilda.

I continued to work as Bryce's publicist until 2002, after Duncan and I married on 23 March 2002 and moved from Sydney to Bowral in the New South Wales Southern Highlands. Our wedding took place at the beautiful naval chapel in Watsons Bay, where I used to attend HMAS *Perth* remembrance services with my parents, Kath and Allan Gee, and my siblings, Bruce and Margaret. Bryce generously paid for our beautiful flowers and lent us his silver BMW sports car. I was very upset that he couldn't share in our happy day, but he was not feeling well and at the last minute reluctantly decided not to attend. Following the wedding ceremony, we stopped by his flat in Rose Bay before hosting the reception at our home. Years later Bryce told me his heart ached that day as he wished he was the bridegroom!

It was to be nearly three more years before anything romantic began to stir between Bryce and me. My marriage to Duncan was under strain even though we shared a passion for adventure and were besotted with our Burmese cat, Cardamon. I didn't enjoy living in Burradoo and missed seeing Nima and my friends in Sydney. Bowral is a beautiful town, but within days I knew it would never replace Sydney in my heart.

There were other issues between us, too, which showed no signs of being resolved. Duncan's loyalty and innate decency had drawn me to him in the first place, even though I had initially been shy of us getting together as he was nearly fifteen years younger than me. He enjoyed being away from Sydney and loved our new home, which we owned free of the mortgage we had carried with our Bronte house. My disquiet about living in Bowral irritated him and we began to bicker. In 2003 he left to fly to America for a trip to California's Yosemite National Park and I wasn't invited.

By early 2005 our marriage was crumbling, which made me feel terribly sad, although deep down I knew things couldn't go on as they were. Around this time Duncan and I were invited to work as assistant expedition leaders on a voyage to Antarctica led by my great friend Robert Swan OBE, a British polar explorer who in 1989 became the first person to reach both poles.

In late February I once again found myself standing on the docks at Ushuaia, this time waiting to board the MV *Ushuaia*. We were about to sail through the notorious Drake Passage to arrive at the Antarctic Peninsula two days later. I had been feeling a bit of a wreck during the previous few days and had not been getting much sleep. Rob could see I wasn't my usual cheerful self and said, 'I hope you're up to the voyage, darling. I really need you to be in top form and you are looking a bit rough.' I apologised and said, 'I feel like rubbish' and told him I was worried about the state of my marriage. He had observed Duncan and me trying to do everything we could to save it and said, 'I'm very sorry, darling. Duncan is such a decent chap whom I admire enormously.' His face then brightened and he said with a cheeky look on his face, 'You'll just have to marry Bryce.' I looked at him as though he were mad and shrugged so hard my shoulders hurt. 'Don't be ridiculous,' I said, before marching up the gangplank and jumping aboard the ship.

On 7 March 2005, Bryce invited me to accompany him to a ceremony at the Sydney Opera House to celebrate the bicentenary of the birth of the Danish storyteller Hans Christian Andersen, hosted by Crown Princess Mary and Crown Prince Frederik of Denmark. Although tempted, I declined as it didn't feel right to go given that I was still married. At the ceremony Bryce was inducted as a Hans Christian Andersen Ambassador along with children's author Mem

Fox, TV presenter Andrew Denton and actor Geoffrey Rush. Prince Frederik described the recipients as 'storytellers in their own right' and Bryce subsequently remarked how charming and down to earth the royal couple were. Afterwards he gave me a magnificent plaque featuring a stunning blue-and-white platter designed especially for the bicentenary. It didn't occur to me at the time that this was a romantic overture, but he later told me that indeed it was.

In April of that year, I was asked if I wanted to go to Russia to travel to the Baikonur Cosmodrome in Kazakhstan to witness a crewed Russian space launch of a Soyuz rocket to the International Space Station. This was associated with my role as a consultant to the American private space exploration company Space Adventures, which is based in Washington, DC. I was dying to go, having been a 'space nut' since watching the moon landing at school on a black-and-white television on 20 July 1969 and hearing Neil Armstrong utter those unforgettable words, 'That's one small step for man, one giant leap for mankind'. The Space Adventures team I was part of were in Russia to take a prospective client to see the launch in the hope that he would sign to go 'up'.

After Duncan and I bought our house in Burradoo, a suburb in Bowral in the Southern Highlands, money was tight and I couldn't justify purchasing the airfare to travel to Russia, which I was required to cover. Bryce was insistent that I should go and, despite my protests, within three weeks I found myself on a plane bound for Moscow via Helsinki – and in business class! I felt like I was the one who had been launched into space. Bryce was thrilled when I brought him back a set of handpainted Matryoshka dolls and loved hearing about the extraordinary trip that had been made possible by his generosity. Our group had been taken on a rare private tour of the hallowed grounds of Star City, where Yuri Gagarin, the first man in space, had trained before his successful mission on 12 April 1961 aboard the spacecraft Vostok 1.

Bryce hugely admired the great Russian writers and was one of the few people I have known who read Leo Tolstoy's War and Peace in its entirety. To my surprise some weeks later he said that one day we should travel to Russia together on a literary pilgrimage to see where legendary authors such as Tolstoy, Alexander Pushkin (considered by many to be the father of Russian literature), Anton Chekhov, Fyodor Dostoevsky and Alexander Solzhenitsyn had penned their works. He told me he never forgot the words of Ivan Turgenev in *Fathers and Sons*: 'We sit in the mud, my friend, and reach for the stars' – perhaps the inspiration behind a book title down the track. I responded, while blushing and not knowing where to look, that it was an enticing idea. I was thinking to myself, well, if we did that what would the sleeping arrangements be?

In June 2005 Duncan and I sold our house in Bowral and returned to Sydney where we rented a small house that reeked of damp in Fletcher Street, Woollahra. We had agreed to separate but remained on good terms and resided together to save money until we finalised plans to go our own way. We had agreed to share custody of Cardamon, who was part of the glue that still bound us together. I used to go and have coffee or a drink with Bryce and regularly made him my famous Goan fish curry, which I once managed to spill on the ground when the container fell on the pavement as I pressed the buzzer for his flat. His place was crammed with books and mementos, and we used to sit on his balcony and chat away for hours. I always left feeling happy and filled with hope for the future.

Bryce was in the middle of writing *Whitethorn*, the novel he later claimed was his most autobiographical. It seemed to be pouring out of him: he wrote for ten to twelve hours a day seated at an antique table pushed against the wall of his bedroom. The book is a more mature reflection of growing up in Africa than the one woven into the pages of *The Power of One*. Similar themes and characters resurface, including Mevrou and his Zulu friend 'Mattress', who takes care of the pigs. In a later interview Bryce referred to Mattress as being akin to Man Friday in Daniel Defoe's *Robinson Crusoe*. The protagonist in *Whitethorn*, Tom Fitzsaxby, was, like Peekay in *The Power of One*, born illegitimately and later incarcerated in a boys farm in South Africa's deep north, run by Afrikaners who regarded themselves essentially as 'Boerevolk' (a farming people). Unlike Bryce's own history, he sent Tom to work in the Kenyan copper mines and then to fight the Mau Mau (the Mau Mau people fought against British authoritarian rule from 1952 to 1960).

I loved chatting to Bryce about his life in Africa, as apart from once having had a South African boyfriend I had never spent time with anyone who grew up there. Bryce loved Australia with an almost evangelical zeal but was in many ways African to his bootstraps. Sometimes when we were discussing a complex issue he would say, 'I know I'm right about this. Remember, darling, I'm an African and I know about these things.'

The incessant pounding of jackhammers from a building site next door and the distraction of a succession of visitors didn't impede his progress in completing *Whitethorn*. It even garnered some good reviews, including one by Cath Kenneally in the *Sydney Morning Herald*:

> The kiss of death for Bryce Courtenay was Kath and Kim's seal of approval. And here's another 680-page doorstop to be avoided by the discerning reader, right? Well, no . . . This isn't a perfectly crafted novel, it's repetitive and has its longueurs. But the boy Tom Fitzsaxby could stand proudly alongside Tom Brown or Tom Sawyer any day.

In September 2005 I was over at Bryce's for lunch. After we finished eating, he said, with his blue eyes gazing intently into mine, 'You know, Christine Gee, you and I would go very well together as a couple, and I want you to think about it.' I was taken aback and felt startled and slightly panic-stricken.

Bryce went on to explain that it was difficult for him to find a partner and he was feeling a bit gun-shy about dating again as he couldn't help but wonder if women were only attracted to him for his money or fame, or both. I completely understood why he felt safer contemplating a relationship with me – I was someone he had known and trusted for more than a dozen years. I think, too, he appreciated that I was financially independent and still running a successful business: he told me how much he admired me for doing this while at the same time raising Nima.

I hadn't the faintest idea that Bryce had been harbouring romantic feelings towards me, but then I was often slow to pick up on this when it came to men. However, even though Duncan and I had agreed to separate, I wasn't in any emotional state to contemplate becoming involved with someone else, not even Bryce. The whole idea of getting together with him felt like madness, and I was certain it could never work out.

Bryce added one proviso to his wish that we be together, and that was that I must consider being prepared to leave Sydney and move to the country. He was making plans to return to his beloved Yarramalong Valley as soon as possible. Having just come back from living in a regional town, I wasn't the least bit interested in leaving the city again so soon. Even though I had grown up on a farm in north-eastern Victoria, I loved Sydney, and I had no illusions about country life, including the distance required to travel for basic services, and the small-town attitudes.

I drove home to Woollahra and consoled myself by thinking, well, at least I have the perfect excuse as to why I don't want to take the next step with Bryce. I did, however, have the distinct feeling he was not going to give up easily. Bryce had travelled a long and hard road and knew how to get what he wanted. Indeed, he continued to be very persistent in his overtures towards me. At first I didn't mention anything to Duncan as it didn't seem fair. He liked Bryce very much and, like me, I am sure never imagined for a moment we would become involved in a relationship. Much later he told me that he had always noticed how well Bryce and I got along and said, 'You only looked happy when you came back from a visit with him.'

After a lot of persuasion, I accepted Bryce's invitation to go to the 2005 Melbourne Cup on the first Tuesday in November. He handed me a wad of cash and told me to go out and buy a new dress, shoes and a hat. A few days later in the early hours of the morning I stepped into a limousine, and we were on our way to Sydney Airport. Bryce liked the green chiffon Alberta Ferretti dress I was wearing, although he didn't much like the large, matching hat bestowed with feathers. We checked in at the Qantas business-class counter and wandered into the lounge, where I noticed a few people staring at us. I wasn't used to such scrutiny and felt uncomfortable. They had recognised Bryce and were probably thinking, who is the new woman on Bryce Courtenay's arm? We returned to Sydney that evening, having enjoyed a wonderful day together, and I was left in no doubt about Bryce's growing feelings towards me.

At the end of November, Bryce drove me up to the Yarramalong Valley to have lunch with friends and we had a peek over the fence at his farm, called *Ikhaya lami*, which means 'My home' in Zulu. He was excited to be returning there soon and to be reunited with Timmy, the kelpie-blue-heeler-cross dog he had rescued a year earlier. A farmer he met had told him, 'This mutt's no bloody good and I'm gonna get rid of the little bastard as soon as I can.' Bryce was aghast and immediately agreed to take the dog. After he put the forlorn creature into his car it promptly vomited in his lap. Ever since, Bryce and Timmy had been inseparable. Bryce loved all animals and had never recovered from losing Tinker as a small boy in Barberton. He wrote about this in *Whitethorn*: 'I was about to lose the one thing I loved the most in the whole world. Without Tinker I was on my own again and my happy days were all over, finish and *klaar*.' (*Klaar* means 'finished' in Afrikaans.)

Leaving Sydney, we travelled on the F3 freeway and turned left at the Peats Ridge exit. After an hour and a half, we arrived in the beautiful Yarramalong Valley and Bryce drew the car to a stop. He was elated to finally have the chance to show me his property. We parked at the boundary of his land, not far from a creek, and I felt apprehensive about leaving the vehicle as it was a boiling-hot day and unbearably humid, and the grass was nearly up to the car windows. As a country girl who had once been bitten by a snake while lying in long grass at Beechworth Primary

School, I was certain we would come across a snake. I was wearing open-toed slingback shoes and was petrified, but I tried hard not to show it.

Within moments of leaving the car, I spotted a diamond python coiled up in the grass. It was at least 3 metres long and its amethyst-coloured skin was shimmering in the sun. I squeaked with fear while wishing I could find a way to be airborne. Bryce rushed to reassure me: 'Don't worry, darling, it's just a harmless python. I promise you it's a pet owned by the family who live up there on the hill.' I rolled my eyes and didn't believe him for a moment. This incident made me feel even more certain that there was no way I was going to move up here to live.

We drove to a property belonging to Greg and Lorraine Woon. Bryce had become good friends with them since moving there and was dying to introduce me. Over lunch he reflected on how he came to purchase the land and in true Bryce style, belted out his version of the story:

> I came across the farmer who owned it. He was hanging over the front fence and tugging on a cigarette while trying to fix his gate. I inquired if his land was for sale and he said, 'This land has been in my family for generations and always will be, so you can bugger off as it ain't for sale.'

Bryce said he pressed the man to name his price and even though the figure was high, he whisked out his chequebook and the land was his.

The Woons were very warm towards me, although I could tell they were sizing me up. They were very fond of Bryce and I expect they didn't want to see him jump from the frying pan into the fire, especially having witnessed the sadness he had felt following the breakup with his former partner.

Bryce was in high spirits that day, and as he downed several glasses of wine he enthusiastically described his plans for his 6 hectares of garden. Since he was a small boy his dream had been to create a water garden, and he had already built a spectacular Japanese-style waterfall surrounded by tropical plants that was the talk of the valley. I had a knot in my stomach as I knew he was confident I would soon be joining him to share in the dream. I also felt he was drinking too much and wondered how we would make it safely back to Sydney. When our hosts expressed similar concerns, Bryce said, 'Don't worry – Christine barely drinks and she will be driving us back, won't you, darling?' I had never driven his racing-green BMW sports car and certainly didn't relish taking it on the motorway teeming with Sunday traffic. So we stayed on chatting to Greg and Lorraine and after Bryce drank a few strong coffees we were on our way back to the city with him at the wheel. Apart from seeing the snake I had enjoyed our day together, but I was certain it was going to be my last trip to the Yarramalong Valley.

Bryce had other ideas. I could see he was falling in love with me, and the pressure was on. One afternoon I had a tearful outburst: 'I am truly sorry, but I can't do this any more. You simply have to give me more time.' He responded gently, 'Darling, when you are young you meet someone, jump into bed and fall head over heels in love. When you are older you first fall in *like* – and then you fall in *love*. I promise with all my heart this is exactly what is going to happen with us.' I was beginning to think he could be right, but wasn't ready to surrender and continued to hold out.

Unbeknown to me Bryce had already confided to his best friend, Alex Hamill, that he was smitten, saying, 'She's the one!' In a television interview in 2012 he explained how we were friends for a long time before coming together as a couple: '[It was a] slow maturation and a huge surprise when she finally liked me beyond friends.' In 2007 he said he thought back to our courtship when he wrote these words in *The Persimmon Tree*: 'I was in love, head over heels, hopelessly, helplessly in love.'

He continued to shower me with lavish gifts, and I was not used to being indulged in such a way. The money I usually spent was the money I earnt by myself, and this had been the case since I left home at seventeen to go to university in Canberra: within weeks of arriving there, I secured a job at the *Canberra Times* a few nights a week to supplement my scholarship. The one exception was in 1973 before I flew to Singapore on my first overseas trip, when my father sold one of his prized Hereford cows for $365 and sent me a cheque to shore up my funds.

Now, after returning to Sydney, I was kept busy with clients. My divorce settlement was also coming up; that was resolved quickly and amicably with Duncan as we valued our friendship enormously.

Bryce didn't much like going out to socialise other than to meet up with his family or a few old friends, and this was especially true when he was in the middle of writing a book. Sometimes, though, he invited me to go to dinner with him at his favourite restaurant, Darcy's in Paddington. It was owned by his old friend Attilio Marinangeli, who seated us at the best table and treated us like royalty. Bryce ordered the same thing from the menu each time: a fillet steak cooked medium rare and served with green beans, creamed spinach and scalloped potatoes, all washed down with a bottle of chardonnay. I loved our conversations, his brilliant mind, great sense of humour and genuine human warmth – as Bryce wrote in *Sylvia*, 'I told myself that I had found a soul mate who, like myself, loved music and stories.' He exuded the kind of confidence that made you feel you could do anything you dreamt of. It bewildered him when people said, 'One day I'm gunna . . .' and then proceed to do nothing to make it happen. He was one of those people who subscribed to the saying 'The harder you work, the luckier you become'. He was incredibly funny, too, and would regularly have me in stitches. It was hard to be serious or downcast for long and I noticed I always left his company feeling like a teenager – perhaps even a teenager who was beginning to fall in love?

Bryce was very proud of my achievements, which included co-founding with Goronwy Price in 1975 the adventure travel company Australian Himalayan Expeditions (later called World Expeditions), which grew to be one of the largest trekking companies in the world; being appointed the royal Nepalese honorary consul general in 1987, a role I maintained for twenty-two years, and attaché to the Nepalese Olympic team during the 2000 Sydney Olympics; and becoming a founding director of the Australian Himalayan Foundation (AHF) in 2002 along with Garry Weare, Lincoln Hall, Mark O'Toole, Michael Dillon, Peter Hillary and Simon Balderstone, to raise funds for health, education and environmental programs in support of vulnerable communities in Nepal, Bhutan and Ladakh. Our current team of directors also includes Julia Booth and Greg Mortimer. Goronwy and I had been married and on 4 November 1979 I gave birth to our wonderful son, Nima – the same date that Bryce's son Damon had been born in 1966.

Bryce believed that along the way I hadn't always been treated with much respect by some of my later boyfriends, and he wasn't wrong about that. He would say, 'Darling, you don't have to be little Cinders any more. It's time you realised this and stood up for yourself.' There was no hiding behind social niceties with Bryce, and if I tried to shy away from a tough question he'd say, 'Come on, darling, spit it out and tell me what's really going on.' If I was feeling tentative about taking on something, he would say, 'What do you mean you can't do that? Of course, you can, and what's more you must.'

As the weeks went by, I knew my resolve not to be with Bryce was beginning to dissolve. In the latter part of 2005 I told him I would move up to Yarramalong and see how things worked out. He was over the moon, although I didn't feel overly optimistic. Nima, then aged twenty-six, was very understanding about my decision and his support meant the world to me as it helped me to summon the confidence to take the next step. Not everyone thought it was a good idea, and they didn't hold back in letting me know. The age difference and my having been recently divorced were among their concerns.

Inevitably word got out that Bryce and I were an item and a story appeared in a weekend newspaper. I had only ever been mentioned in media stories about my adventure travel company or the clients I represented with my marketing company. Being an intensely private person, I didn't like this attention one bit, but Bryce wasn't as bothered. By then he was very famous and understood that journalists writing whatever they wanted came with the territory. It was an early warning sign that the media were going to be a part of our lives whether I liked it or not. At least back then social media was only emerging and so the impact wasn't as intense as it might have been had we been dating today. I remember popping into the chemist shop in Plumer Road, Rose Bay, not far from Bryce's flat. I had my head lowered to avoid being recognised, and quickly made some purchases, which included Panadol to treat a fierce headache. The pharmacist was an old European friend of Bryce's and she said in a caring voice, 'Don't worry, darling, Bryce is a wonderful person, and I am sure you will be very happy together.'

On Christmas Day 2005 we arrived at Bryce's farm. I had a pile of suitcases, several boxes of books, and my collection of paintings and artefacts from thirty-five years of travelling. The 'we' comprised myself and Cardamon, who was not happy to be confronted by Timmy barking excitedly as he raced out the door to greet us. Duncan had driven us up there in his Volkswagen van, which was incredibly decent of him, and he could see during the journey that I was feeling terribly nervous. I wanted to pee every half-hour but was too frightened to leave the vehicle in case I saw a snake.

Soon after arriving we awkwardly bade each other farewell and then Duncan and his van disappeared in a cloud of dust. I remember standing in the driveway and sobbing my heart out. There I was, in what felt like the middle of nowhere, with my cat, a pile of suitcases and all my worldly possessions, about to move in with a man who was twenty-one years older than me and with whom I had never spent a night. I was sure as hell it would turn out to be a disaster.

12

YARRAMALONG

She knew she was in love with him, a thing she had thought impossible. But she also knew that she had heard the breath of the future. – *Tandia*

AFTER I ARRIVED IN the Yarramalong Valley on Christmas Day, Bryce presented me with a gift. As I opened the brown-paper package, I let out a gasp. It was a rare golden cowrie shell from a reclusive marine snail found on coral reefs in the South Pacific. Known for its bright peach colour and distinctive cream curl at one end, it is traditionally worn around the necks of chieftains as a symbol of rank or privilege.

For days I had racked my brain as to what I could give a man who appeared to have everything. I handed over my small parcel and another golden cowrie shell tumbled into Bryce's hand. I had bought it from a village boy on the remote island of Tavanipupu in the Solomon Islands on a trip with my twin sister Margaret, and Bruce, to celebrate our fortieth birthday. Bryce and I were both stunned. What were the chances of us giving each other an identical, highly unusual gift? He beamed with happiness and threw his arms around me, saying, 'Well, kid, this is a sure sign that you and I are going to go splendidly together!' I agreed and began to feel hopeful that we could make this unlikely relationship work.

Once I was installed at Yarramalong, we began preparations to welcome Bryce's family for lunch on New Year's Day. As their cars drew up, the temperature soared to 40°C and the humidity was stifling. To make matters worse we experienced a power failure, probably due to the heat, and were without running water or air conditioning. Fortunately, I had already made our lunch of baked fish, grilled chicken and salads, which everyone tucked into. It was wonderful to see Bryce spending time with his sons Brett and Adam and their wives Ann and Gina, as well as his beloved grandchildren Marcus, Jake and Ben. Little Marcus was about to turn three, and I recall that the stifling heat was even harder for him to bear than it was for us adults and the older boys.

I had felt nervous as to how they would respond to me given that Bryce's most recent relationship had not worked out. Understandably his sons may have been thinking, gosh, Dad, here you go again. But to my relief everyone warmly welcomed me and Bryce was naturally delighted.

As the afternoon unfolded, we heard that a bushfire had broken out near Peats Ridge and was heading our way. Bryce's family wisely made an early exit in case the roads became blocked. I began to feel on edge as I knew we were in for a long night. By early evening ash was landing on our deck and fluttering through the louvres into the house. Cardamon's fur developed a smoky aroma and the neighbour's cattle clustered around the gates and bellowed to be let out.

Come nightfall, the sky had turned an eerie red and flames were forming a menacing ring on the ridge above the valley. Bryce wasn't overly concerned and said, 'Don't worry, darling. Fire doesn't race uphill and as our house sits on a crest we are perfectly safe.' I thought, maybe you should re-read your book *Four Fires*! I recalled the part in the novel where Tommy says, 'What he hasn't reckoned on is there's a wind blowing around twenty knots an hour and it's carrying these embers, which is what we call "radiant heat". It sucks all the oxygen out of the air, like the air burns up . . .'

Bryce sauntered off to bed and within minutes fell asleep, with Timmy snoring on the floor beside him. I barely slept, but by the morning the local fire brigades had contained the blaze and the threat was gone.

Throughout that first long, hot summer I made a big effort to settle back into country life, even though I was not convinced that Bryce and I were going to last. Bryce, on the other hand, was ecstatic to be back in Yarramalong after spending the previous year holed up in his small Rose Bay flat. I anticipated that he would take me out to explore the local area, but this didn't happen. He rarely left home except to go to Tuggerah, a town forty minutes away, to buy plants or to pick up chook food. I had read up about the valley and was fascinated to discover that Yarramalong means 'place of cedars' and that it is the land of the Darkinjung people. It was permanently settled in 1856 by the Stinson and Waters families of Maitland, and prior to that was logged by timber cutters driving teams of oxen from Wollombi.

Once in early February we went to Terrigal, about an hour's drive away, but after lunch and a walk on the beach Bryce said, 'Darling, let's go home. I must get back to my book.' He had started writing *Sylvia*, set in the time of the Children's Crusade of 1212, and it was not going well. Finding the information he needed about the era was proving to be extraordinarily difficult and even Bryce Courtenay couldn't make bricks without straw!

There was no mobile phone reception at Yarramalong, which only increased my sense of isolation. Other problems arose from the antiquated telephone lines, and we had persistent problems with our internet and television links. Bryce would become exasperated when the screen shuddered to black in the middle of a Rugby match. He never missed a game, even if it meant getting up in the middle of the night to watch a live broadcast from England, France, New Zealand or South Africa.

Soon after I moved in with Bryce, my closest friend, Robert Swan, arrived from his home in California to have lunch with us. I was thrilled to see him. Before departing he took me aside and said, 'I admire you sticking it out up here, darling. I don't think I could last for more than a couple of hours.' Oh dear, I thought, and wished I could jump in his car and go with him back to Sydney.

Not long afterwards, Rob was staying at my Sydney flat and I said to him in a tearful outburst, 'I can't do this any more. I think I want out.' I had been feeling a lot of pressure on many fronts and was struggling to cope. I was also still coming to terms with my divorce from Duncan: our breakup had been very amicable, but I found myself grappling with guilt and a sense of failure, which inevitably creeps in when a marriage falls apart. Furthermore, I missed being close by my wonderful son Nima and being able to catch up easily with friends. I spent my days at Yarramalong hanging around with nothing much to do other than housework, cooking and reading, while Bryce tapped away at his computer.

Rob listened to me pouring my heart out and then gently but firmly encouraged me not to give up: 'Darling, I know you are struggling, but I promise you things will come right. You and Bryce make a great team, and he loves you very much. You must dig deep, trust your feelings, and hold the line.' I knew he was right, but also that a long road lay ahead.

In mid-January I was relieved to be able to spend more time back in Sydney. Bryce headed up to Bellingen, not far from Coffs Harbour, to run a writing workshop at Camp Creative, of which he was a patron. It had been founded in 1986 by his old advertising friend Bill Lockley, who had a great passion for music, and Bryce looked forward to this annual pilgrimage as it gave him the opportunity to encourage people of all ages to pursue creative activities. He was delighted that his grandson Jake was able to join him on this occasion. During that week they caught up with the piano virtuoso David Helfgott and his amazing wife, Gillian, who were involved with Camp Creative; David's remarkable story had been captured in the 1996 film *Shine*.

In February Bryce left Yarramalong again to fly to South Africa to participate in a publicity tour for his book *Whitethorn*. I was inwardly relieved, as it meant I could spend a whole two weeks in Sydney. Cardamon came with me and barely left my side. The trip to South Africa was bittersweet for Bryce, with his mother having passed away some seven years earlier. He said, 'My last immediate familial thread with Africa no longer exists.' However, he was delighted to unexpectedly meet up with a couple of relatives he barely knew. He told me they chatted for hours and he learnt a lot about his mother's life and events he had not previously known of. Hearing these stories upon his return was fascinating and gave me a far greater understanding of the new man in my life.

Bryce's strong connection to Africa was always a big part of who he was. In 1993 he wrote a story for the *Sydney Morning Herald* that captured this, called 'The Power of Africa':

> Africa belongs to all of us; it is both our burden in its darkness and, in its magnificence, it is a reminder that once upon a time we all came from its mighty cradle. It is from this place that humankind evolved into the blinding sun. Before you die, come back to where your heart first pumped and your soul began.

He remained convinced that he and I were going to show the world what true love was all about, and after returning from South Africa he said, 'You and I will grow to have a relationship that will be the greatest love story of our lives.' This turned out to be true, but even though I could feel the seeds of a profound love stirring between us, I found his expectation daunting.

It was impossible not to be enchanted by Bryce. I always felt I was in the presence of someone who possessed a great gift and who embraced each day with the boundless energy of a newborn lamb. Whenever I would start to fret, he would say something kind and funny or dream up a grand plan for us to become excited about. One of these revolved around us spending three months in the American South so that he could research a new novel. I was thrilled with the idea, having studied American literature at Canberra's Australian National University (ANU). The novels of James Baldwin, Harper Lee and Mark Twain and the poems of Allen Ginsberg and Emily Dickinson flashed through my mind – particularly my favourite words of Dickinson's from her beautiful poem 'Hope': 'Hope is the thing with feathers / That perches in the soul, / And sings the tunes without the words, / And never stops at all'.

Bryce literally jumped through hoops trying to please me, and my confidence in our relationship began to grow. Another friend, Graham Taylor, who has now been living in Mongolia for over twenty years, saw us together and said, 'Bryce is an old-fashioned gentleman, and it is obvious to me that he has fallen deeply in love with you.'

Bryce never failed to return from the garden without presenting me with a beautiful bloom, and each night he would place fresh flowers on my bedside table. One weekend I came back from Sydney to find a box tied with red ribbon on the kitchen bench. He had bought me a pair of navy Salvatore Ferragamo shoes, and I was stunned to be given such an exquisite and extravagant gift.

As Bryce's readers will know, romance throbs through the pages of his novels, even though the path is not always straightforward for his characters. I used to ponder whether their stories were a metaphor for the love Bryce yearned for, and sometimes wondered if any one woman could give him the amount he needed. In his novel *Tandia* he wrote: 'She would now have someone to whom she could talk, with whom she could share her loneliness, and onto whom she could focus her abundant but unrequited love.' This character trait was without doubt a reflection of the emotional scars he carried from his childhood. We probably all carry childhood scars in one way or another that have an impact on our adult relationships.

While I loved Bryce's divine romantic overtures, I quickly discovered that I needed to be adept at entertaining myself. He maintained a strict routine, as he had done throughout his life, and no new woman on the scene had a chance of altering it. His day started early and was kicked off with strong coffee and a serving of poached eggs on buttered toast, and then he would take Timmy for a long walk. He would let out the chooks, collect the eggs and check on his veggie garden before heading upstairs to write. He rarely stopped for lunch and didn't turn off his computer until 5 p.m., when he would come back downstairs. The fridge door would be opened and out would come a bottle of white wine for us enjoy on the deck. This was my favourite time of the day as we gazed down the valley and listened to the birds making their final calls before darkness descended. Then the frogs would strike up, which would not have gone unnoticed by the snakes lurking in the reeds by the dam.

Bryce and I would chat about anything and everything, including how his day's writing had gone. It was during these interludes that I learnt a lot about his life in Africa, including some very confronting episodes that were fictionalised in *Whitethorn*. Bryce's tales of the dangers of working down the mines on the Copperbelt and his adventures when hitchhiking were also compelling. They sounded so exotic and were from a time long gone. Growing up in Africa during the Great Depression and World War Two and in the era of apartheid had been tough, but it imbued in Bryce a reverence for life and a rare mental strength.

I also loved hearing about what it was like to live in London during the mid-1950s and the heady days of working in the advertising industry from the 1960s to the 1980s. Goodness knows what went on, as Bryce had lived life very much in the fast lane. He confessed to lots of hard drinking and admitted somewhat sheepishly to having had some affairs. I would not have wanted to be his wife during those years, and I told him so.

By March life with Bryce at Yarramalong still wasn't all plain sailing, and I remember on one afternoon I burst into tears in a car park at the Tuggerah shopping centre. The transition from being divorced to moving in with Bryce and living in an isolated valley had me feeling as though I was marooned on an island. Nearly everyone I knew thought I was living the dream, but in fact I sometimes felt utterly miserable. It was the first time in my adult life that I was not running my own business, and I missed that challenge and my independence, the camaraderie of being part of a team, and the stimulation of solving problems and coming up with creative ideas for my clients. I also couldn't get used to not earning my own money, and it didn't feel right to be spending money I hadn't earnt myself.

In other ways, it was easy to be seduced by the natural beauty of the Yarramalong Valley. I especially loved the early-morning mists that descended into our front garden like cream puffs. I would gaze in wonder at the grace of a white-faced heron who landed to forage for fish in our Japanese pond. The pond featured a giant waterfall surrounded by tropical plants and was ringed by huge boulders dredged from the nearby Wyong River. At night, lights came on and the garden was transformed into a fairyland.

Bryce had crammed his large designer home with a breathtaking collection of original artworks, sculptures and treasured mementos along with thousands of books, which lined his study upstairs. He collected frogs in honour of the original title of his debut novel, *The Tadpole Angel*, and readers would send him frog objects fashioned from playdough, crystal, rare wood or precious stones. He had acquired hundreds and used to enjoy handing them out to people who came to visit.

Our master bedroom was bigger than some apartments and included two bathrooms with contemporary Italian fixtures. The elaborate Bose sound system wired throughout the house was state-of-the-art, not that we knew how to make it work. We had a regular cleaner and Bryce employed a capable foreman called Kim Rabbits who ensured that the property and large garden were kept looking pristine. It took a bit of getting used to, especially as Bryce insisted on introducing me to people as 'the lady of the house'! Both of us, though, were far more impressed by the abundance of nature that surrounded us than by living in such a beautiful home. One afternoon Bryce put his arm around me after we returned from a long walk up into the scrub with Timmy and said, 'You know, we are both just a couple of corny country kids, and I couldn't be happier.'

Yarramalong was where I witnessed firsthand Bryce's passion for growing vegetables and herbs on a grand scale. He would say, 'Watching small seedlings mature into food for the table always feels to me like a miracle.' He was living his dream, as written in *Tandia*: 'I shall have a cottage garden. It's all here waiting for spring and a little love.'

Mind you, he had to protect his plants from the wildlife – including wombats, kangaroos and native birds – who believed his crops were being grown for them. Then there were the swarms of insects to contend with, which could appear as if out of nowhere. One summer night they descended and by morning his vegetable boxes had been stripped bare. Bryce was beside himself, even though he held no illusions about the power of nature.

I dared not imagine how many snakes and deadly funnel-web spiders were hiding in the undergrowth. One family member remarked to me, 'You do realise that the Yarramalong Valley is the funnel-web capital of Australia?' Well, in my two-and-a-half years of living there I never saw a snake or a spider except for a snake gliding across our dam during a filming session in April 2006. We were outside with Peter Thompson, who was interviewing Bryce for *Talking Heads* on ABC TV. I had to steel myself not to shriek in fear and resisted the urge to charge back up to the house.

The sight of wombats wandering around in the daylight hours was equally distressing as we could tell that they had gone blind from mange caught from foxes who had used their burrows. We used to call a local woman who would take them home and administer treatment in her living room; after they had recovered, she would release them back into the wild. Bryce donated money towards her costs as protecting wildlife was a passion we shared.

One evening we were watching *Australian Story* on the ABC and they were profiling a Victorian-based park ranger called Sean Willmore, who had set up an organisation called the Thin Green Line Foundation to raise funds to support the families of rangers who were killed by wildlife poachers in Africa. We sent him a cheque with the message: 'Here are some thin black lines to help you continue your work for the Thin Green Line.' I continue to be good friends with Sean, and years later he kindly arranged for me to meet the primatologist Jane Goodall, my wildlife heroine, after she delivered a lecture in Melbourne.

We rescued a sulphur-crested cockatoo who had been confined to a small cage by the couple living in our heritage cottage near the creek. I couldn't bear to see this beautiful creature barely able to turn around and with its cage exposed to the elements. Bryce shared my outrage and arranged for a carpenter who lived close by to build a huge aviary. We decked it out with tree trunks, and watching the poor bird tentatively flutter into its new enclosure brought me to tears. I would gather clumps of fresh grass for him to eat and as the sun went down flocks of wild cockatoos would circle overhead. His plaintive cries made us shake our heads at the cruelty humans bestow with indifference upon innocent creatures. The steel sheds in the valley that housed thousands of chickens in cramped and stifling conditions was also a depressing sight (they persist, sadly). And let's not get started on how domesticated pigs are housed – a great human failure in our midst.

Going to collect the eggs from the chook house at the bottom of our garden was a daily pilgrimage for Bryce. He called his hens 'Les Girls' and became terribly distressed if 'Mr Fox' broke into their roost in the dead of night. The ducks on the dam were also robbed of their ducklings by this artful predator. I used to say to Bryce, 'We need Granpa Chook from *The Power of One* to keep them safe.'

In April 2006 I travelled to the Kingdom of Bhutan on my first overseas trip since Bryce and I had begun living together. It was one of the few countries in the Himalayas I hadn't visited when I owned my trekking company, and I was planning to meet with government officials to discuss an environmental project for the AHF. I was hoping that Bryce would travel with me, but he said, 'You go, darling – I must keep writing my book.'

In 1985 Tenzing Norgay, the first man to climb Mount Everest, with Sir Edmund Hillary, had stayed as a guest at my house in Bellevue Hill.

Before departing Sydney, he had invited me to join a party who were planning to go to Bhutan as a guest of the King and other members of Bhutan's royal family. I had always regretted not accepting his invitation and had promised myself that one day I would travel there.

I invited my twin sister, Margaret, to come with me, and it was a memorable experience. We hiked up to the iconic Tiger's Nest monastery, and at Punakha we witnessed a Buddhist religious festival called a *tshechu*, where hundreds of Buddhist monks of all ages, clad in crimson robes, performed masked dances and ancient rituals in the grounds of a huge temple known as a *dzong*. Locals arrived from all over Bhutan to share in the celebrations, including reclusive Laya and Lunana villagers whose homes and yak camps cling to the sides of mountain passes as high as 6000 metres. Another highlight was sighting at close range a group of black-necked cranes (*Grus nigricollis*) in the Phobjikha Valley. These rare and breathtakingly beautiful birds are a recurring symbol in Bhutanese folklore and mythology, and we were thrilled to see them. We especially enjoyed being welcomed as guests at our good friend Payza's home. He had previously stayed with each of us on a trip to Australia. The chilli chutneys prepared by his mother to accompany a vegetarian feast were delicious, but not for the faint-hearted!

My meetings on behalf of the AHF went well, and we eventually formed a successful partnership with a local non-government organisation called RENEW that is dedicated to the empowerment of women and children in Bhutan. Her Majesty the Queen Mother Sangay Choden Wangchuck is its founder and president, and one of its strong focuses is helping survivors of family violence and gender-based violence.

I arrived back in the Yarramalong Valley with my nomadic yearnings quenched, overjoyed to be home with my darling man, who had missed me terribly. Bryce never really shared my insatiable desire to go travelling. He had already been on dozens of extraordinary journeys and could no longer be bothered queuing at airports, lining up to pass through security and sitting for hours on long flights. As long as he was able to write, watch the Rugby and work in the garden, he was happy.

Reading and listening to jazz and classical music also gave him enormous pleasure following a long day applying lots of 'bum glue'. His passion for music is captured in his final novel, *Jack of Diamonds*:

> If this was jazz, I knew almost immediately that I loved it. This music wasn't slow and tired like on the records upstairs . . . but came at me urgently; it jumped and barked and wailed, hammering into my consciousness. Then it would go smooth all of a sudden and make you smile.

Soon after I returned from Bhutan, Bryce asked me to consider becoming involved in managing the business side of his life. Having co-owned a world-renowned adventure travel company as well as a successful tourism and expedition consultancy, I relished taking this on. I knew it would give me something to do and I looked forward to the challenge of learning more about the world of publishing. Bryce was ecstatic when I said I was happy to oblige, as he was flat out writing and taking care of his sizeable property. When he chose to be involved in business decisions, he was incredibly astute and could be a tough negotiator, but he didn't enjoy handling the day-to-day matters as he found them tedious. Once, in front of an old friend, he said, 'Matey, I have struck gold as not only is Christine very beautiful and loving but she also has a great head for business. I now feel let off the hook and am free to write.' I retorted, 'Lucky Courtenay strikes again!' and we all had a good laugh. Bryce was very trusting and quickly saw that I took the responsibility seriously. He retained his personal assistant, Christine Lenton, who made sure that I was kept abreast of everything.

I was also now the first person to read Bryce's drafts of his *Sylvia* chapters. These were then sent to Penguin, led by Bob Sessions, assisted on this book by publisher Clare Forster and editors Lee White and Anne Rogan. I would read the drafts and give Bryce feedback. His son Adam also read early drafts of Bryce's manuscripts, and he is the author of several superbly written books himself. Adam's latest book, *Three Sheets to the Wind*, was released by HarperCollins in June 2022.

Bryce also continued to involve me with his research, which I thoroughly enjoyed. Over the years he collaborated with a number of talented researchers, each of whom was thanked extensively in the acknowledgements of the relevant book – such as Ann and Lindsay Jarvis for their work on *Four Fires*, teaching Bryce the nature of bushfires from the dry grass up to the blazing canopy.

I had graduated with an Arts degree from the ANU, and writing essays to the university's exacting standards meant having to complete weeks of research. But only Bryce would have decided to write a book as difficult as *Sylvia*. Taking on the subject of the Children's Crusade of 1212 demonstrates a factor that drove him to write. He said, 'One of the things I love about writing is that I get to learn about things I have previously known nothing about.'

While writing *Sylvia*, however, his patience was sorely tested. He said to me, 'This book is such hard going – I cannot get enough information about the medieval era to make the story feel right.' I managed to discover two vital researchers from Macquarie University, Jessica Wynands and Clare Rowan, whose contributions proved invaluable. I frankly don't know what Bryce would have done if I hadn't found them.

The ongoing technology problems were an enduring frustration. Email was only possible via a dial-up process facilitated by the satellite dish outside; and upstairs, where Bryce was writing, he couldn't even receive emails. I had to print them out from my computer and run up and down the stairs all day to ensure he received the material he needed.

Bryce was worried people might not care for the subject of the Children's Crusade. He said, 'I hope my readers will forgive me for writing *Sylvia*. This era is a huge departure from the times and themes I have written about before.' It turned out his readers did forgive him and most really loved the book, although some struggled to embrace it. He said in an interview at home recorded by Michael Dillon on 3 September 2012, 'Thank God there is only one *Sylvia*.'

When not helping Bryce I spent a lot of time cooking, as there were no restaurants or takeaway outlets in the valley. Fortunately, I loved cooking and from the age of ten had helped my mother in the kitchen on our farm in Wooragee. As I put another dish into the oven at Yarramalong, I would reflect that despite the luxuries of modern appliances, not a lot had changed for country women!

My mother, Kathleen (usually known as Kath), did not have the luxury of a dishwasher or a housekeeper, and washing our clothes in the copper took all day. The arrival of summer fruits meant boiling them up on the wood-burning stove to make jams and pickles – I used to tell her, 'You will bottle anything that can be forced into a jar.' Nothing was thrown out, although I always declined the cow's tongue Mum would place in an enamel bowl in the fridge pressed down by an old-fashioned metal iron. But her afternoon teas were irresistible and her cinnamon sponges were legendary. Relatives would arrive at our house on Sunday afternoons, eat everything in sight and then race out the door to be home in time for milking.

The uncertainties surrounding my new life in the Yarramalong Valley appeared to be endless. We were amused to read in the papers that the area was becoming an enclave inhabited by celebrities. The radio announcer John Laws owned the farm next door, and the former New South Wales premier Neville Wran and his wife Jill (who had played a key role in the publication of *The Power of One*) had a property there too. In contrast, some of our neighbours had lived in the valley for generations and a few had never been to Sydney – goodness knows what they must have thought of these 'high-flyers' who had arrived to live in their quiet rural enclave. Mind you, they didn't seem to mind the cheques that were handed over for their parcels of land.

Bryce enjoyed the company of the locals and appreciated how down to earth they were. He was relieved that they weren't especially impressed that he was a famous author. They would say things like,

'G'day, Bryce. Did you manage to get your fence fixed after my bull broke in?'

Bryce had originally thought about buying a property in the Southern Highlands and had once even contemplated moving to Hobart in Tasmania. He had discovered Yarramalong by chance after driving up there one weekend to check it out.

I loved swimming but was not keen on bathing in our creek, so Bryce suggested that we install a swimming pool at the back of the house. He wasn't a keen swimmer, but he encouraged me to supervise this project. I didn't proceed after discussing the idea with a local who already owned a pool. He told me, 'It's great to have one to cool off in, but you have to be prepared to scoop out the occasional funnel-web spider and dispatch the odd snake that arrives for a dip.'

Most people harbour idyllic notions of country life, but having spent seventeen years on a farm I can tell you that the reality is vastly different. You are always at the mercy of the weather, the market prices for selling livestock and the never-ending hard physical jobs, such as fencing. At times these challenges exact a toll on families and relationships, even though there are undoubted rewards.

The local shop was a twenty-minute drive away and, although I was grateful there was any shop at all, it resembled something from the set of a 1970s film, with food choices to match. It had me thinking back to the Ennals store in Beechworth where you had to submit your handwritten list of items and wait as the elderly owners went up and down ladders to fetch tins of sweet corn, bottles of red cochineal food colouring and packets of jelly. Our most coveted treat was a tub of Peter's brand neapolitan ice-cream, which we used to wolf down following the Sunday roast dinner.

One Saturday night during winter Bryce and I went by helicopter to Sydney to see a game of Rugby between the New Zealand All Blacks and the Wallabies, Australia's national team. Bryce's son Adam drove to the stadium to join us along with Greg and Lorraine Woon, who had organised the flight. Bryce enjoyed himself enormously but I was bored to tears and spent most of the match sitting in the women's rest rooms reading a book.

I used to look forward to going to Sydney for a regular fix of city life and during those times Bryce must have felt lonely, even though he was an incredibly capable and independent person who could cook, clean, iron and sew as he had done from a very early age. As I was about to leave he would always put on a brave face and say, 'Go and have a lovely time, sweetheart, and don't worry about me.' He could tell I loved spending a few days at the flat in Rose Bay. I also needed to attend meetings for the AHF and was obliged to fulfil my responsibilities as the Royal Nepalese honorary consul-general.

From the time we came together Bryce was insistent that I maintain my own interests. He would say, 'Remember, darling, you are living with an older man and you must not give up anything which is important to you. If I drop off the perch, your life must and will go on.' Then he would say, 'You must never allow your life to be consumed by the world of Bryce Courtenay.' That sentiment was all very well in theory, but I can assure you my life was indeed consumed by the world of Bryce Courtenay! Make no mistake: he anticipated my unwavering support and it was abundantly clear that he was the centrepiece of our life. Over time I happily adapted to this notion and came to love him 'to the moon and back'.

Friday nights usually saw us hosting a dinner party for some of our neighbours. We looked forward to these occasions and the company, and I would cook up a storm usually featuring fresh seafood I had brought back from the Sydney Fish Market. One evening, however, Bryce's carpentry skills literally came unstuck when a big painting above the dining-room table came crashing down as we were eating dessert. It narrowly missed falling onto the head of one of our guests, and first thing next morning I arranged to have it bolted to the wall. Bryce had a pretty good capacity for drinking, and after one of these dinners he could barely walk in a straight line. He looked thoroughly seedy the next day, but after downing a few cups of strong coffee he headed upstairs as usual and sat down to write.

To my surprise, a small grey cat with a white face turned up in late July. I had first seen her little body pressed against the glass near our front door during a massive thunderstorm. A couple of weeks later my brother, Bruce, arrived for a visit accompanied by his girlfriend Kathleen. He said, 'I see you've got another cat.' He had noticed her under some bushes beside the veranda. Once we started leaving out food, she showed no sign of going and it wasn't long before we had an additional feline in our lives. The arrival of the 'bush cat' we called Muschka was the last straw for my imperious Burmese, who had already made it clear to Timmy she was in charge with a few rounds of hissing and cuffs around his face to put him in his place. It was quite something to later see these two asleep on a bed together beside the fire during cold winter nights.

Not every visitor was quite so welcome. A rather odd fellow began turning up in the evenings having drunk a few too many beers. He would arrive in a battered old ute and an ugly scene occurred on one occasion after he made unwelcome overtures towards me. Without hesitation Bryce rose to his feet and said, 'You need to get going before I show you what I'm made of.' A couple of weeks later the man followed me in his vehicle along the road by our house as I was out walking. I turned and ran home.

Another time I looked up from the kitchen bench to see a woman in her mid-thirties walking towards me having entered the house unnoticed. I had never seen her before and asked, 'Who are you and what do you want?' She said, 'I'm a huge fan of Bryce Courtenay's and I found out where he lived from one of the locals.' Then she held up a pair of plastic, ivory-coloured Asian statues she wanted to give him. Bryce had heard Timmy barking and came downstairs to see what was going on, and he skilfully managed to coax the woman back to her car.

After these incidents I insisted on having a lock placed on the front gate as well as a 'Beware of the Dog' sign. If only they knew what a sweet and gentle dog our Timothy Courtenay really was. Bryce thought it very un-neighbourly and within a few days he removed it, which I reluctantly accepted.

Other colourful characters of the valley became friends, such as Rick, a local farmer who lived nearby and had been born and bred there. He and Bryce loved having a natter together. Both were reluctant to see the local 'quack'. Rick apparently had a heart condition and resorted to some home-grown measures. Bryce told me he said, 'I fixed meself up. See that electric fence over there? It keeps the bull next door from getting my heifers into the family way. So I tied myself to it and got a jolt and ever since my ticker's been right as rain.'

Over the course of that first year in Yarramalong I witnessed first-hand the phenomenal effort Bryce made to complete a book in only seven months. Sometimes people would say to him, 'I'm writing a book too' and to his bewilderment would advise that they had been writing it for five years.

It was especially difficult for Bryce to write quickly as he was a two-finger typist. In addition, he had gnarled arthritic hands and a worn-out spinal fusion that meant he suffered frequent bouts of excruciating back pain. I had learnt to touch-type at Beechworth High School and could do so at sixty-five words per minute. Our teacher used to stride between our desks while clapping her hands to the sounds of the 'Colonel Bogey March'! When watching me type my own work Bryce would say, 'If I could type as fast as you do, I could finish a book in three or four months.'

In late August, just as his book deadline was approaching, he experienced a setback. It was a Saturday afternoon and he appeared downstairs with an ashen look on his face and said, 'Muschka's just deleted the final chapter of *Sylvia* by walking across the keyboard.' I tore upstairs to see if I could retrieve the lost chapter and gently admonished Bryce for not saving it or printing it out as he went along. My efforts to salvage his work failed, and the computer geek from Gosford we depended upon couldn't retrieve the chapter either. With a weary look on his face Bryce walked back upstairs to rewrite it. He didn't finish until 4 a.m. the following morning and was utterly exhausted. Muschka was subsequently placed in the proverbial doghouse, but she was unrepentant.

Bryce submitted *Sylvia* to Penguin on time on 31 August 2006.

Afterwards he could do little more than sit on the front deck with a cup of coffee or a glass of wine and doze off in the afternoons after tending to his garden.

In September of that year we welcomed Bryce's sister, Rosemary, her husband, Esmund, and their daughter, Dorrie, for a visit. They lived in San Diego in the USA and Bryce had not seen them since he was last there in 2001. I had proposed the idea earlier in the year and Bryce had telephoned them in June to confirm our invitation and offer to cover all their costs.

It turned out to be a wonderful reunion, and I was thrilled to meet them and be received so warmly. They were overjoyed to be with Bryce again and marvelled at our beautiful home in its idyllic rural setting. As Bryce wasn't writing he was free to spend a lot of time with them, and I loved listening to their stories about their mother and growing up together in Africa, as well as learning more about Bryce's adventures at the Roan Antelope mine and, later, in London. Those family bonds ran deep, and they had a lot of catching up to do in just a few short weeks. Bryce enjoyed getting to know Dorrie more and learning about her passion for working in education and her love of travelling.

Rosemary, Esmund and Dorrie also had a wonderful time catching up with Bryce's boys, Brett and Adam, and their families in Sydney. We organised shopping excursions for them to David Jones and shared their excitement when they showed us their purchases. In the middle of their month-long visit, we arranged for them to fly to Uluru in Central Australia. Bryce was somewhat amused and bewildered when they returned to Yarramalong and Rosemary said, 'It was an amazing experience all round, and we shall never forget that delicious spaghetti bolognaise we ate at the Yulara resort.'

Bryce did not share Rosemary and Esmund's religious zeal – he had long ago left the fold, and his patience was tested when they occasionally referred to 'the second coming of the Lord'. However, trying to have a rational discussion on the subject proved to be utterly fruitless. These 'discussions', he said, reminded him of the religious dogma he had heard from his mother after she joined the Assemblies of God Church. I expect Rosemary, Es and Dorrie felt similarly exasperated with Bryce and are likely to have been bewildered by his lack of religious faith. I did my best to broker some kind of rapprochement on the matter but didn't make much headway.

Bryce had told me, 'I love Rosemary very much as she's my only sibling, but we squabbled a fair bit while growing up and were never really that close.' Rosemary also told me that they used to bicker often, which is true of most siblings. We should also remember that they grew up in deprived circumstances and would have been under a lot of strain much of the time. When they talked about being separated by their mother, with Rosemary being sent to stay with relatives or kept with Paddy while Bryce was left in a hostel or boarding house (Rosemary also spent some time in these institutions), she went quiet and looked sad. My heart went out to them, even though they always expressed profound gratitude to their mother for doing all she could to take care of them. They also exchanged stories of happy times and amazing adventures, including being chased by wild animals and other narrow escapes that could only have happened in Africa. It was also wonderful hearing stories of Es's family, who had spent most of their lives in Africa, and he and Bryce shared a close bond through their mutual love of Rugby and cricket.

Bryce and Rosemary had spent most of their adult years living in different countries and leading very different lives, often going for years without seeing each other, so this visit felt especially important. On the final evening Bryce asked Rosemary to go outside and sit with him on a bench under his favourite tree, an acacia he had nursed back to life following a big storm. He knew it could be the last time they were together given their age and their residing in different countries. He desperately wanted to resolve some longstanding issues between them, including Rosemary's unease (shared by their late mother) over the extent to which *The Power of One* was autobiographical.

Overall, I observed that they maintained different perceptions about aspects of their mother. Bryce was not at all comfortable with Rosemary's version of some of their family story, which she had handed him in a spiral-bound folder soon after their arrival with a determined look on her face. It was called 'Rosemary's Story' and I heard her say, '*This* is the truth.' While they were staying with us Bryce read what she had written and was left feeling perplexed. I also read it and was especially interested to learn more about their descendants and to see the photos of their forebears and early childhood years. I also enjoyed reading poems written by Paddy.

I tried to calm Bryce down by saying, 'Darling, you of all people would appreciate that siblings always view their childhoods differently. In addition, Rosemary embraced and maintained a profound religious faith which you discarded long ago. It is therefore perfectly understandable that she interprets many aspects of her life through this prism.'

Unfortunately, their discussion in the garden was fairly brief. Bryce told me that Rosemary deflected most of his attempts to engage her in a meaningful chat, and that she kept tugging at her cardigan and looking away before she scurried back inside to finish her packing. It can't have been easy for her, either, as both of them had gone through a great deal and reviving those childhood memories must have been difficult.

As we waved the family off the following morning, Bryce returned to the house unusually downcast. It was one of the few times I ever saw him steeped in sadness, and later that evening he downed one-and-a-half bottles of wine before retiring early to bed. He believed the chance of resolving their differences and acknowledging their differing perspectives of their childhood had been lost.

For now, I tried to reassure him that in spite of all this, Rosemary and her family loved him very dearly and genuinely appreciated all the support he had provided them throughout his life. No one could have done more: he had paid for all his mother's needs for decades and

Rosemary's medical bills after she was diagnosed with cancer in early 2001. In addition, he had paid for her and Esmund to enjoy several trips abroad and had been a generous benefactor of the South African charity they had been closely involved with. The reality was that although he and his sister loved each other, they viewed the world quite differently and didn't have all that much in common. Regardless, the love between them was never for a moment in question, and they shared an unbreakable bond forged during their challenging upbringing.

Bryce and Rosemary never met up again, but I am certain they both cherished the memories from that 2006 Australian visit. I continue to stay in touch with the family including with Dorrie and her brother Owen who so kindly sent me some photos for this memoir. I saw Rosemary, Es and Dorrie in Los Angeles a couple of years after Bryce passed away. It meant the world to me to spend this time with them, and I plan on visiting them again next year.

On Thursday 16 November we attended together as a couple the launch of *Sylvia* hosted by Penguin Books at the Paddington Uniting Church in Oxford Street, Sydney, which was styled in a mediaeval theme in keeping with the new look. There were long tables overflowing with wine and a rich feast of fruit, cheeses and meats. On the way there Bryce flipped open a copy of the book to show that he had dedicated it to me, which was such an honour that I crumpled with tears and mascara ran down my cheeks. Fiona McIntosh, once a student of his writing class and now a bestselling author, was also included in the dedication for having introduced Bryce to the story of the Children's Crusade. We were joined at the launch by Bryce's sons and their families, our friends and the dedicated team from Penguin. We all had a wonderful time, and people later told me they could see a palpable glow between Bryce and me.

A final surprise was in store for me that year. Soon after the launch and prior to his nationwide publicity tour, Bryce told me he had arranged for us to go to New Zealand. He said, 'Darling, we are going to stay at Huka Lodge near Taupo.' The owner was Alex van Heeren CVO MBE, a very close friend of Bryce's, and they thought the world of each other. They had met when Bryce gave a talk at a literary lunch at the lodge years earlier. Alex was responsible for putting Huka Lodge on the world map. Her Majesty Queen Elizabeth II has stayed at Huka on more than one occasion, as have other famous guests, including Hollywood movie stars and rock music legends.

I had always dreamt of going there and knew it would offer Bryce a well-deserved break following his marathon effort to finish writing *Sylvia*. We flew to Auckland and travelled to Huka by limousine before being escorted to the owners' cottage nestling beside the churning waters of the Waikato River. Brown scaup ducks were settling in for the night and I spied the resident marmalade cat curled up on a manicured pathway. The Queen had stayed in these quarters, which were set well away from the other guests. We didn't have any staff in tow, but I was sure we were about to enjoy a right royal experience! It was the most elegant lodge I had ever seen, and felt like we had entered a dream. Alex used to describe his lodge as providing 'barefoot luxury and the ultimate retreat', and that sums it up perfectly.

More surprises were in store. While seated outside before an open fire, we enjoyed a sumptuous degustation dinner prepared by the head chef. Afterwards a waiter appeared with a silver tray holding two crystal glasses of Krug Vintage champagne. I noticed he had a shy grin on his face but he hurried away before I had the chance to thank him.

I began to wonder what was going on. Bryce reached out and clasped my hands. Looking straight into my eyes, he said, 'Darling Christine, I love you so very much and please will you marry me?' I held my breath and my tears welled up as I said, 'Yes, of course I will, darling. I would love to marry you.' Bryce leapt to his feet and, overcome with emotion, shouted to the night sky, 'Good goddles caboddles, she's said yes! Christine Gee is going to be my wife!' He then presented me with a magnificent diamond engagement ring in the 'Tiffany setting'; later he told me the stone had been sourced from his homeland of South Africa.

It was a magical conclusion to a year that had had some highs and some lows, but that in most respects had been unforgettable.

13

MATTERS OF THE HEART

───────────

'In all things, may your heart be as soft and sweet and generous as the fruit of the sacred persimmon tree, your body as resilient as the outer wood, and your mind as strong as its heartwood.' – *The Persimmon Tree*

THE YEAR 2007 WAS a tough one for Bryce. On Sunday 11 March his first wife, Benita, passed away aged seventy-two after a long battle with illness. The night before, we had been about to have dinner when Bryce received a phone call saying that Benita's health was rapidly deteriorating. He raced out the door headed for Sydney, driven by my brother, Bruce, who was staying with us at the time. Upon arrival at St Vincent's Hospital, Bryce met up with Brett and Adam and their wives, Ann and Gina, who had gathered at Benita's bedside. It was a desperately sad time and Bryce was inconsolable when he called to tell me that she had passed away at 8.45 that morning.

Bryce and Benita were married for forty-two years and, although they had divorced in 2000, remained on exceptionally good terms. Bryce never forgot her love and loyalty and how she had been such a wonderful mother to their three sons and a devoted grandmother to Jake, Ben and Marcus. Her funeral service was held at Rookwood Cemetery on 14 March and Bryce delivered the eulogy. As the *Sydney Morning Herald* reported:

He delivered an emotional eulogy in which he acknowledged his former wife's selflessness, saying that he was 'outclassed' by the young woman he met in London in 1955 when he was a 23-year-old South African student on a scholarship and she was an 'amazingly sophisticated' 21-year-old Australian on an extended holiday . . . 'She inspired me – she was the best partner you could have as a writer. She always gave me her full support.'

What Bryce had wanted most in life was to have a family of his own, and his family meant more to him than the achievements of his career. I had met Benita many times, and sometimes she came to stay with us at Yarramalong to have a break from the city. She and I got along very well and I enjoyed chatting to her about her passion for England and Italy, drawing upon her extraordinary knowledge of art and literature. One afternoon we were seated beside the fire and she said, 'You are very good for Bryce. He looks happy, and I think you should get married.' I was completely taken aback and didn't know what to say.

I always felt grateful that Benita was so warm-hearted and gracious towards me, as the situation can't have been easy for her. I could well understand why Bryce had fallen head over heels in love with her when he was studying journalism in London in the 1950s. She had shaped his path in more ways than one – if it hadn't been for Benita, he would probably never have come to Australia, where he had the opportunity to make his mark in the advertising industry, follow his dreams as a writer, and contribute to the shaping of Australian culture.

Benita was ahead of her time in that she forged her own stellar career in a male-dominated industry and after having her children didn't follow the path, expected by many at the time, of a 'typical' wife and mother. Bryce said she was a devoted mother but didn't like cooking or housework overly much, not that this bothered him, and instead she held steadfast to her passion for the arts, and this was something he always loved and admired about her. Benita also had a perspective on life that I found to be enlightened and interesting, and never for one minute was she parochial.

Earlier that year, on 1 February, Bryce had begun writing his next book, which was the sequel to *Sylvia*. He wasn't relishing the prospect as he had found it very difficult to complete the original *Sylvia*. Within weeks he was again battling to find enough research material, and he began to question if he should be writing a sequel at all. He confided, 'My readers forgave me for writing *Sylvia*, but I am not sure they will forgive me for *Sylvia 2*.' Always one to embrace a challenge, he had signed a contract even though Penguin shared his unease about how a second *Sylvia* would be received.

One evening in early February, Bryce said in an unusually agitated voice, 'Christ, I'm finding this book so difficult. I'm struggling to get through a few pages a day.' He looked trapped, but with a contract in place and thousands of readers awaiting a Christmas release, he felt compelled to keep going. Soon afterwards, we were sitting outside in the garden and I said, 'If you are hating this book so much, what is the point of continuing? If you stopped now, could you start writing that other story you mentioned last Christmas?' Friends from a neighbouring property had told him about a group of Australian sailors who had survived their ship being sunk by the Japanese and ended up hiding in the jungles of Java. While this story turned out not to be entirely accurate, it became the inspiration for one of Bryce's best books. He looked relieved as he considered my question – I was in effect giving him permission to stop writing *Sylvia 2*. He went quiet before responding, 'Only if I start straight away, and I will need a lot of help with the research.'

I walked into the house and called Bruce, who was working for Toyota in Melbourne. In 1997, after living in the Pacific for seventeen years, he had started work as Bryce's primary researcher for several books, including *Tommo & Hawk*, *Solomon's Song* and *Jessica*. I managed to talk him into resigning from his job, and Bryce immediately put him to work. I could tell that the Penguins were relieved to know that Bryce had ditched the idea of a sequel to *Sylvia*, and within a few days a new contract arrived for him to sign. He decided to call the new book *The Persimmon Tree*. Straight away I could see he was much happier writing about an era close to his heart. The first few chapters danced off the page and *Sylvia 2* was well and truly buried. Not everyone was happy about this – I'm aware of some dedicated readers very disappointed that the sequel to *Sylvia* was never completed!

Amazingly, a short time later we discovered a grove of persimmon trees in a far corner of our property. They were gnarled and laden with fruit that the birds had gorged on, leaving precious little for us. Persimmons are commonly found in Japan, where they are called Oriental persimmons, and had a wonderful synergy with the themes Bryce was weaving into his story. He told me he had first seen the fruit on a trip to China in 1985 when he was working in advertising. Prior to that he only recalled seeing them in still-life paintings while visiting galleries in Europe with Benita.

The Salmon brothers of Wyong Creek had introduced citrus fruit to the Yarramalong Valley in the early 1900s and it became a major industry there following the decline in timber felling. Before long they introduced persimmons and stone fruits too. Fruit growing in the valley declined after the end of the Second World War and by the 1960s had all but disappeared from the area. These old persimmon groves had survived, and Bryce took our finding them as a sign his book was meant to be.

In 2011 we planted a persimmon tree in the middle of our back garden in Canberra, which always reminded us of the book. As Bryce turned the earth I read aloud from *The Persimmon Tree* the words of one of its characters, Konoe Akira:

These are the metaphors: the core, beyond strength of will; the resilience of the outer wood that will not splinter but always keeps to its resolve; the leaves that, in providing shelter, consider the convenience of others beside themselves; finally, the ripened fulfilment, when the autumn of life comes and with it the soft fruitfulness of wisdom and love to be passed on.

At the start of 2007 we had left Yarramalong to go on a five-week trip to South America. We travelled with three friends and were very excited, having only previously made a stopover in Buenos Aires on the way to Antarctica. We spent the first few days in Santiago and were enchanted by our visit to the home of the Nobel prize–winning poet Pablo Neruda. Bryce loved his writing; he had written poems himself since childhood. He also loved the works of the Argentinian author Jorge Louis Borges, and he loved the Chilean wines – sometimes a little too much! Santiago reminded both of us of the canyons of Los Angeles, and being there was a great start to our trip.

Our arrival in Lima, the capital of Peru, was a different story. Bryce commented, 'This place reminds me of a South American Las Vegas and has a seedy undercurrent', which I agreed was true. We were saddened to see impoverished people lining the footpaths all over the city. They had come from rural areas hoping for a better life but were reduced to selling trinkets to tourists like us to survive.

We were thrilled to visit an Inca site called Huaca Pucllana in the upscale Miraflores district, which housed a superb restaurant serving pisco sours that nearly blew our heads off. This cocktail is made with pisco liquor and lime juice, topped with a dollop of whisked egg white. We enjoyed the modern Peruvian cuisine although we couldn't contemplate eating guinea pigs, the local speciality. It was disconcerting to see guinea pigs housed in hutches in the corner of restaurants waiting to have their necks broken and to be cooked and served to diners.

We paid a visit to the Gold Museum where Bryce bought me a beautiful ring and earrings, and a necklace studded with a selection of Peruvian topaz. Being an accomplished dressmaker, Paddy used to love looking at fine clothes and jewellery but never had the money to buy them. Bryce said that day, 'I feel so happy to be able to indulge my beloved Christine.' I purchased a brightly coloured handwoven rug for him, but he passed it onto Timmy as the texture was 'scratchy' and gave him a rash! Bryce didn't think much of the Peruvian roses, which are an important export for Peru, but I loved them as they were so perfect. Bryce, ever the gardener, thought they were 'over-engineered'.

We savoured our time travelling, knowing he'd soon be hard at work on his next book. But at times on this trip he seemed to be out of sorts, insisting on being right about everything. I brushed it off and attributed it to jet lag, or to him sometimes drinking one glass of wine too many over dinner the night before.

Our next stop was the city of Cusco, situated 8399 metres above sea level and the usual departure point for visiting the UNESCO World Heritage Site of Machu Picchu. Soon after arriving we began to feel short of breath due to the altitude. Even so, we enjoyed ambling along the cobblestoned streets, passing herds of llamas tended by Quechua people wearing traditional dress. Returning to our hotel in the centre of town, we sat down to enjoy another pisco sour. I should have known better – drinking at altitude is never a good idea. Having run trekking tours in the Himalayas, I was aware of the perils of altitude sickness and cautioned Bryce to take things easy when he caught the attention of a waiter to bring us another round. Our local guide, Inti, told us that the best cure for AMS (acute mountain sickness) was to chew on coca leaves, but doing so didn't appear to make any difference for us.

Coping with the altitude was handsomely rewarded when we arrived at the Inca ruins of Machu Picchu, which sit at 2430 metres above the Urubamba River. Inti, who resembled an Inca god, accompanied us on a private tour there at additional expense, but it was worth every sol. We marvelled at the vista of fifteenth-century ruins and tried to imagine the lives of the people who had once lived there. Inti told us grisly stories of alleged sacrifices of children and llamas, made to the mountain gods.

Later that day we visited a poor *barrio* (neighbourhood) on the outskirts of town, where we met an American woman from New York who had walked the Inca Trail and fallen in love with her guide. Now based in Cusco, she had started running classes for children whose families couldn't afford to send them to school. We handed over some copies of the junior edition of *The Power of One* and pledged funds towards this inspiring project.

Over dinner we ate a delicious Peruvian dish made from potatoes called *papa a la huancaína*. I noticed that Bryce didn't look well. His complexion was pale and he continued to be rather short with me, which was totally out of character. Not one to brook being fussed over, he insisted he would be all right after a good sleep. Instead, later that night I became so concerned that I called reception to send for a doctor. The doctor was a Quechuan man who had studied medicine in Lima, and he hooked Bryce up to an oxygen cylinder that resembled a long black unexploded bomb. After taking Bryce's pulse and examining him he said, 'Your husband has a problem with his heart – it keeps missing beats.' This was alarming, as I knew there wouldn't be a heart specialist here on the slopes of the Andes.

After a night on the oxygen Bryce felt much better and to our relief my jewellery, which had gone missing, was handed in by a cleaner who had found it squirreled away in the hotel laundry. With the doctor's guarded blessing, Bryce flew down to the Amazon rainforest, which he had always dreamed of seeing. I should have gone with him but am so frightened of snakes that our friends insisted I stay in Cusco; they were going with him and reassured me they would keep a close eye on him. He loved being in the Amazon and called me to say, 'The forest is as ancient as time itself – it feels as old as Africa', even though he explained 'I barely got a wink of sleep with the howler monkeys screeching all night in the trees surrounding the lodge!'

Before Bryce passed away, he was thrilled to know that his son Adam was writing a book about the Amazon. This fascinating book, *Amazon Men*, was published in 2015 and Bryce would have been so proud to see it in print. It was described in *The Australian* newspaper as: 'Captivating . . . An examination of the complex and contradictory human responses to the development of the Amazon and to its preservation.'

After he arrived back in Cusco, Bryce's breathlessness returned with a vengeance. I thought we should consider returning to Sydney so he could see his cardiologist, but he wouldn't hear of our trip being curtailed. We flew to Punta Arenas, the capital city of Chile's southernmost region and the gateway to Patagonia. Bryce began to feel better at this lower altitude and we were all relieved. *In Patagonia* by Bruce Chatwin was a book we both loved, and we pinched ourselves to be travelling through this vast wilderness that was home to gauchos riding across the Pampas dotted with guanocos, which are closely related to llamas. We were hoping to spot an elusive puma and marvelled at the condors circling overhead in search of prey.

As our bus rumbled along the Patagonian highway, we were in awe of the spires of the Cordillera Paine. I told Bryce that my dear friend the legendary British mountaineer Sir Chris Bonington, along with Don Whillans, had been the first to climb the central tower of Paine, in 1963. Bryce and I embarked on some challenging walks there, including to a glacier-fed lake dotted with icebergs that bobbed like corks by the shoreline. The aqua veins within the bergs reminded us of what we had seen on our voyage to Antarctica and South Georgia in November 2000. Just like in Antarctica the notorious weather didn't let us down, and on one occasion we were almost flattened to the ground by a blast of katabatic winds.

We stayed at an impressive eco-lodge called Explora Patagonia and ran into a couple of Australians who were loyal Bryce Courtenay fans. There was no escaping their overtures towards him, and Bryce characteristically threw his arms around them and told me to post them signed books once we were home. He then invited them to join us for dinner, which of course they agreed to. Although Bryce was a very private person, I came to realise he loved being recognised, and revelled in fans' excitement upon meeting him. I wondered if he needed their attention just as much as they relished his.

I continued to worry about his shortness of breath, which returned within a couple of days. He looked relieved when I said we really must now consider returning home. We boarded the plane in Santiago, and I was having trouble fitting my bag into the overhead locker when a man's hand reached up from behind to help. I turned to thank him and realised it was the Olympic swimming legend Ian Thorpe. After I let out an embarrassing squeak, Ian and I proceeded to spend most of the flight talking while Bryce slept. Ian was delightful and I noticed he had the biggest feet of anyone I had ever seen. I said to him, 'No wonder you were able to swim so fast', to which he shyly smiled.

Bryce was thankful to get home. He couldn't wait to sort out his overgrown veggie patch, visit his harem of chooks, and take Timmy for a walk in the surrounding hills. Tim loved to sniff out the wild goats and wallabies who would take off at high speed, as did the plovers he disturbed from their nests.

Not long after we returned from South America, just prior to Easter, Bryce walked into my study and said, 'Darling, I think you had better give Tony a ring – I'm feeling a bit breathless.' He was red in the face and I knew he must have been crook as he usually brushed off feeling unwell without a word. Dr Anthony Freeman was a great friend of his and a former running mate as well as his cardiologist. Very concerned, I told Bryce we should let Tony know and then immediately head to the emergency department at Gosford Hospital or the Sydney Adventist Hospital (SAN) in Wahroonga. With dread I recalled the day my father had suffered an angina attack on our farm and how he nearly died in Beechworth Hospital when the matron told him to 'stop playing up' after he rang the bell to inform her his chest pains were becoming worse. There was only one GP, the dedicated Dr 'Eb' Collins, for the whole town, and seeing a cardiologist meant having to take a three-hour train ride from Wangaratta to Melbourne.

Bryce wouldn't hear of going to hospital and instead walked back upstairs to continue writing. Cardamon glanced up from her bed while Timmy snored beneath Bryce's desk. I followed Bryce and asked if he was experiencing any other symptoms, such as pain running down his arms or tightness in his chest. 'Yeah, I guess I am,' he said, looking like a child who knows they have just been caught out in a fib. He said, 'I've got a book to write. I'll be fine.' I replied, 'Do you want to be writing this book in heaven?' Bryce ended up getting his way, although I was extremely worried and called Adam straight away. He shared my concerns, and I recall it was he who scheduled an appointment with Tony straight after Easter.

While I was writing this book, Tony reminded me that Bryce had been diagnosed with aortic valve disease in July 2005, around the time we were getting together (hopefully not a coincidence!). Bryce's friend and GP Irwin Light had referred him to Tony for an assessment and he recalled the experience:

> I always remember when he came in for a cardiac assessment prior to undertaking a trek on the Kokoda Trail. He was totally stunned when I said he needed to go into hospital immediately for work on his heart and the Kokoda Trail would have to wait. Initially he refused, but once I explained that he was at risk of a stroke and potential brain damage, he readily acceded to my request.

Bryce was examined in Tony's consulting rooms in Randwick on 12 April 2007, but he wasn't there for long. Tony called an ambulance and Bryce was taken to the cardiac ward at the Prince of Wales Hospital and treated with blood thinners to protect him against a thromboembolic risk – that is, the chance of suffering a stroke. He was admitted under the name of 'Mr Timothy Ryder' to prevent any fans from inadvertently turning up on the ward. He was diagnosed with both atrial fibrillation and moderate to severe aortic stenosis. The aortic valve is the major outlet valve of the heart, and stenosis leads to a restriction of blood flow not only to the heart but to the rest of the body as all the blood pumped by the heart has to travel through this valve. Bryce was told he needed to have emergency surgery to insert a replacement valve. I asked Dr Peter Grant, the cardiothoracic surgeon, how long Bryce would survive if he didn't have the operation. 'About two weeks,' he answered, with a serious expression on his face.

I was feeling distraught but remained focused, staying at Bryce's bedside and making sure his family and close friends were kept up to date. Quite a few of them visited, including his friend and neighbour Dr Ross Hayes, and Bryce looked like he didn't have a care in the world. I also needed to find someone to go and stay at the farm to feed the chooks and look after Timmy, Cardamon and Muschka. Kim Rabbits, Bryce's foreman, came over most days, but ours wasn't a property you could leave unattended overnight. Thankfully, an old friend of Bryce's called Celia Jarvis (also at one time one of his researchers) stepped in and we were hugely grateful to her and her partner, William, for taking on this responsibility at such short notice.

Bryce was the least neurotic person I have ever known. Even following the diagnosis he said, 'Don't worry, darling. Once I'm through the operation, I'll be back home writing in ten days.' I rolled my eyes: both Dr Grant and Tony had told me he would need to rest and take it easy for several weeks. Bryce's heart valve was duly replaced on 17 April. I spent the day pacing up and down the hospital corridors praying like mad that my darling would be all right. I was so relieved when Tony called me to say that everything had gone well, and Bryce's family shared my immense feeling of relief.

Bryce needed to spend the routine twenty-four hours in ICU, but he was soon back on the ward and able to receive visitors even though most of the time he remained fast asleep. Within a few days he was looking better, and he said with a naughty look on his face, 'Darling, can you bring me in a bottle of wine? I'm dying for a drink.' I asked Tony if this would be all right and he nodded with a resigned look, saying, 'I deal with my patients' heart problems, not with their addictions.' I sneaked in a bottle of William Fèvre French chablis, Bryce's favourite, wrapped in a brown-paper bag to make certain it would get past the eagle-eyed nurses stationed on the ward.

After ten days we were back at our Sydney apartment and Bryce was told to stay there for three weeks to be near his medical team. This did not sit well with him, and an additional issue was that a team of tradespeople turned up early most mornings. The lovely old 1920s flat, which I had purchased the previous year, was in the middle of an extensive renovation and was hardly a tranquil place for Bryce to be recuperating in. He was desperately homesick, and it was hard to buoy his spirits. He missed Timmy and the wide-open spaces of his beloved Yarramalong Valley and spent most days dozing on the settee on the balcony with a book across his chest; it overlooks Sydney Harbour and offers the perfect vista of the Manly ferries gliding by and the passing parade of cruise ships as waves swish onto Lady Martins Beach below. At night he would sip a glass of wine while having dinner and watching the news on television.

After about twelve days he was becoming impatient and one evening he said, 'Darling, I know you could happily live here all the time, but I would go crazy. I can't imagine staying in a place where I can't put my hands into the earth and grow things.' He was also very concerned as to how he could finish *The Persimmon Tree* on time. It was already early May, and the deadline of 31 August loomed large in his mind. The following morning I set up his computer on the balcony.

Once he was back to writing he cheered up – that is, until he read what he had just written. He told me in a trembling voice, 'It's utter gobbledygook.' He was distressed at having to accept that his mind was still quite muddled. Both Tony and Irwin reassured him this was due to the after-effects of the anaesthetic and to the medications he was taking for postoperative pain. In addition, they said his heart rhythm was still of concern, which Bryce brushed off with 'Don't worry about that, fellas. I've had that problem most of my adult life.'

We arrived back home in Yarramalong at the end of May and, after attending to some chores, Bryce shot upstairs. Before doing so he said, 'Sweetheart, you aren't going to see me for dust – I need to apply grain silos of bum glue to get this book finished.' Fortunately, the writing quickly gained momentum and Bryce and my brother worked in tandem day and night. I would read the first draft of each chapter and make corrections and then off it went to his other 'readers', including his son Adam and the team at Penguin.

I also hopped in to assist with the research, which Bryce was a stickler for. The storm scene in *The Persimmon Tree* is brilliant and he gleaned every ounce of the knowledge Bruce had acquired from sailing through many ferocious storms in the Pacific. Bruce was able to give Bryce the factual base from which to write his gripping account of a voyage from Java to Fremantle in a small yacht. In fact, Bruce probably did too good a job, as Bob Sessions wasn't sure who had written this part of the book and was none too pleased. He had been aboard ships while serving in the British Merchant Navy and knew as much about storms at sea as anyone. He also knew full well that Bryce had barely stepped aboard a ship except when he had sailed to Australia in 1958 and travelled with me and Bruce on the voyage to Antarctica. Bob called Bruce and was finally reassured when he was told that Bryce had typed every word about the storm himself.

We had further storms to navigate in July as Bryce's heart was still not back into normal sinus rhythm. Tony arranged for him to have an electrical cardioversion, which allowed his heart to perform normally – well, almost normally, as Bryce did end up having to go onto the blood thinner warfarin, which meant he bled easily if he sustained even a minor scratch, such as while gardening. True to form, he then returned to writing at a furious pace and was able to submit the manuscript to Penguin on time on 31 August 2007. He felt very relieved but was also exhausted – the heart surgery and the loss of Benita had taken their toll. His increasingly arthritic hands and worn-out spinal fusion were also giving him hell. He had conquered his own personal

Everest (or, as the Sherpas call it, Mount Chomolungma, Goddess Mother of the World). As Edmund Hillary famously said, 'It is not the mountain we conquer, but ourselves.'

Notwithstanding his physical ailments Bryce felt the book was one of his best, and he loved the cover design by Tony Palmer and Kaz Chiba. He told me, 'This cover is without question my all-time favourite.' With his background in advertising, he always worked closely with the designers as he understood that the front cover was vital for catching the attention of readers. If he didn't like the cover or, for that matter, the title, he would not approve the book for publication.

On 11 November that year we made our way to the Royal Australian Navy Heritage Centre on Sydney's Garden Island for the book launch. This felt very special to me as – like the naval chapel at Watson's Bay – I always attend the memorial services for my dad's ship, HMAS *Perth*, at the Garden Island Naval Chapel.

With the book completed, I had begun to dream about making a return visit to the Himalayas. I wanted to head to the Khumbu region in north-eastern Nepal and attempt the trail leading up to Everest Base Camp. I think I was feeling emotionally worn-out and wanted to be back in 'the hills', as us old trekkers refer to them (many hardcore mountaineers refer to tackling Everest as 'climbing the hill').

Nepal had been a huge part of my life since the mid-1970s when I owned my trekking company, and I was hoping Bryce would be able to come with me. He had been to Nepal several years earlier but had only visited the Chitwan National Park down in the jungle of the Terai lowlands, which are far away from the high peaks. Sadly it wasn't to be, as he said, 'Darling, I'd love to follow you in Hillary and Tenzing's footsteps, but my knees are buggered from having run over two dozen marathons.' He and I had once sat next to Sir Edmund and his second wife, June, at a dinner in Sydney, and he and Ed had spent most of the evening talking about the Rugby! I had known Ed and Tenzing since the 1980s and we were good friends. They were both among the most non-egotistical mountaineers I have ever met. I remember asking Tenzing who had stood on top of Mount Everest first on 29 May 1953. He smiled and with a gentle expression on his face said, 'We stepped on the summit together.' In fact, in his autobiography, *Tiger of the Snows*, published in 1955, he said it was Ed who stepped on top first, with Tenzing following close behind.

Bryce suggested I ask Bruce to join me on the trek, although my invitation would come with the proviso that he had to get fit. Early in his career my ex-husband Duncan had been a mountaineer and he had climbed several small peaks in Nepal as well as many in South America and Antarctica. Bryce suggested Duncan should go with us as an extra safety precaution, which was incredibly magnanimous of him – I am not sure I would have been nearly so accommodating if Bryce had wanted to travel overseas with a former partner. He knew Duncan and I occasionally bickered and made us sign what he called the 'White Flag Agreement', which we laughed about at the time but which turned out to come in very handy!

Bruce had never been to Nepal during the years I co-owned my trekking company, and he was thrilled to be invited to come along. At first he said he wanted to 'just hang out in Kathmandu' but I prevailed upon him to reconsider joining us up in the Solukhumbu. He quickly agreed, realising it was the opportunity of a lifetime to trek amid the highest mountains on earth. Having decided to go, in preparation he then had to endure my marching him up and down every hill and set of stairs I could find.

Bryce was very understanding of my constant yearning to travel to wild places, and he knew how much the Himalayas meant to me. Almost immediately he began to coach me to become really fit, and he showed me no mercy! I felt like Peekay being coached by Hoppie Groenewald in *The Power of One*: 'It was Hoppie's voice that I heard in my head and my resolve became a solid force, a pure, clean feeling, totally controlled by my head.'

While trekking in Nepal, each day you need to be prepared to walk up to 1000 metres in height and then descend just as much. Every morning before our departure I pulled on the shiny red gumboots Bryce had bought me and ran down to the chooks and back a few dozen times. He even hired a personal trainer from a nearby town; his regime was just as brutal, but it was just what I needed. Within two-and-a-half months I was fit and raring to go.

As we hugged goodbye, I knew Bryce was in for a lonely few weeks in the valley on his own with only Timmy and our two cats for company. I told him not to let those 'loneliness birds' wheedle their way back, as my love for him was not leaving home. And I reminded him that it was hardly as though he would be hanging around with nothing to do. The 'farm' was a relentless work in progress, and he was regularly liaising with Penguin on the marketing and publicity tour for his new book, which would be underway once I returned.

I recognised that to some extent it was selfish of me to go and leave him, but I had an insatiable urge to take on this challenge and Bryce was insistent that I continue to lead my own life. So, in mid-November we left Sydney to fly to Nepal via Bangkok. When we landed in Kathmandu we were lucky, as it was a clear day and we were able to glimpse the majestic Himalayan peaks that had caused my heart to miss a beat on my first trip there in January 1976.

My old friend Ravi Chandra, the founder of a pioneering trekking agency called AmaDablam Adventures, had organised everything for us and it was wonderful to catch up with him and his family. A few days later we flew into Lukla Airport (renamed Tenzing–Hillary Airport in 2008), perched precariously on the side of a mountain at 2846 metres. I would have preferred to trek into the Everest region from a town in central Nepal called Jiri to better acclimatise, but I also didn't want to be away from Bryce any longer than necessary, and this would add a further two weeks to my trip.

I felt instinctively at home once we started trekking. It was wonderful to see the familiar sights of Buddhist chortens (stupas) and mani walls beside the track, along with terraced rice fields dotted with thatch-roofed village houses. The friendly smiles of the locals greeting us with their hands clasped as they said 'Namaste' reminded me of the real reason Goronwy Price and I had begun our trekking company all those years ago.

I did notice many changes, with dozens of tea houses set up for passing trekkers and even a few boutique hotels offering the luxury of hot water and flushing toilets; even so, I could see that our Australian Himalayan Foundation projects in the region would need to be sustained for many years to come. Something that hadn't changed was seeing the occasional trekker brought down with a bout of the 'Kathmandu quickstep' – an illness that causes diarrhoea with cramps that rise and fall in your stomach like waves on Bondi Beach.

After a few days on the trail Bruce, Duncan, our crew of two guides and three porters, and I arrived at the Sherpa capital of Namche Bazaar, located at 3440 metres in Solukhumbu. We couldn't have been more excited, even though we began to feel somewhat breathless. I called Bryce and he sounded overjoyed to hear my voice. It was now possible to make calls from there, something that had been impossible during the years when we were operating our treks. The mobile-phone coverage was in fact superior to what we had available in the Yarramalong Valley. The tone in Bryce's voice suggested he was feeling sad not to have come with us, even though I knew that within days his knees would have fallen foul of a painful condition called 'trekker's knee'. He cheered up when I told him that his fame knew no bounds: I had found copies of two of his books (*April Fool's Day* and *Tommo & Hawk*) in a shop in Namche selling second-hand mountaineering gear and oxygen cylinders.

The next day I could have done with one of those cylinders as our Sirdar's oxygen bottle malfunctioned when I needed it (a Sirdar is the leader of a trekking group and their support crew). We had just eaten lunch at the famous Everest View hotel, located at 3880 metres, gazing in awe at the breathtaking views of Everest, Lhotse and Nuptse, when the blood rushed into my stomach and I began to feel woozy. Bruce said I looked as white as a ghost. Duncan didn't hesitate to pick me up and gently sling me over his shoulders to carry me back down the steep slope to Namche. It was a salient reminder of the perils of altitude, and my respect soared for the thousands of climbers who attempt to reach Everest's summit. I was heartbroken: we had planned on pushing up to the village of Khumjung, where in 1961 Ed Hillary and his Himalayan Trust team had opened their first 'schoolhouse in the clouds' for Sherpa communities in Solu.

We returned home as fit as a herd of yaks even though we all then succumbed to a dreadful bout of flu. After a frustrating two weeks recuperating at the Sydney flat so that I wouldn't pass it on to Bryce, it was amazing to finally make it back home. I had missed him terribly and we hugged each other like two teenagers in love – as he wrote so beautifully in *The Persimmon Tree*, 'It never seems to occur to adults that one of the greatest love affairs in literature took place between a fourteen-year-old Juliet and a sixteen-year-old Romeo.'

A week later Bryce and I were walking around the garden when he said he needed to have a serious talk with me. I swallowed hard and wondered what I had done now! To my astonishment he said, 'Sweetheart, I did a lot of thinking while you were in Nepal, and I realise this isn't a place for me to grow old in.'

I was stunned. He loved living in Yarramalong and had created a magnificent garden, the fulfilment of a lifelong dream, that was only going to become more beautiful as the years went by. The idea of leaving it seemed a huge shame and I began to cry. I told Bryce he mustn't contemplate going and that it was all my fault, and I promised I would make more of an effort. But deep down Bryce knew I was never going to love the place as he did. He further explained that having experienced the recent health scares, the distance from proper medical help was starting to bother him. He said, 'It's better we leave here now while I still have time to settle into a new place and can create another beautiful garden.'

His mind was made up, and he asked me to call a local real-estate agent to come over as soon as possible. Inwardly I confess to feeling relieved, even though I knew the job of getting us out of there would largely fall to me. Bryce was one of those people who didn't hold on to things, and when he decided to move on, he quickly let go and embraced the future. Perhaps after all it was he who was the more adventurous of the two of us. Having made this big decision, we were about to step into the unknown.

14

THE QUEEN OF
WERRINGTON STREET

If I don't exorcise this dream, cast out these demons, the
dark shadows of the night will linger throughout this
sparkling day in paradise. – *Fishing for Stars*

EARLY IN 2008 I came close to drowning. Sir Edmund Hillary passed away
on 11 January at aged eighty-eight years. I had known him for more than
twenty-five years and it was a great honour to receive an invitation from
his son, Peter, to attend the state funeral in Auckland on 22 January.

The day before I was scheduled to depart, there was a torrential
downpour in Yarramalong and the only road out became impassable.
The creek below our property had swollen by 6 feet (1.8 metres) and I
broke down in tears, but Bryce said in a gentle but firm voice, 'Darling,
our ute can't cross the creek and as there's no other way out, staying put
is your safest option.'

My frustration and rebellious streak propelled me to defy his wishes
and take my chances. He looked deeply concerned as I hugged him
goodbye and headed out the front gate with my clothes crammed into a
small backpack. After tramping through knee-high grass in the pouring
rain I was piggybacked across the creek by a neighbour who had bravely
offered to help. Kim Rabbits, Bryce's foreman, had rigged up a rope that I

clung to as we fought our way across the raging torrent of water, dodging debris surging towards us, including sawn-off logs and the bloated, rotting carcass of a cow. Finally we scrambled onto the bank on the other side, drenched and exhausted but pleased to have made it. Kim drove me to his house so I could change into some dry clothes before he drove me to Sydney Airport. There I met up with Simon Balderstone, the AHF chairman, who was surprised to see me looking so unusually frazzled.

It was worth the effort. Simon and I both felt privileged to be present at the service honouring Ed's life and in support of Ed's second wife June, his son Peter and his family. Peter is a founding director of the AHF and is now also Chairman of the Himalayan Trust in New Zealand. It was a gathering of the Himalayan community like no other in history. The New Zealand Government, headed by Prime Minister Helen Clark, had flown the surviving members of the 1953 British Mount Everest Expedition team, and their wives to New Zealand for the service and it was an honour to meet up with them all, including Jan (formerly James) Morris, George Lowe, Michael (Mike) Westmacott, Alfred Gregory and the youngest member of the team, George Band. Other honoured guests included Norbu Tenzing, one of Tenzing's sons, who since 1993 has been the vice president of the American Himalayan Foundation, and the late Richard C. Blum.

Witnessing the outpouring of grief for Sir Ed was profoundly moving. The night before the service, thousands of local people queued in the rain for hours to pay their respects. Ed had dedicated his life to improving the lives of the Sherpa people in Nepal, and some of his oldest Sherpa friends were also present. There was enormous love and respect for him among the people of Solukhumbu and among his fellow New Zealanders – and, indeed, people around the world.

While I was in Auckland, Bryce was trapped at our property for a week without water or power. He couldn't flush the toilet or turn on his computer, and he ran low on food as well. I think it was the last straw and emboldened him to embrace the notion that we needed to sell up and move to a place less isolated. I returned to discover that he had set his heart on the Southern Highlands of New South Wales. I had been hoping we would return to Sydney, but Bryce wasn't in the least bit interested in doing that as he had become accustomed to a quieter life.

Bowral felt like the obvious choice, especially as I had lived there before. It was also in an area Bryce had contemplated moving to prior to purchasing his parcel of land at Yarramalong. Bowral was well set up with two hospitals and excellent local amenities, and was only one-and-a-half hours' drive to Sydney. It also had a rail link to the city, not that Bryce was ever one to board a train or a bus. Some of his running mates told him they were disappointed with the decision not to move back to Sydney as they missed seeing him. His family and grandchildren did too, and they were probably perplexed that he continued to choose to live so far away from them. I think Bryce quite liked having everyone a bit at arm's length: it meant less time spent socialising and more time for writing and gardening!

By late February we had sold the farm at Yarramalong. We were lucky to find a buyer so quickly – probably because there had been a lot of summer rain and the garden looked spectacular. To my surprise, potential buyers didn't seem overly concerned about the lack of mobile-phone reception and the poor internet service: perhaps this added to the appeal for some. I worked myself into a frenzy getting the house ready for sale – Bryce even caught me polishing the leaves on the plants outside! He had paid a hefty sum for the land and had overspent on the build, so the financial loss he incurred was eye-watering. With a shrug of his shoulders he said, 'Darling, it's only money, and I'll try and make it back by writing a few more books.' He didn't perceive that being seventy-four years of age might be an obstacle, and the idea of retiring from writing never occurred to him.

A young family from Sydney were our buyers and we invited them to visit. Bryce conducted a grand tour of the house and garden, which in some ways must have been hard for him – he had put his heart and soul into the property and would miss seeing his efforts come fully into bloom. After they departed he put his arm around me and said, 'Well, darling, the clock is ticking. You need to go and find us a new house.' I thought, how in the hell can I do that within just ten weeks? As we had three pets in tow, I knew we couldn't temporarily move back into the Sydney flat even for a short period.

Bryce had already commenced writing *Fishing for Stars*, the sequel to *The Persimmon Tree*, and was determined to keep up his daily word tally. He barely left his office except to feed the chooks and take Timmy for a walk, so it was up to me. In some ways searching for a house in Bowral felt bittersweet, as it was where my marriage to Duncan had crumbled in 2005. I was also concerned that although Bowral was picturesque, it was also far too quiet a place for me. Bryce and I didn't play golf or bowls and I wondered about our chances of finding like-minded friends. It also had that small-town lack of anonymity I hadn't liked while growing up near Beechworth. As Bryce was so well known, I worried he might be endlessly stopped by fans and have to live like a hermit – not that this would have worried him!

Regardless of these misgivings, I was so relieved to be leaving Yarramalong that I decided to count my blessings and do everything I could to find us a home. In the subsequent weeks I made a dozen trips to Bowral but didn't get anywhere. The houses I inspected were either too big or too small or didn't offer enough privacy for my writer in residence!

One day my luck changed. I drove into Werrington Street in a corner of Burradoo (a suburb of Bowral) that the locals call 'the golden triangle'. I had already been told that there was 'Burra do, Burra don't and Burra never!' and this house was definitely in 'Burra do'. When I stepped out of the car I knew I had found our next home. The twelve-roomed house was set in a magnificent 2-hectare garden complete with an orchard and the all-important veggie patch. The perimeter was lined with advanced trees and radiata pines and I noticed a pair of increasingly rare yellow-tailed black cockatoos swinging from the branches. The driveway was flanked by purple agapanthus that shielded the house from the street, and there was a three-car garage and, at the rear, a perfect writer's retreat.

Stately and rendered, with large windows, the house had been constructed in the 1980s. The decor was dated but the spaces were good, and my mind was already mulling over how I could redecorate it. There were open fireplaces, which was Bryce's main proviso aside from the garden. The property looked as though it would be a haven for our pets, even though I was sure the dam in the corner of the front garden would attract snakes. My fears regarding this likelihood were soon to be realised!

I returned to Yarramalong having taken lots of photos and Bryce said in an excited voice, 'Did you make them an offer?' I said, 'Darling, I only saw it today and I really think we should return there together before we take things further.' Bryce quickly responded, 'I'm sure it's lovely, darling. I don't need to go down there. I've fallen behind with my writing and must catch up.' Once again he was displaying total trust in my judgement, but that trust entailed a lot of responsibility. The property had a high price tag that gave our loyal and hardworking accountant, Michael Dean, heart palpitations. It had been on the market for about three years, so I was hoping we could negotiate a good deal. In the end the owners didn't budge that much, which was disappointing, but at least we had somewhere to live.

My next job was to pack up the house in Yarramalong. Apart from the furniture, we had dozens of artworks and decorative items that needed to be carefully wrapped. Friends helped me with this task while Bryce kept tapping away at his book, oblivious to the house being dismantled around him. I had scheduled settlement for our new place on the same day we were due to be paid for the farm, and this scenario gave me some sleepless nights. The next few weeks were frenetic, and the pets sensed that something was up: Cardamon started to pee on the floor and Timmy averted his gaze when I went to give him a pat.

The moving trucks arrived on Ravensdale Road at the crack of dawn on 14 May 2008 and before long the house had practically been stripped bare. I needed to put Cardamon and Muschka into their carrying boxes before setting off, and at the eleventh hour Muschka did a disappearing act. I finally spotted her slinking beside the water tank and had to crawl on my stomach to wrestle the little wretch to the ground. She was unceremoniously placed into her box and strapped into the car. There was no way I would have left without her, but she punished me by yowling in protest all the way to Burradoo.

Before long we reached Burradoo, quite the travelling party. As I walked towards the Mediterranean-style courtyard of our new house, I felt certain it was going to be our 'forever home'. Then I spotted two grey-and-yellow striped reptiles reclining in the garden beds by the back door. My worst nightmare was unfolding and I held my breath, not knowing what to do. Thank goodness they turned out to be two beautiful blue-tongued lizards, which are renowned for keeping snakes at bay.

Once inside the house, I let the cats out of their boxes. Muschka tore off and spent the next three days hiding under a bed, but Cardamon was much calmer and, with her nose in the air, began exploring her new surroundings. I called Bryce and told him I had duly anointed her 'Princess Cardamon'. He responded, 'I have no hope with a princess *and* the Queen of Werrington Street in residence.' As he said, 'Princess Cardamon is a true aristocrat, a mauve Burmese very conscious of her position, imperious and enormously obese, who knows with absolutely certainty she is most loved by the Queen of Werrington.'

Bryce was relieved that the new owners at Yarramalong had agreed to him staying on there for a few more days. I understood he wanted to quietly farewell the place that had meant so much to him. He must have felt a knot in his stomach when he closed the front gate for the last time, knowing his dream of living there was over. I told him he was also clever to stay up there a little longer as it meant that when he arrived at Burradoo I would have already unpacked. Our industrial-quality coffee machine, a gift from Penguin, was switched on and his writing room was set up. I knew he would appreciate being able to get straight back to writing.

While growing up in South Africa Bryce had always been on the move, and having a stable home in his adult life was fundamental to his sense of wellbeing. Once we moved, he only ever returned to Yarramalong once to visit the Woons, but he said he couldn't bear to go and look over the fence at *Ikhaya lami*. I have never returned to the Yarramalong Valley, partly because my memories of living there are mixed. Bryce had come close to dying there from a heart condition, and I always worried something else would happen with us being so far from medical services. Perhaps, like Bryce, I was learning how to move on and rarely look back.

I was panicking that Bryce would not like the new house, but I needn't have worried. On 17 May 2008 his car swept down the driveway with Kim at the wheel. Bryce and I embraced with excitement and he then asked me to show him the veggie patch. He loved everything about the house, and I could see he was already contemplating how to put his own stamp on the garden. I had assured him there were three open fireplaces but hadn't told him they were gas, not wood-burning. That evening we raised our glasses to our new abode and Bryce said that making sure there were log fires was another thing I had got right. It was time for me to confess, and after a long pause Bryce said, 'Well, at least they will be easy to start, and we won't have spiders fleeing burning logs and running across the floor as we did in Yarramalong.' He never sweated the small things, and helped me not to either.

The next morning, I drove into town to do some shopping and after pulling into the car park I began to sob. I am still not sure why I felt so wretched – it was probably just exhaustion following the move. I knew Bryce had decided to leave Yarramalong in part to please me, and he would have been justified in feeling exasperated if I now had the temerity to complain about living back in Bowral. I also didn't want to worry him as he was over halfway to completing *Fishing for Stars*. The novel's main character was Nick Duncan, a semi-retired shipping magnate who resides in Vanuatu living the life of an island patriarch. However he is still grieving the loss of his Eurasian true love, Anna, and battling disturbing flashbacks from the Second World War.

Bryce had barely unpacked at Bowral when he and Bruce flew to Vanuatu to do some research. Bruce had lived in Vanuatu for three-and-a-half years in the mid-1980s, but Bryce still wasn't sure they had the book's settings, or 'take place', quite right and wanted to immerse himself in the locale of his main character. In writing his fiction, Bryce always endeavoured to evoke for a reader the authenticity of a setting so that the reader could imagine the scenery, the smell, the feel. The sky, the landscape, the history, the people and their customs all needed to be rendered authentically. In this research trip they also travelled from Port Vila, the capital, to the island of Espiritu Santo, which during the Second World War, particularly after the attack on Pearl Harbor, was used by American naval and air forces as a large military supply base and airfield. James A. Michener had chosen Santo as the primary locale for his book *Tales of the South Pacific*, which Bryce loved. On returning to Vila he and Bruce hopped aboard an antique yacht to explore the magnificent harbour. Bryce captured this experience in the novel: 'Out to sea on a pristine morning on the gaff-rigged cutter *Madam Butterfly* with the ocean spray hitting your face, when you were young and strong and anything was possible.' They found a magical site for Nick's home in Vila, even though it was currently being used as a fuel depot.

Bryce enjoyed lining up his friends to be characters in his books. Tony's reward for playing a key role in sorting out Bryce's heart condition was to be cast as a psychiatrist in *Fishing for Stars*: 'As it turns out Dr Freeman seems a decent sort of a cove, not at all as I'd imagined: in his early fifties I'd say, lean as a whippet, easy manner, no Sigmund Freud, very Australian.' Tony continued to keep a close eye on Bryce's cardiac situation, and Bryce was relieved to be put on a new blood thinner called Pradaxa. He didn't bleed so easily on this one and didn't need to have frequent blood tests, which he dreaded.

Bryce's family and our friends loved our new home and found the Southern Highlands more accessible to visit than the Yarramalong Valley. We enjoyed popping into the local cafes and having everything close at hand. Being in a bigger town meant Bryce now had access to a personal trainer, and he quickly realised the benefits of this, with the sessions helping to ease his chronic back pain and preventing his arthritic fingers from seizing up. And I was back riding my bike and went swimming in a nearby heated pool.

I no longer felt the urge to constantly rush back to Sydney, which meant Bryce was rarely left on his own. I felt more confidence in our relationship and a level of contentment I hadn't previously known. One day Bryce noted how wonderful it was to see me smiling again and looking more beautiful than ever. I said I felt like Anna in *The Persimmon Tree* with Bryce looking at me just like Nick Duncan: 'I was, after all, a big, clumsy butterfly collector who asked nothing more of her than that she be herself, the nicest and prettiest girl I had ever seen.'

We loved our walks beside the Wingecarribee River with Timmy tottering along behind. Our conversations were always so absorbing, and I rarely felt conscious of the age gap between us. During these walks I did, however, remain alert after I noticed a sign reading 'Beware of snakes'. In a cheeky voice I said, 'Maybe New Zealand should be our next move – they don't have any snakes.' Bryce shook his head vigorously and said, 'We are never moving again!'

I enjoyed reconnecting with David and Carole, old friends who still lived in the same street not far from the house I had shared with Duncan. They loved getting to know Bryce and their kindness and friendship really helped us to settle in. They were also passionate gardeners and Bryce liked talking to them about where to buy plants and how he could enrich the area's notoriously sandy soil.

I also got back in touch with Ken Wilder, the former head of Collins Publishing, who had moved to Bowral many years earlier with his wife, Jean. Ken wrote a moving memoir, published in 1994, called *The Company You Keep* and had started a bushwalking group, which he invited Bryce to join. Bryce loved these excursions and said the walkers chatted about everything, from books to their interest in local conservation projects. In time he discovered a bespoke furniture maker based on the South Coast and engaged him to construct a magnificent wood-panelled bookshelf. The 'library' was where Bryce would retreat to when watching the Rugby, with Timmy at his feet and Muschka sitting on his lap.

In early April Bryce declined an invitation to be the chief guest at Brigadoon, the annual Highland Gathering held in nearby Bundanoon. He was behind with his book and asked me to keep his diary clear. Bundanoon will always have a special place in my heart as on 20 December 2001 I had joined friends from my Himalayan days at the local pub there for an informal meeting to create the Australian Himalayan Foundation. It was lovely to know that one of the AHF's founding directors, Garry Weare, and his wife, Margie Thomas, were still living there.

Bryce sent me to Brigadoon in his place and I watched hefty fellows tossing the caber to the sound of pipe bands and displays of Highland dancing, all washed down with 'wee drams' of whisky. I passed on eating haggis. It was a great day, and when I returned home I reminded Bryce of his mother's stories about their Scottish ancestors, the MacGregors. I also told him that I had dobbed him in to attend next year's games wearing a kilt featuring the clan's red-and-black tartan.

Everyone knew how phobic I was about snakes, and it wasn't long before Bryce saw one in the veggie garden – a 1.5-metre-long copperhead. He didn't tell me about it. Our gardener saw it a couple of days later heading towards our back door and thankfully dispatched it to an early grave. I was relieved, as the species is deadly and I was worried one would strike one of the pets or one of us! Years later Bryce told me he had seen several snakes in the garden but decided not to tell me as he worried I might insist on our selling up. He was right about that – my ignorance was bliss.

We had to contend with other critters as well. Bright-green frogs jumped out of the toilet bowls, possums died in the roof, and there was an unwelcome plague of grasshoppers that wiped out Bryce's entire vegetable crop, which was heartbreaking as he always looked forward to presenting me with freshly picked produce. The grasshoppers even ravaged an oak tree he had successfully grown from an acorn. He thought he had collected the acorn from Sherwood Forest in Nottinghamshire, but it was in fact (I have since been told) given to him by his old friend Harry Blumberg on a visit to Johannesburg. Bryce tended to breeze through these serious incidents, but I found them unnerving. He would put his arm around me and say, 'Sweetheart, the country girl in you is still in hibernation after too many years spent living in Sydney.'

We both pinched ourselves to be living in such a gorgeous region. Bryce used to talk about his childhood spent in and out of institutions and the spartan lodgings his mother occupied, and how in his wildest dreams he never imagined living in a home like ours. I had been raised on a beautiful 120-hectare farm that Dad purchased through the Soldier Settlement Scheme established after the Second World War. My parents did up our old red-brick house beautifully and it was very comfortable, but there were only two bedrooms, a kitchen and a sleepout. The one family bathroom was on the enclosed back veranda next to the laundry, where the dogs slept on sugar bags while Tootsie, our cat, curled up in an apple box lined with a towel. Bryce said it felt as though we were both now living in 'sheer lookzhuree'.

To our delight we were unexpectedly introduced to Sam and Alida Haskins, a South African couple who had moved from London to Bowral a few years earlier. Sam was a world-renowned photographer who had created bestselling books, including the iconic *Cowboy Kate & Other Stories*. He had photographed world-famous figures such as Lauren Bacall, Mick Jagger and Sofia Coppola. A self-confessed workaholic, he still buried his head in his work even though he was over eighty years old. Alida was brilliant too, and Sam acknowledged her as the business brains behind his success. Their Bowral house was filled with antique Cape Dutch furniture and their walls were adorned with original artworks, including Sam's photographs. They had an impressive wooden dining table that Alida told me had belonged to Lord Kitchener, who played a prominent role in colonial victories in South Africa and Sudan.

The Haskins adored Bryce's company and he would frequently break into Afrikaans and a smattering of Zulu during our visits with them. Alida (nee van Heerden) had in fact been born in Witfontein, which is barely a four-hour drive from Barberton where Bryce spent those few happy years during his childhood. I loved hearing their stories of growing up in South Africa. They told me how their Zulu gardener would kill the deadly black mambas that slithered into their garden, and I learnt more about the history of the Boers and how they had established farms after arriving over the mountains with wagons pulled by teams of oxen.

Alida was a sensational cook. She would arrive at our house with a muslin-wrapped ham that had been steeped in beer and cloves and then roasted in the oven, and bags of biltong (dried, cured meat), which was one of Bryce's favourite items of traditional South African fare. Bowral's Empire Cinema, built in 1915, was a real drawcard for me, especially after living in Yarramalong, and I would go with Alida to see a movie while our boys stayed home to toil away at their artistic pursuits.

Tragically, Sam's life ended abruptly on 26 November 2009 when he was aged eighty-three. Understandably, Alida never recovered from his loss after fifty-seven years of marriage. On the night Sam died, Bryce stayed at their house to support her and take care of their little dog, Smokey. Alida sadly passed away in Sydney on the same day as Bryce's funeral, 5 December 2012.

Nima regularly came to stay and he and Bryce always got along incredibly well. Bryce used to introduce him to people by saying, 'This is my best mate, Nima.' He was a wonderful mentor who encouraged Nima never to give up on his dreams. In August they enjoyed watching the events of the 2008 Summer Olympics in Beijing. August was a big month for us in other ways, too: we celebrated our birthdays together as mine was on 13 August and Bryce's was on 14 August.

This year, though, Bryce turned seventy-five and Penguin honoured him with a sensational party at the Sydney Opera House, where over 150 guests raised their glasses in celebration of the milestone. Bryce gave a moving speech, as did Bob Sessions, and I was invited to say a few words as well. In the middle of the party we had to make a frantic dash to the Sydney Cricket Ground to attend a birthday celebration for Bryce's dear friend and GP, Dr Irwin Light. We then returned to the Opera House and didn't make it back to Burradoo until early the following morning.

Bryce handed in *Fishing for Stars* on 31 August 2008. He dedicated it to the corroboree frog, a highly endangered Australian species. Conservationists had declared 2008 the Year of the Frog to heighten awareness of the threat facing frogs around the world, and the Taronga Conservation Society (TCS) was engaged in efforts to save the critically endangered corroboree frog from the chytrid fungus, which attacks the frog's skin and is fatal to many frog species. The TCS had inducted Bryce as Australia's Ambassador for the Year of the Frog, and in *Fishing for Stars* he wrote an 'Epilogue for Frogs'; he also continued to champion the TCS's work after the book was published. We attended a fundraising dinner for the TCS in Sydney on 7 May 2011 and Bryce donated a character in a future novel, an auction item that was fiercely fought over. The winner would have their name used for a cameo or minor character in Bryce's next book.

Completing *Fishing for Stars* was the usual frantic race to the finish line. Bruce had travelled up from Melbourne to be on hand as Bryce battled to finalise the last couple of chapters, working closely with his wonderful editors Nan McNab, Rachel Scully and Anne Rogan. I hopped in too by feverishly sourcing some final bits of research and reading drafts. By the time the last chapter was finished we were all exhausted – especially Bryce, who looked utterly shattered.

I sometimes wondered why he put himself through the struggle of writing a book a year. People would accuse him of churning books out, but if they had witnessed the toll each one took on him and those around him, they may have tempered their remarks. The final round of completing a book guaranteed we were living in a state of high anxiety and securing a good night's sleep was impossible.

Two days after delivering the final chapter, Bryce headed to Sydney Airport on his way to Honolulu to be a guest speaker at the Maui Writers Conference in Hawaii. I stayed home to take care of the pets and look after the garden, and collapsed in a heap after he left. I was happy he was off having a break, even though it wasn't exactly a holiday. I knew he would enjoy being back in Hawaii and going for long walks along Waikiki Beach on Oahu, where the festival was convened that year. He called me each evening while he was sipping on a glass of Californian chardonnay and watching the sun go down from the balcony of the Ala Moana Hotel. I always wish we had travelled more together, but our tribe of pets made that impossible.

With both of us feeling rejuvenated, it was time to celebrate. In September we hosted a housewarming party and Bryce made sure the garden was looking resplendent. He delighted in taking each guest on a tour of the grounds, and they all marvelled at the white standard roses lining the driveway and the magnificent rhododendrons and bushes of fragrant daphne. These two plants reminded me of the Himalayas, where both species are native. The daffodils were out too, and the Japanese maples provided a stunning display of autumnal glory. We hired Pamela Charity, a local chef and restaurateur, to organise the food, and a magician to entertain the children. It was a great celebration, and especially wonderful to see Bryce enjoying the day with Brett and Adam, their wives and his grandchildren, as well as many of our friends. Most of Bryce's friends harked back to his days in the advertising industry and many were former running mates. They were 'brothers in arms' and he had known them and their wives for decades: Alex Hamill, Roger Rigby, Tony Crosby, Ray Black and Peter Keeble, among others.

In early November Bryce left to go on a nationwide book tour for *Fishing for Stars*. The book was a great success, even though some readers preferred *The Persimmon Tree*, and within a few weeks it had shot to number one on the bestseller list, followed by *True Colours* by Adam Gilchrist and *The Guinness Book of Records*. Bryce quipped, 'I feel I have, along with my publisher and my beloved at my side, reached for the stars!'

> Look up, up . . . up there, at the midnight sky
> At the game of chance within the firmament
> Saturn's rings, mooned Jupiter, planet Mars
> All yours if you hoist ambition's sails and set
> A galactic course, then cast a wide-flung net
> To fish for the brightest stars in all creation.

In keeping with his passion for inspiring young people to care about the environment, he paid tribute in this book to Dr Niall Doran, the dedicated founder of Tasmania's Bookend Trust, of which Bryce was a proud patron.

The reviews were good. Patricia Maunder wrote in the *Sunday Age*: 'Detail is something Courtenay obviously enjoys, from the presentation of dialect to the brand of someone's pen.' The success of *Fishing for Stars* meant Bryce rose even higher up the fame ladder, but when he was asked by Wendy Tuohy from the *Herald Sun* whether he cared about this, Bryce told her: 'Not when you've had my beginnings. The two most horrific words in my life are "celebrity" and "icon". I just hate them so much, they grow hair on my teeth.'

On 11 November, in honour of Bryce's seventy-fifth birthday, Penguin launched the Power of One Australian Hero Award.

Nominations were invited from people who had worked for more than three years in the service of others, animals or the environment. The inaugural winner, announced the following year, was the former pop star Ronnie Burns from Tasmania, in recognition of his support for sick and underprivileged children. Bryce told him, 'The power of one is the decision to make a difference without expecting recognition.'

Sometimes he would say things in interviews that made me smile, or occasionally cringe! Prior to Christmas a journalist asked him, 'If you could have a present for one day only, what would it be?' He answered, 'A Harley-Davidson with a sidecar. I'd ride around terrorising the neighbourhood with Christine.' Failing that transpiring, we lazed about reading, went on daily walks and made sure our garden survived the searing summer heat. Our first Christmas in Bowral felt very special, and we both went to town on preparing our festive feast. Bryce baked roast lamb with rosemary and yoghurt while I stuffed a turkey and cooked dozens of golden roast potatoes.

Since our arrival in Burradoo, we had been a little surprised not to receive a single invitation to visit our neighbours. On 27 December, Bryce dropped a letter and a signed copy of *Fishing for Stars* in the mailbox of every house in Werrington Street. The letter said: 'In the eighteen years I have been writing, it has become a tradition to leave a copy of my latest book at every home in the street in which we live . . . Naturally, we have no wish to intrude on your privacy and of course, you should not feel obliged to acknowledge what is, at best, a gratuitous gesture.' In fairness we did receive a couple of very nice notes, but we ultimately came to accept that the neighbours were content to keep to themselves. We also recognised that as we didn't play golf or bowls it was hard to break into the Bowral social scene!

On Tuesday 20 January 2009 we stayed up to watch the inauguration of Barack Obama as the 44th president of the United States. He was

America's first black president and it reminded Bryce of the huge milestone in South Africa when, on 10 May 1994, Nelson Mandela had been installed as president there. Having grown up during the apartheid era, Bryce had a better understanding than most of the enormous significance of America's historic milestone.

It was soon that time of year again when Bryce turned on his computer to begin another book, and on 1 February he started to write *The Story of Danny Dunn*. He had settled on this particular story after chatting with Alex Hamill, who grew up in Balmain and attended Fort Street High School. Despite leaving school at fourteen, Alex had gone on to have an astonishingly successful career in advertising and public life. Balmain felt like the perfect location in which to place Danny, Bryce's central character. Like Alex, Danny was a working-class boy, but in his case he had returned from the Second World War a broken man. Alex's wife Brenda also heralded a mention in the book as Danny's indomitable mother. Danny's love for Helen, the woman who became his wife, and for his mother was what enabled him to pull through.

Balmain was the first place I had lived after arriving in Sydney from Canberra in March 1977. Goronwy Price and I had relocated knowing that Sydney was where we would have the best opportunity of growing our fledgling Himalayan trekking company. My experience of having lived in Balmain ended up being a valuable resource for the research material Bryce needed for the book. In the mid-1970s the suburb had been full of colourful characters who had grown up tough and were committed to improving the lives of working men and women – a far cry from the bijou cafes and designer clothes shops that line Darling Street in the Balmain of today.

So Bryce had the character and the setting, but within weeks of starting work he experienced a severe bout of writer's block and for three long weeks he simply stared at his computer screen and barely wrote a word. Feeling distraught, he rang up Bob Sessions and told him he feared he wouldn't be able to meet the August deadline. Bob was very understanding and wisely encouraged Bryce to take some time off, reassuring him that his creativity would spring back to life.

I have to say I took this as a sign that Bryce needed to consider taking a proper break from writing. After all, is there not a fine line between passion and obsession? I had never witnessed him having writer's block before, but now, seeing him pale, worn to shreds and in agony from long, unproductive sessions at the computer made me wonder if his writing was a kind of monomania – a passion that had got out of hand and needed reining in. I had observed this before with other artists and writers. When I raised the subject with Bryce he seemed slightly offended, but his eyes told me he recognised there was perhaps some truth to my theory. At least he wasn't writing alone. Bryce's yearly output was always a collaborative process with Bob and his team of Penguins waiting in the wings to help, and boy, did Bryce need them now. His commitment to writing was paramount, and I also fully appreciated that having signed a contract for a significant amount of money, he felt compelled to complete the book.

Bryce and I drove up to Sydney for a while. We went out to dinner at Darcy's and took long walks on Bondi Beach, and caught up with our families and spent time with old friends. After returning home to Bowral we invited the grandchildren, Ben, Jake and Marcus, to stay. We always looked forward to spending time with them and Bryce loved trying to nurture their interest in gardening just as his grandfather had done for him during the four years he lived in Barberton. I made sure I cooked some of their favourite meals, which included chicken Maryland, crisp roast potatoes and Thai green curry. Bryce was rather strict, though, when it came to their preference for drinking Coca-Cola! He would buy a couple of bottles but when they were gone, that was it. He absolutely adored the boys and was always so proud of them. It was a pity we didn't see as much of them as we could have if we had been living in Sydney. The boys adored their 'Pa' and I am certain their memory of him continues to be an inspiration in their adult lives.

To everyone's relief, Bryce was soon back at his desk and the book hummed to life – not that Bryce and the Penguins agreed on the title. Bob had come up with *The Dangerous Dance of Danny Dunn*, but Bryce wasn't keen on this. In the end, and after a fair bit of negotiating, *The Story of Danny Dunn* was set in stone. While Bob and Bryce occasionally disagreed, they held each other in great regard and issues were quickly resolved. Any writer on earth would have felt fortunate to have had the wise counsel Bob unfailingly provided to Bryce.

On the Thursday prior to Good Friday I went to the vet in Moss Vale to stock up on biscuits for the pets. In the corner of the reception area was a cage housing a young calico cat. A stout country woman was peering into the cage while pulling on the lead of her Rhodesian ridgeback dog. The cat was cowering in fear, so I politely asked her to move her dog away. That didn't go down too well but fortunately she departed, and I asked the vet nurse how the cat came to be there. She said it had been rescued from a woman who had forty cats, and no one seemed to want this one. I thought perhaps the cat was therefore in line to be euthanised, so I said, 'I'll take her.'

You have never seen a cat bundled into a cage so fast, and she proceeded to meow all the way home while I sang a song about green alligators that I used sing to Nima when he was a baby. Bryce was in the kitchen making himself a cup of coffee. I said, 'Darling, there is something I have to tell you,' and his eyes widened when I told him I'd found another cat and it was in the car. He hung his head and sighed but then grinned when he saw how happy I was. As I was settling our new cat in, Bryce thought she looked disturbed with her golden eyes darting wildly in every direction. He said, 'Darling, only you could find a cat like that,' and walked back into his office.

I called her Ophelia, from Shakespeare's *Hamlet*, even though Bryce reminded me that this particular heroine had come to a rather damp end. Our other cats greeted her with expressions of resigned acceptance.

It took months to calm her down, but I fell in love with this scatty little cat. Bryce used to call her 'the kitten' and correctly predicted that one day she would end up as 'boss cat'. The affection and loyalty of our pets was a source of solace for both of us, and I can't imagine ever living without one or two (or more) in tow.

Ophelia was not the only new pet who came into our lives. One afternoon there was a terrible kerfuffle outside and I saw our three cats scattering in all directions, with one scooting up the trunk of a tree. Before me was a sandy-coloured dog who looked like a cross between a Japanese spitz and a Pomeranian. He was as fast as a whippet, and I discovered he was called Rocky and belonged to a neighbour who was often away, which meant he was a regular inmate of the animal shelter in Moss Vale. One day I picked him up and noticed he was covered in fleas and had a nasty oozing sore on one ear. Our local vet gave him antibiotics and before long the dog, whom we renamed Pemba (Sherpa for 'Saturday'), was again running through the yard and terrorising the cats. I think his owner was relieved when we offered to keep him.

Our cats were unimpressed and ended up lying on the kitchen table sporting stony expressions while Pemba careered around the house barking his head off. This couldn't go on, and luckily, with the help of Russell Coburn, Bryce's regular hire-car driver, we found a local couple willing to take him. The wife had grown up in Africa, like Bryce, and within minutes of meeting Pemba they fell in love with him. Not long afterwards they invited us for lunch and as the wine flowed Bryce started telling them about hitchhiking through Africa after he left the mines. He explained how he and his mate Noel had been welcomed as honoured guests by the Sultan of Zanzibar. The wife's eyes widened and she asked Bryce if they had also met the Sultana – her family had known them and used to visit them during her school holidays. I could see Bryce's mind do a somersault but all I could think of was dates, nuts and sultanas! After we bid a hasty retreat to the car I gently admonished him for embellishing his story. He looked slightly chastened before reminding me he was a storyteller and in our entire time together he had never said anything hurtful to anyone. I said, 'Well, darling, at least you got the history right – the Sultanate was still in place when you were there.'

In May 2009 Bryce was delighted to be appointed Bowral's Tulip Time ambassador as part of a festival that celebrates the blooming of tulips in the town's parks and in the towns of Mittagong and Moss Vale. We were driven down Bong Bong Street in a red fire truck and Bryce waved to the locals cheering from the sidelines. I wanted to sink through the floor with embarrassment, but Bryce enjoyed every minute of it and went on to accept several invitations to attend other festival events.

It was around that time that yet another furry friend joined our fold. I discovered one day another visitor seated on the garden bench I had thought was Muschka, but on closer inspection I realised it was a large tabby wearing a collar that revealed his name as 'Pirate'. He looked up at me and then brushed by my legs before coming inside to eat some biscuits while I rang the phone number on his tag. His owner said she didn't live in Bowral and Pirate now lived with her parents. Later that day a woman arrived at the house and it was obvious she wasn't overly happy to be reacquainted with Pirate. About five days later I was sweeping the front veranda and saw him marching down our driveway with his tail in the air. After another four days Bryce asked me if I had called his owner again and then said with a resigned look, 'Do we really need four cats?' I never did make that call, and Pirate became one of the family. There were now four beds beside the fire each evening, and our darling dog Timmy was hopelessly outnumbered.

In late July 2009 I travelled to South America to embark on a voyage to the Galapagos Islands. Charles Darwin had arrived there on 15 September 1835 aboard the HMS *Beagle* and the information he uncovered on that voyage led him to write *On the Origin of Species*, which fundamentally changed how people thought about evolution. The bird life in Galapagos was spectacular, as were the black lava fields covered with clumps of marine iguanas. The magnificent and great frigatebirds were breathtaking with their distinctive red chests, and the blue-footed boobies were wondrous as well. I felt privileged to see Lonesome George, a male Pinta Island tortoise who was the last of his species and at the time the rarest creature in the world. George died on 24 June 2012 when he was over 101 years old.

The entire trip had me feeling as though I was an extra in a David Attenborough documentary, but the magic was shattered as I was checking in for my flight from Quito, in Ecuador, to Buenos Aires. Bryce called me to say that our dear friend Michael Grace AM had died suddenly on 6 August at the age of sixty-six. This was an untimely and profound loss, and my heart went out to Michael's beautiful wife Megan and their young son, Brighton.

That year, to celebrate my having turned fifty-five, Bryce wrote a poem for me from each of our pets, a most precious gift:

As the Princess of Werrington I naturally go first
With my elegant swelligant Purrrrrfect cat verse
I want you to know you're quite the Queen bee.

Muschka the Bush, I'm a plain-spoken moggy
And I'm lacking in class
But the Princess can stick her wishes up her piss-elegant arse!
It's cats like me who really do care
Have a wonderful, tumblerful Birthday Affair.

'Plain Silly' Phylly . . . I've never written a poem before
But first I'm sorry to my very core
For shitting on the lounge-room floor.

I just want to say in my meowing way
Have a wonderful 55th Queen's birthday . . .

Pirate 'Tucker Man' Macho Cat
Now if you think being 55 is getting quite old
You're as young and sweet as a bangle of gold.

The final chapter of *The Story of Danny Dunn* was handed in on 31 August 2009 and Bryce surprised me by dedicating it 'For my beloved Christine'. He retreated to his garden before heading off in November to do media interviews, literary lunches and book signings.

Then, on 24 and 25 September, a massive dust storm descended that had its origin in far western New South Wales. It was the mother of all storms and the worst in seventy years. There was not a leaf, windowsill or garden seat that was not smothered in red dust and it took us weeks to clean up the mess – even the pets had to be washed, which was a battle royale! The dust storm was followed by torrential rains that flooded the garden. There was a damp corner at one side of the yard, which I had noticed when I first saw the property, and it went on to cause us big problems a few years later.

The Story of Danny Dunn quickly went to number one on the bestseller lists, with the *Weekly Times* describing it as 'A great sweeping novel to lift the spirit'. Against a colourful backdrop of Australian pubs and politics, this novel captures a period of great change in Australia's history, and this family saga went straight to readers' hearts.

On 3 January 2010 we drove up to watch Australia play South Africa in the Third Test at the Sydney Cricket Ground. We were guests of Cricket Australia and had a great time watching the game and enjoying the company of the other special guests, who included a couple of former prime ministers, the author Tom Keneally, and former Australian cricket captain Allan Border. Thanks to Nima I had learnt a fair bit about cricket, and Bryce, being a proud Australian, had long given up barracking for South Africa. Rugby was always more his thing, but it was lovely to see him relaxing, free from the pressures of writing.

Sometimes I pondered whether both Rugby and cricket were a kind of metaphor for how Bryce lived his life, given the discipline involved and how the game was played to win, with losing never an option. We couldn't have known on that happy day that the year ahead would herald the start of the greatest battle of Bryce's life.

15

FORTUNE COOKIES
TO KOEKSISTERS

And there was one more reason for going to Singapore:
I longed for anonymity, to simply walk down a street and be
just another face in the crowd. – *Fortune Cookie*

THE YEAR 2010 HAD started well. In January Bryce was selected as one of Australia Post's six 'Legends of the Written Word'. A set of stamps was issued, and in his typical self-deprecating way Bryce said in an interview, 'Stamps aren't what they used to be . . . it was the King's head on stamps when I was young. Now they just put old shitbags on them.'

The other five Australian authors were Tim Winton, Thomas Keneally, Peter Carey, Colleen McCullough and David Malouf, and Bryce joined most of them for a celebration lunch at a swank restaurant overlooking the Sydney Opera House. This was a rare opportunity for him to meet up with his writing peers. Australia Post also published a commemorative book called *Novel Lives* by *The Age* literary editor Jason Steger. Bryce was accustomed to literary editors giving him a hard time, so he was feeling apprehensive before Jason arrived at our home for the interview. He needn't have worried: after taking him on a tour of the veggie garden, Bryce sat down with Jason to enjoy an absorbing chat about Bryce's life and his most recent novel, *The Story of Danny Dunn*.

I had recently returned from Paris – a city I could easily call home – where I had stayed in an apartment on Île Saint-Louis overlooking Notre-Dame Cathedral and the River Seine. It was a far cry from the squalid digs Bryce had stayed in when he visited Paris in 1957. After I waxed lyrical about my Parisian sojourn Bryce encouraged me to purchase my own *pied-à-terre*. I managed to talk him out of this enticing but extravagant gesture. Soon afterwards I secured a job representing Guest Apartment Services Paris, the inspiring company with which I had just organised my Paris stay. It was founded by Christophe Chastel and Philippe Pée, who continue to be very dear friends.

Bryce had been preparing to start writing his next book, which had the working title *Dim Sum* and was set in Singapore during the 1960s. His main character was Simon Koo, an advertising executive who becomes caught up in the drug trade during the Vietnam War. Bryce had been to Singapore dozens of times during his advertising career and knew he could make this story hum. But he hadn't been back there for a long time and one morning in April he announced that we needed to go to Singapore as soon as possible. I was a bit nonplussed as it was never easy for us both to go away as our big house, garden and five pets had to be taken care of.

However, never one to pass up the chance of a spontaneous trip, I sped into action. On 11 April we were seated aboard a Qantas flight bound for Singapore and Bruce was on his way there to join us from Melbourne, as Bryce wanted him to spearhead the research once again. During the flight I tentatively handed Bryce a piece I had written about my first trip to Singapore in December 1973 when still a student at the ANU. I had written: 'Coming into land I smelt Singapore before I saw it, and I felt like I had arrived on another planet. This little girl from Wooragee was wide-eyed with excitement, and a passion for travel and adventure had been ignited, never to be put out.' After reading my story Bryce said, 'This isn't too bad, darling – you should consider writing something else.' We had later discussed the idea of my writing a memoir about my travels, trekking company and all the extraordinary people I had come to know. Even back then Bryce was insistent that I must write it, warts and all!

He was excited to be back in Singapore and was undeterred by the fierce heat and humidity that assaulted our senses the moment we disembarked. We both adored the luxuriant tropical foliage and the pungent aromas from sizzling woks on every street corner. As he later included in the novel: 'In Singapore, cooking your own dinner is a particular stupidity unless you love to cook – it's the place where all the Asian cuisines meet for breakfast, lunch and dinner.'

On our second night we turned up at True Blue Cuisine, a popular Peranakan restaurant on Armenian Street, next door to the extraordinary Peranakan Museum. We were there to meet family members of Leonard Yong, a Singaporean friend whom I had met when I was studying in Canberra and who had shown me around on my very first trip to Singapore. I remember being introduced to durians at a dinner in the heritage house owned by his family on Bideford Road. Durians have a particularly odorous smell and I was warned that it was inadvisable to drink alcohol when eating them. To their surprise I actually liked the taste although I would always reach for a mango over a durian any day.

One of Leonard's relatives explained that True Blue had originally been a spice warehouse and was later converted into a brothel, whose doors were apparently closed when Lee Kuan Yew was elected prime minister with a landslide majority in 1959 (a position he retained until 1990). Another guest called Oy had worked in a senior role in the police administration and told us, 'All the girls from the brothel were taken to the police station. They were not released for two weeks, but they had a steady stream of "visitors" during that time.'

As a succession of dishes arrived, the stories continued to flow. We were told that in an effort to crush media opposition, the security services seized the house of the editor of one of Singapore's major newspapers before turning it into the Police Officers Club. A family member called Melvin told us that he had resigned his position as a journalist, fearing the prospect of jail if he were to be perceived to have stepped out of line.

All of the dinner guests had been born to affluent Peranakan families, and they described themselves as having been raised more like people with British heritage than people with Chinese heritage. They spoke about the sense of betrayal they felt when Britain largely withdrew from the Far East during the 1960s. Another guest who had worked with the police force said, 'Having been raised speaking English, our Cantonese wasn't very good and it took us nearly two years to pass the police exams in Cantonese, the major Chinese dialect spoken in Singapore at the time.'

The restaurant was crammed with Peranakan antiques and the food was delectable, although I baulked at eating the eyeball in my fish-head curry. The stories we heard provided invaluable material for the book, and Bryce reflected, 'Even I couldn't make this stuff up.' We were cautioned, though, as we prepared to return to the beautiful Four Seasons Hotel: 'Under no circumstances are you to write our full names into your book. The authorities have long memories, and we don't want any trouble.' Naturally Bryce agreed to this request, and it was a sobering reminder of the liberties we often take for granted in Australia.

I was thrilled to be back in Singapore and loved showing Bruce the sights. I told him what it was like back in 1973 – the cab drivers with their black silk pants and white tunics whom we would hail from Raffles Place and along Orchard Road; they drove the famous yellow-top taxis, which had been introduced to Singapore in 1933. We glimpsed the seedy charms of Bugis Street and slurped bowls of spicy laksa, a famous Nyonya dish that Leonard had introduced me to on the first day we met so many years before. Leonard and I continue to be great friends, and he reminded me recently that our friendship goes back nearly fifty years!

Singapore always stirs my emotions as my father, Allan Gee, spent three weeks in the infamous Changi prison camp after being captured in March 1942 following the sinking of his ship, HMAS *Perth*, in the Sunda Strait by a fleet of Japanese destroyers. Bryce, Bruce and I went to the Changi Chapel Museum but left feeling bereft, having seen evidence of the cruelty that Dad and his fellow Allied prisoners of war suffered.

My father always insisted to us children that we shouldn't feel hatred towards the Japanese, explaining that we were growing up in a different time. But his own feelings towards the Japanese were forever soured as a result of what he and his shipmates suffered and witnessed.

Bruce and I paid a visit to the Peranakan Museum while Bryce went for a walk along the historic Clarke Quay by the river. The museum is home to a treasure trove of artefacts, as is the National Museum of Singapore, which we all explored together. We were a bit disorganised as we hadn't set up meetings with the curators prior to our arrival. Bryce sometimes preferred to do his research on the hop and liked to 'feel' places rather than take a more academic approach. Anyway, he said that the formal research was Bruce's job – and mine as well, as it often turned out!

Bryce felt on home ground in Singapore and insisted on taking us for satays at Lau Pa Sat, his favourite hawker food market, built in 1894. He also loved a good curry and we joined him on a pilgrimage back to the famous Banana Leaf Apolo restaurant on Serangoon Road, where ladle after ladle of steaming curry was piled onto platters fashioned from banana leaves. To quell the fire in his throat Bryce downed two bottles of Tiger Beer. Bruce is a fussy eater and he merely looked on, having already had a hamburger back at the hotel.

We couldn't leave without enjoying a Singapore Sling at the historic Long Bar at Raffles Hotel, a haven for authors during its 130-year history. Rudyard Kipling, Noel Coward and Ernest Hemingway all stayed there, and Somerset Maugham proclaimed, 'Raffles stands for all the fables of the exotic East.' It still does, and I adore its dazzling new interiors following a two-year refurbishment completed in 2019.

We went to Chinatown to seek out a tailor to make me a silk cheongsam. I had some difficulty choosing from the shimmering rolls of silk on display, but finally settled on an elegant black and silver design featuring the Singapore orchid. Bryce said with a mischievous look, 'When you wear this, darling, I won't be able to resist calling you my China doll.' On the *Fortune Cookie* back-cover copy he describes the moment Simon Koo first sees Mercy B. Lord:

I'd walked into the reception area at Raffles and seen her in the black cheongsam seated in a peacock-tail wicker chair. I'd come from a forced inspection of my minuscule future office, convinced I'd made a huge mistake coming to Singapore, when, seemingly in seconds, she'd changed everything.

Bruce and Bryce were measured up for tropical linen suits and I teased that they would soon resemble colonial *tuans* from the era of British rule.

All too soon it was time to return home so Bryce could get back to work, his ideas for the new novel bubbling away. After we arrived back at Burradoo, Timothy tore outside barking excitedly, overjoyed to be reunited with his beloved 'father'. The four cats, however, were less impressed and after a cursory glance walked off with their tails in the air.

Our Singapore sojourn spurred on Bryce's writing like the arrival of the monsoon rains. The book that had started out as *Dim Sum* became *Fortune Cookie*, which everyone agreed was a far stronger, more inviting title. In the novel Bryce drew on his lived experience to capture the zeitgeist of the 1960s:

> The winds of change that brought Vietnam and resulted in Kent State became a hurricane that roared through the sixties and ushered in a very different world. Rock'n'roll, Elvis, the Beatles, the Rolling Stones and Bob Dylan musically represented the strident new voices of my generation . . . I've always liked to think I've been involved in some of that change, which may even, perhaps, have been why I chose advertising as my career.

More than any other book, *Fortune Cookie* chronicles the decades Bryce spent in advertising and records the revolution the industry underwent. In the 1960s and 1970s the big American firms started to take an interest in Australian agencies like the ones Bryce was working in: 'We were all aware of the reformation in American advertising – the sixties' creative revolution coming out of New York. The winds of change had been blowing down Madison Avenue like everywhere else.'

Fortune Cookie tells the story of how the tobacco industry was brought to heel and was eventually required to warn people of the dangers of smoking. For decades it had engaged advertising agencies to shamelessly flog a product that caused illness and even death to millions of unsuspecting consumers. The central character, Simon Koo, explains:

> My job was to churn out endless shitty research-guided layouts and then spend hours discussing their subtle differences and how these would turn existing smokers on to the new brand. That was another tobacco industry shibboleth: We don't cause people to take up smoking, we only try to influence them to switch brands . . . The warnings on American packs were, in fact, the first mayday call about the physical harm done by smoking tobacco.

Too late for my darling mother, Kath, who, like so many of her generation, smoked. She passed away from small-cell lung cancer in November 1999.

The weeks flew by until one morning Bryce walked into the kitchen and said, 'Gosh, I feel sick.' Concerned, I looked up and said, 'In what way don't you feel well?' He was generally in robust good health, and I remember the date distinctly: it was 24 June 2010, and I had just seen the news that Julia Gillard, the deputy leader of the Australian Labor Party, had beaten Kevin Rudd in a party-room vote and as a result was appointed as Australia's first woman prime minister.

A bad bout of nausea had arrived for Bryce. His Sydney-based GP and friend Irwin Light diagnosed that he was suffering from severe acid reflux and prescribed some medications. Being mates, these two were usually more interested in talking about the latest Rugby or cricket scores. Irwin and his wife, Erica, were also huge fans of Bob Dylan and we loved chatting to them about the latest concert of his they had gone to great lengths to secure tickets for.

Bryce was never one to fuss about his health and was generally dismissive of any medical concern. He continued taking the reflux medications but they didn't appear to do him much good. I began to worry, mindful of the time in Yarramalong when he had refused to go to the hospital after experiencing symptoms of heart problems. He soldiered on and waved his hand in the air when I prompted him to have another chat to Irwin. The August deadline for his book ensured that he was preoccupied with writing, and he would say, 'Please, darling, no more health checks initiated by Dr Gee.' Frankly, in my experience a lot of men are like this – reluctant to act on early warning signs in health. We women are far more sensible!

In addition to the health worries, Bryce discovered that there was a problem with the book: one of the chapters didn't feel right. If he thought that certain research material wasn't accurate, he never hesitated to make any necessary changes. He well understood that the history had to be bang on to support the narrative and guarantee the integrity of a book.

I discussed the issue with him and then with Bruce, and Bruce reassured me that he would review the research material he had supplied. The same day he called me back, saying, 'I think the facts are actually OK.' My instincts told me to dig deeper, and I forwarded the relevant chapter to Tai Peng, an old friend who lived in Vancouver. Tai Peng grew up in Singapore and was a respected Chinese scholar with whom I was friends when we were both at the ANU. He had learnt English late in life, and I read his masters' thesis to make sure his manuscript would satisfy the eagle eye of his supervisor. Tai Peng's own story was sobering: he was arrested in the 1960s for handing out leaflets during a protest rally at Nanyang University and as a result spent years in solitary confinement.

Tai Peng agreed with me that the history in Bryce's story wasn't entirely correct, and kindly introduced us to Professor Carl A. Trocki, an

American who was then Professor of Asian Studies at the Queensland University of Technology. After reading Bryce's draft, Carl came back with an amazing scenario that Bryce was utterly thrilled about, concerning the alleged drug trade involving the CIA during the Vietnam War. This elevated the book to another level, and after Bryce worked in these new plotlines it really began to sing.

The same wasn't true for Bryce's health. In September he was booked to go on a 160-kilometre trek along the Tsavo River in Kenya. I was scheduled to meet up with him in Cape Town afterwards, but I was so worried I rang Irwin and told him I didn't think Bryce was well enough to travel. I knew he wouldn't be able to keep down the anti-malarial tablets he had been advised to take. I remember Irwin sighing, knowing he would have Buckley's chance of talking Bryce out of going.

True to form, Bryce would not countenance cancelling the trip. Several of his dearest friends were joining him, and he had another agenda as well: he was thinking about writing a novel featuring the extraordinary story of Paul von Lettow-Vorbeck, 'the lion of Africa', a First World War hero of the German East African campaign. Bryce was greatly looking forward to catching up with his old friend Tim Noad, who lived in Nairobi and had promised Bryce that he would be delighted to help him with the research.

Before leaving on the trip, Bryce showed me the synopsis he had written for *The Ghost General*:

As he sees it, his task is to maintain what is good and honourable and expunge what he thinks is unworthy in a system he doesn't control, and one led by a hierarchy who see no fault, ignominy or stupidity in the inculcated beliefs they teach and practise and the traditions they never stop to question. Captain von Lettow, a brilliant young officer in the Prussian military, is in for a bumpy ride.

We had also contacted Bryce's relatives in South Africa and they were hugely excited at the prospect of a family reunion. Bryce told me, 'Darling, we can't let them down. I haven't seen them for such a long time, and I can't wait for you to meet them.' They were his last link to the continent, and I completely understood why catching up with them was something he couldn't bear to cancel. I expect this prospect thrilled him after the revelation of the reunion with some of his half-siblings, the Natal Ryders, in 1991.

His work schedule to finish *Fortune Cookie* book was intense, and by the middle of July he resembled a ghost. He was unusually fatigued and had lost a few kilos. One afternoon I found him slumped over his desk, pale and listless. Even he was now wondering if there was something wrong with him. He said in a barely audible voice, 'Darling, if I become too sick to finish this book, you must ring Geoff Pike. He is the only writer I can think of who would be good enough to complete the story, and in my voice.'

Geoff was a crusty old salt who, like Bryce, had previously worked in the advertising industry. He adored Bryce and always called him *bwana*, a Swahili word meaning 'master'. Geoff had written several superb novels, mostly set in the Far East, under the pen name Pai Kit Fai, and years earlier I had arranged some publicity on his behalf.

Thankfully, Bryce completed *Fortune Cookie* by his deadline of 31 August 2010 and dedicated it to his dear friend, Robbee Minicola. I felt relieved to know he would have a couple of weeks to rest up before heading to Africa. Most afternoons he would fall asleep in his leather chair in the library with Timmy snoring at his feet and a Rugby match blaring away on the television.

Slowly a bit of colour returned to his face, although the nausea didn't subside. His usual hearty appetite was absent and he would leave most of his food on the plate. He used to enjoy an evening glass of wine and rarely failed to request a top-up, saying, 'Darling, please go and get me another titch.' Now, even these requests had all but ceased.

The marketing plans for *Fortune Cookie* were in full swing. Penguin had produced a promotional video about the book, which we were very excited about. Around this time the bookselling landscape in Australia was following global trends and publishers were beginning to see a rise in the sale of ebooks, and were anticipating an increase in the sale of physical books online. Bryce said to the team, 'I'm too old to understand it all, but the writing is on the wall and we mustn't end up looking like a bunch of dinosaurs.'

Despite these changes, and Bryce's conviction that books should be available everywhere, he remained a loyal supporter of bookstores. He hoped they would always be there for readers who, like him, liked to browse before making a purchase and who loved to hold a book in their hands.

Fortune Cookie was reviewed quite favourably, including in the *West Australian* by Alecia Hancock: 'This book is *Mad Men* in a cheongsam with a burgeoning advertising industry and Chinese culture mixed with a healthy dollop of romance, mystery and intrigue.' Bryce even got away with giving some of the characters names I thought were decidedly corny: 'Louie da Fly', 'Chairman Meow', 'Little Sparrow' and 'Chicken Wing'. When I commented on this, he retorted, 'But darling, I am corny, and they deliver some humour into the narrative' – which was indeed the case.

Two weeks before Bryce was due to fly to Kenya, I took the step of ringing St Vincent's Hospital and making an appointment for him to have an endoscopy, performed by gastroenterologist Dr Alissa Walsh. I felt compelled to have him checked out, and this time Bryce didn't object. He said, 'It's probably a good idea. This nausea has been hanging around for months, and I must say I feel as sick as a dog.' I was sorry I hadn't insisted on his having an investigation earlier, even though it had been explained to us that nausea is not always a serious cause for concern.

Bryce was on blood thinners following his heart procedure, which meant the gastroenterologist was limited as to how deeply she could investigate. With the trip coming up fast there wasn't time for him to go off the thinners before having the procedure. The pathology results came back relatively normal, although Alissa wasn't entirely convinced, given Bryce's symptoms. We agreed with her strong recommendation that he have the procedure repeated once he was back from Africa.

On 24 September Bryce flew to Nairobi. He called me to let me know he had arrived safely, but said he was still feeling nauseated. I was beside myself with worry and begged him to consider coming home, but Bryce wasn't a quitter and said he wasn't going to let his friends down. He had invited his old mate Peter Keeble to come on the trip as his guest, and Peter assured me he would keep a close eye on Bryce. They were joined by some other dear friends, including Alex and Brenda Hamill, and Dr Anthony Freeman and his wife, Kerry.

Iain Allan, the owner of safari company Tropical Ice, was leading the trip, called 'The Great Walk of Africa', in Tsavo National Park, where he is an honorary warden. Iain has operated walking safaris and climbs in Kenya since 1978 and looked after my clients when I co-owned Australian Himalayan Expeditions. He has lived in Kenya since the age of nine and is an internationally renowned mountaineer who put up hundreds of new routes on Mount Kenya, famed for its rare lobelia plants that are found up to elevations of 5000 metres. He is unapologetically 'old school' and a fierce champion of authentic African adventures devoid of the overt luxury with which safari operators have become obsessed. Iain is also an accomplished writer and shared Bryce's fascination with Paul von Lettow-Vorbeck. Bryce was itching to spend time with him so that they could chat further about this enigmatic and legendary figure.

The group needed to walk around 15 kilometres a day for ten days, often in temperatures as high as 35°C. Bryce quickly developed terrible blisters, which Kerry, a highly qualified nurse, mercifully treated when they arrived into camp each afternoon. Despite these trials on Bryce's part, Iain later wrote to me, 'He was as tough as hell, Christine. He walked every yard of the 160 kms and never complained . . .You were perfect for each other.' Bryce was seventy-seven when he did this walk and at the time the oldest person to have completed it; his record was superseded in 2021 by two 87-year-olds.

For safety reasons the group was instructed to walk in single file and not say a word – Bryce quipped that I would have found this request challenging. Iain and his loyal team of African guides carried rifles, with some also carrying Masai spears called *assegai*, to protect the group should it be necessary. On the fifth day Iain was charged by a Cape buffalo, considered to be the most dangerous animal in Africa. He shot it in the head at close range before it dropped in its tracks. Bryce said, 'We all stood by in a state of temporary shock.' What Iain didn't tell them was that the shot he fired was the last bullet he had left in his ammo bag.

Further along the trek they came across a deadly black mamba, which Bryce assured me was already dead: 'It was dropped by an eagle flying overhead.' Knowing my fear of snakes, I am certain he said this to make me feel better.

Bryce and his group adored listening to Iain's stories around the campfire, and I remember Tony telling me that for him it was the highlight of the trip. Bryce found the walk with Iain to be extraordinary in every way. It reminded him of his travels through Africa during the 1950s, although he was saddened to see the game so diminished from poaching and climate change. He told me via a satellite call that although he was feeling crook he was loving being back in the African bush: 'Sleeping beneath big African skies, with the dust in my nostrils and listening to the roars of lions at night.'

Iain and Bryce discovered they had a lot in common, and in May 2012 Iain flew to Australia to participate in one of Bryce's final writing courses. In March 2022 he completed a thoroughly absorbing memoir called *Outsider: A Life with the Elephants and Mountains of Africa*, which shall be published in 2023.

*

I felt guilty for not having joined Bryce on this trek, although it was he who had urged me not to go given my phobia of snakes. I think he knew that if I had tagged along, he would have had to spend hours searching for snakes under the beds in our tent! I planned to join a high-end safari at South Africa's Sabi Sands Game Reserve instead.

Knowing Bryce wasn't well made the anticipation of my own safari experience bittersweet. Nevertheless, on 30 September 2010 I flew from Sydney to Johannesburg, feeling hugely excited to be embarking on my first trip to South Africa, Bryce's homeland.

I sensed a security threat from the moment the plane landed at Tambo International Airport. The hire-car driver drove me to the Saxon Hotel in Sandhurst, where Bryce had stayed en route to Nairobi and had hosted a lunch for Lydia Blumberg and her husband, Harry, and I noticed a bevy of security heavies talking earnestly into their phones as we sped into the underground car park. There was a panic button located in a prominent position on the wall in my room, and the hotel receptionist told me under no circumstances to go for a walk in the leafy streets outside the hotel. The barbed wire and high walls protecting the nearby mansions were a sobering reminder of how different daily life in Johannesburg was from life in Australia. Every South African I met had a story of a personal confrontation, home break-in or carjacking. They would finish by saying, 'We have to remain vigilant, even though we love this country and hope we never have to leave.' Australia has welcomed thousands of South Africans whose desire to stay on in their home country was ultimately broken, just as Bryce's had been.

My room was exquisitely decorated with African artefacts and featured a contemporary bathroom with a claw-foot tub. On my first morning in Johannesburg I arranged to go on a tour of the city and we passed by the beautiful Houghton Estate where Nelson Mandela, known by his clan name of Madiba, was in residence. What a staggering contrast this must have been for him after living for nearly twenty-seven years in a spartan and brutal prison on Robben Island.

The late Anglican Archbishop Emeritus of Cape Town, Desmond Tutu, was a good friend of Bryce's and a few years earlier he had invited him to be involved in an extraordinary project called 'Our Icons and Their Wisdom'. In a letter dated 21 August 2007, he wrote, 'Dear Bryce, If we don't share our knowledge, it will be lost. . . by contributing your experience and your wisdom, you are helping to benefit future generations.' The concept and resulting book, *Wisdom*, created by Andrew Zuckerman in New York, featured other prominent 'elders', including Desmond himself, Mandela, Billy Connolly, Jane Goodall, Clint Eastwood, Nadine Gordimer, Judi Dench and Yoko Ono.

While in 'Joburg' I went to a gallery in the leafy suburb of Rosebank and purchased a painting for Bryce by the celebrated artist Vusi Khumalo. Vusi has always insisted his work isn't meant to be didactic even though it displays the harsh realities of life in South Africa's townships where he was raised. The figures in the painting I chose revealed the same resilience that characterised Bryce's own struggle to overcome his childhood challenges. As it turned out he wasn't overly fond of the artwork, saying, 'Although it's beautifully rendered, it reminds me of the inequalities and suffering I witnessed as a child.' I still love it, partly because it's a reminder of how special it was for us to be in Africa together.

The following day I flew to an airfield in the African bush close by the Dulini lodge in Sabi Sands where I was booked to stay. Before departing I noticed a plane about to take off for Nelspruit, which is not far from the citrus estates where Bryce worked after he finished secondary school. Part of me felt like running across the tarmac and jumping aboard – I longed to see more of where he had once lived.

Bryce had told me many stories about growing up in Africa. As I have mentioned, I especially loved the one described in *The Night Country* about a giraffe he came across at sunset after climbing a *koppie* (small hill), so my first sighting of a giraffe was exhilarating as the plane made a bumpy landing on the bush strip. The animal's neck was craning over the whitethorn trees as if to say, 'Oh dear – another planeload of tourists to disturb my peace.'

On my first night at the lodge, I was shown into a rondavel nestled close to the Mabrak River, which I was certain would be crawling with snakes. Certainly it was way more comfortable than the rondavel Bryce had bunked in while working at the mines. Just as I was about to fall asleep, I heard the grunts of lions nearby. As the night went on these sounds intensified and a good sleep remained elusive. The morning call to join a game drive roused me from a restless slumber at around 5 a.m., and after two strong cups of coffee I jumped into an open jeep and headed into the bush.

My first sighting of a magnificent cheetah in the wild is something I will never forget. How sad it was to learn that cheetah numbers were plummeting due to poaching and an outbreak of feline immunodeficiency virus. Just as memorable was what happened when I crouched to pee after a stop for morning tea. I heard an animal noise at close range and felt instantly clammy, and my body began to twitch with fear. I hadn't a clue what I should do, but our guide, Richard, had seen something and said in a calm but firm voice, 'Stand up slowly, Christine, and walk backwards in the direction of our jeep.' I felt the urge to run but did what I was told and was soon safely seated in the vehicle. My late father's advice of 'When you're panicking, you're not thinking' had somehow kicked in. Apparently I was being spied upon by a young and inquisitive warthog, so I guess it could have been worse! The African driver, whose name was Surprise, was quick to hand me a shot of Amarula, a South African cream liqueur, and I swallowed it in one gulp.

Signing up for this 'soft' option had made me the butt of a few rounds of jokes by Bryce's friends, and when the staff on my safari fluttered rose petals into the bath they had drawn for me, I thought about Bryce and his trekking crew washing outside in bucket showers, sleeping on camp beds, and using a pit toilet.

After notching up sightings of the 'Big Five' – the lion, leopard, rhino, elephant and Cape buffalo – I flew down to Cape Town and was immediately transfixed by its beauty. The huge lip of Table Mountain delivered vistas across the city and to the ocean below that rivalled

Sydney Harbour. No wonder so many South Africans felt so much at home after arriving in Sydney. I met up with Shanine Mony (now Cawood), Bryce's first cousin Wendy Bennet's (nee Greer) daughter, making her a first cousin once removed. Shanine is a hugely bright and warm-hearted person with a great passion for staging musical productions, and we had loved having her stay with us in Yarramalong in 2007. It was wonderful spending time with her again on her home turf and I so appreciated that she took the time to show me around.

The day before I was due to meet Bryce, I went on a private tour with a delightful Cape Malay woman called Delilah who had been an activist for the African National Congress during the struggle against the apartheid regime. We walked around District Six, a suburb that is home to descendants of Cape Malays, Indians and Africans who arrived during the days of the hideous slave trade. We wandered past their brightly coloured wooden houses and I couldn't resist sampling the local delicacies. I especially loved the bunny chow – a hollowed-out loaf of white bread filled with a ladleful of goat, chicken or beef curry.

Delilah then suggested we go out to Khayelitsha, a township with which she was very familiar and which is one of the poorest areas of Cape Town. When the apartheid regime was in power, it had been the scene of bloody battles against the security forces. I knew Bryce would have cautioned me against going there, and when I told him about it later, his eyes widened and he said, 'Sweetheart, that wasn't a particularly safe place for you to venture into.' It was a fascinating but confronting place and I did feel a bit on edge. An enduring image was a woman with a baby tied to her back heaving a sheep's stomach covered in flies into a bucket beside her corrugated-iron shack. Groups of young men with stern expressions gazed through the windows of our car, and at first I was reluctant to leave the vehicle. Looking unperturbed, Delilah drove on until we reached a compound ringed with barbed wire. We were there to visit a women's cooperative, and these local ladies could not have been more welcoming. They had created a range of beautiful handicrafts and I left laden with rugs, bags and wall hangings to take home as gifts.

Bryce was never a fan of handicrafts, which he described as being 'happy hands at work', but these were exquisite and I hoped even he would like them. He didn't.

Freedom from the tyranny of apartheid had arrived in the early 1990s, but to be frank I couldn't see that many benefits had trickled down to the people of Khayelitsha. When I expressed this sentiment to Delilah, she sighed and said, 'Corruption is now our greatest enemy. Inshallah, one day things will get better.'

It was dusk and we were about to leave when Delilah noticed that the car was nearly out of petrol. My heart sank and my stomach tightened as we slowly spluttered our way back to the Cape Grace Hotel. The contrast between the luxury of the hotel and Khayelitsha felt uncomfortable. I went straight up to my room, feeling subdued, and remembered Bryce's words: 'Being born with white skin and blue eyes in Western countries gives you opportunities which many people of colour desperately sadly continue to be denied.'

Finally, on 10 October, outside the historic Mount Nelson Hotel in Cape Town, famous for its pink exterior and magnificent gardens, a taxi drew up. Bryce jumped out and threw his arms around me, hugging me so tightly I could barely catch my breath. I felt overjoyed to see him. He looked fit and suntanned, although I noticed he had lost another couple of kilos.

My elation subsided when he said, 'Darling, I'm feeling very sick. I think there's something wrong with me'. Over dinner he struggled to finish a plate of bobotie (minced meat simmered with spices and topped with egg and milk before being baked in the oven). He quietly sipped a glass of Angels Tears sauvignon blanc, produced by the Grande Provence Estate owned by his great friend Alex van Heeren. He only ever drank white wine and said now, 'I like Australian wines, but this one is truly divine.' We raised our glasses and toasted our joy at being in Africa together for the very first time.

Before we went to bed, a bellboy helped us unpack and Bryce started asking him about his life. He told us about his family's struggle and a book he had read that changed his life. Bryce asked him the name of the book, and he answered, 'Sir, it was *The Power of One*.' Bryce told him he was the author and the bellboy fell on one knee and kissed his hand. We kept in touch with him for several months and were able to extend financial help towards the education of his siblings.

The next day Bryce was feeling a bit better, so we visited the spectacular Kirstenbosch National Botanical Garden, founded in 1913 and located on the eastern slopes of Table Mountain. Bryce was in heaven and even the searing heat did not dampen his enthusiasm for exploring its treasures. It was the first garden in the world to have a focus on indigenous plants and I especially loved the spectacular displays of proteas. In addition, we were thrilled to learn that it is home to over 120 species of native birds.

That evening we attended the family gathering at Shanine's house. We were going to meet up at a restaurant, but Bryce was still feeling unwell and we agreed it was better to have a more low-key get-together. I was delighted to be given such a loving welcome from his relatives. Over pizzas and beer, they shared stories thick and fast.

Bryce's first cousins the twins Robyn and Wendy were there, and they shared a lot of memories about Paddy – funny tales of her quick wit and lively sense of humour that had us all bent over with laughter, but also moving stories of how hard it had been for her to raise Bryce and Rosemary. Robyn and Wendy showed a lot of compassion for her and reaffirmed that back then having children out of wedlock was perceived as a terrible sin and led to babies being hidden away or taken from their mothers, with the subject never again being mentioned.

Listening to stories of the hardships Paddy had faced was one of the few times I had seen Bryce's face shrouded in sadness, reminded of the struggles she endured through no fault of her own. In the *Family Confidential* program on ABC television in 2012, the twins said that Bryce saw himself as 'the patriarch of their tribe' and applauded his

340 BRYCE COURTENAY: STORYTELLER

generous financial assistance to their 'Aunty Patty' over her lifetime, from when he was a teenager until her death.

We finished our supper with traditional desserts including koeksisters, an Afrikaner confectionery made of fried dough soaked in sweet syrup or honey. Bryce and I both had a sweet tooth and also loved eating *melktert* (milk tart), a pie-like dessert of sweet pastry with a delicious creamy filling. As the evening drew to a close, Bryce delivered a rousing speech that he concluded by singing a rhyme he sang when especially happy:

> We're off to see the wild west show
> The elephant and the kangaroo-roo-roo
> Never mind the weather, as long as we're together
> We're off to see the wild west show
> Hip-hip hooray, hip-hip hooray!

We all cheered, and Bryce bounded about the room wrapping his arms around everyone with tears of happiness moistening his tired blue eyes. It was close to midnight when we departed, regretting that we had not been able to spend more time with them. We wound down the car windows and waved frantically until everyone disappeared. It was a poignant moment and I wondered deep down if we would see these family members again. We never did.

The following day we went to stay at Alex van Heeren's magnificent Grande Provence Estate at Franschhoek (Dutch for 'French corner'), 75 kilometres from Cape Town. On the way there Bryce told me about the French Huguenots, who had arrived in South Africa in 1689, travelling over the mountains with teams of oxen, to settle this spectacular region.

The houses of the settlers – such as Alex's breathtaking home – were constructed in the traditional Cape Dutch style, with ornate, rounded gables and steep-pitched roofs. Bryce and Alex were as close as brothers, and Bryce was very disappointed that Alex was unfortunately away on business at the time of our visit.

Alex was a founding member of the Duke of Edinburgh's Award program for young people in South Africa and had been awarded an MBE for his contribution. He was also a pioneer of luxury boutique lodges, creating a model that has been copied around the world. His Royal Highness Prince Edward and his wife, Sophie, the Countess of Wessex were once guests at the estate and there was a beautiful photo of them on a side table in the elegant sitting room.

We barely left the house and garden during our stay. Bryce was too unwell even to walk to the estate's fine dining restaurant, run by an award-winning Australian chef who instead arrived at the house to prepare our meals. We were also utterly spoilt by Alex's devoted housekeeper, who would not let me so much as lift a cup and scolded me for making the bed one morning. On our last day Bryce slept for hours, curled up on the day bed on the veranda. While he rested, I went for long walks through the vineyards accompanied by Alex's energetic boxer puppy. The beauty of the vast estate had me spellbound, but all the while I worried about Bryce's health and wondered how we would get home if his condition didn't improve.

Fortunately, our restful stay at Grande Provence Estate did Bryce the world of good and by 14 October he had rallied sufficiently for us to fly to Johannesburg. We left Alex a signed first-edition copy of The Power of One – a new addition for his library, which already housed an impressive collection of first editions.

While we were in transit in Johannesburg, Bryce wandered into an expensive-looking jewellery store and came out with a leather box. It contained a gold and pearl bracelet with elephants encrusted in diamonds and emeralds, and I gasped in awe at this exquisite piece of jewellery. Once again Bryce had spoilt me, and I told him, 'You always make me feel like the luckiest and most loved girl in the world.'

Prior to boarding our flight to Sydney, I asked Bryce if he ever felt like returning to live in Africa. He replied, 'It's been wonderful being here, darling, but I left Africa a long time ago and I can't wait to be home.' Even so, I am certain that Africa always resided in his heart and wish we had made the time to travel back there more regularly.

Our flight was uneventful and we both felt relieved to arrive home and be reunited with our pets. The following morning Bryce was back in the garden tidying up his veggie patch and by the evening he had planted a crop of summer seedlings. However, within a few days he developed an extremely high temperature and I drove him to the emergency department at Bowral Hospital. The doctor on duty asked, 'Have you been travelling to anywhere in the tropics, or to Africa or South America?' The blood tests confirmed that Bryce had contracted falciparum malaria, one of malaria's most deadly strains. Iain Allan was distressed to learn of this diagnosis: after forty-two years of leading safaris in Kenya, Bryce was his first client to come down with malaria.

Bruce had acquired the same strain while he was living in the Solomon Islands. The harrowing symptoms he described reverberated in my mind, and he said, 'Bryce will have a tough time getting over this. You must make sure he rests properly and is kept well hydrated.'

The cure proved to be nearly as bad as the illness: Bryce needed to take a course of Larium (mefloquine), which often causes unpleasant side effects. Without a word of complaint, he swallowed the pills each morning and to my amazement had fully recovered within three-and-a-half weeks.

On 11 November 2010, we arrived at the Royal Motor Yacht Club in Sydney's Point Piper for the launch of *Fortune Cookie*. Bryce greeted his family and friends with a radiant smile and as usual gave everyone a big hug. He couldn't take his eyes off me in my black and silver cheongsam made in Singapore. It was a wonderful evening, and we walked home hand in hand feeling elated and with not a care in the world.

I was immensely proud of Bryce for having overcome so much that year and for having written another remarkable book. I knew his loyal readers would be dying to get their hands on a copy, and they didn't have to wait long: *Fortune Cookie* was soon in the bookstores and shot to number one on the bestseller lists.

But within weeks, our world was turned upside down.

16

THE BUSH CAPITAL

'Jazz ain't about reading music, it about reading the life and the pain that's in plain folk.' – *Jack of Diamonds*

IN EARLY NOVEMBER 2010 we returned to Sydney for further medical investigations into Bryce's condition. Neither of us was particularly concerned, even though Bryce was still experiencing regular bouts of nausea. He had been busy doing media interviews for *Fortune Cookie* and was thrilled the book was doing so brilliantly, as was Penguin.

On 22 November Bryce was booked in for an endoscopy at St Vincent's Hospital – the agreed follow-up to the one he had had prior to leaving for Africa. He was wheeled into a private room to recover and in the early evening a doctor we hadn't previously met walked in. He was accompanied by a nurse carrying a box of tissues, which felt unnerving.

'Hello, Bryce,' he said. 'My name is Koroush Haghighi and I am an upper-gastrointestinal surgeon.' In a quiet and gentle voice, he explained that the results from the endoscopy revealed that Bryce had advanced gastric cancer and an almost complete blockage of his stomach.

We both stared at him in disbelief, holding our breath in shock. Bryce grappled for reassurance by asking if the cancer had been caught early, understandably not managing to integrate the initial diagnosis.

This was not the case, and Koroush told us that he thought Bryce may have had the cancer for up to a year.

The following day Koroush performed a laparoscopy, which uncovered a large tumour involving most of Bryce's stomach and showed that the cancer was growing out to the outer layer of his stomach. Koroush explained that Bryce needed to have an operation as a matter of urgency due to both the bleeding and the blockage. The procedure, he said, was called a radical gastrectomy and meant that 90 per cent of Bryce's stomach would need to be removed.

I slumped next to Bryce and clutched his hand, feeling tears welling up in my eyes. Bryce remained calm, even though he too felt completely shaken to have received this diagnosis. He paused, then said, 'Well, at least we know what has been making me so sick for months.'

On a lighter note, Koroush told Bryce how much he had enjoyed *The Power of One*, which made Bryce's strained expression lighten momentarily. We wondered if this wonderful man might indeed have the power to save Bryce's life. After Koroush left, we held each other tightly and struggled to absorb the gravity of the news. Bryce did all he could to comfort me, saying, 'It's all right, darling. Koroush is one of the world's finest surgeons and he will sort me out. This is just another round on the grizzly bars.' He then added, in a more upbeat tone, 'What is more important is that we get back to finalising our wedding plans.'

The next morning Robert Swan arrived at the hospital and Bryce was more interested in chatting about our impending nuptials than about his health. It was a largely jovial conversation, even though Bryce had just received the most devastating news. Later that night I was in pieces and was grateful Rob was staying at our Sydney flat. He was always a good man to have around in a crisis. When life-threatening incidents took place on his polar expeditions he would say, 'OK, team, it's time to don the "Don't Panic" button and carry on!' This was a nod to his friend Giles Kershaw, the legendary polar aviator, who used to wear a 'Don't Panic' button when flying in Antarctica (tragically, he lost his life there on 5 March 1990). Rob made me promise I would never let Bryce see me looking so broken. I knew he was right and felt I had been weak, but this news of Bryce's diagnosis reminded me of the death sentence my mother had received in mid-1999 after she was diagnosed with stage 4 lung cancer, and triggered the trauma I faced at that time.

Saturday 27 November was the day of Bryce's big operation. He spent the previous night at the Prince of Wales Private Hospital and showed few signs of anxiety. I was filled with apprehension even though I implicitly trusted Koroush. Tony Freeman, Bryce's friend and cardiologist, called me that morning and said, 'Bryce is in excellent hands. If I was ever diagnosed with cancer, Koroush Haghighi is the only surgeon I would want to operate on me.'

After I had spent several hours pacing the hospital corridors, Koroush called me and said in a steady voice, 'The operation has gone perfectly. Bryce did very well.' I was hugely relieved even though he said Bryce had needed to be transferred to the intensive care unit following such a big procedure. When Bryce was returned to the ward, I sat by his bed and thought he looked pale and had aged beyond his years. Brett and Adam came to visit him and this really cheered Bryce up. We were all still trying to come to terms with the reality that he was facing the battle of his life. We had all expected him to live well into his nineties, writing and embracing life as he always had. Many of his running mates, including Alex, Tony, Roger Rigby, Owen Denmeade, Tony Crosby, Ray Black and Peter Keeble, also visited, which really buoyed Bryce's spirits, and within a few days I had once again snuck in a bottle of his favourite tipple, the William Fèvre chablis.

Not long after the operation, Koroush asked if I wanted to see pictures of the tissue he had removed from Bryce's tummy. Glancing at these was illuminating, but I was shocked at the size of the tumour. I tentatively asked Bryce if he wanted to see them, but he said, 'Having Dr Gee look at them is quite sufficient!'

Three weeks later we returned home to Burradoo, where Bryce was able to rest and recuperate. He spent most days sleeping and catching up on his reading, only leaving the house to totter outside to check on his veggie garden.

I knew he was feeling a lot better when he began to discuss his next book. He had already told me he was determined that the cancer diagnosis was not going to change a thing. In an animated voice he told me that his next story would be about a man called Jack Spayd who grew up in a working-class suburb in Toronto. He had felt inspired after reading *Cabbagetown*, a classic tale by Hugh Garner that was published in 1951 and documents what life was like in 'Cabbagetown' during the Great Depression. The name came from the Irish immigrants who moved there in the late 1840s and who were said to have grown cabbages in their front yards to survive.

This would be Bryce's first novel to feature a Canadian chief protagonist, which he knew would delight his Canadian readers. Jack's life did not start well, as confirmed in the novel's opening lines: 'Harry Spayd was a drunk. He was also my father, but the only thing he contributed to my childhood was a sense of unremitting terror.' Harry did, however, make one significant contribution to Jack's life when he handed him a harmonica, which ultimately set Jack free: 'Being a kid, you just go with the flow, but this was a stream that turned into a river until my whole life seemed to be music.'

Bryce told me he was going to introduce an African grey parrot as a leading character, and the initial title of this book was in fact *The Grey Parrot*. Given my passion for birdlife, he asked me to find out all I could about this species.

The idea for the book had gathered pace when Bryce had his unscheduled ten-day stay at the Bellagio in Las Vegas following the September 11 terrorist attacks in 2001. He had been on a train bound for Mexico after visiting Rosemary, Esmund and Dorrie in San Diego. Being in Las Vegas provided him with the perfect opportunity to come face to face with the world of gambling, and he told me, 'I hit the high roller rooms like a kid in a toyshop.' In an interview recorded by Michael Dillon in our home in September 2012 he said, 'Gambling with my background is a nonsense, and I wanted to go inside a gambler's mind.' This book was a perfect example of Bryce's drive to keep writing. He never understood why people gambled and believed that the only way to make a living was from your own efforts. He used to chide me for buying lottery tickets, saying, 'What's the point, darling? The odds are impossible. Can't you see it's a big con, peddling hope when there isn't any?'

Bryce loved jazz and was excited to feature music as a core part of the narrative. In an interview on ABC TV, he explained how as a child he had felt a burning desire to play the mouth organ, feeling sure he'd bring crowds into the local town hall to listen, 'because I realised very early on that a performance was critical to being left alone'. As previously mentioned, things didn't go to plan – he found he had very little talent!

I purchased a Bose CD player and a collection of jazz classics that he listened to as he wrote. Ray Charles, Duke Ellington, Count Basie, Oscar Peterson, Louis Armstrong and Ella Fitzgerald were his favourites. He was also a huge fan of the Australian jazz trailblazer Don Burrows and his protégé James Morrison. I had studied the clarinet for several years while at high school, but now, after I played Bryce a rendition of 'Puppet on a String', he gently told me he would stick to listening to his CDs.

Just before Christmas we attended a consultation with Koroush, armed with an especially fine bottle of whisky as a small gesture of thanks to him for saving Bryce's life. I asked him what stage Bryce's cancer had reached and he answered, 'Stage 4'. I felt alarmed as I knew this was very bad news and had mistakenly thought the cancer may not have been so advanced. When I queried this with Koroush he said without hesitation, 'It was always stage 4.'

Bryce wasn't that clued up on medical terms and asked, 'What does stage 4 mean?' Koroush gently explained as much as he could about Bryce's condition and was as reassuring as he could be, given the grim diagnosis. He asked Bryce how he was finding eating, and showed surprise when Bryce responded that he still enjoyed tucking into a steak and vegetables for dinner, washed down with a glass of wine.

We left Koroush's office feeling well informed but in no doubt that Bryce was facing a monumental battle. I marvelled at Koroush's calmness; he would have had conversations of this nature hundreds of times during his career, and I wondered at the toll this must have taken on him.

Stage 4 cancer is the final stage before the illness becomes terminal, and my hopes for Bryce's survival had been essentially dashed. As we waited by the lifts I almost broke down before I remembered my promise to Robert and pulled myself together. Bryce comforted me as though I were the one having to deal with such bleak news.

He summoned his customary courage and in an optimistic voice would say to people, 'Even if the cancer comes back, I might have another three years and by then I will be over eighty. What's wrong with that?' My heart would sink and I would think, your cancer hasn't gone anywhere, and you'll be lucky to survive for another six to twelve months, let alone three years. I never said this to Bryce, though – what was the point of reminding him of the terrible fate awaiting him? Instead, I focused on doing everything I could to ensure he enjoyed every day to the full. Bryce was someone who lived very much in the present, and that approach felt even more relevant now. His diagnosis was distressing, but I tried not to dwell on it as I knew it would render me a total wreck. Even so, I sometimes needed to take something to get to sleep, as my fears stalked me under the cover of darkness. As Bryce wrote in *The Night Country*, 'In a cloud of blue smoke . . . we moved down the empty road, towards the giant's lair . . .'

Many of Bryce's closest friends were doctors, including Irwin Light, Warwick Selby and Tony Freeman, and they also indicated that Bryce may only have at most one or two years left to live. They would look at us with kind but serious expressions and say, 'Whatever you want to do, you should do it now.'

I started to wonder if staying on in Burradoo was a good idea. Bowral had two good hospitals, but I wasn't so sure about the capacity of the local support services for when Bryce's condition deteriorated. We had our beautiful apartment in Point Piper overlooking Sydney Harbour, but I knew Bryce would go crazy holed up there. The other big consideration was that we had five pets, and I was sure that some of the other owners in the apartment block would be adamant the animals couldn't move in. Mind you, with our pets being used to country life I knew they wouldn't take too kindly to apartment living and would systematically trash our city home. Bryce and I agreed that only Cardamon the Burmese was regal enough to be considered a suitable candidate to live there.

My son, Nima, came up with the idea that we should move to Canberra. He and I had gone for a bike ride and I was discussing my concerns about Bryce's impending needs. He said, 'Well, Mum, why don't you move into your house in Canberra?' I had lived in Canberra for five years when I was studying at the ANU, and in 2008 we had purchased an investment property there in the suburb of Reid, a stone's throw from the Australian War Memorial. It was currently rented out, but I thought it might just be big enough for us and the tribe of pets. I also hoped that Bryce might relish the chance to resurrect the garden, which was in dire need of a Bryce Courtenay makeover.

When I asked him what he thought of the idea, he rejected it out of hand – which was perfectly understandable, given that he loved our beautiful home and had never imagined we would leave. He had only ever visited Canberra a few times, mostly associated with promotional activities around a new book. The only exception to this was when he had joined Alex and Irwin to polish off three or four Canberra marathons during the 1980s and 1990s. As Alex confirmed later, 'Yep, I think that's where he actually fell in love with Canberra. Most of the race ran around Lake Burley Griffin, Old Parliament House and the War Memorial. One of the great marathons.'

Apart from this, like most Australians Bryce believed that Canberra was inhabited by too many overrated politicians and 'fat cat' public servants. His Sydney friends thought even less of it and were largely unimpressed when I mentioned we were contemplating moving there.

Understandably, they were hoping we would live in Sydney, as I am certain his sons would have wanted as well. In hindsight I sorely wish we had done this, but Bryce was adamant he did not want to return to Sydney. He had grown to love the tranquillity of country life. For a writer it was perfect – not that every day was peaceful. One morning I returned home from shopping to find a gas burner alight and the ceiling covered in bits of eggshell. Bryce had been boiling quail eggs to put into a salad but had gone outside to work in the garden and forgotten about them. The kitchen ceiling was badly scorched and repairing it ended up being an expensive exercise. I told him, 'Darling, if you don't mind, boiling eggs might best be replaced with making an omelette.'

Bryce was hoping that the idea of us moving to Canberra would go through to the keeper, but I persisted until he relented. He had witnessed family members and friends go through the final stages of cancer and deep down he knew the medical services in Canberra were better. He was further chastened by the devastating loss of his running mate and brilliant advertising colleague Wayne McCarthy, who passed away unexpectedly at the age of sixty-eight. We attended his memorial service on 7 February 2011 and it was a gathering of everyone who had loved Wayne as much as Bryce had.

Bryce was very quiet and reflective for several days afterwards, and I suspect he was questioning his confidence in thinking he could overcome anything. By mid-February he agreed we could move to Canberra, but on one condition: 'You will have to get us out of here as I am going to keep writing my book. It's probably going to be my last, and nothing is going to stop me handing it in on time.'

T. S. Eliot's poem 'The Hollow Men', which illuminates the space between an idea and the reality, felt spot on as I began to implement the plan. Our Canberra house needed renovating and I knew this would normally take six months or more to complete. However, by engaging two teams of local builders, we quickly got the work underway the moment our tenants vacated. This breakthrough meant that Bryce and I could be installed there by April 2011. I also set to work wrapping up hundreds of pictures and decorative items, and within several weeks our belongings were in cardboard boxes.

Each week I drove down to Canberra to see how things were progressing. The house was not far from Currong Street, where I had lived in after moving out of Garran Hall on the ANU campus. It felt for me like moving back to a familiar place, although I knew Bryce couldn't be expected to feel the same way. Back then, five of us paid $10 each a week for rent and each put $10 into a Fowlers Vacola jar for food. Yours truly ended up doing most of the cooking, which meant I was released from doing the washing-up. We even took in a stray cat I named Pearl. It was two of the happiest years of my life. While there I had the privilege of meeting Judith Wright, the great poet, environmentalist and Aboriginal land rights activist. Her daughter, Meredith McKinney, was friends with a PhD student called Neil Mudford who was one of my housemates.

In late February I organised a garage sale at Werrington Street, much to Bryce's consternation. We had too many belongings to fit into our Canberra house, and he only acquiesced once I agreed to give the proceeds to charity. Garage sales are a source of weekend entertainment in the Southern Highlands and the 'Bryce Courtenay factor' came into play. As our gates were swung open nearly 400 people raced down our driveway like a herd of wildebeest. I had to quickly rope off sections of the garden to hold back the stickybeaks hoping to spy the famous author on home ground. He sensibly laid low and continued writing, blissfully unaware of the mayhem taking place outside.

The garage sale proved to be a time-consuming but necessary undertaking. My friends Connie Wang and her husband, John Adamson, came to help. Connie had migrated to Australia from Beijing and I met her through John, with whom I had studied African history at university back in 1973. Just prior to opening our doors to the public, Connie, an accomplished artist, picked up a drawing I had priced at $10 and with an astonished look said, 'This is an original drawing by Sidney Nolan from his Ned Kelly series!' Thanks to her, the picture was swiftly removed from the garage sale; it continues to give me pleasure. Very sadly, dearest Connie passed away in Sydney on 21 June 2019.

I wasn't saved, though, from selling some books Bryce had given Bruce when we were living in Yarramalong. A wily second-hand dealer who was first on the scene purchased them for a song. I called Bruce to report that the sale had gone well and he said, 'That's great, so long as you didn't sell my set of C. E. W. Bean books recording the official history of Australia during the First World War.' I gulped and put down the phone, then rang the dealer, whose number I had fortunately made a note of. He lived in a nearby town and I begged him to consider allowing me to reimburse him. To my relief he agreed and I jumped in the car and drove to his shop. To thank him, I purchased a pair of beautiful Art Deco vases. However, as I was leaving, I noticed on a table partially hidden by a curtain a badge featuring a German swastika. When I asked what this item was doing there, the dealer opened the curtain fully, and to my horror I saw, lying on the table, a cache of Nazi memorabilia. I was aghast as he explained how he travelled to Germany every year to purchase items to sell to Australian collectors. I couldn't believe that peddling these hateful items redolent of such evil was not a serious criminal offence.

Bryce was happy with how his new book was progressing and was knee deep into weaving in the research material being relayed by Bruce. 'Jack Spayd' was a man who loved jazz as much as they both did, and Bryce had already written about Jack's accelerating gambling habits: 'Years later I would admit to myself that it was at that very moment in my life in Moose Jaw that I took the first step on my way to becoming obsessed with poker. Jazz and then poker – honey mixed with arsenic.'

Bryce's extraordinary gastrointestinal surgeon, Koroush Haghighi, was introduced as a fictional character, which Bryce hoped he would take as a compliment (and he kindly did): '"Jack, may I introduce you to Dr Haghighi . . . Dr Koroush Haghighi is originally from Persia but is now considered one of America's best hand surgeons. He is back from the east and operates out of Albany General Hospital, New York State."' Bryce had woven Koroush into his story as Jack's one chance of having his hands repaired after suffering a devastating injury. Koroush is quoted in the book saying, 'This is an accident no surgeon can fully repair.'

Bryce's friend and GP Irwin Light also had a cameo role: 'The piano was my life and despite the tiny ray of hope Dr Light always left me with, it didn't take much imagination to see that my career as a pianist could be over.' Irwin's remarkable wife, Erica, was not left out, either: 'Dr Irwin Light and his wife Erica are among my few friends in Las Vegas. They've long known about the Chicago Mob and the casino, which isn't exactly a state secret.'

Meanwhile, I had fallen in love with 'Diamond Jim', the African grey parrot. This extraordinary species is renowned for its intelligence and the birds have been known to acquire a vocabulary of 300 to 1000 words. I begged Bryce not to kill him off as the plot unfolded, but he kept me in suspense, writing, 'Diamond Jim's life might well prove to be a short and far from happy one.'

By late March the renovations still weren't finished and the Canberra house looked like it had been hit by a bomb. I had never taken on a big renovation, and it was a fraught process involving hundreds of decisions around changing timelines. I did enjoy selecting the curtain fabrics, carpets and wallpapers, although Michael Dean, our accountant, kept a worried eye on the budget. His demeanour didn't improve when I splashed out on a bathroom featuring a claw-foot bath, Calacatta marble tiles and a custom-made vanity basin. It was inspired by a design I had found in a magazine, and a stark contrast to the family bathroom on the back veranda of our farm in Wooragee where I had been raised.

Bryce selected the decor for his writing room, which overlooked the back garden. He had exquisite taste and chose a bright-red carpet made from pure wool that had been hand-loomed in Argentina. I knew that Timmy's white fur would soon become a permanent fixture but didn't quibble. Bryce decided upon grey linen blinds trimmed with black for the windows, and asked that his bookshelves be transferred from the Burradoo office. Fortunately, there was enough space in his new office for his custom-made brown leather chair and leather ottoman, and for a television. I was especially happy about this as I knew I would be assured of a merciful respite from the Rugby season.

As the weeks went by, the pressure on me mounted. I knew that when Bryce arrived, he would want to tour the garden and then walk into his study and start writing. By early April I was in tears as there had been delays completing the bathrooms and the curtains were 10 centimetres too long and couldn't be hung. I slumped onto the floor, surrounded by boxes, and wondered what the hell I had done.

In addition, I hadn't packed up our vast collection of books. There were so many that I didn't know where to begin. Some were signed first editions, including a biography of Margaret Thatcher and Nelson Mandela's *Long Walk to Freedom*; published five years after *The Power of One*. Bryce was always sorry he never met Mandela, and we used to wonder if he had ever read Bryce's book.

Bryce loved antiquarian books and owned several stories written by the Australian writer Arthur Hoey Davis, whose pen-name was Steele Rudd. He also had an early edition of a book by his hero Charles Dickens, which I recall he may have given to one of his sons as a birthday gift, and multiple copies of *Love in the Time of Cholera* and *One Hundred Years of Solitude* by the Nobel laureate Gabriel García Márquez. He felt they were the two best contemporary novels he had ever read, and would give copies to people he thought might enjoy them too.

We needed to decide what to do with Highfield, our house in Burradoo. The Bowral real estate market was depressed at the time, and it often took years to sell properties there. Our big place needed constant maintenance and with us not living there we feared it would fall into disrepair. As Bryce was unwell, I knew it wasn't practical for us to keep going back to take care of it, and I worried about the possibility of intruders. As an interim measure we invited a good friend, Denis Bertollo, and his lovely family to move in. We knew this would mean the property would be well taken care of. Over time we decided we would quietly put it on the market, even though we were not hopeful of securing a quick sale.

I relocated to Canberra on 15 April 2011 accompanied by our cats Cardamon, Muschka and Pirate. Cardamon nonchalantly wandered onto the back deck while the other two cowered under a bed, refusing to eat or drink. I was met with insolent stares of disapproval when I made any overtures to coax them out. Ophelia, the fourth feline, was missing in action, having run off into the bush in Burradoo. I was beside myself, having loved her to pieces after rescuing her two years earlier. A couple of days later, at midnight, there was a knock on the front door of the Canberra house and I opened it to see our great friend Duncan Thomas, covered in scratches. He told me he had lunged at Ophelia when she returned to the house looking for food. As he brought her in now, she let out a primeval yowl like an animal about to meet its maker.

Bryce arrived in Canberra on 19 April, and although I was over the moon to see him, I worried he wouldn't like the house. In 2008, when I had been keen to purchase it, he had said, 'If you like it, darling, just go ahead and buy it.' I had never been with a man who was so trusting and generous, and it took some getting used to. The one thing he wouldn't agree to my buying were two chocolate-coloured Burmese kittens for which I had been hankering like a woman wanting to bear more children.

Our house in Burradoo had twelve rooms and we were now residing in a three-bedroom California bungalow on barely a quarter of a hectare. The kitchen was functional but unrenovated as I had run out of time to get this done. To make matters worse, Canberra was in the grip of a ten-year drought: the entire city was parched, and strict water restrictions were being enforced. Our garden was nothing more than a pile of dirt apart from a few scorched hydrangea bushes. I immediately set about trying to save what little foliage remained, but most of it was burnt to a crisp.

At first Bryce didn't like living in Canberra at all – and he didn't hold back in letting me know. He missed our magnificent garden at Highfield and was feeling decidedly out of sorts. The drought-stricken landscape was depressing, and there was no sign of rain on the horizon. One evening he announced that it was time to call on the rain gods. He told me about *khulanga ifula*, or African rainmaker knowledge, and said he was preparing to harness its powers to deliver some much-needed rain. When I looked at him askance he said I only had to reread *The Night Country* to understand that this was exactly what he must do: 'In respect of rain, it was known from the beginning of time that Modjadji's power was greater by far than the greatest of the witchdoctors.' I told him I recalled what an inspiring story it was, but privately I thought his plans were utterly fanciful.

That night Bryce launched himself into a trance-like state and began to chant in what he said was a mixture of Zulu, Shangaan and Afrikaans. He leapt about the garden like a man possessed, and Timmy started barking, which I knew would wake up the neighbours. Sure enough, lights went on next door and our lovely neighbour popped her head over the fence to see if everything was all right. I could only smile weakly and splutter that Bryce was working up an idea for his latest book.

I know it sounds preposterous, but within two days the rains arrived and Canberra's drought was broken, just as in *The Night Country*:

> Soon puffs of cloud like early morning breath would appear. Then, cotton clouds, strung across the horizon like herds of grazing, pure white goats, after which would follow great towering cliffs and mountains of tumbling air filled with moisture.

Was this a case of 'Courtenay luck', or had the rain queen heard his call?

Following the downpours Bryce cheered up immeasurably and went back to writing at full tilt. He also began to resurrect our forlorn-looking garden. A persimmon tree was planted in the middle of the backyard and the privet hedges were pulled out and replaced with rose bushes.

As the garden bloomed, so too did Bryce's spirits and he began to say things like 'You know, sweetheart, the bush capital has a lot going for it.' He also began to take an interest in the origins of Canberra, first settled thousands of years ago by Indigenous communities. The city's name derives from the Ngambri people.

Our new home town certainly ensured we experienced a welcome blast of energy in contrast to our more sedate life in Burradoo. It had been a privilege to live in Bowral, but it had sometimes felt like an outpost of Sydney's deep North Shore. We came to discover how cosy and intimate our Canberra bungalow was and grew to love it more than any of the larger homes we had lived in previously.

Furthermore, we could now enjoy occasional visits to Canberra's superb cultural institutions, such as the National Library and the National Gallery. Questacon, the incredible National Science and Technology Centre, was a place Bryce loved visiting with his grandson Jake, who was a gifted science student.

Sometimes we would go out to dinner, our favourite restaurant in this city being Mezzalira, a refined Italian eatery on London Circuit in Civic. Most Saturday mornings we headed to the farmer's market at Exhibition Park, and the plant nurseries at Pialligo soon had one of their best customers in Bryce.

One morning when we were trudging up Mount Ainslie, Timmy panting alongside, Bryce put his arm around me and said of Canberra, 'What's not to like?' We had earlier spotted an eastern grey kangaroo nibbling on a lettuce in our front garden, and as it took off and bounded up the street Bryce had said, 'What other city in the world would be home to such a beautiful native creature?' To my relief he had discovered that Canberra had a soul after all!

On 25 April 2011, we attended the Anzac Day Dawn Service at the Australian War Memorial, which was a ten-minute walk from home.

Many of Bryce's novels are set against the backdrop of theatres of war, and he regarded the AWM as the holy grail for remembering all those men and women (and animals) whose service enabled us to live in peace. He had sought help from the AWM with research material for several of his books, including *Solomon's Song*, *Four Fires*, *Smoky Joe's Cafe*, *Brother Fish*, *The Persimmon Tree* and *The Story of Danny Dunn*.

It was a bitterly cold morning and our fellow Canberrans told us that Anzac Day always heralds the start of winter. The service was a moving experience, with the distinguished newsreader Ross Symonds being the time-honoured MC. We swallowed hard as the Last Post was played at the conclusion. Then, as the dawn broke, the magpies warbled a chorus, which lightened the sombre mood.

Feeling hungry, we walked into the AWM to savour the Anzac Day 'gunfire breakfast' in memory of the First World War troops, who were given tea with a splash of rum before heading into battle. We inquired whether we could join a table of others already seated. The men were clad in Royal Australian Air Force dress uniforms complete with braces of medals. Bryce shook each person's hand, saying, 'Hello, I'm Bryce, and this is Christine, my beloved fiancée.'

One woman who introduced herself as Stacey did a noticeable double-take before exclaiming, 'Bryce, I've read everything you've written, and *Jessica* is my favourite book. I've read it twenty times and keep it at my bedside to dip into whenever I need some words of encouragement.' Bryce chatted with her as we ate breakfast beneath the wings of the Lancaster bomber named 'G for George'. Stacey explained that she and her husband had been in the air force for many years but had moved to Canberra to take up civilian roles in the Department of Defence. Bryce interrupted by saying, 'That's lovely to know, but if you could now do one other thing in life, what would it be?' Stacey blushed and replied tentatively, 'I'd be a writer.' Bryce beamed and said, 'Tell me the story you want to write.'

Stacey told him she was already writing a book about Nancy Wake, Australia's most awarded war heroine, whom she was fortunate enough to have met. Nancy had fought alongside the French Resistance during the Second World War, famously nicknamed 'The White Mouse' by the Gestapo because she could not be captured. Bryce confessed he would have loved to have written her story, grasped Stacey's hand and said, 'I'll make you a deal. You start writing and I'll read it and give you feedback, as well as doing whatever I can to help you get it published.' Stacey looked at her adoring husband, who said in a steady voice, 'Shake his hand, Stace.'

From the outset we were warmly embraced by the Canberra community. Stacey and her husband were the first new friends we made in Canberra, and they continue to offer me their love and support. We also became reacquainted with friends I had met while at the ANU, including David Hawking and his partner, Kathy Griffiths. David, like me, had attended Beechworth High School and had left with big dreams on his mind, and both he and Kathy had outstanding careers. Duncan's father, Don Thomas, was another long-term resident of Canberra; he had fled Japan in 1941 with his parents on the second-last boat out. It was lovely to reconnect with Duncan's siblings, Susan, Penny and Rohan, and their families.

I felt so happy when Bryce said, 'You know, sweetheart, I wish we had never lived in either Yarramalong or Burradoo. We should have instead moved straight to Canberra – this city is Australia's best-kept secret.' Most of the time he appeared to be relatively well, and he continued writing, but I noticed he was in fact slowly deteriorating before my eyes. I could see that we had transitioned into living 'one day at a time' – a mantra my father, Allan, said had enabled him to survive being a prisoner of war on the infamous Thai–Burma Railway.

Aside from writing, Bryce spent as much time as he could with Brett and Adam and their families who, like his old friends, regularly drove down to visit. A particular source of joy was when the grandchildren, Ben, Jake and Marcus, came to stay. The youngest, Marcus, had started to take an interest in gardening and Bryce helped him plant some flowers in a pot on the back deck that he labelled 'Grown by Marcus'.

On 27 April we were invited to Freedom Day at the South African embassy in Yarralumla. I loved its distinctive Cape Dutch architecture and Bryce tucked into a traditional barbecue called a *braai*. We also ate *mieliepap*, a porridge-like breakfast dish made from maize, and other traditional delicacies. Bryce remarked to Her Excellency the high commissioner Koleka Mqulwana that it was an honour to meet a black South African in this role and, even better, a woman. He said that in his wildest dreams growing up there he couldn't have imagined such a thing ever happening.

The local Canberrans mostly left us in peace, and Bryce was relieved as he was able to relax and focus on his writing. Sometimes people would come up to him to ask for an autograph or to have their picture taken with him. He never declined as he remembered that the loyalty of his readers allowed him to keep fulfilling his lifelong dream of being a writer. Within a few months we began to lend our support to several local charities, and Bryce accepted their invitations to deliver keynote speeches at fundraising events and we donated signed collections of his books for auction items. Aside from this, he spent long days writing *Jack of Diamonds*, with the 31 August deadline looming large.

Unfortunately, in the middle of 2011 Bryce succumbed to a bout of shingles, a painful viral condition that if not treated promptly can take months to recover from. To make matters worse, I had joined an expedition cruise to the High Arctic region in Norway, not far from the North Pole. Bryce unfortunately didn't let me know he had fallen ill soon after I had departed. I did wonder if something wasn't right when I called to see how he was via a satellite phone on the ship. He said, 'I'm just a little tired, darling, and you're the first person I've spoken to all day.' I had an amazing but potentially dangerous experience when I sighted a polar bear while on shore, but I decided to share the details with Bryce after I was safely back home.

When he opened our front door to greet me, he looked dreadful. He said, 'I'm in a lot of pain, darling, and I don't know what to do.' I immediately drove him to a doctor and we were referred to a specialist who, fortunately, lived in our street. Bryce slowly began to improve, but I naturally felt guilty for having left him in the first place. He begged me not to fret and instead said how much he loved hearing my stories of the spectacular journey. However, he did say that there had been some days when he wondered how much longer he could carry on.

It was becoming clear that he was not going to finish *Jack of Diamonds* on time. He had barely written a word while I was away due to the debilitating pain from shingles. Having cancer was also draining his energy: he could no longer sit and write for eight to ten hours at a time.

Bryce had never not delivered a manuscript on time, and he felt mortified to have to call Bob Sessions at Penguin and say, 'Mate, I can't finish my book by the end of August.' He tended to be hard on himself and even with his health in serious decline, never forgave himself for being late with this book, telling me, 'I've failed, I've failed, I've failed.' Bob was incredibly understanding and begged Bryce not to worry. I think he and his team were amazed that Bryce was writing at all. Bryce left Bob in no doubt that by early the following year he would hand in the book.

On 30 September Bryce was humbled to be invited to deliver the keynote address at the Australian Capital Territory's first Older Persons Assembly, convened in the ACT Government's Legislative Assembly chamber. He looked grey and drawn as he climbed into our car, but after a strong cup of coffee he strode in and set the room on fire. I was so proud of him, and the atmosphere was one of jubilation as he acknowledged the enormous contribution of senior Canberrans. Earlier he had been interviewed by the *Canberra Times* and said:

I have this theory we live through three distinct sections of our lives . . . The first is that disastrous section called growing up, then the second is that travesty we call marriage, children, mortgages, struggle and anxiety and then suddenly someone says you have enough superannuation. It's that third stage you need to watch very carefully, it's time to do all those things you couldn't do in the other stages.

He noted that he despaired for people who spent their older years playing golf, and said he would rather sit down and write than 'chase a white ball across a green field and into a hole'. Not surprisingly, he didn't receive any invitations from Canberra's golf clubs after that!

Bryce looked shattered after delivering the speech, his face rigid with pain. He said to me in an urgent tone, 'Have you got one of those tablets, darling? The pain in my stomach is excruciating.' The cancer had let him know it was ready to strike, like a tiger snake lying in wait on a hot summer's day.

In early October 2011 Bryce took time out to be interviewed for an ABC TV series called *Family Confidential*. The two programs called 'The Courtenays' were broadcast in February 2012 and included interviews with Bryce, me, Brett and Adam, Alex Hamill and Celeste Coucke as well as some other friends and relatives. The film crew even travelled to South Africa to film Bryce's first cousins, the twins Wendy Bennet and Robyn Davies (nee Greer). The director, Ili Baré, executive producer Laurie Critchley and their crew were incredibly professional and unfailingly considerate, but even so Bryce was exhausted from his illness and in considerable pain, and didn't feel he was up to giving his best. Ili was interviewed by Graeme Blundell for *The Australian* shortly after, and said:

Courtenay is driven by a fear of failure dating back to a life that began in poverty and illegitimacy in South Africa: 'I've got to be first . . . I'm climbing up this perpetual cliff, watching bodies fall on either side of me, saying, "All I have to do is hang in here and I'm going to win."'

I felt a bit remorseful as I was the one who had pressed him to go ahead with the show, thinking it would give him a chance to discuss his remarkable life for his readers and record some precious reflections for his family. In many respects this indeed happened, but after the series was broadcast he told me, 'Well, darling, I hope the viewers found it of interest, but for me it felt bittersweet.'

A far more challenging media encounter was to arrive later, when he was in an even more vulnerable state.

The most joyous occasion of that year took place when Bryce and I were married at the Royal Motor Yacht Club (RMYC) in Point Piper at 5.30 p.m. on 21 October 2011. He had asked me to marry him in 2006 but our wedding plans kept being delayed due to his writing commitments, our house moves and his recurrent health issues.

On the ABC's *Family Confidential*, Alex said, 'He's found the right woman in Christine. They are soulmates and very compatible. He has wanted to marry her for a long, long time.' We had indeed been friends for over eighteen years, and Bryce described our relationship on the program as 'a slow maturation and a huge surprise when she finally liked me beyond friends . . . What a way to finish up. You finish life with a glorious lady you want to be with forever . . . Maybe she'll sing me "Summertime".'

On a trip to Paris I had purchased a stunning Jenny Packham couture gown (she is a favourite designer of Her Royal Highness the Duchess of Cambridge) – thank goodness it was on sale! – made from mint-coloured silk chiffon and featuring a hand-tooled silver clasp. It needed altering and arrived by international courier only two days before the wedding. I had bought Bryce a superb blue and rust-coloured tie designed by Lanvin at their signature store on Rue du Faubourg Saint-Honoré, not far from the Élysée Palace.

Prior to the big day I had embarked on a massive fitness and diet regime. Over several months I rode hundreds of kilometres on my bike, attended Zumba classes and ate as little as possible. It worked a treat and Bryce was delighted. He said, 'You are sprouting muscles I have never felt before!'

I had contacted a well-regarded florist in Sydney's eastern suburbs to obtain a quote for the flowers, but it came in at $8000. Bryce agreed this was absurd and offered to take charge. At dawn on our wedding day, he drove to a flower market and came home laden with armfuls of roses, gerberas (like the ones his grandfather had grown in Barberton) and Australian native species. Like his mother, Paddy, he loved arranging flowers in vases, and they looked magnificent on the day. One guest couldn't believe that Bryce had arranged them himself, and Bryce said with a trademark twinkle in his eye, 'There's a lot of things you don't know about me, and this happens to be one of them!'

As I prepared to leave our apartment, the press ran down the street with their cameras flashing but I managed to make a quick getaway in my old friend John Atkin's Mercedes. He had earlier managed to whisk Bryce away without being detected, but his plans came unstuck when it came to me. John had thought that getting me to the church on time would be straightforward, but it wasn't to be.

After our arrival the RMYC staff did an excellent job of keeping the press at bay. Bryce said to the assembled mob, 'Boys and girls, I'm sorry, but this is our wedding day, to be shared with our families and friends and not with the rest of the world.' Even so, a story that included a picture of me climbing into John's car ran in the newspapers that weekend.

Nima walked me into the ceremony, smiling broadly while shooting me shy smiles of wholehearted support. Bruce was in the bridal party too, and Lili Price, Nima's half-sister, was my beautiful flower girl. (Lili is now studying law in London, and I couldn't be prouder of her.) The two resplendent bridesmaids were my two closest girlfriends, Liz Courtney and Christine McCabe, and Karen Thomas was matron of honour. Bryce's best man was his great friend Alex Hamill, and little grandson Marcus officiated as the ring bearer – his beautiful smile caused everyone's hearts to melt. Janet Morice was our gracious wedding celebrant.

Bryce and I were bursting with happiness throughout the proceedings. Our families could not have been more loving, and having my siblings, Margaret and Bruce, there, as well as Bryce's two sons and their families, was especially wonderful. It was a magical wedding shared with our sixty guests, and we felt honoured that some had travelled long distances to be with us. My friend Graham Taylor flew in from Ulaanbaatar in Mongolia and arrived wearing a traditional Mongolian *deel*, to everyone's delight (especially mine!), while Alex van Heeren travelled from Cape Town, as did Bryce's warm-hearted relative Shanine Mony. Robert Swan flew in from London and was joined by his son – and my godson – Barney, who now lives in Queensland's Daintree rainforest, where he heads up an environmental project called ClimateForce.

It was a divinely happy occasion, mostly because everyone dearest to us was there to help us celebrate. Our guests feasted on gourmet canapés washed down with French champagne, and a paella stand was popular. The Messina ice-cream parlour had the longest line, led by the delightful Miss Lili Price.

My wedding gift to Bryce was to engage a soprano, Evelyn Duprai, who had been born in Uganda, to sing his favourite song, 'Summertime' accompanied by Joseph Calderazzo. (He told me much later that he had gone up and asked Evelyn, 'Will you please sing at my funeral?') After her performance, everyone got up to dance the night away. Bryce's feet eventually got the better of him – he had donned a thirty-year-old pair of handmade Italian shoes that were too small – and it was time anyway to farewell our assembled guests. We walked back to our apartment in bare feet. We had both been far too excited to enjoy the gourmet wedding fare, so we sat down and over a plate of hot buttered toast and Vegemite polished off a bottle of our favourite William Fèvre Chablis.

Bryce was over the moon that I was now his wife and the woman he could finally introduce as Mrs Christine Courtenay. I felt as though I was in a dream, and my only wish was that we had married earlier as Bryce had wanted. His cancer diagnosis was always at the back of my mind, but on our wedding day our hearts soared and we felt as though stars of happiness had fluttered from the heavens.

If you are imagining that we embarked on a romantic honeymoon, you are mistaken. Our wedding date coincided with the Rugby World Cup matches being played in New Zealand, and Bryce headed off to Auckland on 23 October, two days after our wedding, with his friend Greg Woon; they met up with friends who loved Rugby as much as they did. Their visit was hosted by Andy Hayden, a legendary former New Zealand Rugby player and All Blacks captain, and his wife, Trecha. Alex van Heeren, who had introduced Bryce to Andy and Trecha, was also there, having travelled on to New Zealand after attending our wedding. They watched a thrilling final in which the All Blacks beat France 8 points to 7.

I was delighted that Bryce was well enough to go, as attending these Rugby World Cup matches was the fulfilment of a lifelong dream for him. I might add that he had flown 'across the ditch' to watch his beloved Wallabies in the semi-finals against the All Blacks on 16 October, just five days before our wedding! The Wallabies, by the way, were beaten by the All Blacks 20 points to 6.

We weren't the only ones to travel that year. Bryce felt very proud when his eldest son, Brett, took his son Jake on their first visit to South Africa. They went there to meet Bryce's surviving family members and to go on safari, and even paid a visit to Soweto in Johannesburg. It gave them a chance to learn more about Bryce's early life, which Brett told me his father had rarely spoken about with them. Brett described it in an email to his father as 'a trip of a lifetime that I will never forget'. Bryce buried so much about what happened to him growing up in Africa, except when he chose to weave aspects of it into his books. Perhaps that felt like the only safe place to share what had really happened. He had dreamed of taking his grandchildren to Africa and told me it broke his heart to know he probably wasn't now well enough to do so.

When people ask me about Bryce's life, I suggest they consider reading his novels *The Power of One*, *Tandia*, *Whitethorn*, *Fortune Cookie*, *The Night Country*, *Four Fires* and *Jack of Diamonds*, among others. Not that they are intentionally autobiographical, but at times his main characters appear to me as being Bryce Courtenay camouflaged as Peekay, Billy O'Shannessy, Tommy Maloney, Tom Fitzsaxby, Nick Duncan, Simon Koo and Jack Spayd. As I said on *Family Confidential*, 'You are the fly on the wall listening to those intimate conversations' – the conversations of a complex man who was a great and rare spirit who never forgot where he came from, and who possessed an empathy for others that knew no bounds.

Bryce returned from New Zealand with an idea racing through his mind. We had been given two particularly extraordinary wedding gifts: a stay on Alex van Heeren's Dolphin Island in Fiji, a luxury private retreat nestled on 5.6 hectares and catering exclusively for just eight guests, and an invitation from Robert Swan to join him on a voyage to Antarctica he hosts each year on behalf of his 2041 Foundation. Naturally I thought we would be partaking of one of these very special gifts, but it turned out that this wasn't what Bryce had in mind.

I should have twigged that something was up when he began playing 'The Chorus of the Hebrew Slaves' from Verdi's opera *Nabucco* with the volume turned up high. One evening as we were enjoying a glass of wine in the garden surrounded by our cats vying for attention, he took me by surprise.

'Darling, I don't know how much time I've got left,' he said. 'We must therefore make plans to go on our honeymoon as soon as possible.' I answered quietly, 'Do you think we should travel to Dolphin Island, or go on Robert's voyage to Antarctica?' Bryce shook his head and said, 'Neither of these, darling. I have decided we will be spending our honeymoon on a journey to the Promised Land.'

17

THE PROMISED LAND

'And then one day I found you, Mrs Moses, who will lead us through the wilderness to the promised land.' – *The Family Frying Pan*

BRYCE HAD ALWAYS DREAMT of going to Israel. This is perhaps surprising, as he wasn't in the least bit religious. However, he saw Israel as being at the crossroads of civilisation and the home of more stories than any other place on earth. It held a special allure for Bryce the storyteller, and the prospect of going there on our first trip as a married couple was enchanting in every way.

The imagined stories of their ancestors his mother had told him as a child, and as described to Diana Ritch in her 1991 interview, echoed in his mind: 'I discovered that the first crusader king who went out and conquered Jerusalem was a Courtenay.' In September 2012 Bryce told me how much it had meant to him to travel to Israel: 'It was hugely important for me to go there. I wanted to touch the same stones, I wanted to walk the cobbles, sense the same air, and imagine what it was like for those conquering crusaders who made this region the centre of Christianity for a thousand years or more.'

Bryce's recent grim health diagnosis gave further impetus to his desire. He wanted to travel to Israel before it was too late. His son Adam had already been, and his experiences, I believe, further inspired Bryce to go. While Bryce and Benita were not observant, their backgrounds were steeped in religion. Benita's family was Jewish and some of her ancestors had fled Russian pogroms in the nineteenth century in search of safety. Parts of their remarkable stories are retold by her in *April Fool's Day*: 'Bryce loved my nana's fried fish, which she prepared every Friday in the large ancient frying pan which she claimed was the same one her mother had carted on foot across Russia, when she was fleeing from Jewish persecution.'

Benita's great-grandmother was the inspiration for Bryce's book *The Family Frying Pan*, which he confirms in the dedication: 'To my two sons Brett and Adam who would not be who they are if their great-great-grandmother had not walked across Russia carrying a large cast-iron frying pan.' In the book, Bryce relates the chilling history of the Russian pogroms:

> In Tsarist Russia, the Jews were not, as a general rule, among the wealthy classes, but mostly existed in small rural villages which were known as *shtetls*. Most of them worked the land and were in every way a peasant class, though the Russian peasants, themselves devout Russian Orthodox Christians, were deeply anti-Semitic and, even after hundreds of years of living side by side, resented their presence . . . It became a common practice for Cossacks, the Tsar's elite mounted troops, to raid a Jewish village for no other reason but an afternoon's sport . . . A raid on a *shtetl* was therefore thought of as an afternoon's entertainment and as a cleansing of vermin from the Motherland.

Mrs Moses, the protagonist in *The Family Frying Pan*, is the only survivor of a Cossack raid on her village. She escapes carrying her cast-iron frying pan, and in her travels across Russia to freedom feeds other refugees from her pan. In return, each must tell her a story around the campfire at night, and these unfold in the book. The *Sydney Morning Herald* said of

The Family Frying Pan, 'It comes from inside Courtenay's soul, which is the soul of a storyteller and a pilgrim . . . get out the tissues.' Indeed.

By December 2011 Bryce was still struggling to finish *Jack of Diamonds*. I remember saying to him, 'Perhaps we should go to Israel in September next year, once you have handed in your book and when the weather there will be cooler.' However, we both knew his health was a ticking time bomb. He answered, 'I think we should go now, darling, while I am still feeling well enough.' That evening I went online and found a boutique travel company called Touring Israel. Within a few days our reservations were confirmed and we were scheduled to depart Canberra on 4 January 2012 to travel to Tel Aviv via Paris. Until the moment we departed Bryce was in his office writing his book, ever conscious of his promise to Penguin to submit the manuscript as soon as possible.

During childhood Margaret, Bruce and I were dispatched to Sunday school at the Beechworth Anglican Church in Victoria's north-east by our darling mother, Kath, who was a devout Anglican. Miss Betty Collins, the unfailingly kind sister of the town's only doctor, was our teacher and I remember being transfixed by the silver hairs that sprouted from her chin like palm fronds. The baby Jesus, Mary and Joseph and the Three Wise Men in her stories always seemed like mythical figures in far-off lands, but they made a lifelong impression. The prospect of now visiting these hallowed lands was intoxicating, and I could barely contain my excitement.

A few of our acquaintances could not understand why Bryce and I wanted to go to Israel. One was decidedly frosty because of his views concerning the fraught situation of the Palestinians. Bryce and I felt empathy for the Palestinians' enduring plight, but this did not diminish our desire to travel there. Bryce also reminded this friend that Israel was still the only democracy in the Middle East.

While Bryce felt that religion had played an overbearing role in his childhood, as he described in an interview at home with Michael Dillon, he ultimately felt a debt of gratitude to his mother for forcing him to memorise great swathes of the Bible:

I'd be given two days to learn an entire chapter of one of the books
of the Bible by heart. . . At the time it was well the most severe
punishment, but it taught me the language of English. . . I learnt
grammar and how to say things, and how to give a lyrical feel to
words and how to give rhythm to words and structure and so on
and so forth.

He also loved the time-honoured Christian hymns, as did my father
Allan Gee. I wondered if going to Israel would feel like a pilgrimage for
him to pay homage to those lessons and hymns that had contributed so
much to his writing skills.

When we arrived in Paris, Bryce was left in no doubt about my passion
for the City of Light. He marvelled at my efforts to speak French when
ordering his favourite meal of *steak frites* and the accompanying bottle of
Chablis. We went to the top of the Eiffel Tower to enjoy the breathtaking
view and then walked to Place des Vosges, the oldest planned square in
Paris. The Grand Synagogue in the Rue de la Victoire, consecrated in
1874, was not far from our beautiful apartment. Bryce especially loved
wandering through the Luxembourg Garden, which he told me had been
inspired by the Boboli Gardens in Florence, and seeing Monet's waterlily
murals at the Musée de l'Orangerie in the Tuileries Garden.

It is always chilling to recall that France was once occupied by Nazi
troops. The story has it that Dietrich von Choltitz, the last commander
of Nazi-occupied Paris, did not carry out Hitler's orders to level the city.
It was Choltitz who also later signed the formal surrender, on 26 August,
and later that day General Charles de Gaulle led his liberation forces
down the Champs-Élysées. Bullet-riddled walls are still visible in Paris
as a sobering reminder of the terrible events that took place during the
Second World War.

We were delighted to be able to catch up with Irwin and Erica Light,
who had arranged to meet us in Paris during their year-long stay in
France. They treated us to lunch at the historic Bofinger brasserie as a
belated wedding present. Bofinger is famous for its Alsatian specialities

and Belle Époque decor, which includes a spectacular domed ceiling of stained glass above the central dining room.

We couldn't leave Paris without dropping by the iconic Parisian bookstore Shakespeare and Company on the Left Bank. It was opened in 1951 by an American ex-serviceman, George Whitman, and is the oldest English bookstore in the city. The original bookstore, which was also a lending library, was located at 12 rue de l'Odéon and founded by Sylvia Beach in 1919, and it became the centre of literary life in Paris. Bryce was amazed to see a few copies of his books on the shelves, and we were enchanted to see the store had a resident cat. It's also one of the best places to find an Australian-strength coffee in Paris!

We touched down at Ben Gurion Airport in Tel Aviv on 13 January 2012. The security procedures were robust and it took hours to clear customs, even though we had paid for an 'express service'. The experience was a reminder of Israel's preoccupation with security, which frankly we welcomed – and we didn't feel uneasy during our stay. In fact, quite the opposite, as we knew security measures there are the best in the world. Mind you, Bryce did comment that the airport staff were suffering from 'a serious case of a humour bypass'. I nodded in agreement as we hurriedly left the terminal.

We were handsomely compensated when we first laid eyes on Jerusalem and checked into the legendary King David Hotel, which overlooks the Old City and Mount Zion. Bryce said he instantly recalled his mother reading to him from Revelation, the last book of the New Testament: 'Then I saw a new heaven and a new earth, for the first heaven and the first earth had passed away, and there was no longer any sea. I saw the Holy City, the new Jerusalem, coming down out of heaven from God . . .'

Our hotel was named after David, a biblical king, and constructed entirely of locally quarried pink limestone. The ornate mouldings and decor are exquisite and it's worth a visit even if you aren't staying there. It's easy to see why world dignitaries have beaten a path to its door since it opened in 1931. I had been learning more about the hotel in the book *O Jerusalem!* by Larry Collins and Dominique Lapierre, which I started reading on the plane. Tragically, in 1946 it was targeted by the Zionist paramilitary group Irgun and ninety-one people were killed. We arrived there on a Friday and were seated for dinner among locals who had gathered for Shabbat, the Jewish day of rest. During Shabbat, Jewish families remember the story of creation from the Torah, when God created the world in six days and rested on the seventh. Bryce had written about Shabbat in *Four Fires*, and the Friday-night dinner prepared by Mr Morrie Suckfizzle and Mrs Sophie Suckfizzle: 'Tonight we eat chicken soup and *geroicherte flaysh mit kroit* (I only learned how to say that later, but it's stew with cabbage) and *honig lekach* (which turns out to be honey cake).'

Bryce and I didn't always stay in fancy hotels – far from it, as he thought all that mattered was sleeping between clean sheets and having access to a flushing toilet! He had worked incredibly hard all his life, as I had since the age of seventeen, and we didn't believe in wasting money. We also understood that in a moment your life can change, and that all that matters is family, friends and your health. However, as Bryce was now so unwell I felt he deserved to be spoilt, and this beautiful hotel exceeded our expectations.

Bryce's favourite meal was breakfast, and the hotel buffet laden with local specialities was amazing. The flatbreads, creamy dips, marinated olives, raw honeycomb, and pastries crammed with almonds, pistachios and walnuts were divine, so we made the most of the feast on our first morning before visiting the Mount Scopus observation decks for a breathtaking view of the city. This was an emotional experience, and brought to mind what Bryce wrote in *April Fool's Day*:

The next morning as the sun rose gloriously over the desert, Moses was standing on the summit of Mount Sinai. Far below him he could see the Israelite tents, tiny white dots on the desert floor arranged in neat rows; from each rose a wisp of smoke into the sharp, clean air as ten thousand families prepared breakfast.

From there we visited the Garden of Gethsemane at the foot of the Mount of Olives, where it is believed Jesus was arrested before his crucifixion. Bryce was especially enchanted by the ancient olive trees, some of which date back to 1092 CE. What was absent were the cedar trees referred to in the Bible as the 'Cedar of Lebanon'; they had apparently been decimated by timber felling and, more recently, climate change. A local guide was astonished to learn that our street in Reid in Canberra was lined with blue Atlas cedars (*Cedrus atlantica* 'Glauca') that were over ninety years old. Bryce looked startled when I purchased a small wooden cross from a monk who resembled Friar Tuck and who administered a blessing, but his eyes shone with joy when we later spied stands of river red gums (*Eucalyptus camaldulensis*), which are among the most iconic of Australia's eucalypts.

We were driven to the Western Wall (also known as the Wailing Wall), which has been a place of pilgrimage for thousands of years. Constructed from ancient limestone rising to 57 metres, it dates from about the second century BCE, though its upper sections were added later. We stood among hundreds of worshippers dressed in traditional attire who were chanting prayers. I placed a prayer I had written into a crevice on the wall before leaving, and it shouldn't be hard to guess what I was praying for. I told Bryce I had done this and he answered, 'So long as you haven't prayed to get those Burmese kittens!'

We went to see the magnificent Dome of the Rock, an Islamic shrine located on the Temple Mount in the Old City. Being non-Muslims, we weren't permitted to enter; Bryce appreciated this but also felt disappointed as he was hoping to see the exquisite tiled mosaics of its interior. Instead, all he was granted was a ticking-off from a resident imam who became offended when Bryce put his arm around me. He shouted at us, 'No touching, no touching!' Bryce didn't warm to this overt rebuke, and we held hands as we dashed down the steps to return to our guide.

Travelling to Bethlehem in the West Bank to visit the Church of the Nativity and Manger Square felt like a pilgrimage. However, as soon as we crossed the border into Palestine, we began to feel a little tense. A massive concrete wall festooned with barbed wire and smeared with graffiti divides the two countries. It is a confronting sight and testament to the divisions that never seem to end. We needn't have worried, though, as we were warmly welcomed by the local guides, who receive thousands of tourists each year from all over the world.

I knelt beside the manger where Jesus is said to have been born. You can run your hands across this very spot, and believe me, it is a well-polished site. It's a place of pilgrimage almost without equal for Christians, and I lingered, feeling overcome with emotion. Bryce saw what I was doing and looked slightly bewildered. He had never expressed any religious convictions whatsoever, and I think he presumed that given my extensive Himalayan travels I would be more drawn to Buddhism than Christianity. I wanted to explain to him that I was in fact drawn to aspects of both but by then he had sauntered off.

My expressions of faith that day triggered memories for him of being hounded by religious dogma throughout his childhood, which he said was usually associated with punishment. What we agreed on was that we both gained spiritual succour from being immersed in nature. This was especially true when Bryce was gardening. He always said that watching things grow 'felt like a miracle'.

Returning to our vehicle, Bryce sighed deeply and said, 'I think I've had enough of God for one day.' In a conciliatory gesture, he put his arm around me before wandering into a nearby shop. When he returned, he handed me a box containing a beautiful Jerusalem cross (a Christian cross surrounded by four smaller Greek crosses) encrusted with semi-precious stones, and my ruffled feathers were instantly settled. I wore this beautiful necklace during our entire stay and began to think what gift I could buy Bryce in return.

My chance came after we had lunch at the American Colony Hotel on the southern side of Jerusalem. We knew that this 100-year-old property noted for its Ottoman architecture had been the backdrop for many historical events, and were keen to see it. It is also a muezzin's call to prayer away from several of Jerusalem's most beautiful mosques. Like the King David Hotel, it has welcomed a stellar line-up of guests, including Bob Dylan, Lawrence of Arabia and Mikhail Gorbachev. I said to Bryce, 'And now they can add Bryce Courtenay!' Bryce said wistfully, 'My preference would still be to sleep beside you in a tent in the Negev beneath starlit skies.'

The Negev is a desert region in southern Israel whose name means 'dry land' in Hebrew. During the Exodus journey to the Promised Land, Moses sent twelve scouts into the Negev, and Bryce naturally knew that the Negev desert is mentioned in the Bible verses Genesis 12:4–9, 20:1 and 24:62. Its main city is Be'er Sheva (Beersheba), and we had both read stories of the Battle of Be'er Sheva when, on 31 October 1917, the 4th and 12th regiments of the 4th Australian Light Horse Brigade galloped on Be'er Sheva. In less than an hour they overran the Turkish trenches, and by the evening they had captured the city. It was the regiment's first major battle fighting as mounted infantry and marked a decisive turning point in both the battle for Gaza (which fell a week later) and in the Allied campaign in the First World War. As Bryce stated, 'This battle will always provide a significant historical connection between Israel and Australia.' I agreed, and asked if he was perhaps working up another idea for a book. He smiled, saying, 'Kid, you could be on to something here. We should talk to Bob about it as soon as we are home.'

After lunch at the Colony Hotel, we visited Balian Armenian Ceramics on Nablus Road in East Jerusalem. The studio was crammed with a spectacular range of handpainted decorative tiles and murals, created by the world-renowned tile artists and master potters of the Balian family from the former Armenian Soviet Socialist Republic, who arrived in Jerusalem (then in Palestine) in 1919. Bryce had to physically haul me out of there, but not before I purchased a decorative vase featuring dancing gazelles (derived from the Arabic *gazal*), a traditional theme in Persian love poetry, which I thought was the perfect honeymoon gift. He was thrilled with my gift, although we weren't sure how we would get it home intact. (We did!)

Touring Israel of course knew that Bryce was a famous writer. Jonathan Rose, their marketing manager, who was originally from Australia, had enjoyed reading *The Power of One* and was pleased to know it had been translated into Hebrew. Before we departed Canberra he informed us that the Australian embassy was planning a dinner in Bryce's honour that would give him the opportunity to meet some of Israel's finest authors, including Etgar Keret, Gadi Taub and Nava Semel. I immediately ordered copies of their books and Bryce set about reading every single one of them. I only managed a couple as I was still reading Simon Sebag Montefiore's *Jerusalem: The Biography*.

As a teenager the only books I had read about Israel (aside from the Bible) were *Exodus* by Leon Uris, published in 1958, and *The Source* by James A. Michener, published in 1965. I had also read *My Life*, the extraordinary autobiography of Golda Meir, the first (and only) woman prime minister of Israel. She famously said, 'We can't do a zigzag,' as she drove the 1948 Israeli Declaration of Independence through with a bare majority of 6 to 4 in the provisional government. The Ukrainian-born Golda had herself escaped a Russian pogrom in 1906 before being raised by her family in Milwaukee in the United States. Years later, in Israel, she was remembered fondly for hosting government ministers in 'Golda's kitchen', where she prepared chicken soup with *kneidlach* (matzo balls) along with gefilte fish and Turkish coffee. Bryce felt hugely honoured to attend this dinner in Tel Aviv hosted by the Australian ambassador, Andrea Faulkner. Predictably we enjoyed animated conversations about writing, art and politics that carried on late into the night.

On another evening we attended a dinner with distinguished Israeli-Arab journalist and documentary filmmaker Khaled Abu Toameh, who filed stories for the *Jerusalem Post* and NBC News. This was a fascinating experience. As a young and naive sixteen-year-old Khaled had somehow ended up working for a short time in the office of Yasser Arafat, the former chairman of the Palestine Liberation Organization (PLO), and some of his stories about his encounters with Mr Arafat were hair-raising. It was a memorable evening and Khaled's insights gave us a lot to think about.

It was a revelation to witness people of so many faiths and nationalities residing in Israel. Christians, Jews, Arabs and even small communities of Druze, who make up about 2 per cent of the population. Within the Jewish faith there are many sects, including the ultra-orthodox communities who largely reside in East Jerusalem. I said to Bryce, 'I am certain you could uncover some amazing stories here for another book.' He sighed wearily and said, 'Darling, so many brilliant books have already been written that I would need to really dig deep.' He added, 'However, I am sure I could find a good story and we would then need to spend several weeks here completing the research. If it wasn't for the cancer, I would jump at the chance.' I was equally certain that, sadly, this book would never come to fruition.

I reminded Bryce that he had already recorded some incredible stories concerning Jewish history, such as in *Four Fires*, where he wrote about the European families who arrived in Melbourne as refugees and remade their lives working in the rag trade in Flinders Lane: 'The Jewish workers and the bosses have usually come from a Europe destroyed by the war where most have suffered personal tragedy and some have lost their entire families.' I shall never forget going to Melbourne to carry out research for the book and meeting with some of these fashion industry leaders and their descendants to hear their stories of survival and hope amid unimaginable loss. I was deeply moved by their courage, humour and determination to create new lives in our beautiful country at the bottom of the world.

Bryce's book *Tommo & Hawk* also records a remarkable story of survival: 'My brother Tommo and I were born to a Jewish mother, who died, then we were given the name Solomon by Mr Ikey Solomon, who was our father of sorts.' And in *Matthew Flinders' Cat* Bryce tells the story of one of his characters, Nathan Goldstein, who 'was probably the best-known medical name in Sydney':

> He was the son of a Jewish heart surgeon who'd survived the Warsaw Ghetto and the Holocaust and who, after the war, had migrated to Australia . . . His son, Nathan, had attended Waterloo Public School, where he earned the respect of his peers by belting the crap out of anyone who called him 'Dirty Jew' or 'Reffo!'

Local folkore says that during the British Mandate for Palestine, cats were brought over from England to deal with a rat problem; now, there are over two million strays. Cat-loving locals tend to them, and I raced into a supermarket to buy some cat biscuits. I was always feeding cats as they sat in clusters on motorcycle seats or hovered under stalls at the markets. One day Bryce said in exasperation, 'I don't know why you bothered coming to Israel – all you have done is feed hundreds of cats!' Later on, he bought me four small wooden cats at a stall in the Old City, which he said, smiling, were undoubtedly 'holy cats', to present to our four felines at home.

Young Israeli conscripts wearing battle fatigues asked to be photographed standing next to us – not that they knew Bryce was a famous Australian writer. Bryce said seeing those boys in uniform reminded him of his days as a young conscript in the Rhodesia Regiment at Bulawayo. I used to enjoy chatting to Israelis in Chile and Peru who were travelling, having completed their national service. However, sometimes I saw signs outside hostels that said 'Israelis not welcome'. Anti-Semitism is a disturbing undercurrent that persists unabated in communities worldwide, and Australia is not immune from it.

Visiting Yad Vashem, Israel's official memorial to the victims of the Holocaust, was a profound, heartbreaking experience. As we entered, I thought of Bryce's dedication in *Tandia*: '"Together since the world began, the madman and the lover." – Discovered by Allied troops written on a latrine wall at Dachau.' After our visit we felt overcome with sadness and sat down on a bench and wept. It was a privilege to be there to pay our respects to those innocent people who suffered so much.

We then visited the grave of Oskar Schindler, a German industrialist who saved the lives of 1200 mostly Polish Jewish refugees from the death camps by employing them in his factories. Oskar's grave lies in the Roman Catholic cemetery on Mount Zion, and his story was recorded by Australia's internationally acclaimed author Thomas Keneally in his book *Schindler's Ark*, published in 1982. This powerful book was deservedly awarded the Booker Prize, and in 1993 the film *Schindler's List*, directed by Steven Spielberg, was released, starring Liam Neeson, Ralph Fiennes and Ben Kingsley. The film, too, was internationally acclaimed. I recall going to Tom's house with his close friends Iain Finlay and Trish Clark while he was writing this book; I think he may have originally given it the title of *Oskar*.

The next day we were driven to the city of Haifa in north-western Israel, which is the country's major seaport. My father's ship, HMAS *Perth*, had docked there on 25 June 1941. I used to gaze at Dad's black-and-white photographs of Haifa, and I had read about the ship's war experiences in the diaries of Petty Officer George Hatfield, but I never dreamed I would one day have the chance to visit.

There is a huge Baha'i temple in Haifa called the Baha'i World Centre that was inscribed as a UNESCO World Heritage Site in 2008. The Baha'i religion grew out of the Babi faith, or sect, and was founded in Iran in 1844. It is the only religion apart from Judaism that has its world headquarters in Israel. The Baha'i Terraces or the Hanging Gardens of Haifa are located on the slopes of Mount Carmel, and we were enchanted by their splendour although we didn't manage to climb the 1500 steps up the mountain.

Before leaving Haifa we ducked into a little Arab cafe to have lunch with Joe Yudin, the charismatic founder of Touring Israel. We were spellbound by his stories, including from when he was a paratrooper in the Israeli Air Force prior to starting his travel company. We all agreed that the cafe served the best falafels we had ever tasted. We reluctantly said goodbye to Joe and told him we wished we could spend many more days in Haifa exploring its 3000 years of history and its cultural and archaeological sites.

We returned to Jerusalem and the following evening dined at a well-known restaurant featuring modern Israeli food. It was utterly delicious, and we had begun to feel that Israeli cuisine was on par with the food we loved from Italy and France. Bryce said, 'The food in Israel is like eating Yotam Ottolenghi's food on steroids.' He wasn't quite as fond of the locally produced wines from the Golan Heights, which seemed to be the only ones readily available. Before leaving Paris, I had purchased a bottle of Chassagne-Montrachet chardonnay from Burgundy – the king of white wines, as far as I am concerned. It had disappeared down our throats within hours of our arrival as we raised our glasses and said, 'L'chaim', which in Hebrew means 'To life'.

We loved our day spent in the Armenian Quarter of the Old City. This magical place is one of four neighbourhoods within the ancient precinct, the others being the Jewish Quarter, the Muslim Quarter and the Christian Quarter. It was enchanting to wander the ancient alleyways and to bargain with local traders selling carpets, brass hookahs and tiers of spices. There was even frankincense for sale. I couldn't resist purchasing an ostrich egg painted with an intricate Persian design. We feasted on sickly-sweet pastries and drank glasses of fresh pomegranate juice, which later played havoc with Bryce's bowels!

Leaving Jerusalem, we travelled for over 100 kilometres to reach Masada, an ancient fortress in southern Israel's Judean Desert that occupies an isolated rock plateau overlooking the Dead Sea. It was the site of the infamous siege of Masada by Roman troops from 73 to 74 CE at the end of the First Jewish-Roman War, which according to legend ended in a mass suicide. I confess that the memories of my childhood Sunday school lessons were proving elusive, but not so for Bryce, who knew as much about the history of Masada as our well-meaning but at times overbearing guide. At one point Bryce was so frustrated by his incessant banter that he said to him, 'I want to *feel* Israel – I don't want to hear everything about it!'

Not far from Masada was the Dead Sea, a salt lake bordered by Jordan to the east and Israel and the West Bank to the west. Its shores are the lowest land-based elevation on earth, and the water is so salty it is possible for a human to float unaided. I took a fantastic photo of Bryce lying on his back reading *The Power of One*. It was his idea to set up the shot, and it typified his great sense of fun. I told him, 'Everyone will think that you do indeed have superhuman powers!' Bryce laughed uproariously and it was wonderful to see him having such a great time.

We then travelled to Tiberias for an overnight stay at the Scots Hotel on the western shores of the Sea of Galilee, overlooked by the Golan Heights. The hotel was founded in 1834 by a Scottish doctor called David Watt, who welcomed patients from all faiths and nationalities, and its nineteenth-century buildings are made of basalt. I gazed in wonder at the Sea of Galilee, but I could see that recalling his Bible lessons wasn't something Bryce was overly fond of doing. Despite this, he faithfully answered my many questions about any biblical references. What he did enjoy was chatting to the hotel gardeners about the extraordinary plants native to the area.

It wasn't hard to understand why Bryce believed that Israel was always at the crossroads of history. Over dinner that evening he said, 'It's a mirror to the sands of time from every civilisation which at some point has passed through here.' Later that night I had a dreadful nightmare and woke up fearing we were going to be attacked, although I didn't know by what. I was overtired and anxious, having grasped the reality of the grave issues facing Israel, which is pretty much surrounded by nations that are none too keen on its long-term survival.

On the way back to Jerusalem we were stopped at several checkpoints, and bomb disposal units checked underneath our vehicle and carefully perused our passports. This is par for the course when travelling in Israel. As Bryce said, 'They are only doing this, darling, to make sure we are kept safe.' Dusk fell as we waited, and I shall never forget watching a long line of camels crossing the road – a scene straight out of the pages of the Bible.

Throughout our trip to Israel Bryce appeared to be well, but sometimes he looked more tired than I had ever seen him. He napped during our road excursions and didn't have his usual healthy appetite at mealtimes. I wondered if he was feeling any pain in his stomach, but he reassured me, saying only, 'It's nothing to worry about, darling,' and 'I'll just take some Panadol.' He was occasionally a bit tetchy, which was extremely rare, and looking back I am sure this was because he wasn't feeling great. Recently I was browsing through photos of our trip and was shocked to see how pale he looked. It was a miracle we ever got there. Perhaps some divine intervention made our honeymoon trip possible after all.

Earlier on I had been hoping we could extend the trip and travel across the border into Jordan as I had always dreamt of visiting Petra, the famous rose-coloured archaeological site dating back to around 33 BCE. In the end we decided not to go, and Bryce looked very relieved. He said, 'Darling, I have loved being here with you for our honeymoon, but now I just want to go home.'

We departed Israel on 20 January and felt very relaxed when we arrived in Rome – not that we had ever really felt uneasy in Israel, but it was an intense experience at times. You can't help but sense the vulnerability of the nation, and the subjects of security and politics always crop up in conversations. Even so, we found the Israelis' passion for life, humour and abiding faith in the future to be uplifting. As Bryce observed, 'When life is too easy, people become complacent and look half asleep. In Israel everyone lives each day with a zest for life, which is rare and wonderful.' It is one of those places you just know deserves another visit, and I am planning on going back there soon. This time I will cross the border into

Jordan to visit Petra to complete the final stage of the journey Bryce and I undertook in 2012.

In Rome we stayed at the Baglioni Hotel Regina on Via Vittorio Veneto, which is swathed in Italian Art Deco and accents of Murano glass dating back to 1892. It was lovely to dine al fresco, even though we sometimes shivered in the crisp winter air. We ate bowls of pasta washed down with glasses of pinot grigio, and invariably had gelato for dessert (pistachio was Bryce's favourite flavour). Bryce had been to Italy several times before with Benita and said he found himself reflecting on those memorable trips. I could see how sad he was feeling, especially with Benita having passed away just a few years earlier. While we were in Rome, I wore a lovely necklace and earrings created from tiny seed pearls that Benita had given me as a birthday present. Bryce was always so proud of her and very grateful, as I was, that she had been so warm and kind to me.

While in Rome I thought Bryce might want to go to the Vatican to see Michelangelo's Sistine Chapel ceiling, but he had been there previously and wasn't interested. Instead, he headed up to the Spanish Steps to reach the gardens of the Villa Borghese. A garden always took precedence over a museum or a shopping arcade unless Bryce was buying shoes, bags or jewellery for me. He also looked rapturous when he saw the fresh produce being sold in the Campo de' Fiori market. He held up a bunch of tomatoes and said, 'Why can't we grow tomatoes in Australia that smell as good as these do?'

I was hoping we might do something a little crazy and romantic like hiring a Vespa for a ride around the city. Bryce's eyes shone with excitement at the thought, but he reminded me how he had fallen off his pushbike in Canberra a few weeks earlier and teased me that I should instead find a local 'spunk' with slicked-back hair and a leather jacket to take me for a spin à la Audrey Hepburn in the classic film *Roman Holiday*.

It was soon time to leave the Eternal City, and we arrived back home in Canberra feeling jet-lagged but in high spirits. The four cats were, however, not impressed and gave us withering looks as we opened the front door. Timmy was far more forgiving and jumped excitedly all over Bryce before begging to be taken for a walk.

After a few days Bryce came inside from working in the garden and asked me to sit down on the red leather sofa in his study. With an unusually strained look on his face, he said, 'Darling, I think the cancer has come back. I have been getting some bad pains in my stomach and bowel and thought you should know.'

I was shocked to hear this, although in retrospect it wasn't surprising. I put my arms around him and said, 'This is terrible news, darling. Overall you were so well during our honeymoon in Israel.'

Bryce answered in a quiet voice, 'Darling, I think we probably only just made it home.'

My heart sank as I walked to the phone to call Dr Koroush Haghighi. I think Bryce and I both had a feeling of dread that his final chapter was on its way.

18

THE FINAL CHAPTER

'Life is all beginnings and ends. Nothing stays the same,
lad,' my granpa said at last. Then he puffed at his pipe and
seemed to be examining his fingernails which were broken
and dirty from gardening. 'Parting, losing the thing we love
the most, that's the whole business of life, that's what it's
mostly about.' – *The Power of One*

AT 11.30 P.M. ON 22 November 2012, my beloved husband Bryce
Courtenay passed away at our home in Canberra. He was seventy-nine
years old and his long battle with cancer was over. He had fought it with
the same courage he had summoned throughout his life.

In the lead-up to his passing, Bryce noted that our social life
increasingly revolved around attending medical appointments – and this
was true. His cancer diagnosis in 2010 continued to be deeply worrying
throughout the two challenging years that followed, but we remained
hopeful despite Bryce's proclamation in May 2012 that 'There's a time to
live and there's a time to die, there's a time to laugh and there's a time
to cry; there's a time to love and there's a time to hate, but we all have a
use-by date.'

That date felt even closer after 25 June, when Bryce underwent
a Hartmann's operation at Sydney's Royal Prince Alfred Hospital,

performed by Professor Michael Solomon. It was necessary because Bryce had a large bowel obstruction after his cancer metastasised from his stomach to his colon, which had been confirmed following an investigative procedure on 21 May performed by Associate Professor Warwick Selby, a running mate of Bryce's who was also a leading Sydney gastroenterologist. After the operation, Professor Solomon called me to say that Bryce had come through OK but his cancer had reached a very advanced stage. I feared this might have been the case, but even so the news was a terrible shock.

I arrived at the hospital early the next morning and Bryce said, 'Darling, I'm not going to make it.' In a quiet voice I told him I already knew. All we could do was hug each other and quietly sob. He looked me in the eyes and bravely said, 'It's all right, darling. Everything possible has been done to save me. My final round on the grizzly bars is coming up. All we must do now is make the best of whatever time I have left.'

Bryce's sons Adam and Brett were also very shocked. They came to visit with their families and were wonderfully caring and supportive.

Inevitably, the subject of Bryce having chemotherapy arose. We had seen friends go through it and Bryce was not convinced he wanted it. We were offered some salient advice by his extraordinary and caring gastric surgeon, Dr Koroush Haghighi, when we met with him on 16 July. Koroush explained to Bryce that having some chemotherapy might delay the recurrence of further tumours and provide him with relief from the symptoms of his cancer for a longer period. After considering this, Bryce agreed to go ahead and Koroush organised a consultation with Associate Professor Eva Segalov, an oncologist at St Vincent's Hospital. Eva and Bryce immediately clicked, and she further discussed with him how a course of chemotherapy might give him more time, although she wasn't understandably able to determine how much.

On 31 July he commenced the treatment and seemed to tolerate it quite well, although he was warned he might feel sicker in the coming days. I was disappointed to learn that after a few days he planned to escape from the hospital! He said, 'If this is not going to save me, darling, what's the point? After a lot of thought, I have decided to ask the doctors to cease the treatment as I want to go home. I want to spend the time I have left with you, my boys and their families – and I am determined to finish my book.' I sighed deeply but respected that he was really the only person who had the right to decide what he should do.

He was very happy to be back home in Canberra, despite having to take some heavy-duty pain medications that had unpleasant side effects. He didn't complain one bit, only saying, 'I know how dedicated the medicos are, but it's such a relief to be free from being poked and prodded in hospital.' Eva valiantly tried to prevail upon him to recommence the treatment and ever so kindly came down to see us in Canberra. However, Bryce's mind was made up. We shall never know if taking Eva's and Koroush's advice would have impacted his cancer or extended his time.

Medical concerns aside, we needed to attend to some practical matters. Our former home in Burradoo had been on the market for twelve months, and in July we finally secured a buyer. It wasn't a great result for the bank balance, and I told Bryce that the amount we had lost would have covered the cost of being in France for as long as we wished. He rolled his eyes and said, 'I don't think our pets would be too happy about that.'

We knew that no amount of money could save Bryce, and I told him I would willingly sell everything we had if it meant his health could be restored. I asked what he would like to do if he had more time and he answered sheepishly, 'I'd probably write another book. There are at least five other books I would love to write.' He also said he wished we could go on a barge trip down the Burgundy Canal in France. We had discussed the possibility of doing this, but it was now too late.

At home in Canberra we pretty much carried on with life as normal, but it didn't feel the same. It felt very much as though Bryce was being stalked by an enemy who would devour everything precious to us and whom we were powerless to stop. We welcomed a steady stream of visitors – probably too many, but Bryce understood that people wanted to say goodbye. He usually ended up talking more about what was going on in their lives than in his own. One afternoon I heard him pleading with a friend who was hesitant about taking on a new challenge: 'None of this "One day I'm gunna . . ." Dare your genius to walk the wildest unknown way.'

Professor John Rasko AO, a world-renowned clinical haematologist and scientist, was among those who spent time with Bryce. Their close friendship had grown from Bryce's passion to see a world free from the suffering that haemophilia had brought to his family. He was the first patron of John's Cure the Future foundation, a remarkable organisation that funds ground-breaking research into the treatment of haemophilia, muscular dystrophy, cancer and various other genetically acquired and rare diseases.

Another very special visitor at this time was Noel White, who travelled with his wife, Judy, all the way from Seattle, Washington. He and Bryce had worked down the mines together on the Copperbelt in Zambia during the 1950s and had travelled together afterwards in the Belgian Congo and to Zanzibar before Bryce left to study journalism in London – a formative time in Bryce's life. It was wonderful to listen to the two men reminisce about their adventures. After we waved goodbye, Bryce commented how strange it felt to be seeing friends for the last time.

On the writing front, he was still struggling to complete *Jack of Diamonds*, which of course he'd commenced the year before. The forced interruptions in writing created challenges in the continuity of plot and timelines, which brought further headaches for Bryce and his editors Rachel and Nan McNab. Bryce had also received a forthright letter from Bob Sessions, who rarely interfered but was concerned the pace of writing wasn't up to scratch. Bryce accepted that there were issues he needed to address, but this meant he had to undertake the gruelling process of rewriting large sections. And it was a race to the finish line for all concerned. One afternoon he was so fatigued that in exasperation I begged him to forget about finishing the book. I said, 'Darling, you may only have weeks to live, so what is the point? You need to be resting, and spending time with your family!' Bryce acknowledged that this was true but nonetheless insisted on ploughing on. Looking weary beyond words, he got back to work and by the end of August, with help from his editors, the book was finished.

He then wrote an epilogue, knowing that it would be impossible for him to write the sequel he'd planned and that his readers would want to know what happened next in the wild adventures of the enigmatic Jack Spayd. It was a brilliant solution to an unfinished story, and Bob called it 'a masterpiece of vintage Bryce Courtenay writing'. Bryce took the opportunity in the final words of the book to thank his loyal readership: 'It's been a privilege to write for you and to have you accept me as a storyteller in your lives. Now, as my story draws to an end, may I say only, "Thank you. You have been simply wonderful."' With its striking cover designed by Adam Laszczuk, the files were rushed to the printer. As these final files were sent to print, there was a deep sadness among the team at Penguin, knowing that Bryce was dying. For just as Bryce referred to his Penguin family, they too felt that Bryce was very much part of theirs. Many of the team had worked closely with Bryce for fifteen years, and he was a perennial favourite at Penguin sales conferences and held in high esteem by all who had the privilege of collaborating with him.

And then it came to planning the book's publicity. As we sat around a table with Bob, publisher Julie Gibbs, publicist Anyez Lindop and marketer Sally Bateman discussing how to market *Jack of Diamonds*, Bob was rendered speechless. Although Bryce's body was in serious decline, his finely tuned marketing instincts were still very much alive and kicking. He wasn't well enough to go on a publicity tour but he didn't see this as a problem, saying, 'This is a great marketing opportunity, Uncle Bob. With my help Penguin can promote this as Bryce Courtenay's final book – we should sell twice as many as usual!'

Bryce dedicated *Jack of Diamonds* to the brilliant surgeon and gracious human being who, in November 2010, had saved his life: 'For Dr Koroush S. Haghighi, with my gratitude and thanks'. Bryce would have been so proud to know that Koroush was honoured with being appointed as an associate professor in 2021.

Upon the completion of each book, Bryce always tried to be at the printers to see his latest effort coming off the presses. For this final book the ritual was undertaken by Bob, who travelled to McPherson's in Maryborough, north-west of Melbourne. It was a poignant moment when he arrived at our front door and handed Bryce the first copy of *Jack of Diamonds*. Bryce held the book with both hands and was visibly moved. In a trembling voice he thanked Bob before ushering him inside. Afterwards we celebrated with lunch at a nearby cafe and then it was time for Bob to return to Melbourne. It was a bittersweet meeting – Bob and Bryce were publishing brothers and knew they may never see each other again. I later invited Bob to come and see Bryce in the final week of his life, but in a dignified voice he said, 'I want to remember Bryce as he was, and I think he would probably prefer that too.'

In the precious weeks leading up to his death, Bryce continued to write and tend to the garden as often as he could. I was hoping he would turn off his computer to rest, but he chose not to. He began writing some stories simply for the joy of it, and said how nice it was to be writing without the pressure of a deadline – 'apart from my own', he quipped! He wrote a heartbreaking piece called 'The Unfortunate Process of Dying Slowly', a reflection on 'the curiosity of dying over a roughly measurable prognosis' that touched upon his life lived and confronted the experience of his illness and how it felt to come towards the end of his life:

> As I write, spring is just about done and summer about to commence. My spring flowering is returning to seed, the daffs slipping back into their long two-seasonal slumber. This year the tulips will have to remain underground together with the daffodil bulbs. Alas, if I should raise them ready for replanting again in autumn, I'm not sure they will be returned to the soil. Non-gardeners have the misfortune of having stressful matters on their minds.

Bryce described these last sketches as 'a mishmash of ideas about my life'. To be honest, he wasn't writing at his best, but a year later I sent them to Ben Ball, who succeeded Bob as publishing director, and Rachel Scully. By this time Penguin Books had merged globally with Random House, to form Penguin Random House. Rachel combined the new pieces with other shorter ones written throughout Bryce's life, together with quotes from interviews he had done over the years and his thoughts on life, death and writing. We named the collection *The Silver Moon* and it was published on 22 October 2014. While Bryce never imagined these final stories would be published, his readers loved them. Soon after *The Silver Moon* was released, I was at Sydney Airport after arriving on a flight from Canberra. I knew it would be the last time I would walk past airport lightwalls beaming the news that a new Bryce Courtenay book had hit the shelves.

Every afternoon Bryce and I continued to take Timmy for a walk to the Reid Oval so that he could have a sniff and a romp with the other dogs, who regarded him as their elder statesman. On Bryce's final birthday on 14 August we were there again with tiny pots of sunflower seedlings to hand out to our friends, including the lovely Beatrice Guppy. We all sipped champagne from plastic cups and it was a bittersweet experience. On the way home I couldn't hold back my tears. To my astonishment Bryce insisted on returning to the oval in the last week of his life to hand out copies of *Jack of Diamonds*. By this time he was in a wheelchair. *The Silver Moon* captures the emotions of this time:

> For the first time I am experiencing on a daily basis the 'never again' feeling. That is, sensing that some task or experience will never again occur in one's life. It is a distinctly unique physical and mental catharsis, like the sudden automatic application of brakes to avoid an accident.

The City of Canberra warmly embraced Bryce being in its midst. In January 2012 he had been named as Canberra's Australia Day ambassador, and on 14 September we were guests at the official opening of Floriade, the annual flower spectacular created on the shores of Lake Burley Griffin. Megan Doherty from the *Canberra Times* was there to interview Bryce, who said, 'We've only been here a year and a half but it is the loveliest surprise. It is just the nicest, nicest city . . . I can't quite manage Mount Ainslie now but I used to do it two or three times a week.' He also said, 'You can quote me as saying I'm dying, but I'm not sick.'

Bryce had become an enthusiastic supporter of the local Brumbies Rugby team, and on 24 March their coach, Jake White, invited him to present the new season's jerseys to the players. He then gave them a rousing talk before they ran on to the field and won! On 29 May 2019, while celebrating the thirtieth anniversary of *The Power of One*, I was quoted in the *Canberra Times* as saying, 'People said I was a writing widow, but I was really a Rugby widow.'

The media were not always kind to Bryce, even during his illness that year. He was low in resilience at that time anyway, so these episodes left him distraught. Vanessa Stoykov, the CEO of Evolution Media, produced an interview with Bryce and Alex Malley, best-selling author of *The Naked CEO*, for a series called *The Bottom Line*, and commented:

> I have to say I find this both pointless and typical of the tall poppy syndrome that often happens in Australia. After all, Bryce was a fiction writer, not a politician. To throw into public question his integrity feels both wrong and cruel. Australia needs to believe in people like Bryce Courtenay. Their intellect, passion and determination shape our culture, determine a global view toward Australia, and inspire the next generation of leaders to do great things.

In the ABC television program *Family Confidential*, Bryce's first cousins, the twins Robyn Davies and Wendy Bennet, both cheerfully confirmed that embroidering stories was something of a family tradition. With great affection they said that Bryce, as well as their father Bryce, and Bryce's grandfather Robert Greer were renowned for doing this.

They pointed out that their grandfather told lots of stories about his experiences during the Boer War that changed each time he told them. Many families would relate to this. Bryce's sister Rosemary confirmed in an email to me in July 2013 that 'Bryce's story was much more dramatic I guess – understandably as he was the writer.'

Bryce's final media interview was arranged with the legendary television journalist Tracy Grimshaw, the host of the Channel 9 program *A Current Affair*. As soon as she walked into our living room in Canberra, Bryce said, 'Trace, I hope you're going to go easy on me.' Tracy's face shone with warmth and she gave him a big hug. During this exclusive interview Bryce revealed that he was terminally ill. The deeply moving segment was broadcast on 7 September 2012 and followed with an announcement on Bryce's Facebook page: 'It is with great sadness that I am writing to let you know that *Jack of Diamonds*, my new book due out in November this year, shall be my last. I have been diagnosed with terminal gastric cancer.'

During Tracy Grimshaw's interview Bryce addressed the recurring issue about the accuracy of his childhood recollections. He explained, 'I am a storyteller – my job is to tell stories', and confirmed that he had been telling stories from the age of five to fend off bullies in the orphanage and institutions he was placed in:

> Your question is, do I exaggerate – you bet I exaggerate. So I take a fact, and I put a top hat on it, a silk tie and striped trousers and tailcoat and a pair of tap shoes and I do a Fred Astaire with a fact, but I don't ruin the fact . . . I never ruin the fact, I just give it life, I give it ebullience, I give it joy and people say, 'Jesus, Courtenay – you really can bullshit.'

I remember becoming emotional when Tracy asked Bryce if he was ready to go, but I have since drawn comfort from his response: 'Yes, yes I am, in the sense that I have achieved those things that seemed at one stage in my life to be absolutely impossible.' He reflected further on the stuff of life:

We all have tragedy in our lives . . . it is the great substance of our lives – we have joy, and we have tragedy . . . We can't exist without mistakes, and that's the thing that youngsters these days don't appear to be embracing – that you have to make mistakes before you can go forward. You've gotta crash, you've gotta break your nose, you have to do all those things, you have to make mistakes, because that's how you learn. You don't learn from success, you don't learn from getting a degree – you learn from buggering up!

When Tracy asked what he was most proud of, Bryce answered, 'I think there is only one answer to that, and it's having a family.'

Following the interview there was an outpouring of love that demonstrated the huge and positive impact Bryce had made on millions of people's lives. The advice of Count Tolstoy to Miss Showbiz, Tamara Polyansky, in *The Family Frying Pan* comes to mind: 'That's right, my child, never let them get the better of you. Not until your final breath. Never give up!'

Bryce's terminal diagnosis did not preclude us from enjoying some 'romantic final dates', as Bryce called them. In June we went to the Canberra Theatre Centre to see a Barry Humphries show called *Eat, Pray, Laugh!* starring the Moonee Ponds housewife-turned-global-megastar Dame Edna Everage and the inebriated cultural attaché Sir Les Patterson. Bryce said that this hilarious show reminded him of the great fondness he had for his fellow Australians.

The last film we saw together was the French comedy-drama *The Intouchables*, which earned its star, Omar Sy, the César Award for Best Actor in 2012. I booked a premium seat so that Bryce could stretch out, and he held my hand while sipping a glass of wine and eating fried calamari. The food did not agree with his stressed constitution, but we felt like two teenagers in love out for a night on the town.

Bryce's grandchildren, Ben, Jake and Marcus, were still quite young when they were told that their grandfather, whom they called 'Pa', didn't have long to live. I asked Bryce if he would like to record a message for them, and on 3 September our dear friend the world-renowned documentary filmmaker Michael Dillon arrived with his camera and microphone in hand. Bryce's message for his beloved grandchildren was: 'It's so obvious and it's so corny but here it is. Fellas, live your dreams. Don't listen to what anybody says. Live your dreams. Do that thing that makes you wake up in the morning, and say thank you, thank you, thank you for giving me this day.' I am proud to say that Bryce's three grandchildren are indeed doing just that in following their dreams. Jake will graduate as a doctor of medicine in December 2022, while Ben is forging a career in corporate cybersecurity and Marcus is undertaking a tertiary degree that includes a course in creative writing. They adored their Pa, and Jake says, 'It is such a pity he isn't here to see how we are doing, and that we weren't able to get to know him as adults.' I was overjoyed when Jake said about this memoir, 'What a grand undertaking. I'm very excited to read it.'

Bryce loved teaching writing and championing the dreams of writers coming through. He taught for many years, including in Hobart at the University of Tasmania, at writers' festivals in Australia and overseas, and, as previously mentioned, even onboard a ship bound for Antarctica and South Georgia. In the second week of September he said, 'Darling, I want to deliver a final writing course, and I would like it to be filmed. I want to ensure that my lessons teaching people how to write will be passed on to the next generation.'

I loved the idea, but with the clock ticking on his health I knew I needed to get everything organised at lightning speed. What also worried me was that Bryce was desperately tired and the tumours that had spread to his bowel were causing him hell. I was already having to call the palliative care nurses at all hours of the day and night to ensure he was comfortable. But he was determined to go ahead, and we planned a five-day course that he decided to call 'The Last Class'. Within days of its announcement, a few hundred people had applied to enrol. Bryce said he could only cope with ten or twelve students, but due to the demand he accepted twenty. I worried it was too many for him to manage, but there was no turning back.

On the morning of 21 September 2012 he walked into a room at Canberra's National Library and said, 'I want everyone to stand up, place your right hand over your heart and repeat after me, "I am a writer."' He made sure his students repeated this mantra at the start of each day of the course. It was all filmed by Kyle O'Donoghue, a South African–born documentary filmmaker who loved Bryce's books and travelled all the way from his home in Norway to do the job. Kyle is Robert Swan's filmmaker, and it was Rob who insisted that he was the best person to produce the film. The lessons were highly charged, and Bryce urged his students to revisit everything they wrote. He said, 'Words just jump and down with excitement when you use them properly' and 'Stories are essentially emotional creatures' and 'I want you to walk away from this course and say "I now know how to do this, and I am fearless".' He was genuinely thrilled to discover the diversity of his students' stories. One was writing a novel set in Martinique about a black doctor, another was writing their family history, and Stacey Truscott, whom we had met on Anzac Day, was well into her book about Nancy Wake.

A highlight of the course was when Bryce read from his original manuscript for The Power of One, which he had not looked at since 1987. He also discussed his passion for growing sunflowers, which he believed offered a great talking point and were a brilliant way of bringing people together. Together, the class agreed to call themselves 'The Sunflowers'.

On the afternoon of the fourth day Bryce was very red in the face and seemed confused. He said, 'Darling, I can't remember us driving to the library and now I can't hear anything.' These revelations were alarming, and I had sufficient medical knowledge to realise he may have sustained a minor stroke called a transient ischemic attack (TIA). I told him I was calling an ambulance but he wouldn't hear of it. Not to be put off, I asked one of our guest presenters to take over and drove him to Royal Canberra Hospital. The brain scans they organised didn't show any obvious abnormalities; even so, the medical staff were concerned and told Bryce he must go home and rest. I was feeling sick with worry, but the following morning he insisted on returning to teach the course.

After it was completed, Bryce assembled his students on the front steps of the library and delivered a traditional Zulu blessing. Many broke down in tears, and their emotions continued to run high as they formed a guard of honour holding up sunflowers. Bryce and I ran through this floral corridor joyfully before jumping in the car and heading home.

Co-producing *The Last Class* with Kyle was challenging, but we were both happy with how it turned out. The late Chris Richards, who had completed two of Bryce's writing courses, wrote a beautiful endorsement for it: 'Not only was Bryce Courtenay a Master Storyteller, but he was also a gifted teacher. This film is his legacy, and possibly his greatest gift.'

Speaking of writers, several began circling, hoping to gain access to Bryce with a view to writing his biography, but Bryce told me he wasn't interested in cooperating with them – and besides, by then he was feeling chronically tired and was frequently in pain. The only writer he had allowed to interview him was the Sydney-based author and journalist Roger Maynard, who arrived at our home in April and, as referenced in this book, recorded some outstanding interviews with Bryce that can still be viewed on YouTube.

On 28 September Bryce attended a graduation ceremony to receive an honorary doctorate from the University of Canberra. In 2005 he had been awarded the honorary degree of Doctor of Letters (*honoris causa*) from the University of Newcastle. We were thrilled that his eldest son, Brett, and his grandson Ben were able to attend the event in Canberra. The doctorate was awarded at a grand ceremony convened at Parliament House and hosted by the university's vice-chancellor, Professor Stephen Parker. Bryce addressed the staff and students with an almost evangelical zeal and received a standing ovation. However, the newly inducted Dr Bryce Courtenay AM felt so exhausted afterwards that he didn't have the strength to join the boys and me for lunch. Instead, he collapsed into bed and within seconds was dead to the world, as he later teased me!

Following our work on *The Last Class*, Bryce announced that he wanted to choose where he was going to be buried. I contacted Bill Cole, the owner of William Cole Funerals, which is run by Bill, his wife, Christine, and their lovely daughter, Judy. Bill said that he had never dealt with a request quite like Bryce's, but he was unfailingly kind and helpful. Early one morning he fetched us to be taken on a personal tour of Canberra's cemeteries. Seeing row upon row of graves was very confronting, and Bryce asked Bill if we could bid a hasty retreat. Bill completely understood and suggested we head out to Hall Cemetery instead, which lies in pristine bushland on Canberra's outskirts and was established in 1883, making it the oldest public cemetery still in use in the Australian Capital Territory.

Soon after our arrival it was clear that Bryce had found the place where he wanted to be laid to rest. When he surveyed the beautiful setting, the strain on his face was replaced with a look of serenity. He said, 'When Timmy goes, I want him to be buried here with me.' I put my arm around him and said, 'Darling, I hope you are going to extend the same invitation to me?' He grinned and said, 'Come here, kid, and give me a hug.' He then wandered over to meet a local botanist who was there to do some research, and was delighted to learn from her that these burial grounds were home to several rare and endangered plants, including the Tarengo leek orchid (*Prasophyllum petilum*).

Bryce said he wanted to be buried vertically in a recycled cardboard box with a tree planted on top of it. I stifled a rush of tears – the looming reality of him not being around suddenly felt very real. He recorded this request in his last writings:

Now that my use-by date is almost upon me my last remaining ambition . . . is to be buried vertically in a cardboard box and then have a ghost gum planted over me. No tombstone, no name plaque, no given place except a place in the Australian bush of sunshine and cold, wild wind and calm, where fire renews growth, somewhere natural where my flesh and bones might be useful to the eternal renewal of life.

Now, wouldn't that be a way to go – there grows the ghost gum of Bryce Courtenay.

Bryce was adamant he wanted to have his funeral service in a church, even though we had barely set foot in one while we were together. At first Bryce had hoped his service would be conducted at St. Peter's Anglican Church in Watson's Bay, opened in late 1864, but when I called their office I was told this beautiful church could only accommodate sixty to sixty-five mourners, which we knew wouldn't be sufficient for the number of people whom Bryce wished to have invited. I therefore arranged for David Crain, the acting rector at St Mark's Anglican Church in Darling Point, to call us. Bryce thanked him for agreeing to preside at the service and admitted he hadn't been a churchgoer since leaving South Africa other than to attend a wedding or a funeral. David warmly responded, 'Bryce, we are all God's children, and your service will be conducted at St Mark's just as you wish.'

Bryce planned his celebration-of-life service down to the last detail. As the plans became more elaborate, I said, 'Darling, please don't take this the wrong way, but it's going to be incredible and the terrible thing is you won't be alive to see it.' Bryce broke into laughter, and while still chortling I said, 'I especially love your idea of making a recording of Timmy barking.' (Getting that recording done deserves a chapter of its own!)

To my astonishment he remained confident that he could muster the strength for us to go on a second honeymoon to Alex van Heeren's Dolphin Island in Fiji. It was a magical idea, but I wondered how I could manage his health in such a relatively remote location. Bryce came up with the bright solution that we would travel with his long-term Sydney GP and old friend Irwin Light and his gorgeous wife, Erica. This felt like it might work, and with Irwin and Erica's blessing I made reservations for us to arrive at Dolphin for a six-night stay on 1 October. However, it was not to be. In the end Irwin advised us not to go as he felt the risks were too great. Bryce was terribly disappointed, and with a heavy heart picked up the phone to let Alex know. Alex's response was ever-gracious: his only concern was for Bryce's and my wellbeing. After putting down the phone Bryce said in a resolute voice, 'Alex van Heeren is in a class of his own.'

He felt hugely grateful when on Sunday 4 November Dr Koroush Haghighi flew down to see us, taking time away from his family and his responsibilities at the hospital. We sat on the deck outside and Koroush talked us through Bryce's current health situation and his options. Although Bryce's predicament was dire, it gave us a great deal of strength to know that Koroush cared so greatly. We also loved hearing more about his own life and his extraordinary career. Bryce told him it contained all the ingredients for a very good book.

Within days of our meeting with Koroush, Bryce somewhat unexpectedly entered the realm of what he described as 'my endgame'. One afternoon his pain become acute but he still insisted on taking Timmy for a walk. Within fifteen minutes he was back home and could barely stagger onto the deck. I helped him come inside and got him to lie down on the sofa in his office. To my alarm he started to convulse with pain and his eyes began to roll back in his head. I rushed to the phone and shortly afterwards a medical team arrived. I am certain their intervention saved his life, and we both felt enormously grateful to them.

Bryce's pain continued to accelerate. The tireless efforts of his excellent Canberra GP, Dr Stephen (Steve) Jamieson, and the amazing palliative care nurses could not stem the tide of his escalating condition. Even so, he insisted on signing a book for every member of the team and they all said they had never known a patient like him. His palliative case manager suggested we pay a visit to a hospice located on the shores of

Lake Burley Griffin. It was a beautifully appointed facility and expertly managed, but we had only been there for about ten minutes when Bryce said, 'Darling, we must go.' I promised him he would be cared for at home until his final breath. I think most of us would hope for that. As one of Bryce's doctors explained, 'If you are lucky, you can essentially have a good death. But if you are unlucky, you can have a bad death.' I felt relieved when he added, 'Not that there is anything good about being dead.'

Unlike many of us, Bryce wasn't in the least afraid of dying. This was testament to his innate courage as well as his practical approach to whatever came his way. I asked if he felt scared about what was coming and he said without a shred of fear, 'Darling, I know exactly what is going to happen. I'm going to become humus and return to the earth and things will grow from the remains of my body, as it should be. It's all going to be wonderful.'

He felt enormously grateful that he would be leaving the earth with his mind fully intact. He had always said that having dementia would be an unbearable fate and far worse than having cancer. He had watched his beloved first wife, Benita, suffer a degree of memory loss and it was the one thing he was terrified of going through. During his interview with Alex Malley he had stated:

> I watch people get older and lose their intellectual acuity. You lose that sharpness, that cleanness, that brain you worked so hard on and that you were gifted with, and lose the gifts that were given . . . I'm going to die with my mind intact. And to me that is the most exciting way you could possibly die.

Bryce also said in the interview filmed at home by Michael Dillon in early September, 'The idea that I will actually die and be able to hold my darling in my arms and kiss her and say goodbye is a wonderful idea.'

On 10 November 2012, Bryce wrote a letter to the editor of the *Canberra Times*:

Some twenty-four years ago I was given, as part of a winter promotion by your newspaper, a sloppy joe inscribed with your logo . . . As it happened, this was the winter in which I wrote *The Power of One* and I wore your sloppy joe with every page completed. With the surprising success of my first novel, I continued to wear it every winter for the next twenty-one novels, coming to believe that without it I couldn't possibly write a bestseller . . . It occurred to me that you might like to have the sloppy joe?

The sloppy joe was duly returned, along with a signed hardcover edition of *Jack of Diamonds*, which was released on 12 November, just ten days before Bryce passed away.

Bryce's life ended in a challenging way, like his birth and the first few months of his life. Towards the middle of November he reluctantly accepted that it was necessary for him to have emergency surgery. By this stage he was not well enough to be transferred to Sydney to be treated by Koroush and his usual medical team. We were fortunate that Canberra had excellent medical services and felt grateful that we weren't living out in the sticks. We were due to arrive at Calvary Hospital in the suburb of Bruce in the early afternoon, but Bryce kept delaying our departure, saying, 'I have so many jobs I still want to finish in the garden.' Sadly, those jobs were destined to remain unfinished.

The highly regarded Canberra surgeon discussed the risks of this palliative surgery, especially given Bryce's precarious condition from his cancer and his history of heart disease. Bryce bravely nodded that he accepted the risks, and gave me a cheery wave before he was wheeled into the operating theatre. Within seconds I began to feel terribly anxious, and in the late afternoon while I was taking Timmy for a quick walk I received a call from the hospital asking me to return at once. I felt frantic as the caller said she was sorry but she could not tell me over the phone what was going on. Naturally I assumed the worst, and my fears were quickly realised: Bryce had suffered a serious heart attack at some stage of the procedure. I was devastated to learn this, but I later understood it wasn't overly surprising given his cardiac history and advanced medical issues from cancer. The specialist doctors at Calvary explained that Bryce's heart had been severely damaged and they weren't confident he would pull through. I thanked them for their valiant efforts before blurting out in a tearful voice, 'You don't know Bryce Courtenay. He will somehow fight his way out of this, just as he's done his entire life.'

Adam arrived from Sydney, and together we were caught up in a desperate unfolding drama where every minute felt like an hour. The hospital's medical team agreed to my request to let Timmy come into the ward, naturally via the tradespersons' lift. He barked excitedly when he spied his 'father' lying in bed, and to everyone's relief Bryce opened his eyes and moved his arm to pat his beloved dog. Later, Bryce even managed to walk slowly through the ward leaning on a frame. All the staff and the other patients cheered, their eyes moistened with tears.

Bryce's condition, however, was approaching a terminal stage. I promised I would bring him home, even if it meant carrying him to the car myself. Having said that, it was a daunting task to get the house set up sufficiently for him to be adequately cared for. It all needed to be arranged within hours, and looking back I honestly don't know how I managed it. I would do it again in a heartbeat, and I knew Bryce would have done the same for me – not that he had a clue about medicines, and even less first-aid training than I had. I ordered in the necessary equipment, including a hospital bed, and by nightfall the medical support systems were in place, including a live-in nurse and regular visits by Dr Steve Jamieson and the team of palliative care nurses. Bryce's Sydney and Canberra team of doctors were also in constant touch, and their support and reassurances were galvanising. It was an overwhelming undertaking, but the only thing that mattered to us all was that Bryce was at home surrounded by his loved ones, including our pets, far removed from the clinical environment of a hospital.

One afternoon Bryce was enjoying being in the front garden with Alex Hamill and Tony Crosby, who had driven down from Sydney, and I said, 'I imagine us being together in Claude Monet's garden at Giverny [a place we had planned on visiting]. Instead, here we are in our beautiful Reid garden, although it feels like a scene out of *Picnic at Hanging Rock*.' In a flash Bryce responded, 'No, darling, it's more like the Picnic at Clanging Clock – tick, tick, tick, tick.' That was Bryce: even in the direst of circumstances he brought a smile to our faces.

During those final days Adam, myself and the rest of our team provided twenty-four-hour care, and Bryce's son Brett was also in constant touch with us. Bryce loved watching our wedding video while sucking on cotton swabs dipped in French chablis, and he ate only Peters Frosty Fruits icy poles. He listened to classical music and jazz, including his favourite song, 'Summertime', sung by Ella Fitzgerald. I occasionally heard him murmuring songs he must have learnt from his African friends during childhood. The five pets never left his side, especially Cardamon and his ever-loyal dog, Timmy. Bryce snored like a warthog and the hired hospital bed would be dotted with four snoring cats and Timmy would be adding to the chorus close by. I remarked to our amazing live-in nurse, Effie, 'As you can hear the orchestra is still in full swing.'

One morning Bryce asked me in an urgent tone to fetch a notebook and proceeded to talk in an animated voice about many aspects of his life, especially his childhood while I scribbled down as much as I could. It felt as though he wanted to get a few things off his chest, and one of the nurses told me this often happens with people in the final hours of their lives. A couple of things he divulged made me raise my eyebrows slightly and say, 'Thank you, darling, for telling me, but it's all right – I am not in the least bit upset.'

Not long before Bryce died, he pointed his finger towards the end of his bed. At first Adam and I couldn't work out what he wanted, but I finally twigged that he wanted to be facing south, to the Great South Land. He nodded vigorously and we moved him to the other end of the bed. Having a hospital bed that could be raised and lowered proved to be invaluable in managing his care.

In one of our last conversations, I asked Bryce in a trembling voice what I should do after he was gone. He answered quietly and gently, 'Darling, I want you to embrace the gift of life as I have.' Not long after, he told me he could feel his life force beginning to retreat. I asked him if he was afraid and he shook his head while staring at the wall on the other side of the room, which was bathed in morning light. His heart condition had overtaken his cancer, and the doctors explained that he was going to pass away from what is called congestive heart failure (CHF).

Late at night on 22 November I noticed that his extremities had begun to feel cold, and I called out in an urgent voice to Adam. In the final moments of his life, Bryce opened his beautiful blue eyes and looked straight at us. His eyes then rolled back in his head and we knew he was gone.

The shock and grief of that moment is something I shall never forget. Even when you know the end is coming, when the moment arrives your whole being is catapulted into a state of shock. I remain hugely thankful that Adam was there: his unfailing support and that of Brett and their families, as well as my family, was a great source of comfort. What mattered most to us all was that Bryce felt totally and completely loved, which was all he had ever wished for. I believe that he went in peace just as I prayed he would. Dear, brave Timmy went to pieces and couldn't stop shaking as he too knew his beloved 'father' was now gone.

Because Bryce was a significant public figure, news of his death was in the media the next day and went around the world. Within days I had to brace myself for the challenge of finalising the plans for the funeral. I remain eternally grateful to the team at Penguin, especially Bob Sessions and the amazing Julie Gibbs, Sally Bateman, Anyez Lindop and Rachel Scully, as well as to to Luke Bonanno of LAB & Co., who handled the logistics. I simply couldn't have managed without them.

Simon Balderstone AM, the hugely dedicated chairman of the Australian Himalayan Foundation, called me to extend his deepest condolences. He had got to know Bryce well and greatly valued his counsel and support (both personal and regarding the AHF). He remembered that he had met with Julia Gillard in Canberra when she was prime minister, and that Bryce had been appointed by her government as an ambassador for the National Year of Reading in 2012. Julia had been a good friend of Simon's since his days as a senior adviser to prime ministers Bob Hawke and Paul Keating, and when he worked closely with Midnight Oil's Peter Garrett in his roles as Minister for the Environment, Heritage and the Arts, and Minister for School Education, Early Childhood and Youth. Simon told me he had rung Julia's office to see if she would like to attend Bryce's service. At first she said thank you for the invitation but she was very sorry, she couldn't come as she had some important meetings scheduled that day in Melbourne. However, the following day Simon received a call from her office: 'Julia says to tell you she has postponed those meetings and can come – and she would be honoured to be there.'

I was very moved to hear this and recalled chatting with her on 23 July 2012 when we were at the National Library to attend the Prime Minister's Literary Awards. But I worried that having her at Bryce's service would add another layer of complication – I wasn't sure what was involved in hosting the prime minister as a guest. In the end everything was organised without my having do a thing, and I felt honoured that Julia and her partner, Tim Mathieson, attended. They were seated with Simon and his partner, Jenny Hunter, and their son, Fergus Hunter, who had attended Bryce's final writing course. The *Daily Telegraph* noted Julia's presence at the service as 'the surprise special guest'. It was also uplifting to have our friends the former senator and leader of the Australian Greens, Bob Brown, and his partner, Paul Thomas, in attendance.

Bryce's 'Celebration of Life' memorial service was held at St Mark's Church in Darling Point, Sydney on Wednesday 5 December 2012. It was as colourful and memorable as Bryce's life had been. Darling Shanine Mony arrived all the way from South Africa and provided a brilliant recording of the Children's Choir from Ocean View, Cape Town singing a favourite song of Bryce's, 'Who Killed Cock Robin', in Zulu. 'Summertime' was sung by Evelyn Duprai, the African vocalist who had sung at our wedding, accompanied by Joseph Calderazzo. Dozens of cottage garden roses, just like the ones Bryce had grown with his grandfather in Barberton, adorned the church. The Reverend David Crain officiated with a traditional Anglican service complete with the time-honoured hymns 'Battle Hymn of the Republic' and 'Jerusalem', which Bryce had requested. David held my trembling hands and said a prayer before the proceedings commenced, and I was seated beside my wonderful and caring son Nima who continues to bring me such joy.

Bryce's coffin was draped with silk prayer scarves from the Himalayas called *khatas* that had been blessed by Buddhist monks, and his Wallabies' team scarf was there too, along with a beautiful handmade quilt created by our friend Carole from Bowral. We even had portraits of the four cats and Timmy our dog on display, just as they would surely have insisted. Tim Bauer's stunning photographs of Bryce were shown, and his portrait of Bryce (which graces the cover of this memoir) was selected for the Order of Service, which was designed to resemble one of his book covers. Bryce's printer wouldn't accept a cent from me for printing them. On the back was a picture of the Bryce Courtenay cymbidium orchid 'Sylvia' especially propagated by Royale Orchids, Peats Ridge, not far from our former home in Yarramalong.

Brett and Adam shared moving tributes of their father, and his grandson Ben read from *Four Fires*. Alex Hamill and Simon Balderstone also spoke, as did I. I felt loved and supported by family and friends. Robert Swan delivered a message with his trademark charisma via a pre-recorded video. We also played that recording of Timmy barking, which gave us all a moment of happiness, and screened memorable footage from *The Power of One* movie and from the television series of *Jessica* and *The Potato Factory*, as well as footage from *The Last Class* writing course.

Bob Sessions delivered a magnificent eulogy that later formed the basis of the foreword in *The Silver Moon*:

> Bryce was quite simply Australia's most popular novelist, and a storyteller without peer. All of us who knew him will remember those blue eyes, the husky compelling voice and the way he engaged with everyone he met.
>
> Not to have a new Bryce Courtenay novel to work on will leave a hole in my publishing life. Not to have a new Bryce Courtenay novel to read will leave a hole in the lives of hundreds of thousands of his loyal readers. Not to have Bryce Courtenay in my life will be to miss the presence of a very special friend. Bryce wrote his own epitaph when he said: 'If in the end, someone says: "Here lies Bryce Courtenay, a storyteller", my life will have been worthwhile.' For all his success in advertising and as a writer, Bryce always maintained that his proudest achievement was that of being a father.

In all, around 300 guests filed into the church to pay tribute to Bryce's life, including family, friends, his publishing family from Penguin and others from the writing community, and the founders of several charities he had been involved with, including Sean Willmore and Nicholas Duncan. The church resonated with emotion and quiet reflection. Bryce had been a powerful and treasured presence. It was an overwhelming day and we all struggled to accept that our beloved Bryce was forever gone from our lives.

The pallbearers comprised a group of Bryce's oldest friends, including Dr Anthony Freeman, Dr Irwin Light, Alex Hamill, Tony Crosby, Peter Keeble, Alf Field, Roger Rigby and Owen Denmeade. As people departed, the Sunflowers writing class formed a colourful guard of honour to the sounds of the recessional music, 'The Chorus of the Hebrew Slaves' from Verdi's *Nabucco* and 'Fantasía para un gentilhombre' by Joaquín Rodrigo. The Sunflowers handed out packets of sunflower seeds and there was a display of Bryce's final book, *Jack of Diamonds* and a barrowful of vegetables to celebrate Bryce's passion for growing things.

Finally, Nima and I stood at the back of the hearse and clasped our hands in the traditional Himalayan greeting of *namaste*. It felt surreal to see Bryce's coffin lying in the back of the vehicle, which slowly moved off on its way to Canberra and Bryce's final resting place. I remember saying to myself the Zulu words of farewell that Bryce had taught me: *Hamba kahle mngani wami*, which means 'Go well'.

Michael Dillon and Adrian Reinhardt filmed the service, and I sent a copy to Rosemary and her family in America and to many others who were not able to attend. Koroush was very sorry not to be there, but as ever he was performing lifesaving surgery for his patients. Rosemary sent me an email on 11 December 2012: 'We tremendously appreciate all you've sent on to us about our beloved Bryce. I still struggle to realise that he's not there with you – at the other end of the e-mail. We will ever be thankful for you Christine, and for the happiness you gave Bryce to the very end of his life.'

When I returned to our home in Canberra, the silence was deafening. Late one night I remember calling my twin sister, Margaret. I was overcome with grief, and for once I could barely speak. Picking up the handset in Bryce's office later, I discovered there was a message that he had left me prior to his final operation. I listened to it countless times and felt distraught when after several days it automatically disappeared from the system.

Thousands of cards and letters of condolence arrived, and obituaries were published by media outlets throughout the world, which was incredibly moving, but I realised I was too emotionally exhausted to take it all in. I arranged for my dear friend Stacey to come and mind the pets so that I could go to South Durras on the New South Wales South Coast for a much-needed break.

When I got home I was able to take in the heartfelt messages. I also read a memorable article written by Jason Steger and Steve Dow for the *Sydney Morning Herald* that included tributes from Bryce's fellow writers. Thomas Keneally was quoted as saying, 'Writers such as Courtenay and J.K. Rowling, have allowed thousands of flowers to bloom', their bestsellers financing 'the publication of books that might sell more humbly'. Matthew Reilly stated in an additional article published by the *Sydney Morning Herald*, 'I think we've lost one of Australia's greatest storytellers. He single-handedly paved the way for mass-market authors like me, and I thank him for that.' And Di Morrissey enthused, 'What I loved about Bryce was his passion – for everything!'

It was a great honour to listen to the federal parliamentary debates on 27 November. Several members of the House rose to offer moving tributes to Bryce and his contribution to Australia's cultural life. Simon Crean, the Labor minister for regional Australia regional development and local government, whom we had met, stated:

> He was a mentor, a friend and a true advocate for storytelling, the importance of reading and the importance of literacy . . . He ignited an interest in Australian history in people who had never had one before . . . From the ripping yarns to the heart-wrenching stories, his books adorned the Christmas trees and bookshelves of millions in Australia and the world . . . The annual report of the Australian government's Public Lending Rights Committee shows that, of the 100 highest scoring Australian books since 1974, 15 are by Bryce Courtenay, with four in the top 10.

The National Party's Michael McCormack spoke in part about Bryce's success born of his incredible work ethic:

Bryce Courtenay once wrote: 'intelligence is a harder gift. For this you must work, you must practise it, challenge it, and maybe toward the end of your life you will master it' . . . Bryce Courtenay was a splendid storyteller whose legacy will live on as long as the printed word endures.

Dan Tehan of the Liberal Party spoke of his legacy: 'He was a great storyteller; he was a great author. He has left a legacy with his books, which will mean his life is remembered in time immortal.' And Andrew Leigh of the Australian Labor Party captured what it was about Bryce and his work that won the hearts of Australians:

> Bryce Courtenay's power to tell a compelling story saw him sell more than 20 million books worldwide – nearly a book for every Australian . . . What was it about Bryce Courtenay the man and the writer that so enthralled us? I believe it was his ability to tell stories about the strength and triumph of the human condition. His own life was testimony to that . . . Bryce Courtenay, like all of us, was very much human – a man with his own imperfections – and he showed us through his life and his writing that we should not hide from them; the imperfections and hardships of life are what makes a story worth celebrating.

Bryce was buried at Hall Cemetery in the Australian Capital Territory on Monday 10 December at noon. He was honoured with a customary ceremony performed by the inspiring Ngambri Elder Mingku (aka Shane Mortimer). The Ngambri people, who were called the 'Canberry' or 'Nganbra' tribe by the white settlers, are the First People of Canberra and the origin of Canberra's name. Shane had visited our home several times and Bryce had been astonished to learn from him that Canberra is located on what was once a grassland, devoid of trees, and was never in fact a 'bush' environment as Bryce had always believed. On one occasion Shane told Bryce he wanted to bestow upon him the name

'Wynu murinya', meaning 'Sunny man'. Bryce said this was the single most meaningful and special honour he ever received.

As the ceremony began, light rain started to fall and we watched as Mingku, decorated in white ochre, draped in a possum-skin cloak and clutching clapsticks, stood on one leg. His little dog, Heidi-Ho, and Timmy joined our small gathering of close family and friends. One of these friends, who had also been raised in South Africa, whispered in my ear that the setting reminded him of the Eastern Transvaal, where Bryce had lived during his childhood.

While Bryce had previously mentioned not wanting a headstone, as his final days approached he had a change of heart. His headstone was fashioned from a yellow-ochre rock from the Yarramalong Valley that had been unearthed by our dear friends Greg and Lorraine Woon. The words that were later carved into it were penned by Bryce:

In loving memory of Bryce Courtenay AM
Writer & Storyteller
1933–2012
'This is what happened'
YOU DONE GOOD

As we walked back to the car, I could hear Bryce saying with a twinkle in his eye, 'Given your fear of snakes, darling, I'm not expecting you to visit me over summer.' This reality was recently greatly exacerbated by the COVID-19 pandemic lockdowns, during which I wasn't able to travel from Sydney to the cemetery for nearly eighteen months. A professional gardener who lives nearby and loves Bryce's books kindly did her best to ensure his resting place was well tended.

On 23 May 2014, I flew to Sydney to attend the 14th Australian Book Industry Awards (ABIAs) held at Doltone House in Pyrmont. I had been invited to accept the prestigious Lloyd O'Neil Award for outstanding service to the Australian book industry, which was being posthumously awarded to Bryce. I thought the best way of honouring him at the event would be to read from one of his stories, so I stood on the stage and read 'Where the Giraffe Comes to Drink from the Silver Bowl of the Moon', which is included in *The Silver Moon*. I felt so much love and affection in the room for Bryce from booksellers and publishing people, and as I returned to my seat, I so wished that Bryce had been given this special award during his lifetime.

Within days of arriving back from Sydney I received a call from Alex van Heeren inviting me to stay on Dolphin Island where Bryce and I had hoped to enjoy our second honeymoon. He generously invited me to travel there with some close friends so that I wouldn't feel lonely. So on 11 June 2013, five of us clambered up the steps onto Dolphin's jetty after a twenty-minute boat ride from the tip of Fiji's Viti Levu.

Being there was a divine experience, although of course it felt bittersweet without Bryce. The magic of Dolphin Island enveloped me like soft rain after drought and I could feel myself slowly rejuvenating after years of heartache. Dawn Simpson, Alex's long-term island manager, treated us like royalty, and with the warmth and kindness for which Fijians are renowned. World-class diving and snorkelling are easily accessible in the pristine Bligh Waters surrounding Dolphin. At night local villagers treated us to spectacular displays of drumming and dancing as a huge bonfire sent flames into the night sky.

When the tide was out I loved wading into the shallow lagoon and rushing back to shore as the tide came flooding in. I smiled recalling Bryce's response to a question posed by Peter Thompson on what Bryce would like his legacy to be, and Bryce said, 'Peter, we have to be careful about talking about legacies. I keep reminding myself that the tide comes in twice a day and it wipes out the footprints. You just do the best you can, and whatever's left is left.' I also remembered what Bryce said to Andrew Zuckerman when he was interviewed for the spectacular book *Wisdom*: 'Wisdom is a very specific thing. It's not about brains. It's not about the accumulation of knowledge. It's about being decent.'

As the moon rose over Dolphin Island, the closest place to paradise I have ever been, I hoped with all my heart that Bryce's soul was resting peacefully. I like to think that part of his soul has returned to Africa, the continent of his birth, even though he lived in Australia for fifty-four years. Throughout his writing life, Africa remained an essential part of his very being. As he wrote in *The Night Country*:

> Now see again, it is gone only a moment and immediately it begins to rise once more, see how it rises silver from the water, the moon over the Night Country. It is here you can come whenever you are sad, or frightened. It is here where you can re-think your courage and find the way to go and the path to take.

I had every intention of staying on in Canberra, where I had so many precious memories of us living there, even though I struggled to maintain the garden to Bryce's standards of imagination and excellence. However, one day my handsome tabby cat, Pirate, was badly injured by a neighbour's dog and subsequently died on 16 January 2013. I was distraught, and some of the grief I had probably suppressed following Bryce's death poured out in a torrent I could barely contain. I know this sounds strange, but I began to feel that he was saying to me, 'Go home, darling. Go back to Sydney where Nima lives, and where you have lived for most of your adult life.' That same week a magnificent male king parrot with a scarlet-red head, electric-blue tail and emerald-green wings and back, a pale-green strip running from his shoulder and down his wings shimmering in the sunlight, landed on our persimmon tree. I could feel Bryce's presence, and once again he was telling me it was time to leave.

It was a very tough decision as I loved living in Canberra, but in early 2015 I knew the time had arrived. With the expert asssistance and kindness of Mary Debus, a highly respected real-estate agent, the house was listed for sale on 19 February. The Bryce Courtenay factor was in evidence at our first open for inspection, with over sixty groups arriving. The house was sold within thirteen days, and it was soon time for me to pack up and move on. Sadly, I did not leave Canberra with my Burmese cat, Cardamon, who passed away on 18 March, or with Timmy, who died on 23 May after a protracted illness. His ashes were scattered on Bryce's grave after I discovered that interning him, as Bryce had wished, was not possible.

On 14 June 2015, I returned to live in Sydney. Walking in the door of our apartment was a lonely experience but it felt good to be back, even though it was strange knowing that Bryce was never going to come through that door again. We had shared a lot of time there – mostly happy times, but also weeks of him recuperating from various bouts of ill health. I thought of selling up and starting anew, but it didn't feel right. I was comforted once I'd hung in the hallway the portrait of Bryce painted by Paul Newton. To this day I always bid the portrait goodnight, and if something is troubling me I look at it and say, 'Darling, what should I do?'

Ophelia is now the only surviving pet of our five, as Muschka died a few years ago. In late February 2022 I did finally sell my lovely apartment in Point Piper and in June I moved into a small house. The cat needed a garden, and after the COVID-19 lockdowns, so do I! I can't wait to plant vegetables and grow herbs and sunflowers just as Bryce would have. I look forward to seeing Ophelia reclining in the sun on the red wooden garden bench that was a gift to Bryce from Penguin, and once sat in our garden in Canberra.

I am planning to return to South Africa next year to retrace Bryce's childhood years. I will spend time with Shanine and Bryce's other relatives and visit Alex at his Grande Provence Estate at Franschhoek. I hope to then travel up to Luanshya in Zambia where Bryce worked down the mines, and visit Bulawayo in Zimbabwe where he was conscripted into the army before he headed to London to study journalism.

Who knows? Having now completed what seemed at the outset to be a monumental task – the writing of this memoir, a tribute to the extraordinary man I had the great privilege to call my husband – I might even try my hand at writing something else. But for now it feels only right to conclude Bryce's memoir in his own words – the words that close his iconic novel *The Power of One*:

Outside, high above me, a full moon, pale as skimmed milk, floated in a day sky. I felt clean, all the bone-beaked loneliness birds banished, their rocky nests turned to river stones. Cool, clear water bubbled over them, streams in the desert.

SOURCES

THIS BOOK IS A result of many years of research. Hundreds of references were checked and accessed in reviewing materials. The following list summarises only the main sources cited in this book. Every endeavour has been made to ensure details are correct but there may be some omissions and errors, for which I sincerely apologise.

Works by Bryce Courtenay

BOOKS
Words, Smith & Miles Ltd, Sydney, 1981.
The Power of One, William Heinemann, Melbourne, 1989.
Tandia, William Heinemann, Melbourne, 1991.
A Recipe for Dreaming, William Heinemann, Melbourne, 1992.
The Pitch, Margaret Gee Publishing, Sydney, 1992.
April Fool's Day, William Heinemann, Melbourne, 1993.
The Potato Factory, William Heinemann, Melbourne, 1995.
The Family Frying Pan, William Heinemann, a part of Reed Books Australia, Melbourne, 1997.
Tommo & Hawk, Penguin Books Australia, Melbourne, 1997.
The Night Country, Penguin Books Australia, Melbourne, 1998.
Jessica, Penguin Books Australia, Melbourne, 1998.
Solomon's Song, Penguin Books Australia, Melbourne, 1999.
Smoky Joe's Cafe, Penguin Books Australia, Melbourne, 2001.
Four Fires, Penguin Books Australia, Melbourne, 2001.
Matthew Flinders' Cat, Penguin Books Australia, Melbourne, 2002.

Brother Fish, Penguin Group (Australia), Melbourne, 2004.

Whitethorn, Penguin Group (Australia), Melbourne, 2005.

Sylvia, Penguin Group (Australia), Melbourne, 2006.

The Persimmon Tree, Penguin Group (Australia), Melbourne, 2007.

Fishing for Stars, Penguin Group (Australia), Melbourne, 2008.

The Story of Danny Dunn, Penguin Group (Australia), Melbourne, 2009.

Fortune Cookie, Penguin Group (Australia), Melbourne, 2010.

Jack of Diamonds, Penguin Group (Australia), Melbourne, 2012.

The Silver Moon: Reflections and Stories on Life, Death and Writing, Penguin Group (Australia), Melbourne, 2014.

CO-AUTHORED BOOKS

Kennedy, Ian & Courtenay, Bryce, *The Power of One to One*, Margaret Gee Publishing, Sydney, 1995.

Pike, Geoff & Courtenay, Bryce, *Rumble the Redgum Yowie and the Mean Earth-Munching Grumkin*, Five Mile Press, Melbourne, 1997.

Pike, Geoff & Courtenay, Bryce, *Nap the Honeygum Yowie and the Fiery Flame-Fanning Grumkin*, Five Mile Press, Melbourne, 1997.

Pike, Geoff & Courtenay, Bryce, *Crag the Mangrove Yowie and the Yukky Mukky-Poo Grumkin*, Five Mile Press, Melbourne, 1997.

Pike, Geoff & Courtenay, Bryce, *Squish the Fiddlewood Yowie and the Murky Ooze-Making Grumkin*, Five Mile Press, Melbourne, 1997.

Pike, Geoff & Courtenay, Bryce, *Ditty the Lillipilli Yowie and the Smelly Rotten-Rubbish Grumkin*, Five Mile Press, Melbourne, 1997.

Pike, Geoff & Courtenay, Bryce, *Boof the Bottlebrush Yowie and the Tigertoothed Tree-Chomping Grumkin*, Five Mile Press, Melbourne, 1997.

OTHER WORKS

A selection of letters written by Bryce Courtenay, copyright Christine Courtenay.

A selection of poetry, short stories and cartoons created by Bryce Courtenay, copyright Christine Courtenay.

'The Window She is Open and the Brains She's Coming In', unpublished, 1985.

'The Greatest Rugby Player on Earth Comes from Mars', unpublished, 1996.

'The Ghost General Synopsis', unpublished, 2011.

'The Grey Parrot Synopsis', unpublished, 2011.

'On matters such as "the elephant in the room"', unpublished, 2011.

PRINT MEDIA

'China: The great Australian culture shock', *The Australian Weekend Magazine*, 15 February 1986.

'The Pitch' weekly columns, Archive of Press Cuttings, *The Australian*, 1986 – 1992.

'The power of Africa', *Sydney Morning Herald*, 26 August 1993.

'Blood sweat & tears', *Sydney Morning Herald*, 2 September 1993.

'The forgetting of wisdom', *Sydney Morning Herald*, 13 October 2008.
'Bryce Courtenay: Author', *Sunday Life*, *Sunday Age*, 21 December 2008.

Television & Radio

'Bryce Courtenay', *This Is Your Life*, presented by Mike Munro, TCN Channel Nine, Episode 5, 12 October 1995.

'Bryce Courtenay', *Talking Heads*, presented by Peter Thompson, ABC Television, 8 May 2006.

Profile interview with Bryce Courtenay, by Sheridan Voysey, Hope 103.2FM, Sydney, 8 December 2009.

'Bestsellers & Blockbusters', *Jennifer Byrne Presents – The Book Club*, ABC Television, 11 May 2010.

Peschardts People – Bryce Courtenay, presented by Michael Peschardt, BBC World (United Kingdom), 2010.

The Book Show, ABC Radio National, 9 February 2011.

'The Courtenays', *Family Confidential*, directed by Ili Baré, executive producer Laurie Critchley, Southern Pictures, ABC Television, 9 February 2012.

'Modern Day Dickens', interview with Bryce Courtenay by Karina Carvalho, *News Breakfast*, ABC Television, 14 May 2012.

'Bryce Courtenay: Fact or Fiction?', interview with Bryce Courtenay by Karina Carvalho, *News Breakfast*, ABC Television, 15 May 2012.

Exclusive interview with Bryce Courtenay by Tracy Grimshaw, *A Current Affair*, Nine Network Australia, 7 September 2012.

'Bryce Courtenay: Australia's Master Storyteller', by Tim Ayliffe, *ABC News*, ABC Television, 23 November 2012.

'Vale Bryce Courtenay – a *Conversation Hour* Special', by Samantha Stayner, *The Conversation Hour*, ABC Radio, 23 November 2012.

'Bryce Courtenay: A Brief Encounter', by Elaine Harris, ABC Radio, 18 December 2012.

Alex Malley interviews Bryce Courtenay, *The Bottom Line*, Joint venture by CPA Australia and Evolution Media Group, TCN Channel Nine, 2 March 2013.

Electronic Media – not broadcast

Bryce Courtenay interviewed by Diana Ritch, 6 March 1991, National Library of Australia, ORAL TRC 2728.

Interviews with Bryce Courtenay by Roger Maynard, recorded at the Courtenay home, Canberra, in April and May 2012, produced and presented by Roger Maynard, and available (Parts 1 – 5) on YouTube.

Bryce Courtenay interviewed by Christine Courtenay, filmed and produced by Michael Dillon AM at the Courtenay home, Canberra, 3 September 2012.

Bryce Courtenay: Celebration of Life Service, filmed and produced by Michael Dillon AM and Adrian Reinhardt, 5 December 2012.

The Last Class DVD, filmed and directed by Kyle O'Donoghue, produced by Christine Gee, published by Bryce Courtenay International Pty Ltd, 2013.

Interviews and films recorded by Penguin TV, Penguin Books Australia: 'Bryce Courtenay – *Fishing for Stars*', 21 October 2009; 'Penguin Presents Bryce Courtenay', 9 November 2009; 'Bryce Courtenay *The Story of Danny Dunn*', 23 October 2009; 'Bryce Courtenay *Fortune Cookie* Film Trailer', 15 November 2010; 'Bryce Courtenay – *Jack of Diamonds* TV Ad', 12 November 2012; 'Bryce Courtenay – Thank You', 12 November 2012.

Film & Television Series

The Power of One, feature film written by Bryce Courtenay (novel) and Robert Mark Kamen (screenplay), directed by John G. Avildsen, produced by Arnon Milchan and Regency Enterprises, distributed by Warner Brothers Pictures and Roadshow Entertainment, 1992.

The Potato Factory, television series written by Bryce Courtenay (novel) and Alan Seymour (screenplay), directed by Robert Marchand, produced by Anthony Buckley, Golden Square Pictures and Screentime, distributed by Seven Network and Columbia Tristar Television Pty Ltd, 2000.

Jessica, television miniseries written by Bryce Courtenay (novel) and Peter Yeldham (screenplay), directed by Peter Andrikidis, produced by Anthony Buckley, Power and Powercorp, distributed by Network Ten, Screentime, Umbrella Entertainment and Powercorp, 2004.

Further Books & Writing

Achebe, Chinua, *Things Fall Apart*, William Heinemann Ltd, London, 1958.

Bornman, Hans, together with the Baberton Museum, *Photo history of Baberton 1884 – 1984*, published and distributed by the Town Council of Barberton, 1984.

Courtenay, Rosemary Ann, *Rosemary's Story: An Autobiography*, unpublished work copyright Rosemary Ann Anderson 2006, USA - Registration number TXu 2-226-541. With kind permission from Rosemary Anderson and her family.

Crossle, Philip et al., *The Courtenay Family in Ireland*, compiled by Philip Crossle et al., Newry, Ireland, 1904, with transcriptions of notes, letters, and other genealogical material added by St. John Courtenay III, 1993, Courtenay Publications, Arlington, Virginia, USA, 1993. Note: this item kindly provided by Owen Anderson (son of Rosemary and Esmund Anderson).

Dickens, Charles, *Oliver Twist*, Bentley's Miscellany, London, first published as a serial, 1837–1839, printed edition published by Richard Bentley, London, 1838.

Finlay, Iain, *A Hitch in Time*, High Adventure Publishing, Tumbulgum, 2490 Australia, 2016.

Greer, Luanshya, *Reap the Whirlwind*, Century, London, 1991; and *Shadows in the Wind*, Orion, London, 1993.

Hatfield, P.O. George, *Through the Eyes of P.O. George Hatfield*, H.M.A.S. *Perth 1939–1941*, published by George Hatfield, Sydney, 2009. Extracts of letters kindly supplied by George Hatfield, Jnr.

Steger, Jason, *Novel Lives: Legends of the Written Word*, Australian Postal Corporation, Melbourne, 2010.

Zuckerman, Andrew, *Wisdom*, Andrew Zuckerman Studio and Abrams, New York, 2008.

PERSONALLY PENNED DOCUMENTS

Personal Letter to Bryce Courtenay from The Most Reverend Desmond M. Tutu, OMSG DD FKC, Anglican Archbishop Emeritus of Cape Town, 21 August 2007.

Eulogy for Bryce Courtenay's Celebration of Life service by Bob Sessions, 5 December 2012.

'Bryce Courtenay: a Celebration, 14 August 1933 – 22 November 2012' Order of Service, 5 December 2012.

Print Media

Bagwell, Sheryle, 'Books, books and more books', *Australian Financial Review*, 1 December 1995.

Baum, Caroline, 'The strategy sessions behind Penguin's rise', *Australian Financial Review*, 31 January 1998.

Blundell, Graeme, 'Bryce Courtenay is telling stories on *Family Confidential*', *The Australian*, 16 November 2012.

Butt, Craig, '"Months to live": Bryce Courtenay reveals', *Sydney Morning Herald*, 8 September 2012.

Cadzow, Jane, 'The world according to Bryce', *Good Weekend Magazine*, *Sydney Morning Herald*, 17 March 2012.

Canning, Simon, 'Boardroom fit', *The Australian*, 3 September 2011.

Dean, Paul, 'Aussie ad executive shares the secret of how he remade his life', *Los Angeles Times*, 3 August 1989.

Dean, Rowan, 'Not dead yet – why Louie the Fly has more lives than a cat', *Sydney Morning Herald*, 23 September 2011.

Dempsey, Dianne, '*Whitethorn*', *The Age*, 17 December 2005.

Doherty, Megan, 'Author reveals love affair in final chapter', *Canberra Times*, 15 September 2012.

Doherty, Megan, 'Remembering Bryce Courtenay, 30 years after *The Power of One*', *Canberra Times*, 29 May 2019.

Dow, Steve, 'The Power of Bryce: writers speak of their debt', *Sydney Morning Herald*, 23 November 2012.

Dow, Steve, 'Writers salute the skills of a master', *Sydney Morning Herald*, 23 November 2012.

Dubecki, Larissa, 'Mighty unclean maybe, but he's no fly by night', *The Age*, 6 October 2007.

Elder, James, 'The Bryce is right', *Sydney Weekly*, 5 June 1997.

Ellis, Bob, 'Bob Ellis on the Bryce Courtenay he knew', *Independent Australia*, 25 November 2012.

Endacott, Michelle, 'Courtenay's Crusade', *New Idea*, December 2006.

Fitzgerald, Ross, 'Amazon explorers' adventures revisited by Adam Courtenay', *The Australian*, 20 November 2015.

Ford, Sean, 'Top author hails Burns a hero', *The Advocate* (Tasmania), 11 May 2009.

Fortescue, Lou, 'The power of one sad story', *Daily Telegraph*, 16 October 2008.

Hancock, Alecia, Book Review: *Fortune Cookie*, *West Australian*, 25 January 2011.

Hornery, Andrew, 'Courtenay enthused about the power of one last big sell', *Sydney Morning Herald*, 5 December 2012.

Hush, Ian 'Bestselling author visits Sheppie', *South Coast Herald*, Port Shepstone, South Africa, 28 April 1989. Kindly provided by David Rush, Editor.

Kalman, Aaron, 'Chicken soup à la Golda Meir', *The Times of Israel*, 4 December 2012.

Kenneally, Cath, '*Whitethorn*', *Sydney Morning Herald*, 8 December 2005.

Lehmann-Haupt, Christopher, 'Everything but sex (lack of time)', *New York Times*, 19 June 1989.

Lynch, Michael, 'Bryce Courtenay: A Tribute', *Campaign Brief*, 12 December 2012.

Lynch, Michael, '*Family Confidential* profiles former agency CD', *Campaign Brief*, 8 February 2012.

Lynch, Michael, 'Valé Bryce Courtenay: the legendary adman and author dies, aged 79, after long battle with cancer', *Campaign Brief*, 23 November 2012.

Lynch, Michael, 'Valé Michael Robinson', *Campaign Brief*, 24 July 2008.

Mason, Meg, 'The Power of Two', *Stellar* magazine, *Sunday Telegraph*, 16 June 2019.

Masson, Sophie, 'Middle Ages in a preachy muddle', *Sydney Morning Herald*, 16 December 2006.

Maunder, Patricia, 'Book of the Week: *Fishing for Stars*', *Sunday Age*, 14 December 2008.

Maunder, Patricia, 'The man who made Christmas presents', *Sydney Morning Herald*, 23 November 2012.

Maunder, Patricia. 'Great storyteller has his final word', *Sydney Morning Herald*, 24 November 2012.

Meacham, Steve, 'The power of Bryce Courtenay: let me tell you a story', *Sun-Herald*, 29 November 2009.

Shapiro, Larry, 'The Power of One by Bryce Courtenay: An adventure of mind, heart and fists', *Book of the Month Club News*, Pennsylvania, USA, August 1989.

Sharp, Annette, 'PM pays tribute to Bryce Courtenay', *Daily Telegraph*, 5 December 2012.

Shoebridge, Neil, 'An author sells his books as a cereal', *Australian Financial Review*, 23 October 1995.

Shoebridge, Neil, 'Is Reckitt's 'reprieve' for Louie the Fly real?', *Australian Financial Review*, 29 September 2011.

Shoebridge, Neil, 'The power of promotion: when writers become brand names', *Australian Financial Review*, 3 November 1997.

Steger, Jason and Dow, Steve, 'Bryce Courtenay writes his final chapter', *Sydney Morning Herald*, 23 November 2012.

Steger, Jason, 'Bestselling author Bryce Courtenay dies, aged 79', *The Courier*, 23 November 2012.

Tate, Meredith, 'Adventures in the exotic East', *Sun-Herald*, 20 February 2011.

Tuohy, Wendy, 'Bryce power', *Herald Sun*, 22 November 2008.

Wyndham, Susan, 'Australia Post gives the stamp of approval to literary legends', *Sydney Morning Herald*, 21 January 2010.

'Sad serenade for Courtenay' *Sydney Morning Herald*, 12 March 2007.

'Bryce Courtenay … doesn't care for five-star "nonsense" or Zanzibar's Cheapest Digs', *Sun-Herald*, 21 November 2010.

'Bryce Courtenay opens new chapter', *Canberra Times*, 5 September 2011.

'Great storyteller has his Final word', *Sydney Morning Herald*, 24 November 2012.

'Triathlon veteran Alex Hamill, 73, on why Noosa beats them all', *Australian Financial Review*, 24 October 2016.

'Marketing man built LEGO sales with engaging TV advert', *Sydney Morning Herald*, 25 March 2019.

Web References

Akle, Cheryl, 'A powerful legacy: Bryce Courtenay's *The Power of One*', betterreading.com.au, 11 June 2019.

Akle, Cheryl, 'What does *The Power of One* mean to you? Authors and publishers reflect on Bryce Courtenay's classic novel', betterreading.com.au, 11 June 2019.

Akle, Cheryl & Tara, Jane, 'The book that won hearts: celebrating the 30 year anniversary of *The Power of One* by Bryce Courtenay', betterreading.com.au, 4 June 2019.

Akle, Cheryl & Tara, Jane, 'Bryce Courtenay's *The Power of One*: an ode to the power of education and a reminder of our past', betterreading.com.au, 11 June 2019.

Byrnes, Holly, 'Bryce Courtenay reveals he was "excited about dying" in his final interview', News.com.au, 2 March 2013.

Clark, Blanche & Metcalf, Fran, 'Tributes to author Bryce Courtenay, a great storyteller who inspired readers and writers', News.com.au, 23 November 2012.

Bryce Courtenay Facebook page, facebook.com/BryceCourtenay

Diaz, Amanda, 'Louie the Fly: the making of an iconic jingle', nfsa.gov.au

Estera, Christine, 'Why the Louie the Fly Mortein ads created by late author Bryce Courtenay remains a favourite six decades later', celebrity.nine.com.au, 2021.

Isle, Mike, 'Bryce Courtenay – The Power of Creativity', Partisanadvertising.co.nz/blog, 14 August 2018.

King Edward V11 School, Johannesburg, South Africa, kes.co.za

Krause, Tom, 'Hamburgers on the road to apartheid', gonzomeetsthepress, 29 November 2018.

'Louie the Fly' Mortein jingle (1962), nfsa.gov.au/collection/curated/louie-fly-mortein-jingle-1962, mortein.com.au/about/about-louie/.

Metcalf, Fran, 'Bryce Courtenay bids farewell with *Jack of Diamonds*', News.com.au, Nationwide News Pty Ltd, 12 November 2012.

Parliament House Canberra (Australia): Condolences, Courtenay, Bryce AM Official Hansards: 26 November 2012, and 27 November 2012, aph.gov.au

Patterson, Amanda, 'The Writers Write Interview – Bryce Courtenay', Writers Write, Johannesburg, South Africa, Writerswrite.co.za, 08 February 2006.

Penguin Random House, penguinrandomhouse.com.au

Stoykov, Vanessa, 'Why believing in Bryce Courtenay is good for Australia', Evolution Media Group blog, vanessastoykov.com.au, 2012.

ACKNOWLEDGEMENTS

IT HAS BEEN A PRIVILEGE to write this book honouring the life and legacy of my beloved late husband Bryce Courtenay AM. My hope is that people will enjoy reading it, and that it may even provide readers with some inspiration in their lives. I remain indebted to the many people whose support, love and kindness has been invaluable in writing it. There are too many people to cite in full, but they will know who they are. In the space available I would however like to especially thank the following:

Members of Bryce's immediate and extended family in Australia, the United States and South Africa, some of whom helped me fill in the gaps by generously sharing with me their recollections of Bryce. A special thank you to Bryce's grandchildren Jake, Ben and Marcus Courtenay, whom he loved so much and was always so proud of. Heartfelt thanks also to Brett Courtenay for his support and for providing some family photographs. Profound gratitude to Bryce's sister Rosemary Anderson, her husband Esmund and their children Dorrie and Owen, who were incredibly kind and helpful. I'd like to extend thanks also to the wonderful Shanine Cawood, and Bryce's first cousins Pamela Edith Carson (nee Greer), also an acclaimed author of historical fiction published as Luanshya Greer, Wendy Bennet (nee Greer) and

Errol Greer. I'd like to acknowledge too the late Robyn Davies. My thanks also to Victor Solomons.

To the following people for their invaluable contribution, encouragement, and unwavering support:

Alex Hamill, Associate Professor Koroush Haghighi, Alex van Heeren, Hon. CVO, MBE, Nima Price, Dr Anthony and Kerry Freeman, Dr Irwin and Erica Light, Duncan Thomas, Bruce Gee, Lili Price, Stacey Truscott, Shane Mortimer (Ngambri Elder Mingku), Robert Swan OBE, Barney Swan, Sir Chris Bonington and Lady Loreto Bonington, Trish Scott, Tracy Grimshaw, Diana Ritch, Rhys Cardew, Thomas Keneally AO, Iain Finlay and Trish Clark, Peter Thompson, Roger Maynard, Jennifer Byrne, Ramona Koval, Louise Adler, Cheryl Akle, Albe Falzon, Andrew Zuckerman, Laurie Critchley, Ili Baré, Vanessa Stoykov, Leonard Yong, Michael Dillon AM, Simon Balderstone AM, Greg Mortimer OAM and Margaret Mortimer, Garry Weare and Margie Thomas, Norbu Tenzing, Peter Hillary, Iain Allan, Professor John Rasko AO and Associate Professor Simone Strasser, Angus Finney and Diane Jackson, Michael Frankel, Greg Duffy, Adrian Van Dam, Denis Bertollo, Roger Rigby, Carolyn Hamer-Smith and Kinzang Chhogyal, Barbara Goldin, Sigrun Baldvinsdottir, Jane Corbett-Jones, Liz Courtney, Christine McCabe, Denise Goodfellow, Lyn and Cec Clark, Allan and Wilma Gee, Diane Summers, George Hatfield Jnr., Dr Michael and Jacky Finkelstein, Christophe Chastel and Philippe Pée, Patrick Benhamou, Jonathan Rose, Joe Yudin, Susan Haynes, Suellen Dainty, Kate Maclaren, Gary and Nicola Kennedy, Rigstal Dorji, Mary Debus, Megan Grace and Brighton Grace, Judy Cole and Bill and Christine Cole, Graham Taylor, David and Carole Baird, John Adamson, John Atkin and Dr Janet Drewitt Smith, Sherri Reginato, Alex Bullough, Jenny Smith, Dominic Smith, James J Howard, David Hawking and Kathy Griffiths, Richard and Ruth Rosebery, John Borthwick, Catriona Terris, and finally the headmaster and staff at King Edward VII School, Johannesburg, South Africa.

To Julie Burland, the CEO of Penguin Random House, who

has honoured Bryce's legacy by publishing this book, and to Rachel Scully my editor and publisher who championed my book, and whose contribution has been simply extraordinary. Thank you also to the wider team at Penguin Random House, and particularly to Katie Purvis, whose copyedit was exceptional; Saskia Adams, my talented proofreader; Bella Arnott-Hoare, my dedicated publicist; Adam Laszczuk, who designed the stunning cover; Tony Palmer, the text designer; Julian Mole, the typesetter; and Ben Fairclough and Nikla Martin in production. I'd also like to thank here Bryce's former long-term publisher at Penguin Books Australia, Bob Sessions AM, and Bryce's former publicist Anyez Lindop.

My profound gratitude to Tim Bauer for the gift of his iconic photos of Bryce, and the pictures he took of me for this book: timbauerphoto. myportfolio.com

Bryce and I were committed to supporting many charitable organisations, including the Australian Himalayan Foundation (I am a founding board member), Cure the Future, SAVE African Rhino Foundation, the Thin Green Line Foundation, the Bookend Trust and Camp Creative, and I wish to acknowledge these organisations here.

Thanks must also be extended to my adorable cat Ophelia – the last of our tribe of pets – who never left my side as I wrote this book.

Finally, I wish to acknowledge the incredible support and kindness of Bryce's loyal readers from around the world who asked me to write this book, and who regularly join me in championing Bryce's life and enduring literary legacy.

My warmest wishes,

Christine Courtenay

Christine Courtenay AM
3 August 2022

075 81428827

Discover a
new favourite